Telesage

Building Integrated Business Intelligence Solutions with

SQL Server® 2008 R2 & Office 2010

D1456728

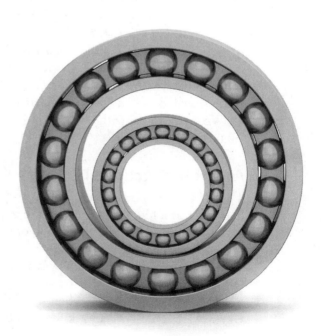

About the Authors

Philo Janus has a very diverse background, and is still trying to decide what he wants to be when he grows up. A graduate of the U.S. Naval Academy and Georgetown University Law Center, he has been developing software since 1995, and specifically C# since the .Net Framework was in beta. Ten years as a "guerilla developer" has given him a distinct preference for agile development frameworks, and six years as a sales engineer working for Microsoft has built an appreciation for how much Microsoft products can enable rapid solution development and deployment. He has written *Pro InfoPath 2007*, *Pro PerformancePoint Server 2007*, and *Pro SQL Server Analysis Services 2008*. Philo lives in Virginia with his wife Christine and his daughters Samantha (GO NOLES!!!!) and Antoinette. You can reach Philo at philo@saintchad.org.

    Stacia Misner is the founder of Data Inspirations (www.datainspirations.com), which delivers global business intelligence (BI) consulting and education services. She is a consultant, educator, mentor, and author specializing in business intelligence and performance management solutions that use Microsoft technologies. Stacia has more than 25 years of experience in information technology and has focused exclusively on Microsoft BI technologies since 2000. She is the author of *Microsoft SQL Server 2000 Reporting Services Step by Step*, *Microsoft SQL Server 2005 Reporting Services Step by Step*, *Microsoft SQL Server 2005 Express Edition: Start Now!*, and *Microsoft SQL Server 2008 Reporting Services Step by Step* and the coauthor of *Business Intelligence: Making Better Decisions Faster*, *Microsoft SQL Server 2005 Analysis Services Step by Step*, *Microsoft SQL Server 2005 Administrator's Companion*, and *Introducing Microsoft SQL Server 2008 R2*. She is also a Microsoft Certified IT Professional-BI and a Microsoft Certified Technology Specialist-BI. Stacia lives in Las Vegas, Nevada, with her husband, Gerry. You can contact Stacia at smisner@datainspirations.com.

About the Technical Editor

Thierry D'hers is the Group Program Manager for the SQL Server Reporting Services team. His group oversees the requirement gathering, features definition and design, as well as evangelization of the product. Prior to this position, Thierry occupied various roles in the SQL Server Analysis Services team and the Microsoft Performance Point team. Thierry is an 18 plus–year veteran in the BI software industry, having been at the source of many products at Microsoft and Hyperion Solution before his joining Microsoft. When he is not building teams and designing BI software, Thierry enjoys skiing, climbing mountains, and playing classical guitar.

Building Integrated Business Intelligence Solutions with

SQL Server® 2008 R2 & Office 2010

Philo Janus and Stacia Misner

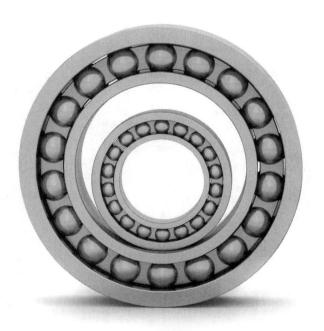

New York Chicago San Francisco Lisbon
London Madrid Mexico City Milan
New Delhi San Juan Seoul Singapore
Sydney Toronto

The **McGraw·Hill** Companies

Cataloging-in-Publication Data is on file with the Library of Congress

McGraw-Hill books are available at special quantity discounts to use as premiums and sales promotions, or for use in corporate training programs. To contact a representative, please e-mail us at bulksales@mcgraw-hill.com.

Building Integrated Business Intelligence Solutions with SQL Server® 2008 R2 & Office 2010

Copyright © 2011 by The McGraw-Hill Companies. All rights reserved. Printed in the United States of America. Except as permitted under the Copyright Act of 1976, no part of this publication may be reproduced or distributed in any form or by any means, or stored in a database or retrieval system, without the prior written permission of publisher, with the exception that the program listings may be entered, stored, and executed in a computer system, but they may not be reproduced for publication.

All trademarks or copyrights mentioned herein are the possession of their respective owners and McGraw-Hill makes no claim of ownership by the mention of products that contain these marks.

1234567890   QFR QFR   10987654321

ISBN   978-0-07-171673-4
MHID   0-07-171673-4

Sponsoring Editor Wendy Rinaldi	**Indexer** Claire Splan
Editorial Supervisor Janet Walden	**Production Supervisor** James Kussow
Project Manager Manisha Singh, Glyph International	**Composition** Glyph International
Acquisitions Coordinator Joya Anthony	**Illustration** Glyph International
Technical Editor Thierry D'hers	**Art Director, Cover** Jeff Weeks
Copy Editor Lisa McCoy	**Cover Designer** Jeff Weeks
Proofreader Claire Splan	

Information has been obtained by McGraw-Hill from sources believed to be reliable. However, because of the possibility of human or mechanical error by our sources, McGraw-Hill, or others, McGraw-Hill does not guarantee the accuracy, adequacy, or completeness of any information and is not responsible for any errors or omissions or the results obtained from the use of such information.

For my wife, Christine, whose unending support has gotten me through so very much.
–Philo Janus

For my husband, Gerry, whose support makes it possible to do more than I ever imagined.
–Stacia Misner

Contents at a Glance

Contents

Foreword

When earlier last year I was approached to tech edit this book, I couldn't have been more delighted. Having worked with Philo for many years at Microsoft, I knew his passion and the extent of his knowledge of the BI practices and of Microsoft technologies in particular. And Stacia has, herself, has been practicing Microsoft BI for almost as long as Microsoft has had a BI offering. She usually hangs out in all Microsoft events where business intelligence is being discussed and always spends time around the product team so as to be among the first to get the latest and greatest news from Microsoft development. So when I heard that Stacia had joined the project as well, I knew this book had two of the best talents in the industry working on it. This was going to be good, real good.

Yet, writing a book about BI is always a challenging dilemma. Business intelligence is such a big area that it can be covered on multiple levels, from different angles: business needs and impact, technology review, implementation best practices, customer/industry scenarios, and examples. The authors chose for this book to bring all these together in a clever mix that makes it a valuable tool, not just for the BI novice but for the knowledgeable BI practitioner as well. It not only provides a great introduction to business intelligence; it also covers how BI is evolving in a business world influenced by social networking and by a highly collaborative professional workplace. It does so while also describing the most up-to-date Microsoft BI technology available through Microsoft Office 2010 and SQL Server 2008 R2.

In addition to providing a great introduction to business intelligence and Microsoft BI offerings for the novice reader, this book contains many valuable insights from years of implementation experience from both authors. For example, it will help you figure out what part of the Microsoft BI offering is best optimized for specific business scenarios, or which specific technology to use if you have a particular feature requirement. This type of insight can be invaluable to the BI practitioner, who can sometimes be lost in the wide array of Microsoft technologies available.

This book will prove to be a great aid to whoever has a business intelligence project in sight and needs to learn how to best leverage investments in Microsoft Office and Microsoft SQL Server. So I hope you will enjoy reading this book as much as I have enjoyed working with Stacia and Philo through the editing of it. May it be a useful tool and guide to make you successful in your business intelligence projects.

Thierry D'hers
Principal Group Program Manager, Microsoft SQL Server Reporting Services
Microsoft Corporation

Acknowledgments

I owe the strongest thanks to my coauthor Stacia for her incredible effort in making this book a reality. Her BI expertise was invaluable, and without her you'd be holding half a book. I also thank Thierry D'hers for his knowledge of the Microsoft BI stack and helping us stay aligned with the goals of the product group. Of course, thank you to Manisha Singh for her work in keeping everything readable. But my deepest appreciation goes to Wendy Rinaldi and Joya Anthony for their dedication, support, and patience. If you find this book worthwhile, they are the people to thank.

–Philo Janus

I'd like to thank my coauthor Philo Janus for his contributions to the book. In addition, thanks to Thierry D'hers for providing a technical review of the book and offering advice on how to make it better. I must also thank Lisa McCoy for polishing up my words during the copyedit process and Manisha Singh for managing that process smoothly. Joya Anthony also deserves thanks for nudging me along firmly but gently through the book development process, as does Wendy Rinaldi for her role in introducing me to McGraw-Hill and this project. I'd also like to express my appreciation to Mark Tabladillo Ph.D, of MarkTab Consulting and Associate Faculty at University of Phoenix for his help reviewing the chapter on data mining.

–Stacia Misner

Introduction

The Microsoft business intelligence suite contains a comprehensive set of tools that you can use for a variety of tasks, from building a data mart or data warehouse to producing a sophisticated presentation layer for reporting and analysis. The purpose of this book is to introduce you to business intelligence in general, and to explain the supporting role that each of the tools plays. To help you understand how the tools work, and hopefully to inspire the development of your own business intelligence solutions, we provide examples that you can follow on your own computer.

We start with two chapters to introduce you to some essential business intelligence concepts. In Chapter 1 we will discuss the underlying concepts in business intelligence and give you some perspectives on business intelligence solutions to lay the foundation for the material in this book. Then in Chapter 2 we expand on the traditional concepts of business intelligence to include the collaboration necessary to make a business intelligence solution successful.

One of the daunting topics in business intelligence is online analytical processing, or OLAP. The ability to draw data from multiple data sources and create multidimensional "cubes" for analysis is a core competency in business intelligence. In Chapter 3 we introduce you to SQL Server Analysis Services, the OLAP engine that's part of Microsoft SQL Server. Then in Chapter 4 we show you one of the best tools for reporting and analysis of dimensional data—Excel 2010 and Excel Services in SharePoint Server 2010.

The Office 2010 "wave" introduced a new tool for the business intelligence toolkit—PowerPivot for Excel and SharePoint. PowerPivot enables analysts to create smaller dimensional models in Excel and then publish them to SharePoint where others can use them as data sources. While putting data in Excel helps out the analyst, you also want to understand the tools available to get data into the enterprise data stores that are the bedrock of business intelligence. In Chapter 6 we discuss the various ways you can get data into your solution.

For a long time the only "business intelligence" available was a report. While this book shows you all the different ways to pick your data apart, the basic report is still a vital part of business intelligence. Chapter 7 shows you SQL Server Reporting Services and covers both standard reporting as well as the advanced features available in the new 2008 R2 platform.

Following the chapters that cover the core business intelligence components available as part of the SQL Server platform, we continue in Chapter 8 with an overview of the business intelligence features in SharePoint Server 2010 that you can use to build dashboards. In Chapter 9, we cover the additional scorecard and dashboard features in PerformancePoint Services that integrate with and extend the capabilities of the SharePoint dashboard.

By this point in the book, you might have noticed there is overlapping functionality among the tools for developing charts and graphs. In Chapter 10, we compare and contrast your options for data visualization within each tool. We also provide advice for choosing the right type of chart or graph for the type of information that you want to communicate. Then, in Chapter 11, we delve into the intricacies of using maps in Reporting Services as a data visualization tool. We cover more advanced data visualization and other analysis techniques in Chapter 12, which explains the data mining capabilities in Excel 2010 with the Data Mining Add-ins and in Analysis Services.

Of course, once you build a business intelligence solution, you must also build processes to maintain it. In Chapter 13, we explain how you can use Master Data Services to manage the reference data for your solution. In the final chapter, we review the necessary processes to put your solution into production and implement security.

For the most part, there are no dependencies between each chapter in this book, so you can start by reading any chapter that interests you. However, if you're new to business intelligence or to the Microsoft business intelligence suite, we recommend you start by reading the first two chapters. That way, you can develop a better understanding of the background for the subsequent chapters as well as an appreciation for how the tools in the suite fit together. An exception to the statement about no dependencies between chapters—the exercises in Chapters 9 and 10 assume that you have successfully completed the exercises in Chapter 8.

Chapter 1

What Is Business Intelligence?

In This Chapter

► **Business Intelligence**
► **Aggregating Data**
► **Cleaning Data**
► **Reports**
► **Dashboards**
► **Summary**

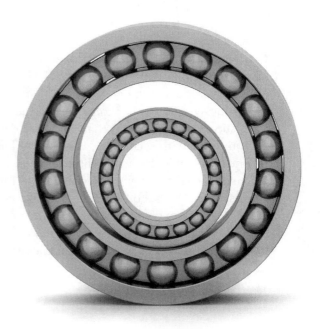

This book is going to talk a lot about "business intelligence" (BI). One of the most important things to remember as you read is not to worry about what "business intelligence" is. The issue is not about satisfying an abstract definition of a marketing phrase, but using the data locked up in your systems to solve business problems.

However, in order to have a working definition, we'll go to The Data Warehousing Institute:

> "The processes, technologies, and tools needed to turn data into information, information into knowledge, and knowledge into plans that drive profitable business action. Business intelligence encompasses data warehousing, business analytic tools, and content/knowledge management."

That last sentence is intriguing. The definition was published in 2002, more than seven years ago. Yet in the time since, only one company has really put any effort into the idea of content and knowledge management as part of a business intelligence solution. We'll come back to that in Chapter 2.

Essentially, business intelligence is about extracting business value from the data that runs the business itself. Every organization generally has a collection of business systems they have accumulated over the years. Each of these business systems is generally designed to solve a single problem or set of problems. We have human resources systems that contain personnel records; financial systems that have the company's balance sheets; enterprise resource planning systems that hold materials, inventory, and order data; and so on.

The data in these systems is designed to serve the system, not the business. For example, consider a financial budgeting system—it stores the budgeting and planning data necessary to produce the budgets for each fiscal year and quarter. In general, a budgeting system will not automatically be designed to interface with other systems. (We even worked with one customer that had a multibillion-dollar budget whose budgeting system was not connected to the execution system.) So we have a number of "data stovepipes"—systems that each have data pertinent to the business but that do not communicate with each other, as shown in Figure 1-1.

The problem is that while these systems may serve their primary purpose well, we're somewhat stuck when we need to perform business analysis on something that crosses system lines. For example, what if we want to evaluate the cost of personnel over time? We need to combine data from the personnel and financial systems. However, that means we have to get to the data in those systems, which has significant security implications, and determine how to relate the records.

Financial Data   Personnel   Warehouse   Customer   Retail Returns   Scientific
                     Data   Management   Account   Data Analysis
                                                 Management

Figure 1-1   *Data stovepipes in business*

If we only want to do the analysis once, then maybe getting extracts into Excel spreadsheets and manipulating these by hand would be fine. But experience teaches us that in general, once a report like this is created, if it is useful, there will be an ongoing demand to see the report on a recurring basis. Often, the solution here is to assign an analyst to create the report manually every month. This is exceptionally problematic for a number of reasons:

▶ The task could be automated easily, yet an analyst is being paid to create a report instead of doing analysis.

▶ Manual manipulation of data invites error.

▶ It can be difficult to perform historical analysis. ("Go pull the report from this time last year.")

▶ There may be legal requirements to retain these records, which the analyst isn't aware of or enforcing.

▶ Traditionally, the analyst is a single point of failure—if he or she is on vacation, then the business goes without the report.

In this case, we're talking about just one report to merge two data sources. What we can really expect to see in a business is something similar to Figure 1-2.

The analysts generally collect the data they need in Excel spreadsheets, and over time may create robust data extraction and storage macros to pull the data they need into the spreadsheet. The truly talented analysts will have their system so automated that they can actually extract data from the Excel spreadsheet—it is acting as a mini-data mart for their reporting.

This problem is so pervasive that Wayne Eckerson of The Data Warehouse Institute (TDWI) coined the term "spreadmarts" ("Taming Spreadsheet Jockeys," "TDWI Case

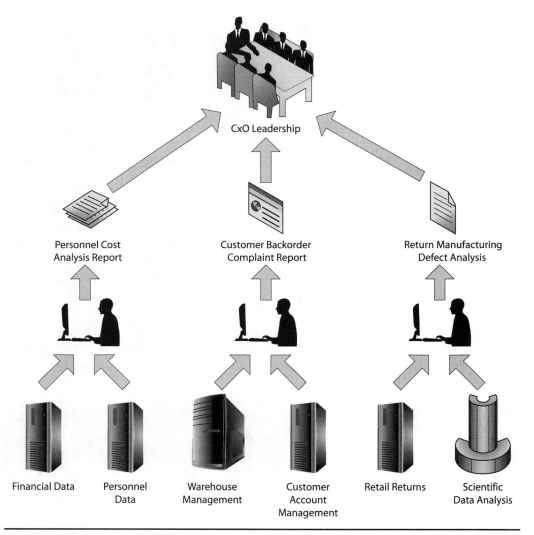

Figure 1-2   *Analysts generating reports for an executive audience*

Studies and Solutions," July 8, 2004) to describe this proliferation of business analysis data on the desktops of our analysts. The issue is that we have the data that's being used for strategic decisions to run the business living in office documents on the desktop hard drives of individuals in the company.

The solution is to build a true data warehouse or data mart that aggregates all the business data we need for our analysis and decision making, as shown in Figure 1-3.

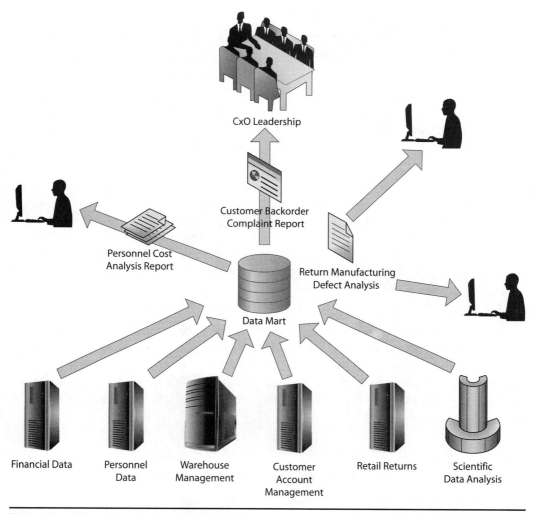

Figure 1-3   *Using a data mart to combine business data*

Then that data mart could be used by both the analysts (who are now doing analysis, not report generation) and the executives who need the various reports and status updates. In addition, since the process is automated and kept up to date, reports can be viewed at any time, or in almost real time.

This is our goal with a business intelligence solution. We can add frilly bits on the front end—dashboards, scorecards, reporting engines, and data mining. We like to refer to these as the thin candy shell on the chocolate that is our data infrastructure. Now let's take a look at the bits and pieces that we expect to see in our business intelligence solution.

Business Intelligence

The beginning of a business intelligence solution is collections of data residing in existing stovepiped systems, and the end is some form of user interface that enables the user to derive business value from the information. To accomplish this, we generally need to extract the data from the source systems, transform it to match what's needed in our data mart, and load it into the data mart repository. Once in the data mart, we'll use business intelligence tools to deliver the combined data to our users.

NOTE

One thing to keep in mind as we go through our discussions on business intelligence is the reason these systems exist. When we look at data analysis, reporting, and other aspects of getting value out of the systems, let's not lose sight of the fact that they are in place to serve the business as a transactional system. Financial systems are generally for tracking purchase orders, invoices, revenue, and expenses. Customer relationship and account management systems are designed to keep track of customer contacts, projects, and initiatives, as well as to proactively interact with customers and track workflow. What this means is that as we pursue getting value out of these systems beyond their original design, we have to be mindful not to interfere with their primary duty.

Before we proceed on our quest for business intelligence, we need to decide what value we want to get out of our solution. Many BI initiatives fail because they try to "boil the ocean"—create a data repository encompassing the entire business, or to deal with every system. A more realistic approach is to deal with a single or small number of "tactical" problems that need solving. There are a number of advantages to this approach:

► The smaller scale makes for a shorter timeline.

► There is less likelihood of running into strategic conflicts in the data.

► A narrower scope allows more focus on solving the problem.

► Most importantly, a smaller scope confers the ability to deliver results more quickly, keeping interest in the project high.

So in the case we've been looking at, we might not want to try to unify the data from all the systems shown, or produce all the analytic reports as our first effort. Perhaps we'll start with a data mart to serve the sales group—pulling data from the financial system, customer accounts, the sales system, and warehousing. We want to be able to show reports to the sales group and to executive management regarding quota attainment, sales, "just-in-time" stock reports (was a product in stock when a customer ordered it?), customer purchasing history and demographics, and other metrics. So let's start by looking at pulling together the data we need and the tools we'll need to do it.

Aggregating Data

Considering the stovepipes we're looking at, we need to think about how we're going to get this data together. Often, if the data is highly structured, we can pull it together from the sources directly—Microsoft's PowerPivot allows end users to do this, as shown in Figure 1-4.

The first roadblock we'll usually run into here is that we don't want to burden the business systems with our users' queries—there's a dual risk of individual users requesting too much data or complex queries and simply having too many users that can bring a production system to a crawl. ("I'm sorry, I can't take your order—our computers are down.")

The next problem we're generally going to face is that the data is *not* structured and clean enough for our analyst to play with. For example, the warehouse management system has part names and manufacturer part numbers ("Westinghouse 21-234098"), while the retail return system indexes parts by company product ID and bill of materials part number ("Roadster Frame RF-140 #132"). There's also a good chance of running into data that's not exactly clean (misspellings, typos, changes in manufacturer billing systems).

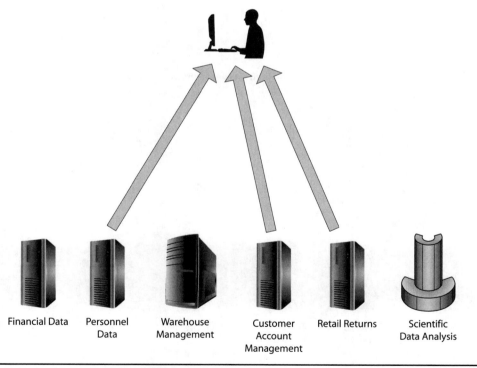

| Financial Data | Personnel Data | Warehouse Management | Customer Account Management | Retail Returns | Scientific Data Analysis |

Figure 1-4   *End-user analysis using PowerPivot*

We probably don't want to access the business system data directly due to loading issues, and we may have to scrub or transform the data before it's usable. So what we want to do is create a shadow copy of the data in the business systems. Two concepts evolve from this: relational data warehouses and analytic or dimensional data warehouses.

There is a fairly major problem in the BI space, in that the architecture and nomenclature of what happens between the business systems and the end-user tools are not well defined, and there is a lot of ambiguity—note the duplication of the term "data warehouse" earlier. Essentially, the part that everyone agrees on is that there are a number of business system stovepipes and an analyst that wants to combine the data, as shown in Figure 1-5.

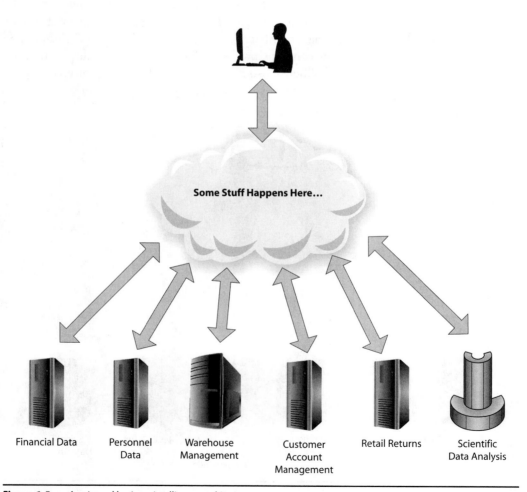

Figure 1-5   *A universal business intelligence architecture*

A major part of the issue is that we have different things going on in our miracle cloud. Generally, there are many considerations:

- ▶ Scrub and normalize the data.

- ▶ Merge the data from different repositories.

- ▶ Take the load off the production systems.

- ▶ Optimize the data for reporting, as opposed to transactional operations.

- ▶ Pre-aggregate the data.

These can be distilled down to a functional diagram, as shown in Figure 1-6.

The *staging database* is exactly that—a place to land data after extracting it from the business system. The goal here is minimal impact on the production system, so we want to essentially bulk-extract the data from the production system and into the staging database. Once in the staging database, we can start performing analysis on the state of the data, then prepare to manipulate it as necessary to move it into the data warehouse.

"Data warehouse" is a term that gets abused a lot. Sometimes it is used to describe the relational database that is the aggregation point for the company's data. Alternatively, it may be used to refer to the entirety of the architecture in Figure 1-6: the staging database, the relational storage, and the analytic functionality. In this book, we'll use "data

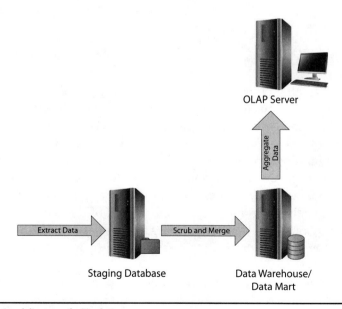

Figure 1-6   *Functional diagram of a BI solution*

On the Term "Data Warehouse"

Personally, we try not to use the word "warehouse" when dealing with a business intelligence initiative. Traditionally, data warehouses were projects to pull together *all* the data in the company into one monolithic data store to service all the analysts in the company.

A 2003 Gartner Report found that 50 percent of data warehouse projects failed.

When you consider the potential size, complexity, and political minefield involved in trying to unify all a company's data, you might think "only 50 percent fail?" These issues are fairly well ingrained in the executive mindset, so a mention of a "data warehouse" may either result in a roadblock from senior management, who fear cost overruns; a turf war with someone else who has "the data warehouse project"; or the project being sidelined for an expensive, long-term analysis.

In *Performance Dashboards* (John Wiley & Sons, 2006), Wayne Eckerson makes the point that "quality not quantity counts." He cites a strategic dashboard at a Halliburton subsidiary that used just a handful of metrics and a small amount of data, but that brought the company from losing money to number one in its market niche.

For those reasons, we always refer to the central data store in a BI initiative as a "data mart," which better communicates the idea of a more narrowly focused, agile approach.

warehouse" or "data mart" to refer to the relational data store optimized for reporting and analysis.

The final piece of our architecture is the OLAP server. OLAP is short for *online analytical processing.* Most business analysis doesn't work with line-by-line transactional reports; analysts are more interested in aggregated data. For example, instead of seeing purchase order records for each widget ordered by a customer over the course of a year, we want to see a breakdown of how many widgets were sent to each state by month.

Figure 1-7 shows a page of transactional records. Your eyes are probably already glazing over just looking at the image. Now consider that there are 120,000 records in that report—we're really not going to get much use out of this data in this format; we want to look at distributions of the sales among various aspects of the order (geographic location, model, over time, color, size, etc.). We need a way to roll the data up into those details.

If you've ever done any analysis of data in Excel, you've probably used a pivot table. A pivot table takes transactional records, as shown in Figure 1-7, and aggregates them together. We want to see the breakdown by state/province, so we collapse the sales

	A	B	C	D	E	F	G	H	I	J	K	L
1	SalesOrderID	OrderDate	LastName	FirstName	ShipToState	TotalDue	Name	Color	Weight	OrderQty	UnitPrice	LineTotal
2	43659	7/1/2001 0:00	Hendergart	James	Georgia	$27,231.55	Mountain-100 Black, 42	Black	20.77	1	$2,024.99	$2,024.99
3	43659	7/1/2001 0:00	Hendergart	James	Georgia	$27,231.55	Mountain-100 Black, 44	Black	21.13	3	$2,024.99	$6,074.98
4	43659	7/1/2001 0:00	Hendergart	James	Georgia	$27,231.55	Mountain-100 Black, 48	Black	21.42	1	$2,024.99	$2,024.99
5	43659	7/1/2001 0:00	Hendergart	James	Georgia	$27,231.55	Mountain-100 Silver, 38	Silver	20.35	1	$2,039.99	$2,039.99
6	43659	7/1/2001 0:00	Hendergart	James	Georgia	$27,231.55	Mountain-100 Silver, 42	Silver	20.77	1	$2,039.99	$2,039.99
7	43659	7/1/2001 0:00	Hendergart	James	Georgia	$27,231.55	Mountain-100 Silver, 44	Silver	21.13	2	$2,039.99	$4,079.99
8	43659	7/1/2001 0:00	Hendergart	James	Georgia	$27,231.55	Mountain-100 Silver, 48	Silver	21.42	1	$2,039.99	$2,039.99
9	43659	7/1/2001 0:00	Hendergart	James	Georgia	$27,231.55	Long-Sleeve Logo Jersey, M	Multi		3	$28.84	$86.52
10	43659	7/1/2001 0:00	Hendergart	James	Georgia	$27,231.55	Long-Sleeve Logo Jersey, XL	Multi		1	$28.84	$28.84
11	43659	7/1/2001 0:00	Hendergart	James	Georgia	$27,231.55	Mountain Bike Socks, M	White		6	$5.70	$34.20
12	43659	7/1/2001 0:00	Hendergart	James	Georgia	$27,231.55	AWC Logo Cap	Multi		2	$5.19	$10.37
13	43659	7/1/2001 0:00	Hendergart	James	Georgia	$27,231.55	Sport-100 Helmet, Blue	Blue		4	$20.19	$80.75
14	43660	7/1/2001 0:00	Collins	Takiko	Georgia	$1,716.18	Road-650 Red, 44	Red	18.77	1	$419.46	$419.46
15	43660	7/1/2001 0:00	Collins	Takiko	Georgia	$1,716.18	Road-450 Red, 52	Red	17.42	1	$874.79	$874.79
16	43661	7/1/2001 0:00	Elson	Jauna	Ontario	$43,561.44	HL Mountain Frame - Black, 48	Black	2.8	1	$809.76	$809.76
17	43661	7/1/2001 0:00	Elson	Jauna	Ontario	$43,561.44	HL Mountain Frame - Black, 42	Black	2.72	1	$714.70	$714.70
18	43661	7/1/2001 0:00	Elson	Jauna	Ontario	$43,561.44	HL Mountain Frame - Black, 38	Black	2.68	2	$714.70	$1,429.41
19	43661	7/1/2001 0:00	Elson	Jauna	Ontario	$43,561.44	AWC Logo Cap	Multi		4	$5.19	$20.75
20	43661	7/1/2001 0:00	Elson	Jauna	Ontario	$43,561.44	Long-Sleeve Logo Jersey, L	Multi		4	$28.84	$115.36
21	43661	7/1/2001 0:00	Elson	Jauna	Ontario	$43.561.44	HL Mountain Frame - Silver. 46	Silver	2.84	2	$722.59	$1.445.19

Figure 1-7 *Transactional sales records*

values down, adding them together for each state or province. Those become our row labels down the left side.

Then we want to break the data down by quarter and month. Again, we collapse the values down, adding them together by month. Now we take that column of months and rotate, or *pivot,* them so they are our column headings along the top. Thus, the name "pivot table." States down the left, months along the top, and dollar amounts of sales "in the middle," as shown in Figure 1-8.

We can do this in Excel rather easily. However, what if we have millions of rows of data? What if we want to break it down by size, then geography, and then by date?

	A	B	C	D	E	F	G	H
1								
2								
3	Sum of LineTotal	Column Labels						
4		Qtr1			Qtr2			Qtr3
5	Row Labels	Jan	Feb	Mar	Apr	May	Jun	Jul
6	Alabama	$24.29	$12,823.36	$6,478.06	$3,288.92	$1,045.34	$4,346.08	$402.88
7	Alberta	$106,347.56	$168,794.43	$2,000.32	$163,795.49	$176,274.07	$14,363.01	$195,972.09
8	Arizona	$202,858.81	$12,694.56	$65,453.36	$261,595.79	$7,182.35	$79,717.56	$298,944.90
9	Bayern	$17,674.09	$76,360.47	$36,070.28	$50,125.61	$87,868.45	$47,314.31	$23,818.98
10	Brandenburg	$28,275.26	$6,091.73	$4,271.29	$32,545.48	$9,899.62	$9,743.93	$33,807.10
11	British Columbia	$302,854.77	$401,324.54	$605,975.39	$400,291.96	$416,616.89	$609,418.66	$387,799.23
12	Brunswick	$52,155.77			$74,493.24			$121,558.39
13	California	$740,865.91	$1,354,982.72	$1,324,359.87	$887,860.31	$1,817,063.83	$1,531,642.85	$772,520.81
14	Charente-Maritime	$2,971.21	$6,267.49	$2,065.37	$5,383.61	$3,216.90	$2,157.39	$2,445.92
15	Colorado	$42,868.78	$376,091.01	$85,529.02	$59,556.54	$431,808.34	$75,430.83	$127,295.47
16	Connecticut	$107,923.90	$67,364.48	$61,919.68	$141,160.05	$97,182.14	$46,574.35	$138,058.10
17	England	$409,133.40	$569,812.51	$728,141.80	$428,246.60	$616,434.20	$918,977.51	$448,571.10
18	Essonne	$17,599.49	$59,753.94	$25,064.46	$31,869.26	$54,152.35	$19,648.61	$25,282.70

Figure 1-8 *A pivot table showing aggregated values*

Or perhaps we want to create a hierarchical breakdown of product categories, then product subcategories, and then individual products. If we try to crunch all that data and slice it in various ways as we examine it in Excel on our desktop, we will spend a lot of time waiting for it to calculate all those aggregated values.

That kind of number crunching doesn't belong on the desktop. What we should do is set up those structures of data we can anticipate our users needing and establish them, and then create the necessary aggregations in advance so that when an end user wants to see sales by model and color, the matrix is created on the server and sent down the wire to the desktop. We'll dig into this more in depth in Chapter 3 and Chapter 5.

So this is our fundamental business intelligence architecture—a staging database for whatever data manipulation we may need, a data warehouse/data mart as the repository for data structured to serve reporting and analysis needs, and an OLAP server to preaggregate our data for pivot reporting and analysis. This isn't the "only right answer," but it's a good baseline for the functionality we'll be looking at in this book.

Cleaning Data

Several times so far we've mentioned moving data, cleaning data, etc. "Moving data" is generally referred to as *ETL* for "Extract, Transform, Load." This is the exact description of what happens—data is extracted from a data source (for example, the business system we've been talking about); then it is transformed in some way. The transform may be grouping similar records, cleaning data entries ("Mississippi," "Missipi," and "Mississippi" all refer to the same state), assigning identifiers or foreign keys, and so on. The final step is to take the transformed data and load it into the destination—our data mart, for example.

Data cleansing can be more advanced as well—there are ways to analyze existing data to evaluate new data. For example, if your sales history shows that nobody has ever bought more than 5 bicycles in one order, then an order for 500 bicycles might be worth raising an alert flag. The data may be valid, but it's such an outlier that you want to double-check it.

Each of the transfers—between the source data system and the staging system, and the staging system and the data mart—is an ETL action (even if there's no "transforming" going on). The connection between the OLAP server and the data mart is different—OLAP servers generally map to data sources directly, so the server will read the data from the data mart just as a report would run a query against a database.

In the Microsoft world, ETL is performed with SQL Server Integration Services, which we'll take a look at in Chapter 6.

Now that we have our data extracted, cleaned, and loaded into a data mart, and we've set up an OLAP server to optimize and preaggregate the data in the data mart, what do we do next? Let's take a look at *consuming* the data we've worked so hard on in reports, scorecards, and dashboards.

Reports

Reports are fairly straightforward—generally a structured document that presents a specific set of data in a specific way. Back in the mainframe era, reports were simply reams of figures printed out on green-bar paper, as shown in Figure 1-9. As computing evolved, so did reporting, and enterprise reporting added summary reports, pivot tables, charts, graphs, and so on. Today, reports are rarely printed—they are created and evaluated directly on the monitor, copied and pasted into PowerPoint for executive presentations, and the files saved to server hard drive space for archiving.

Reports in a modern business intelligence solution are generated on a dedicated reporting server. This is the software that runs just like a web server, allows IT to create structured reports, and then publish them to the server to execute against data from various sources. Reports may run against the business systems directly (if the business systems support access to their data), against a data mart or data warehouse, or there may be a dedicated data mart set up for reporting purposes (generally referred to as a "reporting database").

From a business intelligence perspective, "reports" are everywhere. Modern tools embed charts and graphs on webpages or dashboards, as seen in Figure 1-10, and analysts have

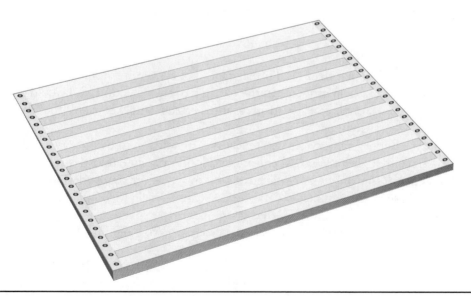

Figure 1-9   *Green-bar reports—the reason people still hate reports*

Country	Subcategory	CY 2005	CY 2006	CY 2007	CY 2008	
Australia	Mountain Bikes	$304,749	$651,980	$1,155,980	$741,111	
	Road Bikes	$1,004,298	$1,502,305	$1,435,419	$1,062,526	
Canada	Mountain Bikes	$20,275	$79,711	$243,896	$271,559	
	Road Bikes	$126,555	$541,891	$143,674	$123,497	
France	Mountain Bikes	$30,450	$109,231	$382,141	$377,439	
	Road Bikes	$150,122	$405,711	$457,811	$298,289	
Germany	Mountain Bikes	$44,025	$113,263	$361,898	$484,615	
	Road Bikes	$193,760	$407,968	$477,854	$300,760	
United Kingdom	Mountain Bikes	$54,275	$159,102	$467,893	$481,710	
	Road Bikes	$237,316	$432,485	$586,848	$341,569	
United States	Mountain Bikes	$132,200	$449,170	$1,377,831	$1,458,258	
	Road Bikes	$968,350	$1,677,527	$850,422	$793,627	

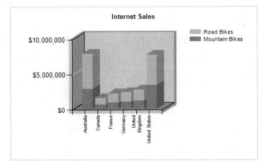
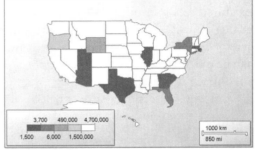

Figure 1-10   *Modern reporting dashboard*

their own tools to drill into data. And often, instead of consuming a static report, a user will simply create their own in Excel. In the past, a report created in Excel would either have to be e-mailed around as a spreadsheet, or the screen simply copied if the report designer wanted to share it.

SQL Server Reporting Services was released as an add-on to SQL Server 2000 in late 2003. Since then, it has enjoyed enormous adoption as an enterprise reporting platform. While Reporting Services is hosted on SQL Server, report designers can build reports based on a number of data sources, from Oracle to Teradata. The latest edition, Reporting Services 2008 R2, has geospatial maps, sparklines, KPI, and gauge indicators, and can use SharePoint lists as data sources. We'll dig into Reporting Services in Chapter 7.

Microsoft introduced Excel Services with Microsoft Office SharePoint Server in 2007. Excel Services allows end users to publish spreadsheets to a SharePoint Server, and then other users can view the spreadsheet in a browser without needing Excel. Excel Services also provides a way to create ad hoc reports in Excel and then publish them to a dashboard, where they can interact with other parts of the dashboard. We'll look at Excel Services in Chapter 4.

Ad Hoc Reporting

A standard requirement for an advanced reporting system is "ad hoc reporting." The term generally refers to the ability of end users to create their own reports from data sources they choose. The issue here is that generally, enterprise report design tools are complex and targeted towards developers, as the resulting reports will be consumed by hundreds or even thousands of users. As a result, there can be scalability concerns with respect to the underlying data design.

On the other hand, reports designed by users in an ad hoc fashion have a narrower focus, and therefore will have a reduced number of users. Often, the only user will be the person who designed the report—the scenario here is that they have a report they need on a recurring basis, so if they can design it themselves and publish it somewhere, they can call it up when they need it.

NOTE

We have run into cases where the request for "ad hoc reporting" was actually a request for rich filtering and sorting. The requirement wasn't about end-user design of reports from the ground up, but rather simply about reports being configurable to some degree. So be sure you truly understand what the user wants, instead of relying on keywords and assumptions.

Many vendors have had tools to allow end users to easily create their own reports for a long time. In the Microsoft world, there are two approaches: SQL Server Reporting Services has an end-user report builder, which we'll cover in Chapter 7; alternatively, users can create reports in Excel and publish the spreadsheet to Excel Services.

With all these reports floating around, some of which relate to each other, we should start looking for a way to organize them and display related reports on the screen at the same time (in addition to some other "things," which we'll get to in a minute). If we want something that will display all the metrics we need to drive our business in one place, what else could we possibly call it but a "dashboard"?

Dashboards

Generally, a dashboard is an online application that presents an aggregated view of various aspects of performance management, assembled to provide the information necessary for the anticipated user base. For example, an executive dashboard may have a collection of strategic measures, charts showing historical trends, and other reports. The focus with this executive dashboard is weekly and monthly data collection. On the other hand, the manufacturing floor may have a dashboard that has real-time indicators on operating cycles, downtime, defects, personnel hours, etc. It may also then show historical trend data, or have those reports available on other screens.

Dashboards are a critical component of a business intelligence initiative, as they are the presentation layer that delivers all the data we've painstakingly assembled in our data marts and OLAP servers. Months or even years of work may go into the analysis, data mapping, architecture, and implementation of the databases necessary to run the dashboard. After all of that labor, the actual implementation of the dashboard can often be relatively trivial, if the requirements were followed, the data analysis performed properly, the stakeholders kept involved, and so on.

NOTE

In Performance Dashboards, *Wayne Eckerson presents an iceberg as an analogy for a business intelligence solution: 10 percent visible above the water, 90 percent hidden beneath the waves. We've always referred to the data management architecture as the rich chocolate center, while the dashboard is the thin candy shell. Either example will help to understand where most of the labor is in a BI project.*

However, it can also be possible to expertly craft a robust data warehouse and then find when building the executive dashboard that the data in the data warehouse isn't appropriate to provide the information necessary for the executives to drive the business. This can be the result of "losing sight of the forest for the trees." We'll talk a bit about the dangers here in the section on key performance indicators (KPIs).

A common feature found in executive dashboards is the ability to "slice" the dashboard. For example, a dashboard may show a scorecard, a few graphs, and some reports on the business as a whole. The user will then want to see how a certain district is performing, or perhaps review the data from last year. Dashboard applications provide a filter interface similar to that shown in Figure 1-11 so that end users can select a filter, and it will act on all the items on the dashboard (or at least the appropriate ones). So, for example, selecting the "Brakes" product subcategory would filter charts, graphs, and scorecards to reflect the metrics on brake sales, instead of all products.

Microsoft's dashboard tool is PerformancePoint Services, part of SharePoint Server. PerformancePoint was introduced in 2007 as a separate product—PerformancePoint Server 2007. In January 2009, Microsoft announced they were ending PerformancePoint as an independent product and rolling it into SharePoint (at that time, Microsoft Office SharePoint Server, or MOSS). We'll get a full introduction to PerformancePoint in Chapter 2, and then dive into it later in the book.

So—dashboards can have charts and graphs, and some folks seem to have a thing for gauges. But at the executive level, when running a multibillion-dollar corporation, executives don't want to be reading through charts, parsing numbers, trying to remember statuses, etc. What they want is a straightforward way to look at an indicator and

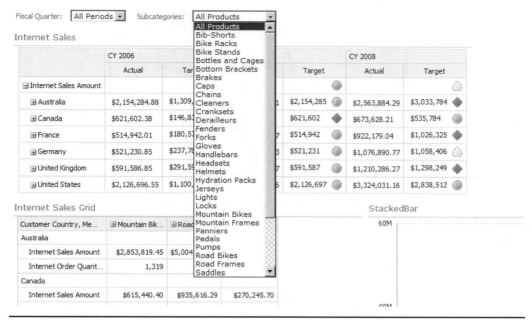

Figure 1-11   *Filters on a dashboard*

understand if it's good or bad. That indicator is a "key performance indicator" (KPI), and we put collections of them on scorecards.

Scorecards

A scorecard is, essentially, a collection of key performance indicators (more on those in a moment). A scorecard is shown in Figure 1-12. This particular scorecard shows a sales amount broken down by geographic region and calendar year. This kind of arrangement should look familiar (hint: pivot tables).

Scorecards can be designed to be hierarchical as well. Figure 1-13 shows a scorecard where the KPIs are grouped into higher-order *objectives*. The objectives are business driven, while their subordinate KPIs are data driven. Generally, in scorecard tools, KPIs can be *rolled up* so that the objectives, even though they are not directly linked to data, have scores and indicators. The goal here is that a complex scorecard, perhaps with dozens of KPIs, can still provide an easy way to identify problem areas at a glance.

For example, consider the scorecard in Figure 1-13. Note that a quick scan of the objectives will show them all as green (round), except for Profit Margin—that objective is yellow (triangular). Looking at the subordinate KPIs shows a number of metrics in

Internet Sales

	CY 2006			CY 2007			CY 2008		
	Actual	Target		Actual	Target		Actual	Target	
⊟ Internet Sales Amount			●			●			△
⊞ Australia	$2,154,284.88	$1,309,047	●	$3,033,784.21	$2,154,285	●	$2,563,884.29	$3,033,784	◆
⊞ Canada	$621,602.38	$146,830	●	$535,784.46	$621,602	◆	$673,628.21	$535,784	●
⊞ France	$514,942.01	$180,572	●	$1,026,324.97	$514,942	●	$922,179.04	$1,026,325	◆
⊞ Germany	$521,230.85	$237,785	●	$1,058,405.73	$521,231	●	$1,076,890.77	$1,058,406	△
⊞ United Kingdom	$591,586.85	$291,591	●	$1,298,248.57	$591,587	●	$1,210,286.27	$1,298,249	◆
⊞ United States	$2,126,696.55	$1,100,549	●	$2,838,512.36	$2,126,697	●	$3,324,031.16	$2,838,512	●

Figure 1-12 *A scorecard showing sales values*

	Actual	Target	
⊟ **Business Performance**			△
Facilities	78%	85%	△
⊟ Manufacturing			●
Build Time	1.4	1.5	●
Backlog	23	15	●
Quality	89%	100%	◆
⊟ **Customer Focus**			●
Acquisition Cost	$85	$90	●
Complaints	4.2	5	△
Customer Volume	127,000	125,000	●
Repeat Business	72%	75%	△
⊟ **Employee Metrics**			△
Attrition	8%	5%	●
Workgroup Turnover	18%	10%	△
⊟ **Financial Performance**			●
⊟ Increase Revenue			●
New Product Revenue	$235,000	$250,000	△
Quota Attainment	113%	100%	●
⊟ Reduce Costs			△
Travel Expenses	$185,234	$175,000	△

Figure 1-13 *A hierarchical scorecard*

yellow and red (diamond shape). This is the ideal of a scorecard—instead of parsing through reports and charts, comparing numbers, reading graphs, etc.—a manager simply has to scan the scorecard to identify problem areas.

Now that we see we have a problem, what can we do? Some scorecards are relatively static—they present the metrics and that's it. However, modern BI solution scorecards will offer what are called *drill-down* capabilities, where a user can right-click a scorecard and view the underlying data, structured in a way that's analogous to the KPI presentation.

Another way to provide amplifying data is by putting the scorecard in a dashboard and then adding components to provide contextual data around the scorecard. Most scorecard tools also provide dynamic capabilities so that clicking an objective or KPI can either change which components are presented, or they might act as a slicer/filter against the data in the charts. For example, in the scorecard in Figure 1-12, clicking "Canada" may filter all associated charts on the dashboard page to show values for Canada alone.

NOTE

Usage of the terms "scorecard" and "dashboard" can get fuzzy—many people use the term "dashboard" to describe what we've been calling a "scorecard" here. However, we don't recall anyone ever referring to an integrated dashboard as a scorecard. Wayne Eckerson covers the traditional differences in Performance Dashboards.

So now that we have a rough understanding of scorecards, let's take a closer look at the most important part of this exercise—the KPIs that make up a scorecard.

Key Performance Indicators (KPI)

Above KPIs in a schematic are objectives, perspectives, the scorecard, dashboard, etc. All business-driven objects. Below the KPI is the data. Data drives the measure of a KPI, the target, the trending. Thus, our descriptions of KPIs as "where business meets data." As such, KPI design is the critical part of a business intelligence initiative.

Be wary of trying to "boil the ocean." In the sidebar on the use of the term "data warehouse," we mentioned avoiding the impulse to include everything in the underlying data store for a BI initiative. The same advice applies here, on top of the initiative. A project group may be tempted to create key performance indicators for every aspect of a business, map out the data requirements in advance, distill the required metrics, and so on.

In *The Balanced Scorecard: Translating Strategy into Action* (Harvard Business Press, 1996) by Drs. Kaplan and Norton, they indicate that a working balanced scorecard can be implemented in 16 weeks. Obviously, with only four months to work with, you're not going to create metrics for every facet of the company. In our opinion, keeping this

Balanced Scorecard

The balanced scorecard was first created in 1987, but the idea was formalized by Dr. David Norton and Dr. Robert Kaplan in 1992. A balanced scorecard is simply a specialized type of scorecard that uses top-level *perspectives* as the top level of analysis for the aggregated data. Most robust scorecard applications that have some flexibility are capable of creating a balanced scorecard.

The idea is that, left to their own devices, it seems like a lot of scorecard designers tend to focus on the financial aspects of the business a little too much. So Drs. Kaplan and Norton created a framework for business excellence that proposed *perspectives* as top-level groupings on a scorecard to drive awareness towards nonfinancial aspects of the business that are every bit as essential for success as profit and loss.

The four perspectives in a standard balanced scorecard are:

▶ **Financial** This perspective contains the traditional money-focused objectives in a business.

▶ **Customer** This perspective contains objectives regarding customer satisfaction, retention costs, turnover, etc.

▶ **Internal Business** This perspective looks inward. There should be objectives in areas such as facilities management, business processes, and so on. This is often phrased as "What must we excel at to succeed?"

▶ **Innovation and Learning** Here is your investment in your people. This includes training and attrition, for example, but also maturation and evolution of the business itself.

The hard part of building a balanced scorecard is in the business analysis. For the tools themselves, they only have to be able to handle several levels of hierarchy in the scorecard (for perspectives, objectives, and KPIs).

"16 weeks" timeframe in front of you is a good way to keep your mind on the goal of implementing a strategic scorecard, instead of trying to map out every nook and cranny of the company.

There are numerous methodologies and characteristics of successful KPIs. In *Key Performance Indicators* (John Wiley and Sons, 2010), David Parmenter advocates seven characteristics, and details them well. Wayne Eckerson, on the other hand, details

Agility in Creating KPIs

Once again we're going to raise the issue of trying to stay agile when working in business intelligence. We worked with one customer that already had a balanced scorecard for their organization—it was printed on paper, and once a quarter, executive management would push to update all the metrics (by hand). This had been going on for a few years.

We met with the strategic coordinator, and we reviewed the scorecard. It was a solid set of metrics to define success in the organization. The problem was that nobody seemed to take it seriously except when they had to submit their metrics. We helped him set up a web-based scorecard package, and we hand-coded the perspectives, objectives, and KPIs, with manually entered data from the most recent published metrics.

The strategic coordinator then called a meeting of the stakeholders to show them the current scorecard and discuss project plans to wire it up to live data. As soon as they saw the scorecard and KPIs on a web portal, criticism came out of the woodwork: "That measure isn't accurate!"; "Where did you get those numbers?"; "That's not the right way to measure my business!"

The point being that when working on a scorecard initiative, consider hand-coding the scorecard with manual values as soon as possible so that stakeholders and metric owners can start vetting the details early.

12 characteristics of effective KPIs in *Performance Dashboards*. Personally, we tend to rely on good old SMART:

- ▶ Specific
- ▶ Measurable
- ▶ Attainable
- ▶ Relevant
- ▶ Time-oriented

SMART originates from the project management world, and refers to setting project objectives. We happen to feel this is a short, easy-to-remember mnemonic that will keep you on track when defining the KPIs.

A KPI is generally going to consist of a text description, an actual value, and a target value. From there, you may have additional data, such as a performance indicator, trend

	Actual	Fiscal Year Target	Ultimate Target	Trend	Comment
Customer Satisfaction	86.0%	85.0% ● 1%	95.0% △	⤴	Long Term Target is 12/31/2012

Figure 1-14   *A detailed KPI*

indicator, additional targets (for example, a long-term target and a short-term target), and perhaps even annotations and sparklines. Figure 1-14 shows a detailed KPI; we'll walk through the parts of it.

First we have the label—this is straightforward. Next we have the actual value—the number we really care about. Note in this case it's measured in percent, but it can have any units (dollars, days, gallons—whatever the measure of the thing we care about). There may also be a historic value (last quarter or last year). Next is what brings our scorecard to life—the target value. This KPI has two target values, a short-term and a long-term, but we'll focus on the short term target. Note that we have a target value (85 percent) and an indicator. Generally, you are able to set thresholds on the indicator as to when it changes from green to yellow to red.

NOTE

You're not limited to green, yellow, and red. Most scorecard packages will allow you to select from different indicators or even design your own (we had a customer with a scorecard for a helicopter assembly line—they created an indicator that used red, yellow, and green helicopters). You can have more than three states as well. For example, if a KPI isn't implemented yet but you want it on the scorecard for awareness, you might give it a neutral indicator—blue or gray. Just remember as you redesign indicators that people have come to expect red, yellow, and green for underperforming, near target, and on or above target, respectively. You don't want to have to train everyone who looks at the scorecard what fuchsia means.

Next is an "ultimate target," which is a longer-term goal. Having short-term and long-term goals can help keep your folks energized. Trying to care about a five-year goal on a day-to-day basis can be challenging. The trend arrow simply gives the KPI a sense of being in motion, as opposed to a static snapshot. The final piece is a comment field. KPIs can have any number of additional information, either static (hand-entered) or data driven. Often, a web-based KPI will have a hyperlink for detailed information or to view a definition of the KPI.

One important value that KPIs will have, but which generally isn't visible, is a weighting factor. Because KPIs will be assembled into a scorecard, you may want some metrics to count more than others. Adding weighting factors allows, well, weighting the indicators as they are rolled up by the scorecard.

So we have business data linked into key performance indicators, KPIs collected into objectives and perspectives, and all of this glued together in a scorecard. However, how do we keep track of relationships between KPIs, and how they may affect our business strategy? For example, if our customer satisfaction drops, while that metric itself will drop, and the customer perspective will drop, we will likely also see a financial impact as we lose returning customers. Is there any way to keep track of which KPIs may affect which perspectives?

There is—it's one of the outcomes of the work done by Drs. Kaplan and Norton, and it's the *strategy map*.

Strategy Maps

In *Strategy Maps* (Harvard Business Press, 2004), Drs. Kaplan and Norton describe strategy as "a step in a continuum" and lay out a hierarchy, from mission and values down through vision, strategy, balanced scorecard, targets and initiatives, and objectives. Between strategy and balanced scorecard is a map to "translate the strategy." Just as the KPI was where business meets data, the strategy map is where big-picture strategy is translated into execution.

An example strategy map is shown in Figure 1-15. You can design a strategy map in a specialized tool, or Visio, or on paper with a pencil. The important thing is to ensure that you understand the relationships between the perspectives and the objectives and KPIs that drive them.

Many BI tools will include strategy map tools, and may include a way to publish the strategy map. Some will also have a method to link the objectives and KPIs in the strategy map to the actual metrics in the scorecard so the strategy map will "light up" to reflect the real-time values of the underlying data.

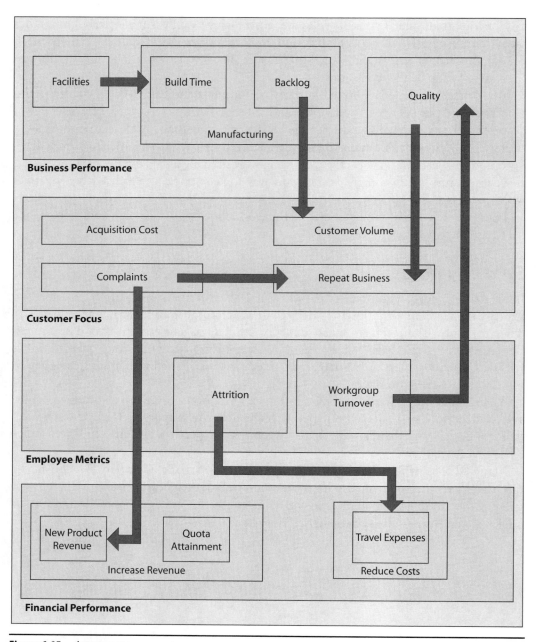

Figure 1-15   *A strategy map*

Summary

We currently have six business intelligence books lying open on our desk—literally thousands of pages written about this topic, and we've covered it in less than 30. Needless to say, there's so much more we could add. However, ultimately, this book is not about the business side of business intelligence. We do recommend that you read further on the subject, whether you're a business analyst, consultant, or software developer who has to make the stuff work. It's important for everyone to be aware of the ultimate goal.

We've tried to keep this chapter vendor-agnostic. Moving forward, we'll spend more time talking about specific Microsoft products and technologies to bring the concepts we've learned here to life. After an overview of the platform in the next chapter, we'll start to dig into specific technologies, such as SQL Server Analysis Services, Excel and Excel Services, and the new bridge between the two—PowerPivot, introduced in SQL Server 2008 R2.

We'll discuss SQL Server Integration Services for ETL, and Reporting Services for enterprise reporting and reporting as an adjunct to a business intelligence solution. Then we'll move into the collaboration space and look at SharePoint Server 2010 and the business services that will aid our BI initiatives.

Then on to a discussion about charts and graphs (they're not just lines and pies). SQL Server 2008 R2 improves on the spatial capabilities introduced in SQL Server 2008, and we'll look at how to add maps and cartographic information to our dashboards. As we round the home stretch, we'll talk about data mining, then using PerformancePoint Services for scorecarding and dashboards (which builds on all the previous material, so no cheating and skipping ahead).

Finally, we'll finish up by discussing Master Data Services, introduced in SQL Server 2008 R2, and how we use it to bolster our "one version of the truth" in our business intelligence platform. The last chapter will cover publishing, administration, and other "keep it running" type tasks.

So, let's step forward into the world of Microsoft Business Intelligence…

Chapter 2

Collaboration Meets Business Intelligence

In This Chapter

- ▶ SQL Server
- ▶ Business Intelligence and Collaboration
- ▶ SharePoint
- ▶ PerformancePoint Services
- ▶ Visio Services
- ▶ Business Connectivity Services
- ▶ Summary

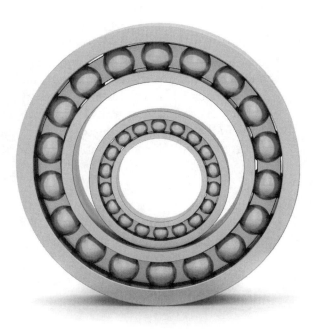

As we were researching this book, we found a curious theme throughout the business intelligence community. A lot of time and effort was expended discussing how to deal with semistructured and unstructured data, and how to bring them into a BI infrastructure:

> "More complex text analysis tools are used to try to transform the data embedded within the text into a structured form." – David Loshin, *Business Intelligence: The Savvy Manager's Guide* (Morgan Kaufmann, 2003)

> "The incorporation of text analytics with traditional business intelligence is still in its infancy." – Cindi Howson, *Successful Business Intelligence* (McGraw-Hill/ Professional, 2007)

> "Therefore, it is much more appealing to bring the unstructured data to the structured environment than it is to recreate the analytical infrastructure in the unstructured environment." – William Inmon and Anthony Nesavich, *Tapping Into Unstructured Data* (Prentice Hall, 2007)

Each of these statements takes the approach of treating the structured business intelligence environment as the one-stop toolset and brings the unstructured data (e-mail, documents, and slide decks) into it. What we find fascinating is that Microsoft has done the exact opposite—they have brought business intelligence into the middle of the collaborative stack. Integration between structured and unstructured data isn't going to be about moving data from one side to the other—the data will stay in place; the tools will reach out as necessary.

We've given you a basic foundation in business intelligence, and you should now have an appreciation for the requirements on the BI side to clean data; bring it into a data mart; create OLAP structures; and then build reporting, analysis, scorecards, and dashboards on top. In this chapter we're going to start by looking at SQL Server and understanding how it fits into the whole "BI stack." Then we're going to look at SharePoint Server and the services that supplement the hard-structured data integration with the collaborative framework that SharePoint is known for.

SQL Server

When most people think of SQL Server, they think of the relational database—tables of data, running queries, etc. However, that's just the beginning of what SQL Server is capable of. Consider "SQL Server" to be an umbrella technology label that encompasses:

▶ SQL Server Relational Database Management System (RDBMS), the database engine

▶ SQL Server Integration Services (SSIS), an enterprise-class ETL

▶ SQL Server Analysis Services (SSAS), multidimensional data analysis

▶ SQL Server Reporting Services (SSRS), web-enabled reporting from any data source

With SQL Server 2008 R2, two new technologies are introduced that have enormous implications for a business intelligence solution: PowerPivot for Excel and SharePoint, and Master Data Services, which provides a service-based framework for managing standard data structures for an organization.

This makes SQL Server a powerful basis for a business intelligence platform. With a SQL Server installation, you have everything you need to move and clean data, create dimensional OLAP repositories, and achieve enterprise-class reporting. You also have data mining, end-user ad hoc reporting, and now end-user ad hoc modeling. When you couple this with the user interface capabilities of Office and SharePoint server, it's a complete BI suite.

Let's take a look at the services in SQL Server and how they create the foundation for our business intelligence solution.

Business Intelligence Development Studio (BIDS)

Actually, before we start, let's introduce one of the most compelling aspects of the SQL Server BI experience—BIDS, shown in Figure 2-1. SQL Server uses a Visual Studio shell with specialized projects to develop Integration Services packages, Analysis Services cubes and data mining solutions, and Reporting Services reports. The benefit here is that by using a common tool for all the BI tasks, it's easier for BI developers to move from one task to another, and to learn the various services.

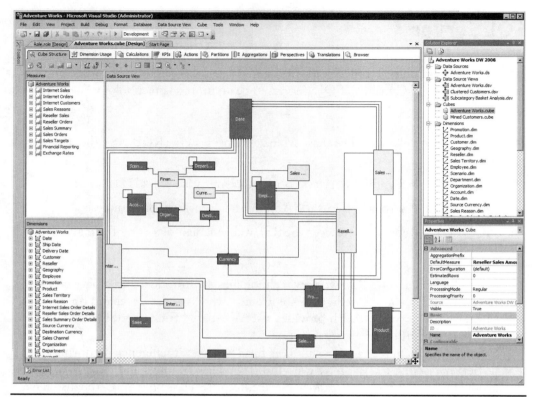

Figure 2-1   *The Business Intelligence Development Studio*

While the shell is based on Visual Studio, there's no licensing necessary to install BIDS—all you have to worry about is the licensing of SQL Server with respect to your developers. Beyond that, BIDS is installed with the SQL client tools. If you already have the appropriate version of Visual Studio installed, then installing the client tools will just add the BI templates to Visual Studio, as shown in Figure 2-2.

Now that we understand our toolset, let's look at the services. This is just a quick introduction to ease the transition from the vendor-agnostic BI material in the first chapter to the Microsoft BI platform that we will be using moving forward.

SSIS

SQL Server Integration Services was introduced with SQL Server 2005 to replace Data Transformation Services (DTS). SSIS is an enterprise-class Extract, Transform, Load (ETL) engine for moving data from one place to another. One of the most compelling

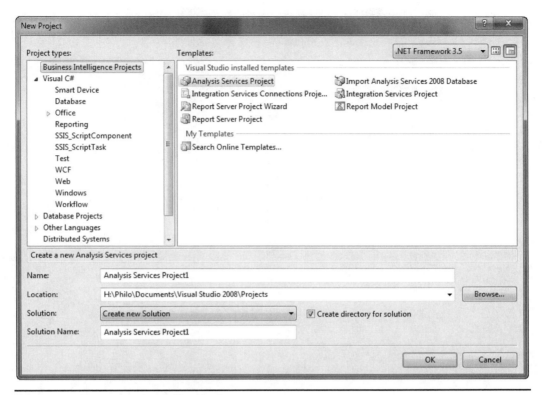

Figure 2-2   *BI project templates in Visual Studio*

aspects to the designer is that the component/canvas approach allows for the creation of some complex processes, as shown in Figure 2-3.

NOTE

While SSIS is a SQL Server service, there is no requirement for its data to be in SQL Server. For example, you can use SSIS to load data from a text file into Oracle, or to extract data from SAP and load it into MySQL.

The components in SSIS cover dozens of tasks—processing Analysis Services cubes, profiling data, sending mail, interacting with a message queue, operating on the file system, or any number of database maintenance tasks. This is so that SSIS packages can perform maintenance operations in conjunction with moving data. For example, you may want to compact a database before loading a large-batch data dump. Or, you may want to process an OLAP cube after loading new data.

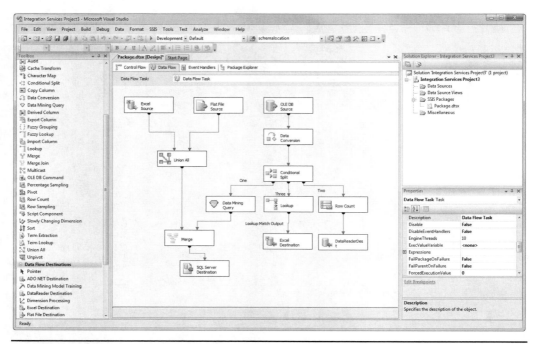

Figure 2-3   *Integration Services package in BIDS*

With respect to moving data, SSIS can extract from any OLE DB source, and has a number of data destinations, from OLE DB to more specific destinations (such as data mining, to train mining models, or an ADO.Net data reader). Between the source and destination, there are a number of data transformation tasks to manipulate the data while it's in transit.

Once you've built an Integration Services package, you can deploy it to SQL Server and use the SQL Server agent to execute the package as necessary (on a schedule, as the result of another job running, etc.).

We'll dig into Integration Services in Chapter 6.

SSAS

Analysis Services has been part of SQL Server in various forms since SQL Server 7. SSAS is an online analytical processing (OLAP) server that provides a means for creating a business model for structured data, and then aggregating and caching numerical data in structures to enable fast response times when end users do analysis on the data.

As we discussed in Chapter 1, when analyzing data, we are generally more interested in aggregations of the values than the atomic values themselves. We want to know how many bicycles were purchased in California in October; we don't care that John Smith bought a Red Touring 150 on October 15. SSAS lets a database administrator (DBA) design a model that reflects the business needs of analysts and then map underlying data sources into that framework. By creating *dimensions* in business-aware terms like "product categories" or "sales territory," we can make it easy for an analyst to understand the data and how it relates. Figure 2-4 shows an example of working in the semantic layer and focusing on results instead of worrying about queries.

Analysis Services acts as a data source for various front ends—Excel, SharePoint, various reporting engines, PerformancePoint, and third-party vendor tools. One of the

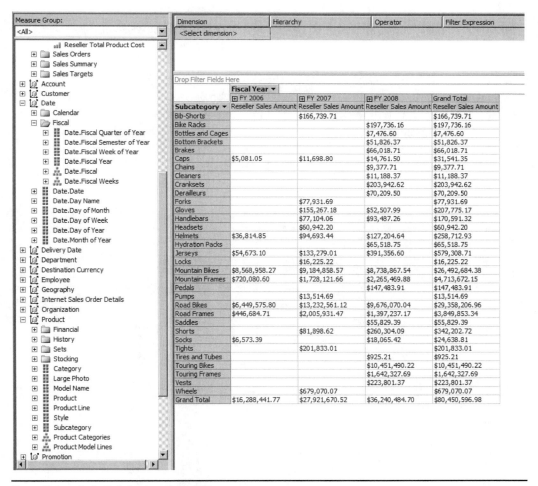

Figure 2-4   *An Analysis Services cube in BIDS*

most important aspects of using SSAS to unify data is that as a single point source for analytic data, each user gets what is referred to as "one version of the truth."

PowerPivot

SQL Server 2008 R2 introduces what is effectively a new capability, called PowerPivot. This is an OLAP engine that integrates with SharePoint Server and (with a free download) Excel 2010. This enables an end user to use Excel to connect to various data sources directly (providing they have the right credentials) and build a model in Excel. Essentially, they are creating an Analysis Services cube on the fly, on their desktop.

NOTE

PowerPivot is actually an Analysis Services instance. However, it can only host PowerPivot models; it cannot host standard SSAS cubes.

Once a user is happy with their PowerPivot model, they can publish it to Analysis Services running in PowerPivot mode, and it can be accessed via the SharePoint Server. From there, it will look like a standard cube in an Analysis Services instance, so other users can connect reports to it, Excel spreadsheets (shown in Figure 2-5), PerformancePoint—any application that can connect to SSAS.

ID	Name	Purchase Price	Original Sale Price	Discount	Actual Sale Price	Profit Margin	Number in Stock
3242-4342	"Ready-To-Grow" Fertilizer (XL)	$79.99	$189.99	20%	$151.99	90%	16
4534-3409	Brick Barbeque Set "Make it Yourself!"	$149.99	$199.99	0%	199.99	33%	4
8943-3244	Charcoal	$4.99	$9.99	20%	$7.99	60%	49
4235-4324	Decorative Stones	$1.99	$9.99	20%	$7.99	302%	198
7803-4321	Electic Hedge Clippers	$19.99	$39.99	30%	$27.99	40%	14
7892-4324	Electic Push Lawn Mower	$89.99	$149.99	20%	$119.99	33%	10
2342-7879	Elegant Crystal Vase	$49.99	$129.99	30%	$90.99	82%	12
4323-4325	Elegant Steel and Glass Table	$109.99	$209.99	10%	$188.99	72%	8
4324-7899	Elegant Steel Chair	$79.99	$149.99	30%	$104.99	31%	12
8903-4213	Garden Hose	$4.99	$9.99	10%	$8.99	80%	28
8932-4324	Garden Hose Spray Nozzle	$2.99	$4.99	0%	$4.99	67%	34
8234-5534	Gas Powered Push Lawn Mower	$99.99	$179.99	10%	$161.99	62%	24
2343-4324	Hand Saw	$4.99	$29.99	20%	$23.99	381%	18
5443-4342	Hedge Clippers	$4.99	$9.99	10%	$8.99	80%	27
4324-8943	Outdoor Sink	$109.99	$189.99	20%	$151.99	38%	4
3232-4323	Reclining Fabric Lawn Chair	$24.99	$49.99	0%	$49.99	100%	11
7888-7878	Regular Barbeque	$109.99	$149.99	0%	$149.99	36%	18
8902-3532	Riding Lawn Mower	$299.99	$599.99	10%	$539.99	80%	7
3424-4354	Shovel	$9.99	$29.99	30%	$20.99	110%	36
4242-7873	Sod	$0.99	$4.99	0%	$4.99	404%	503
3249-3255	Spade	$2.99	$9.99	40%	$5.99	100%	42
3243-4235	Stainless Steel Barbeque	$249.99	$499.99	15%	$424.99	70%	4
9232-4324	Starter Fluid	$1.99	$4.99	0%	$4.99	151%	74
4233-5324	Stone Tiles	$1.99	$4.99	0%	$4.99	151%	412
7833-4321	Weeder	$9.99	$29.99	20%	$23.99	140%	18
2314-4234	White Plastic Lawn Chair	$29.99	$79.99	40%	$47.99	60%	42
3433-3425	White Plastic Table	$34.99	$129.99	40%	$77.99	123%	12

Figure 2-5 *A PowerPivot report in Excel, hosted in SharePoint*

In addition to the modeling aspects, PowerPivot technology is woven into the SharePoint Server infrastructure, giving administrators powerful capabilities regarding management and scalability. Performance metrics are tracked and rolled into a cube so they can be displayed in a dashboard, reported on, and so on.

Data Mining

Reporting is simply presenting a detailed list of records—answering structured questions. OLAP analysis lets analysts dig into data to ask various questions and try to find the answers. Data mining is what you do when you don't even know what question to ask.

Essentially, data mining is about identifying patterns in large volumes of data. Data mining is how grocery stores identify purchases that are generally made together, or alternatively, purchases that are *not* made in the same trip. Data mining feeds the question when the fast food cashier asks, "Would you like a side of coleslaw with that?"

There are a number of definitions or explanations of data mining. We like the following:

> "Data mining is the analysis of (often large) observational data sets to find unsuspected relationships and to summarize the data in novel ways that are both understandable and useful to the data owner." – David Hand, Heikki Mannila, and Padhraic Smyth, *Principles of Data Mining* (MIT Press, 2001)

SQL Server Analysis Services has a data mining engine built in. This data mining engine provides a number of different algorithms to perform different types of analysis, from basket analysis (who will buy what based on what's in their shopping cart), classification (estimating what a customer will purchase based on their demographics), to time-series analysis (predicting future values based on past performance).

Data mining in SQL Server was largely ignored until Office 2007 was released. Excel 2007 had an add-in available that enabled end-user creation of data mining models and performing mining analysis on data in Excel. This made data mining far more accessible, for experimentation and hands-on learning. Models created in Excel can be published back to Analysis Services for consumption in other front ends.

Reporting Services

Speaking of front ends, SQL Server Reporting Services is an amazing tool for creating enterprise reports. Reporting Services was designed by the SQL product team for SQL Server 2005. However, after the initial alpha release, customer demand for it was so great that they released Reporting Services as an add-on to SQL Server 2000.

Reporting Services is a web-based application. IT professionals design reports in BIDS, shown in Figure 2-6, and then publish them to the server. From the server, users

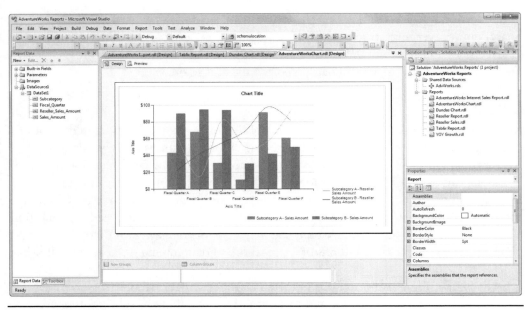

Figure 2-6 *Designing a report in BIDS*

can view reports through the Report Manager website, or the URL for a report can be linked from any other website. Reports can also be embedded in webpages.

In addition to simply looking at reports via a browser, reports can be exported to Excel, Word, XML, PDF, or TIFF formats. Reporting Services 2008 R2 adds the ability to make reports available as an Atom data feed. Users can also subscribe to reports and have them e-mailed on a regular basis or when specific data points change value. Through a .Net control, reports can also be embedded in Windows applications or ASP.Net websites.

If you've dealt with enterprise reporting in the past, you will know that often, reporting servers can get to be a bit of a mess—old reports that aren't used, no configuration management, new reports created because users can't find an existing one, and so on. SSRS offers one option out of that madness: SharePoint integration.

Starting with SQL Server 2005, Reporting Services can be integrated with SharePoint Server. In this case, there is no longer an independent report manager—all report management is performed via SharePoint. In addition to making it easier to collaborate on reports and put reports in a location where they make sense, this means the capabilities of SharePoint are available—workflow for report approval, version control, publishing, and content management capabilities.

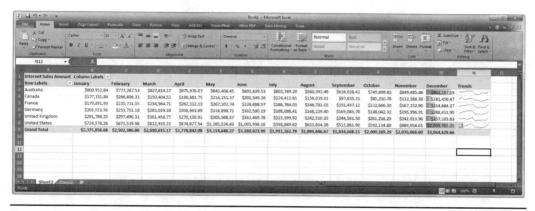

Figure 2-7   *A report with sparklines and data bars*

Charts

Reporting Services continues to improve on the charting engine. In 2008 R2, you now have the ability to add data bars, sparklines, maps, and KPI indicators to a report or chart, as shown in Figure 2-7. This gives us a lot more flexibility to design charts that can speak visually at a quick glance.

If you haven't worked with charts in Reporting Services since 2005, you absolutely must upgrade. The shift from 2005 to 2008 was remarkable, and 2008 R2 just adds to that.

Maps

SQL Server 2008 introduced the spatial data type, allowing DBAs to capture geometric and geographic data with their records. There were some interesting architecture changes to accompany this, but not a lot surfaced in the tools. SQL Server 2008 R2 changes this—Reporting Services now has a map control that can parse spatial data for display graphically, as shown in Figure 2-8. You can see how powerful this is for data that has a geographic component.

Report Builder

Reporting Services 2005 included an ad hoc report builder, which was a client application that end users could use to create reports and publish them back to Reporting Services. The big problem was that the Report Builder would only work against special reporting models created and published in Reporting Services. The combination of lead work required and limitations on the client meant Report Builder didn't see much use.

Worldwide Sales of FY08 (thousands $)

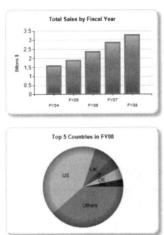

Figure 2-8   *Report with a map*

SQL Server 2008 saw Report Builder 2.0, which no longer had the requirement for models—it could work directly against data sources, or even create data sources and publish them back to Reporting Services. SQL Server 2008 R2 introduces Report Builder 3.0, shown in Figure 2-9, which is a huge stride forward (again).

Report Builder also has all of the capabilities of BIDS with respect to Tablix, charting, sparklines, indicators, and maps.

Master Data Services

One problem often faced in large organizations is ensuring that the same thing is referred to in the same way across the organization. Whether it's a project name, customer name and information, or job title, there is a tendency for semantics to drift across the organization. And if you want to change a name, there can be a dozen places or more to change it. You can see how this can get a bit nightmarish when talking business intelligence.

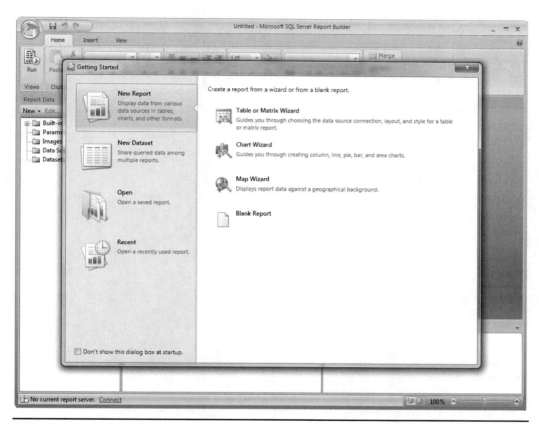

Figure 2-9   *Report Builder 3.0*

SQL Server 2008 R2 includes a new technology called Master Data Services. This is a web-based service that lets the business maintain a standard set of definitions for objects and standard values for those objects. In other words, the address of vendor companies will always be Street1: and Street2:, not Street & Apt, or Address & Suite. And the names and addresses of vendors will be uniform, and if they change, they only need to be changed in one place. Figure 2-10 shows the master data model for "Product."

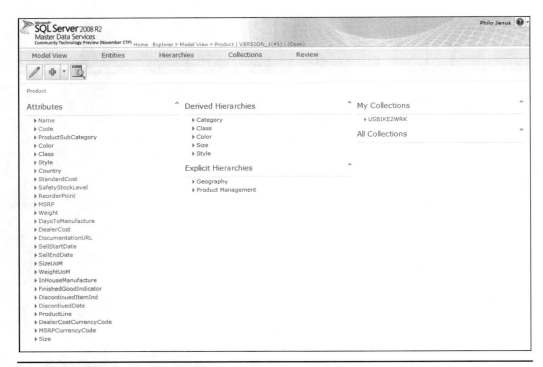

Figure 2-10   *Master data model for "Product"*

Business Intelligence and Collaboration

We've reviewed the data infrastructure that will serve as the foundation for our business intelligence solution. As mentioned earlier, the BI data and enterprise collaboration have traditionally been viewed as two separate worlds that had to interact on rare occasion somehow. However, Microsoft has successfully merged them; not by pulling the unstructured data into the BI world, as often suggested—they have pulled the BI world into the collaboration space.

In *The Jericho Principle* (Wiley and Sons, 2003), Ralph Welborn and Vince Kasten define a "Jericho Zone" (as in "bring down the walls of..."). They say:

> In the Jericho Zone, you can rapidly create high-value collaborative relationships with other companies. Based on everything we have seen [...], operating in the Jericho Zone means that you and your partners have found rapid and efficient ways of:

> ▶ Quantifying the value each of you brings to the relationship

> ▶ Controlling the risks associated with high intimacy

> ▶ Equitably sharing the rewards of the collaboration

Now in *The Jericho Principle,* the discussion is about collaboration between two business entities or companies. But we found the approach also appropriate for considering merging business intelligence and collaboration. In an established organization, merging BI and collaboration will bring disparate groups into close proximity—it is worth remembering that this merger is nontrivial, but the payoff can be great.

NOTE

We highly recommend The Jericho Principle. *Although it is about enterprise collaboration, there is a lot of salient advice regarding collaboration and business agility. If you're in the collaboration space, you should have this on your bookshelf.*

SharePoint

SharePoint debuted in 2001 as a collaboration platform leveraging Exchange as a data store. Everyone hated it. After a significant redesign, it was relaunched in 2003 as an ASP.Net application with SQL Server as the data store. Despite some interesting drawbacks (nobody ever did figure out what area pages were for), it took off like wildfire as a collaboration platform.

In 2007 Microsoft rebranded SharePoint to Microsoft Office SharePoint Server (MOSS). There were a lot of revolutionary changes (no more area pages), but what we're most interested in are Excel Services, the Business Data Catalog, and the architecture that made PerformancePoint Server possible. MOSS was definitely the foundation for a capable business intelligence platform.

SharePoint returns in 2010 with a facelift, as shown in Figure 2-11. Now Windows SharePoint Services is termed SharePoint Foundation, while MOSS has gone back to simply being called SharePoint Server. Add in PowerPivot capabilities, tighter integration with Reporting Services, improvements to Excel Services, and the fact that PerformancePoint Services is now included instead of a separate product, and SharePoint Server *is* a business intelligence platform in its own right.

SharePoint is really just the platform, though. The heavy lifting is done by the services under the SharePoint umbrella. Let's take a look at them.

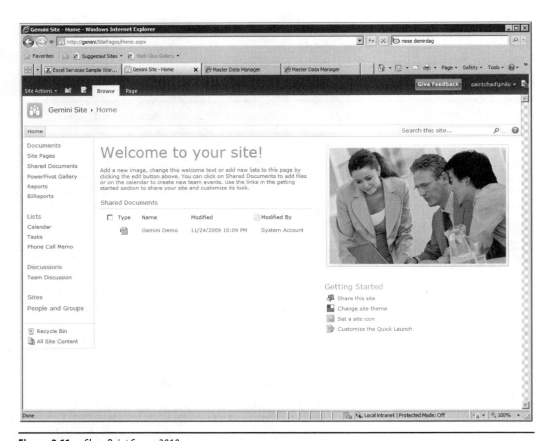

Figure 2-11 *SharePoint Server 2010*

Excel, Excel Services, and PowerPivot

The SharePoint service here is Excel Services, but it's so tightly integrated with Excel and PowerPivot we wanted to be sure that was clear. Excel Services is an engine that runs in the SharePoint space and can emulate the behavior of the Excel desktop client. A lot of power Excel users will have incredibly complex spreadsheets with macros and reams of data. This gives rise to them having the most powerful desktop in the organization, and they still have to leave a "do not turn off" sign on it when they leave it crunching at night. With Excel Services, that same spreadsheet can be published to a server, where it will leverage the server hardware (and failover), and the results can be published to a webpage or other output.

Excel Services provides three key scenarios:

▶ Using server hardware to process heavy computing jobs, either by publishing the spreadsheet into Excel Services or by leveraging the Excel Services object model from a custom code base

▶ Publishing interactive spreadsheets to a server for public consumption

▶ Publishing spreadsheets for secure consumption

Spreadsheets published to Excel Services can be displayed via a web browser and have some interactivity. They can be wired to live data and parameterized, but end users can't just use the spreadsheet on an ad hoc basis. Thus, Excel is necessary as a front end for Excel Services. SharePoint 2010 adds Office Web Apps, which includes a web-based edition of Excel as an interactive end-user application. This enables the creation and editing of Excel spreadsheets via a browser.

Excel is also the front end for PowerPivot, the modeling engine in SQL Server Analysis Services 2008 R2. With PowerPivot, the primary scenario is publishing to SharePoint, so again they're pretty well welded together. Figure 2-12 shows a PowerPivot gallery in SharePoint 2010. Note the automatic thumbnails created and presented.

PowerPivot gives us the data modeling and analysis, but for a full BI implementation, we also need a scorecard and analytics. Let's look at PerformancePoint Services.

Figure 2-12   *A PowerPivot gallery in SharePoint 2010*

PerformancePoint Services

PerformancePoint Server launched in 2007. It had the ability to build scorecards, create and associate analytic charts, and it had a modeling engine for doing what-if analysis and budgeting. The reception was interesting—the BI community *wanted* to like it, but it had a lot of rough edges, and to really get the full benefit out of it, you needed MOSS Enterprise Edition, which was a commitment many organizations weren't ready to make.

In January 2009, Microsoft folded PerformancePoint into SharePoint. It became a "feature" of SharePoint, available to users who had or bought MOSS Enterprise Edition. The planning module, which had shown a lot of promise but still had a way to go, was end-of-lifed. Its modeling functions would eventually be picked up by PowerPivot, while its budgeting and financial capabilities were migrated to Microsoft's Dynamics line.

NOTE

If you are planning to stay with MOSS 2007 for some time, and are interested in PerformancePoint Server, allow us to recommend our book Pro PerformancePoint Server 2007 *(APress, 2008). Although written when PerformancePoint was a separate product, it's still relevant.*

In SharePoint Server 2010, PerformancePoint Services has been fully integrated into SharePoint. To create a scorecard or dashboard, you start at SharePoint at a PerformancePoint site, as shown in Figure 2-13. This site makes it easy to organize the content in PerformancePoint dashboards. (And, of course, you can have multiple sites, so as to keep everything clean.)

To build a dashboard in PerformancePoint, launch the Dashboard Designer—a click-once application that is deployed from SharePoint on demand. The Dashboard Designer allows users to create KPIs and connect them to data sources, as shown

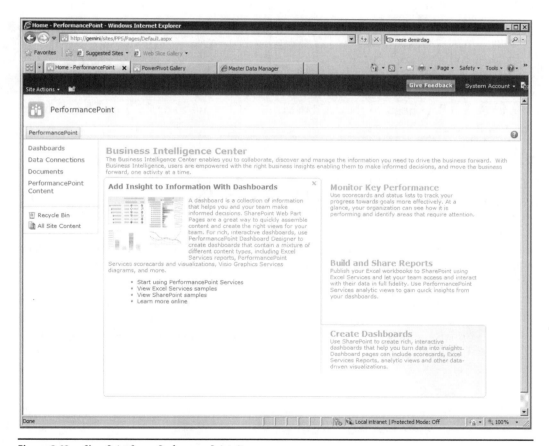

Figure 2-13 *SharePoint Server PerformancePoint site*

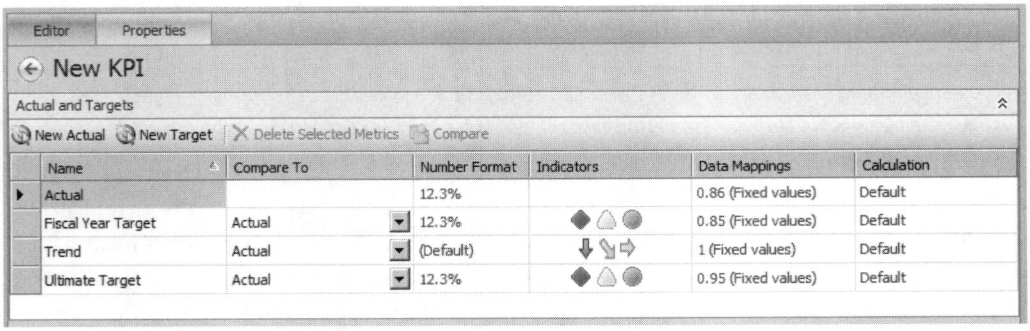

Editor	Properties

New KPI

Actual and Targets

New Actual New Target X Delete Selected Metrics Compare

Name	Compare To	Number Format	Indicators	Data Mappings	Calculation
▶ Actual		12.3%		0.86 (Fixed values)	Default
Fiscal Year Target	Actual	12.3%	◆ △ ●	0.85 (Fixed values)	Default
Trend	Actual	(Default)	⬇ ⬊ ⇨	1 (Fixed values)	Default
Ultimate Target	Actual	12.3%	◆ △ ●	0.95 (Fixed values)	Default

Figure 2-14   *The KPI designer in Dashboard Designer*

in Figure 2-14; collect KPIs into scorecards; create analytic reports; and combine everything into dashboards.

The scorecard designer is WYSIWYG (what you see is what you get)—if you've made data connections, you can see the scorecard as you build it. You can also build a scorecard from a dimension, automatically creating KPIs for every district in the state, for example. Dashboard design, however, is not WYSIWYG—there's a block designer where you can drag items to the dashboard, but you'll have to deploy it to SharePoint to see how it looks.

Dashboards can have scorecards, reports, embedded webpages, filters, and so on. Reports can be linked to scorecards, so clicking a KPI on the scorecard will filter the reports. In addition, the dashboard is active—there are means to drill down into data, drill up or down hierarchies, annotate KPI values, etc. A sample dashboard is shown in Figure 2-15.

Another feature in PerformancePoint Services is the ability to connect a strategy map to a scorecard. Strategy maps are just Visio diagrams, and the Dashboard Designer will open an editor that allows you to link shapes to KPIs, resulting in the KPIs being color-coded based on the KPI status. The cool thing here is that the Visio diagram doesn't have to be a strategy map—any Visio diagram will work. So you could show a shop floor and color machines based on the status read from performance metrics.

And, on the topic of Visio, let's talk about another brand-new feature in SharePoint Server 2010: Visio Services.

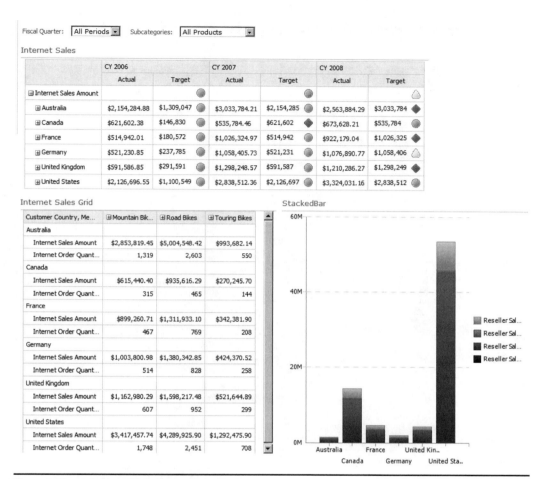

Figure 2-15   *A dashboard in PerformancePoint Services*

Visio Services

Since Visio 2003, Visio has been getting increasingly data-connected. Visio 2010 has amazing capabilities to connect it to data, and hopefully what we've covered so far in the Microsoft suite has you thinking in terms of pervasive data availability. However, the problem to date has been the ability to create actual reports out of Visio diagrams—you always had to have Visio to view a .vsd file.

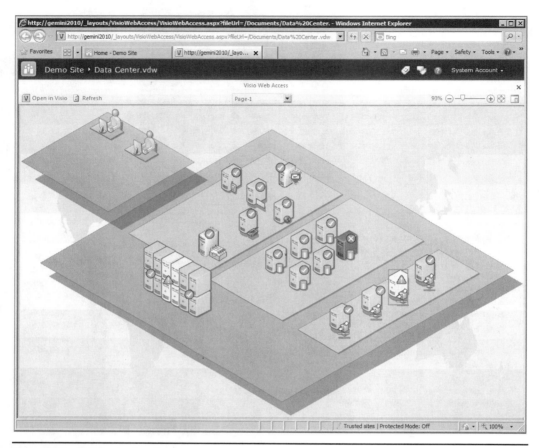

Figure 2-16 *Visio Services in action*

In SharePoint Server 2010, there is a Visio Service that is similar to Excel Services. It allows you to publish a Visio diagram to SharePoint, enable live updates of the data-connected shapes, and dynamically zoom and pan around the diagram. Although this sounds like limited functionality, if you think about it, it's just opened the door to Visio as a report designer. An example of a published Visio diagram is in Figure 2-16.

Business Connectivity Services

MOSS 2007 introduced the Business Data Catalog (BDC). This was an XML-driven modeling library to enable SharePoint developers to create business data connections to any business system. The idea was that then business data could show up in searches and be read by reporting applications. Unfortunately, the BDC was read-only, hard to configure correctly, connections required hacking XML, and the usefulness was somewhat limited.

Enter SharePoint 2010 and Business Connectivity Services (BCS). Business Connectivity Services provides "no-code" connectivity to external business systems so that using them internally is uniform and easy to understand for SharePoint users. In addition, the connections are now read/write, governed by the security around the connection ID.

With BCS, a DBA creates a *model* of the business system, which is then maintained in a metadata catalog. From that catalog, SharePoint users can access and leverage connections to any business system mapped.

Summary

Hopefully, these first two chapters have given you a general feel for business intelligence in general, and then how the SQL Server and Office technologies fit into a BI world. From here, we're going to dive deeply into these technologies to give you a working understanding of their features, limitations, and how to use them, both as a content creator and as a content consumer.

Chapter 3

SQL Server
Analysis Services

In This Chapter

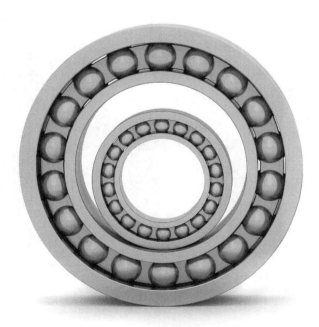

We've talked about OLAP and Analysis Services. Now it's time to dig in and understand what this is all about. Fundamentally, SQL Server Analysis Services provides the ability to read in data from external data sources, align it with multiple *dimensions,* and aggregate the numerical data into *measures* so that end users can perform analysis on that data.

We talked about business system stovepipes in Chapter 1 and analysts who pull the data together into Excel, similar to what is shown in Figure 3-1; each of the analysts

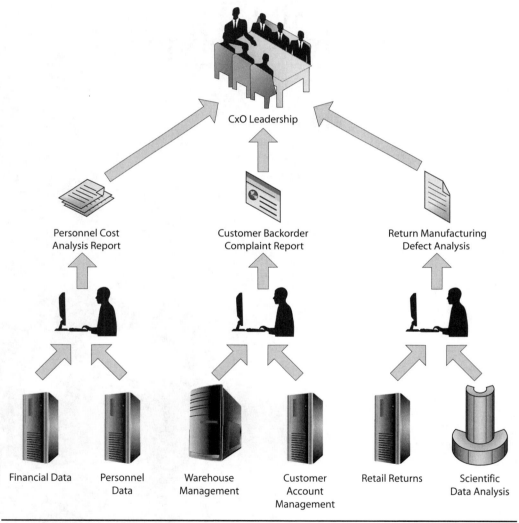

Figure 3-1   *Business system stovepipes*

is probably pulling data from the business systems shown. They have queries they've written specifically to pull the data from systems, using their specific user credentials. They're copying and pasting the data into a spreadsheet that probably has complex macros to merge the data and do some analysis before producing the output—either a spreadsheet report or perhaps something pasted into PowerPoint.

Using Excel spreadsheets this way is acceptable for reporting or analysis—as an endpoint for data. The problem is that over time, as a result of business logic added through formulas and macros, the Excel spreadsheet files become actual repositories of business data themselves. These are the "spreadmarts" (spreadsheet data marts) that can be so problematic in an enterprise.

These "spreadmarts" are problems because:

- ▶ The user who owns the spreadmart is generally a single point of failure.

- ▶ Potential inaccuracies aren't audited.

- ▶ Reviewing historical data is problematic.

- ▶ Unifying data between separate spreadmarts generally involves creating a new spreadmart.

- ▶ They don't scale.

OLAP cubes on data marts, when properly designed, can solve all these problems.

NOTE

Analysis Services is a complex server, and there are a lot of nooks and crannies to get lost in. This chapter is simply meant to be an introductory overview to the subject of multidimensional data sources, and Analysis Services in particular. If you are interested in digging more deeply into SSAS, we recommend the book Pro SQL Server Analysis Services 2008 *(APress, 2010).*

OLAP Technical Overview

We're pretty familiar with pivot-type reports that break down data between two groups of variables, similar to what's shown in Figure 3-2. Here we've grouped the numbers for a report by country and by year. This type of capability is built into most reporting platforms, including Excel. However, even at this level, consider the amount of loading we're putting on the database—all the records covered by these fields need to be queried out, aligned with the matching values, and summed.

That's just breaking down the values two ways. What if we also want to break down the data by product category, as shown in Figure 3-3? Now we have three axes to deal with, and far more complex queries. The biggest thing to notice here is that when we

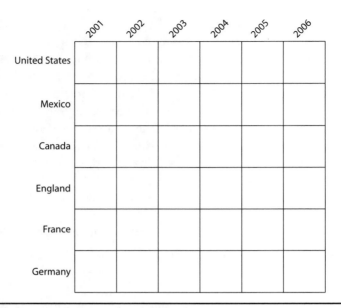

Figure 3-2 *A pivot-type report*

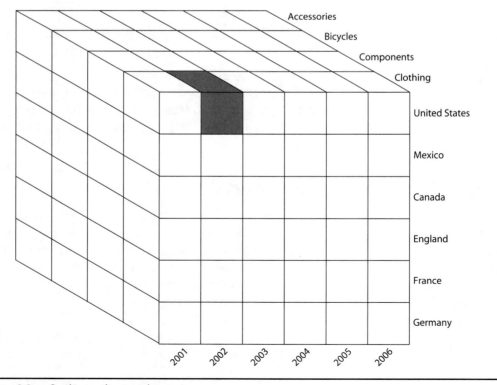

Figure 3-3 *Breaking up the report data again*

add one more *dimension* to the data breakdown, we now have a *cube* of values. Thus, we call OLAP data sets cubes. Note, of course, that we can have more than three dimensions—customer geography, purchase order date, currency, promotion, and so on.

Imagine each small cube containing the purchase order data for the dimensions that match. For example, the colored area is a "box" holding the purchase order numbers for clothing in the United States in 2002. So we could take the collection of boxes for clothing and get a pivot chart breaking down clothing sales by year and by country. Or take the horizontal slice for Canada and get a pivot chart showing sales in Canada broken down by year and by product category.

OLAP systems are designed to take relational and record-based data and create structures like this—enabling end users to break down the numerical data through various predefined dimensions. The engine rolls the numeric data together as indicated in the cube's design—it's usually summed together, but in some cases, we may want numbers averaged, or even just a count of records ("Twenty-five orders from the United States in 2003 included bicycle seats").

To review our terminology—our unit of data is the *cube;* the numeric data we're rolling together is referred to as *measures.* The semantic values we use to break down the numeric data are referred to as *dimensions.* In Figure 3-4, we have three dimensions—years along

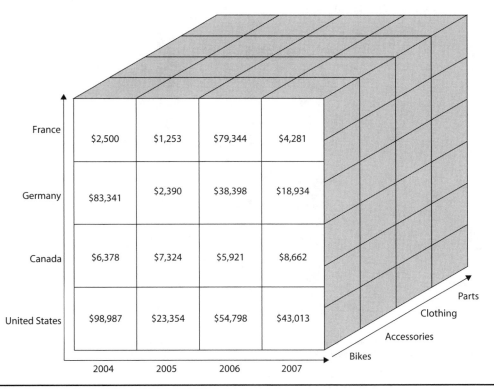

Figure 3-4   *Cube terminology*

the horizontal axis, countries along the vertical axis, and product categories going into the page. Each of the items on the dimension axis is called a *member*.

Often, when designing a cube, it can be confusing as to whether a particular collection of data should be a dimension or a measure. There's one easy rule of thumb that will help you until you figure it out: dimensions are strings, measures are numbers. Collections such as cities, product names, or people—they're nouns, and would be members of a dimension. On the other hand, measurements like population of a city, sales of a product, or number of people—those are numbers, and would be measures. One area of confusion might be labels that are numerical, for example, years or line numbers. If you're not sure, the best thing is to ask yourself, "Am I ever going to add two of these together?" If the answer is "no," then consider it a text label and members of a dimension.

There's one more term we need to consider, and it's another powerful feature of OLAP—the *hierarchy*. In Figure 3-3, we have the data broken down by years. However, we will often want to see the numbers broken down by quarter or by month. This is when OLAP really starts to make sense. For example, let's say that fabrication time on the factory floor had gone up significantly during one quarter. We could dig through the performance records of several hundred machines, looking for an anomaly. Alternatively, if we've been feeding performance data for the equipment into a data mart, we can break the data down by month and compare the performance to other quarters easily. A date hierarchy is shown in Figure 3-5.

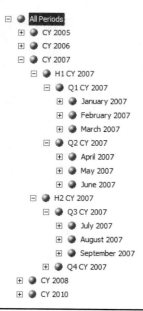

Figure 3-5   *A date hierarchy showing calendar years down to the month level.*

This still requires sifting through a lot of data. However, we can look at a report like the one in Figure 3-6, which shows Internet sales by product and by year. By reviewing the data in this compact format, we can quickly spot an anomaly. Can we narrow it down even further? In this case, we can break down the year into its constituent quarters, and the product category into subcategories, then individual products. Now we again find an anomaly, so we can dig into the months in the quarter and the specific product.

NOTE

There is a difference between "drilling down" (as in a hierarchy) and "drilling through." Generally in an OLAP solution, "drilling through" refers to accessing the underlying records themselves. We'll cover this later.

Online Analytical Processing (OLAP)

To achieve this kind of reporting, we need a system that will take transactional records and create ready-made pivot tables for us. The trick is in optimizing the architecture to produce the maximum flexibility and responsiveness. Ideally, you would precalculate

Internet Sales Amount	Column Labels ⏷					
	⊞ CY 2006	⊟ CY 2007				⊞ CY 2008
		⊟ H1 CY 2007		⊟ H2 CY 2007		
Row Labels ⏷		⊞ Q1 CY 2007	⊞ Q2 CY 2007	⊞ Q3 CY 2007	⊞ Q4 CY 2007	
⊞ Accessories				$118,674.53	$175,035.18	$407,050.25
⊟ Bikes	$6,530,343.53	$1,413,530.30	$1,623,971.06	$2,569,678.24	$3,751,923.02	$9,162,324.85
⊞ Mountain Bikes	$1,562,456.76	$626,184.78	$780,916.25	$1,081,342.74	$1,501,194.71	$3,814,691.06
⊞ Road Bikes	$4,967,886.77	$787,345.52	$843,054.81	$1,028,986.54	$1,292,642.34	$2,920,267.67
⊞ Touring Bikes				$459,348.96	$958,085.97	$2,427,366.12
⊟ Clothing				$55,987.71	$82,260.26	$201,524.64
⊞ Caps				$3,299.33	$4,656.82	$11,731.95
⊞ Gloves				$5,681.68	$8,547.01	$20,792.01
⊟ Jerseys				$28,622.50	$41,747.96	$102,580.22
Long-Sleeve Logo Jersey, L				$3,599.28	$5,898.82	$13,097.38
Long-Sleeve Logo Jersey, M				$3,699.26	$4,649.07	$13,747.25
Long-Sleeve Logo Jersey, S				$2,899.42	$4,549.09	$13,997.20
Long-Sleeve Logo Jersey, XL				$3,199.36	$5,648.87	$11,797.64
Short-Sleeve Classic Jersey, L				$4,103.24	$4,373.19	$11,715.83
Short-Sleeve Classic Jersey, M				$3,887.28	$5,776.93	$12,309.72
Short-Sleeve Classic Jersey, S				$3,563.34	$5,992.89	$12,363.71
Short-Sleeve Classic Jersey, XL				$3,671.32	$4,859.10	$13,551.49
⊞ Shorts				$12,668.19	$17,777.46	$40,874.16
⊞ Socks				$890.01	$1,339.51	$2,876.80
⊞ Vests				$4,826.00	$8,191.50	$22,669.50
Grand Total	$6,530,343.53	$1,413,530.30	$1,623,971.06	$2,744,340.48	$4,009,218.46	$9,770,899.74

Figure 3-6 *Breaking down the report by product and quarter*

any sum that the user is going to need. But what does this really mean? Looking at our example to date, we have dimensions for the calendar, geography, and products. Let's look at what those dimensions mean in the AdventureWorks sample database, as shown in Table 3-1.

Now if we have a few hundred thousand purchase order line items, those all have to be allocated to the proper members, and then the matrixes have to be calculated. For example, to have totals for each combination of City, Product, and Date, we need $1{,}460 \times 395 \times 587 = 338{,}522{,}900$ cells (obviously not every cell will have data, since there are more cells than line items). If we want to break down data by Country, Subcategory, and Month, that would take $6 \times 37 \times 48 = 10{,}656$ cells. You can start to see how complex this process is. Calculating totals on the fly quickly bogs down the server, especially for larger data sets; but precalculating every possible combination will take huge amounts of disk space.

SQL Server Analysis Services addresses this by walking the line between the two approaches. Once you've designed your cube, it calculates aggregations to provide a "best guess" foundation to minimize the amount of on-the-fly calculation necessary

Dimension	Level	Members
Date		
	Year	4
	Half	8
	Quarter	16
	Month	48
	Week	208
	Day	1,460
Product		
	Category	4
	Subcategory	37
	Product	395
Geography		
	Country	6
	State-Province	71
	City	587

Table 3-1   *Members in the Date, Product, and Geography Dimensions*

when a user runs a query. For example, while it may not precalculate the sums for every country, if it *has* calculated the totals for every province, then grouping by country is much quicker (add the states or provinces) than actually totaling the values from the source data.

SQL Server Analysis Services

SQL Server Analysis Services first appeared with SQL Server 7 as OLAP Services. Microsoft released SQL Server Analysis Services with SQL Server 2000. However, this edition suffered from not having any significant client tools in the box—virtually all administration, development, and management were through add-ons and third-party products.

SQL Server Analysis Services 2005 was the first version of Microsoft OLAP that approached what we have today. SSAS runs as a service on the server and provides online analytics for relational data sources. Although SQL Server 2008 had some minor improvements, they pale in comparison to the changes made in SQL Server Analysis Services 2008 R2. SSAS 2008 R2 introduced *Vertipaq mode,* also known as *PowerPivot* or sometimes *IMDB* (for in-memory database).

Code-named "Gemini" before release, Vertipaq mode is an isolated session of Analysis Services that runs and provides aggregation and multidimensional query services to a single application. For PowerPivot, those applications are SharePoint on the server and Excel on the desktop. This new technology provides the powerful multidimensional capabilities of Analysis Services to users to leverage on an ad hoc basis from Excel. The idea is to bridge the gap between lightweight pivot tables in Excel and full-blown cubes on SSAS servers.

Architecture

SQL Server Analysis Services runs as a service, and you can have multiple independent instances running on the same server. Within an instance you will have a single Server object, which can contain one or more databases. A database on the server is equivalent to an SSAS solution in the Business Intelligence Development Studio, which we'll look at in a moment.

Within an SSAS database, you will have three collections of objects:

▶ **Helper objects** Basic housekeeping objects—Assemblies (for SSAS stored procedures), Roles (for security), and Traces.

▶ **OLAP objects** This is the heart of what we'll be looking at in this chapter; these cover the multidimensional collection of objects—cubes, dimensions, data sources, and data source views.

▶ **Data-mining objects** These are a separate collection of objects to manage the data-mining capabilities of SSAS, including data-mining structures and mining models.

The most important thing to remember is that there are instances on a Windows Server. Instances have databases; and databases have data sources, data source views, cubes, and dimensions. You may want to think of cubes as "owning" the dimensions, but they don't—dimensions are separate and equal objects. Cubes will have references to dimensions, as we'll see later in the chapter.

From a physical perspective, SSAS is a service, and the repository for the objects structures are XML files, and the data (caching, aggregations, writeback values, etc.) are all stored in a hashed file structure. You shouldn't ever need to interact with SSAS at the file level—everything you need to do will be performed through server tools and web services.

Speaking of tools, let's take a look at the tools used to create SSAS cubes and manage the server.

Administrative Tools

The two primary administrative tools for Analysis Services are SQL Server Management Studio (SSMS) and the Business Intelligence Development Studio (BIDS). We find the easiest way to understand Analysis Services is to walk through an Analysis Services database in BIDS.

Business Intelligence Development Studio (BIDS)

BIDS, shown in Figure 3-7, is the primary development platform for the SQL Server "BI Services"—SQL Server Integration Services (SSIS), SQL Server Analysis Services (SSAS), and SQL Server Reporting Services (SSRS). BIDS may look familiar to you—it uses the framework for Visual Studio 2008. (SQL Server 2008 R2 will still use Visual Studio 2008 for BIDS.) Note that since BIDS is a stripped-down version of Visual Studio, your DBAs and BI developers don't need a Visual Studio license to install it—it's just part of the SQL Server client tools.

In the top-right corner of BIDS is the Solution Explorer. The primary parts of a solution we're going to worry about right now are data sources, data source views, cubes, and dimensions.

Data Sources

To build cubes in Analysis Services, you need access to the source systems, whether you are connecting directly to transaction business systems, reporting systems, or unified data warehouses/data marts. Data sources in an Analysis Services solution are effectively a collection of sockets that SSAS will use to connect to the data repositories.

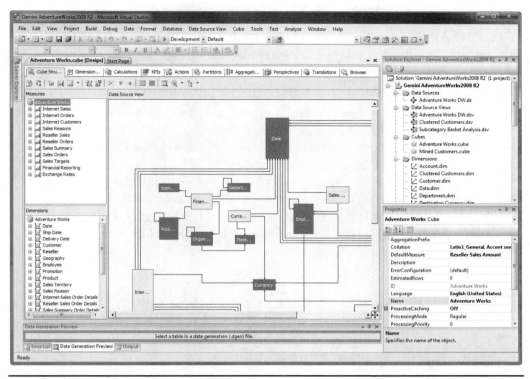

Figure 3-7   *Business Intelligence Development Studio*

There seems to be some belief that for SSAS to build cubes, the data must first be in SQL Server. This isn't true. In fact, you could build a cube with data from an Oracle database without having a SQL Server relational instance running! Having said that, for various scenarios (such as ROLAP, discussed later), SSAS does use SQL Server as a relational repository.

Out of the box, Analysis Services supports connections to:

▶ SQL Server 7, 2000, 2005, 2008

▶ Oracle 9.0

▶ IBM DB2 8.1

▶ Microsoft Access

▶ Teradata v2R6 (with OLE DB 1.3 provided from NCR)

Additional data sources may be available through third-party providers (for example, there is an SAP BW native adapter available from SAP). When connecting to another database, Analysis Services can use its own credentials or a specified user account.

Data Source Views

Once you have your data sources defined, you need to create a data source view. The data source view is the heart of the *unified dimensional model (UDM)*. Essentially, it provides a virtualized data mart structure that can be used to assemble the data for the cubes without making a copy of the data into a data mart.

Now you're confused. We spent several pages talking about bringing data together into data marts, and now we're saying you don't need data marts. What's going on?

Before the UDM, an OLAP solution would need two (or sometimes more) transitional database stores, as shown in Figure 3-8. In this architecture, the staging

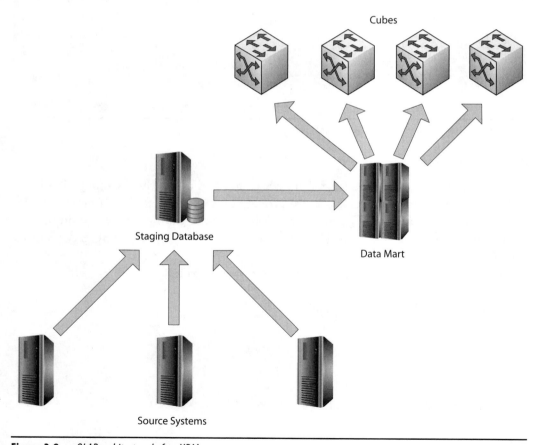

Figure 3-8 *OLAP architecture before UDM*

database and data mart are split. The staging database is, as we've discussed previously, a temporary repository—the data generally needs to be scrubbed after being extracted from the source systems. After it's scrubbed, we would put it in the staging database simply as a "waypoint" en route to the data mart.

As we'll see later in this chapter, the data structure requirements for an OLAP solution are different from the standard relational model. There are ways to denormalize the data to optimize it for dimensional processing. We extract the cleaned data from the staging database, manipulate it as necessary, and then load it into the data mart. Once there, cubes can be built from the data in the data mart.

The unified dimensional model approach in SSAS addresses this requirement for multiple copies of the data by providing a capability for creating a "virtual data mart" within an Analysis Services database. With the data source view, you can create a schema based on tables, views, and even queries created within the data source view itself. The data source view is then the data source for all the dimensions and cubes within the solution. Part of the data source view for the AdventureWorks database can be seen in Figure 3-9.

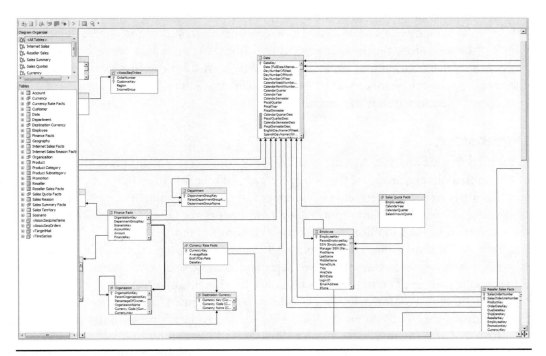

Figure 3-9   *Data source view in BIDS*

As you can see, it looks pretty much like a database diagram from SQL Server Management Studio. Designing a data source view is just like building a database schema—adding and connecting tables and views. Relationships can be created in the data source view even if they don't exist in the underlying database, or they can be created between two different databases. You can add views in the data source view editor, again from disparate data sources. You can also create calculated columns in tables to represent data in different ways.

So to review—in the past, when you wanted an OLAP solution, you would design a data mart based on data feeds from various sources, create a schema, and create the views and derived columns for the OLAP cubes to consume the data. In SSAS, the data source view virtualizes that data mart, eliminating the need for a dedicated server.

Now data marts aren't just for a single OLAP solution—they can also be used as reporting databases and for other analytic solutions. So there still may be both a staging database and a data mart. Or if Analysis Services is your primary analytic solution, the data source view replaces the data mart; you can engineer the staging database to take on the additional responsibilities of the data mart. Thus, there are source systems, SQL Server Analysis Services, and a single database in the middle, which is a staging database/data mart hybrid.

Once you've created the data source view, you can start building cubes. In SSAS, an OLAP cube actually consists of a collection of dimension objects and a cube object, which is the repository for the measures of the cube. There is a cube wizard, which will evaluate a selected data source view (DSV) and then create the necessary dimensions and measures; of course, once you have the fundamentals down, you can create everything by hand without the wizard.

Dimensions

Within an Analysis Services database, all the dimensions are shared. This is another facet of the unified dimensional model—you can create a dimension once (say, for the products your company sells) and then reuse it in numerous cubes. Designing a dimension consists of creating a "mini data source view" (not a new data source view—this is just a virtual representation of the DSV for the cube showing a subset of its tables) to build the data structure for the dimension. The Dimension Designer in BIDS is shown in Figure 3-10. The right-hand pane displays the tables selected from the data source view, which the dimension is built on. The left-hand pane shows the dimension *attributes*.

Each member of a dimension has a collection of attributes that describe it. In the Product dimension, each member is a single product, and each product has values for the attributes of Category, Class, Dealer Price, Model Name, and so on. Hierarchies are created by defining attributes, which can be used to gather dimension members into groups.

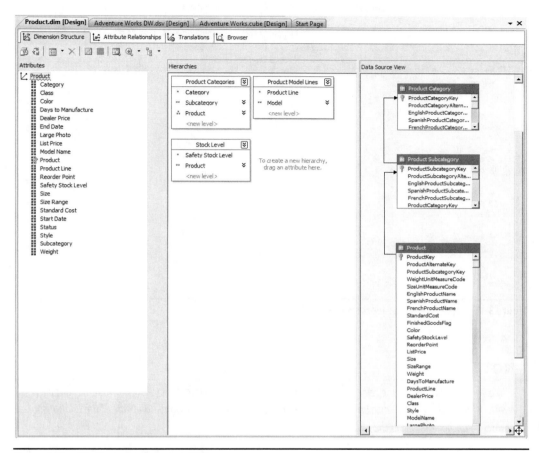

Figure 3-10   *The Dimension Designer in BIDS*

For example, each product has a category and subcategory attribute. As a result, we can create a hierarchy based on the categories and subcategories of the products. Hierarchies are created by assigning attribute relationships in the Attribute Relationships tab, shown in Figure 3-11. You can see the attribute relationships between the Product primary key, Subcategory, and Category (also Product > Model Name > Product Line and Product > Safety Stock Level). Each of these creates a hierarchy we see back in the Dimension Structure tab. It is even possible to connect to dimensions from other databases, called "linked dimensions," further improving the reusability of dimensions.

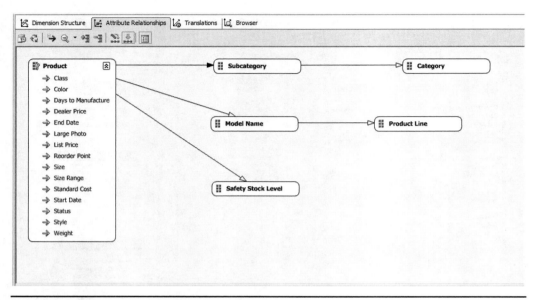

Figure 3-11   *Attribute Relationship Designer in BIDS*

NOTE

When you create the attribute relationship, BIDS will check the underlying data sources to validate that each relationship is 1:N and will raise an error if the number of members on the right-hand side of the relationship is greater than the number on the left.

Time Dimension

Most analysis is going to involve some form of time analysis. As a result, having a standardized, structured dimension for time is very important. You could try to use an existing date field to build the time dimension, but you'll probably have issues. For example, if you wanted to use the Order Date field, if there were no orders on Christmas Day, you could find some unintended consequences.

It's best to have a dedicated date table for use as the data structure for a time dimension. Luckily, BIDS provides a wizard to create a dedicated time table. When you use the dimension wizard, two of the options are to generate a time table—one in the data source, one on the server. You can select where to put the authoritative time table depending on your needs (and, possibly, whether you can even access the data source).

The wizard then gives you options on how much data to generate (beginning and end dates), what time periods to include (year, quarter, month, etc.), and what alternate calendars to include.

Through calculated fields and multiple hierarchies, Analysis Services can provide multiple calendars in a time dimension. In addition to a standard calendar, you can have a fiscal calendar, reporting calendar, manufacturing calendar, and ISO 8601 calendar (an international standard date reporting format for exchanging date- and time-related information). Once the data tables are generated, the data source view schema is created and the dimension is in place; then, it's simply a matter of joining the date table to the appropriate fact tables in the data source view and mapping the dimension to the appropriate measures.

NOTE

The dates in the date dimension have a time of 0000Z. If you plan to join the date table to other data tables, you may have to create a view to normalize the time before creating the join.

Now that we have our dimensions in place, let's take a look at cubes.

Cubes

Cubes are the final part of an Analysis Services solution/database we're going to look at. A cube object will contain references to dimensions and the measure groups related to those dimensions. *Measure groups* are created in the Cube Structure tab of the Cube Designer, shown in Figure 3-12. Each measure group is based on a single fact table in the data source view.

The definition of an individual measure is shown in Figure 3-13. A basic measure is simply a field from one of the fact tables with some form of aggregation defined. In the case of the Internet Order Quantity measure shown, it takes the OrderQuantity field from the Internet Sales Facts table, as indicated in the Source properties. Then the AggregateFunction property indicates how the values should be combined—the default is to sum them, but there are also options for count, min, max, average, and so on.

As mentioned, the cube is defined as a collection of measures and dimensions. Dimensions are added to the cube in the Dimensions pane, located in the lower-left area of the Cube Structure tab of the Cube Designer. Here you can add dimensions to the cube, either existing dimensions in the solution/database, or you can link in dimensions

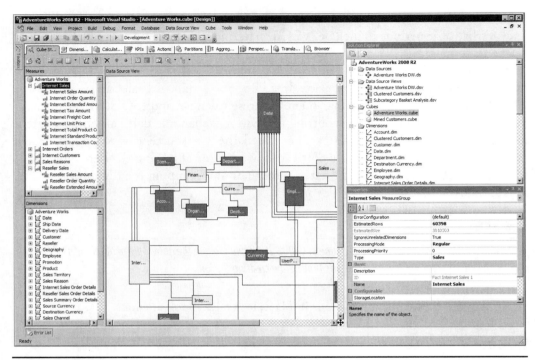

Figure 3-12 *Measure groups in the Cube Designer*

from other Analysis Services databases. However, just adding the dimension to the cube is not enough; you also have to create the relationship between the dimension and one or more measures.

Figure 3-14 shows the Dimension Usage tab of the Cube Designer. Measure groups are along the top, and dimensions are listed down the left side. At each intersection, the cube design shows the relationship (if any) between the two. Note that not every dimension is used in every measure group—this helps to minimize processing time by not investing aggregation processing into dimensions that aren't needed or that don't make sense.

For example, the Geography dimension is mapped to the Reseller Sales measure group indirectly through the Reseller dimension table. This allows reseller sales to be

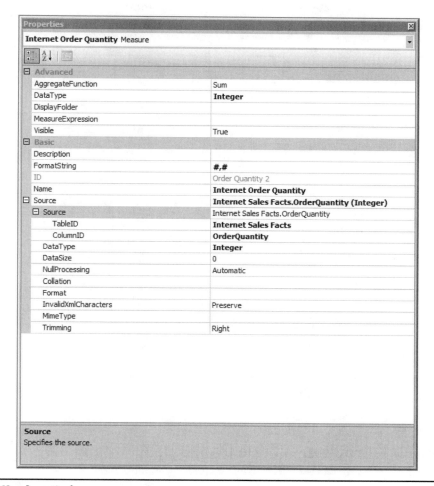

Figure 3-13   *Properties for a measure*

broken down by geography—not that the Geography dimension is not associated with the Internet Sales measure group. In this case, if we look at the Customer dimension, we'll see there is a Customer Geography hierarchy within that dimension, so we don't need a Geography hierarchy associated here.

Now let's jump to the last tab in the Cube Designer—the Browser—and start to apply some of what we've learned.

Dimensions	Internet Sales	Internet Orders	Internet Customers	Sales Reasons	Reseller Sales
Date	Date	Date	Date		Date
Date (Ship Date)	Date	Date	Date		Date
Date (Delivery Date)	Date	Date	Date		Date
Customer	Customer	Customer	Customer		
Reseller					Reseller
Geography					Reseller
Employee					Employee
Promotion	Promotion	Promotion	Promotion		Promotion
Product	Product	Product	Product		Product
Sales Territory	Sales Territory Region	Sales Territory Region	Sales Territory Region		Sales Territory Region
Sales Reason	Sales Reasons	Sales Reasons	Sales Reasons	Sales Reason	
Internet Sales Order Details	Internet Sales Order	Internet Sales Order	Internet Sales Order	Internet Sales Order	
Reseller Sales Order Details					Reseller Sales Order
Sales Summary Order De...					
Source Currency	Source Currency Code	Source Currency Code	Source Currency Code		Source Currency Code
Destination Currency	Exchange Rates				Exchange Rates
Sales Channel					
Organization					
Department					
Account					
Scenario					

Figure 3-14   *Dimension Usage tab in the Cube Designer*

Exercise 3-1: Browsing a Cube from BIDS

NOTE

This exercise assumes you have BIDS for SQL Server 2008 or 2008 R2 installed and access to the AdventureWorks 2008 cube. You can get the AdventureWorks databases and SSAS project from CodePlex.

1. Either open the BIDS project for AdventureWorks that you used to build the cube, or open BIDS and select File | Open | Analysis Services Database.

2. Double-click the AdventureWorks cube in the Cubes folder in the Solution Explorer, as shown in the following illustration.

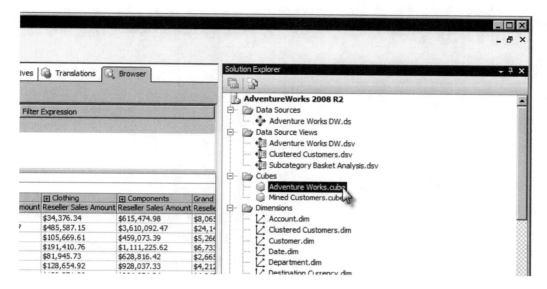

3. Click the Browser tab in the Cube Designer.

NOTE

If you see an error instead of the browser, make sure you have the Office Web Components installed. (The BIDS browser uses the OWC 2003, which isn't installed with Office 2010.)

4. The left-hand pane lists the cube objects—measure groups, measures, and dimensions.

5. Open up the Measures folder and then the Internet Sales folder. Drag the Internet Sales Amount measure to the area of the chart labeled "Drop Totals Or Detail Fields Here" as shown here:

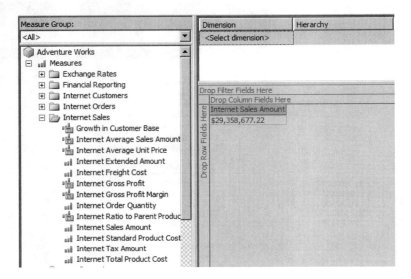

6. Next, scroll down to the Geography dimension, and open that. Drag the Geography hierarchy to the area of the chart labeled "Drop Row Fields Here." You should see something like the following illustration:

What's going on? Were the sales in every country identical? Of course not. Remember back when we looked at the Dimension Usage chart and pointed out there was no relationship between the Internet Sales measure group and the Geography dimension? This is the result—hierarchies from that dimension don't have any effect on the numbers from the measure group. Let's try this again.

1. Click the Country header in the browser and drag it away—as soon as it's off the grid, you should see an "X" icon and it will then be removed from the chart.

2. Open the Customer dimension, and then drag the Customer Geography hierarchy to the Drop Row Fields Here area. Now we should have a breakdown of Internet sales by country. Click the plus (+) icon next to Canada to open the list by province, as shown here:

Drop Filter Fields Here		
		Drop Column Fields Here
Country ▾	**State-Province**	Internet Sales Amount
⊞ Australia		$9,061,000.58
⊟ Canada	⊞ Alberta	$22,467.80
	⊞ British Columbia	$1,955,340.10
	⊞ Ontario	$36.96
	Total	$1,977,844.86
⊞ France		$2,644,017.71
⊞ Germany		$2,894,312.34
⊞ United Kingdom		$3,391,712.21
⊞ United States		$9,389,789.51
Grand Total		$29,358,677.22

3. Now open up the Date dimension and then the Calendar folder. Drag the Date. Calendar hierarchy to the Drop Column Fields Here area on the chart. Now it should look like the illustration here:

Drop Filter Fields Here						
		Calenda ▾				
		⊞ CY 2005	⊞ CY 2006	⊞ CY 2007	⊞ CY 2008	Grand Total
Country ▾	**State-Province**	Internet Sales Amount	Internet Sales Amount	Internet Sales Amount	Internet Sales Amount	Internet Sales Amount
⊞ Australia		$1,309,047.20	$2,154,284.88	$3,033,784.21	$2,563,884.29	$9,061,000.58
⊟ Canada	⊞ Alberta	$3,578.27	$8,203.18	$4,363.18	$6,323.17	$22,467.80
	⊞ British Columbia	$143,251.54	$613,399.20	$531,384.32	$667,305.04	$1,955,340.10
	⊞ Ontario			$36.96		$36.96
	Total	$146,829.81	$621,602.38	$535,784.46	$673,628.21	$1,977,844.86
⊞ France		$180,571.69	$514,942.01	$1,026,324.97	$922,179.04	$2,644,017.71
⊞ Germany		$237,784.99	$521,230.85	$1,058,405.73	$1,076,890.77	$2,894,312.34
⊞ United Kingdom		$291,590.52	$591,586.85	$1,298,248.57	$1,210,286.27	$3,391,712.21
⊞ United States		$1,100,549.45	$2,126,696.55	$2,838,512.36	$3,324,031.16	$9,389,789.51
Grand Total		$3,266,373.66	$6,530,343.53	$9,791,060.30	$9,770,899.74	$29,358,677.22

4. Finally, drag the Internet Sales Amount out of the grid, and drag in the measure "Internet Gross Profit Margin." Instead of dollar figures, you'll see percentages. We'll talk percentages after the exercise.

5. Experiment with dragging and dropping other hierarchies and measures to the grid—this is the best way to learn your way around a cube and get used to how cubes operate.

Calculated Measures

So what about those percentages? They weren't added, obviously. In fact, there really isn't any math you can use on a collection of percentages to get a reliable answer. Consider two classrooms—Classroom A with 10 students and Classroom B with 100 students. All 110 pupils take an exam. Classroom A averages a 95 percent; classroom B averages a 70 percent. What is the overall average for the two classrooms? You can't just average the averages—70 percent and 95 percent —to get an 82.5 percent. You have to either calculate a weighted average or go back to the base data. If we have all 110 scores, then the class average is the sum of the scores divided by the count of the students.

Wait—"Sum"? "Count"? Those *are* methods we have of combining values in Analysis Services. So if we have a measure that gives us the total of the scores and another measure that gives us how many scores there are, at any time we can divide the count into the total and get the average. (And the average score for all the students is 72.3 percent.)

In Analysis Services, we can create what's called a *calculated measure* and enter a formula which will be applied to measure values to determine the resulting value, no matter how the cube is sliced. The expression language for the calculations is called MDX, for MultiDimensional eXpressions. (This language is also used for queries against an OLAP source.)

Key Performance Indicators

Another significant feature in Analysis Services is the ability to define *key performance indicators* (KPIs). This is similar to calculated measures, but with a bit more structure. An example of SSAS KPIs is shown in Excel in Figure 3-15 (the browser in BIDS doesn't render KPIs). Key performance indicators in Analysis Services consist of four expressions: a value expression, a goal expression, a status indicator, and a trend indicator.

The *value expression* is just that—the number being reported on. The KPI editor in BIDS provides a script editor—it may be simply a measure or a more complex calculated measure. You can also select which measure group to associate the KPI with.

The *goal expression* is, again, simply a script. This is likely to be more complex— differentiating based on different dimension members, or building goals dynamically

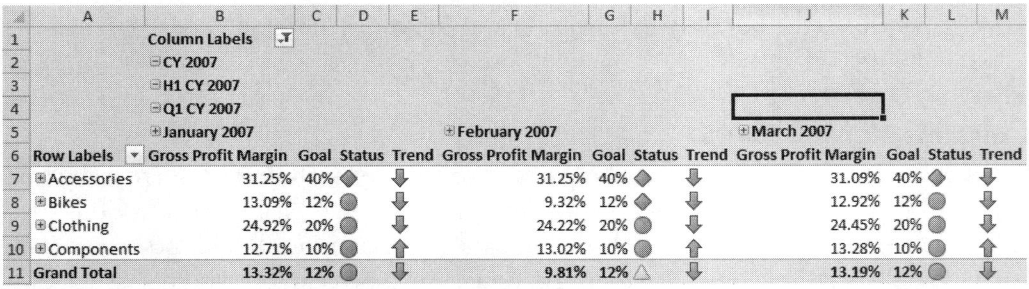

Figure 3-15   *Key performance indicators in Excel*

so they change over time (for example—this year's quota will be 5 percent more than last year's revenue).

The *status indicator* and *trend indicator* are special cases for two reasons. First, they have several discrete states (such as red, yellow, green or up, even, down). This is handled with a CASE statement that returns –1, 0, or 1. The WHEN clause of the CASE statement is the logic to determine when the indicator shows what. The second special case is that indicators are generally represented as icons, as shown in Figure 3-16.

However, it is worth noting that these specific images are not necessarily what may show in the client application. Analysis Services returns the name of an icon with the KPI when answering a query—it's up to the client application to implement and apply a suitable icon when displaying a KPI status indicator or trend arrow.

KPI indicators can be displayed in Excel, in SharePoint through KPI lists, in SQL Server Reporting Services, and in PerformancePoint scorecards. The strong benefit is that once the KPI is defined in Analysis Services, it is presented uniformly no matter what client you choose. The downside is that there is some inflexibility in the KPI structure—only one value, one target, one indicator, and one trend indicator. If you find that the KPIs in Analysis Services don't meet your needs, look into using PerformancePoint Services in SharePoint—we'll be digging more deeply into this topic in Chapter 9.

Now that we have a basic understanding of how Analysis Services pieces together dimensions and measures to create a cube, let's take a look at some of the practical aspects of OLAP that will affect your BI architecture—storage modes, schemas, and a closer look at the time dimension.

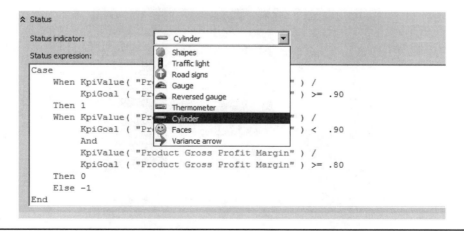

Figure 3-16 *Status indicators in BIDS*

SQL Server Management Studio (SSMS)

SQL Server Management Studio connects to Analysis Services by selecting Analysis Services from the Server Type drop-down list in the Connect dialog, as shown in Figure 3-17. Then enter the server and, if necessary, the instance. If SSAS is installed as the default instance, you only need to enter the server name. If there are multiple instances, then enter server\instance.

NOTE

When you install SQL Server Analysis Services in integrated mode with SharePoint, it is installed by default as an instance.

Once you have connected to the server, you will initially have two folders: Databases and Assemblies. If you open the Databases folder, you will have a list of databases on the server instance. Opening a database will show the familiar list: Data Sources, Data Source Views, Cubes, Dimensions, Mining Structures, Roles, and Assemblies. Open each of the folders and browse through the objects on the server. Right-click various objects to understand how you can interact with them.

With Data Source Views, for example, you pretty much have just basic properties. But with Data Sources, you can change the connection string—which is vital for maintaining cubes in a dynamic server environment. You also have the ability to process cubes, dimensions, and partitions from SSMS.

You can enable or disable writeback for Measure Groups, and when you get down to the Partition level, there is a significant amount of capability in how the DBA can work

Figure 3-17 *Connecting to SSAS with SSMS*

with partitions without firing up BIDS and getting into the wiring of the database. The DBA can create a new partition, edit the existing partitions (particularly, the query that defines the partition), run the Usage Based Optimization wizard, and design the aggregations for the partition. He or she can also design the storage modes for partitions and dimensions.

Storage Modes

To calculate all those totals, Analysis Services cubes must be *processed*. This pulls the data from the source system, aligns it with the dimension members, and performs the calculations. Since processing is generally an intensive operation and takes the cube offline for a time, it is done infrequently. The downside is that this means cubes are always outdated to some degree.

To address this problem, SSAS offers three different ways of storing data:

▶ **MOLAP**   Multidimensional OLAP is what we've been discussing—the data is read from source systems and aggregations are calculated and stored. All queries are answered from the cubes.

▶ **ROLAP**   Relational OLAP addresses the latency concerns of MOLAP. The data is stored in relational format and calculations are performed in real time. Some form of notification process will be put in place so that the SSAS relational store can be updated when the source data changes. As you can imagine, for larger data sets this is very demanding on the server and can tax the source systems.

▶ **HOLAP**   Hybrid OLAP tries to provide a compromise between the two extremes. In HOLAP, some portion of the structure is processed and stored in aggregated format; other parts of the cube are maintained in relational format. The goal is to have as much precalculation performed as possible, but data that is very volatile is kept in relational format and calculated in real time.

Another part of this puzzle is the concept of *partitions*. Measure groups can be partitioned—this allows for flexibility both in scaling the cubes as well as in processing and storage. Partitions are divided by criteria defined by the DBA—using the WHERE clause of a query string. Generally, the net effect is that a measure group will be split between members. For example, in the AdventureWorks cube, the Internet Sales measure group is partitioned by year—a single partition for each year.

Each of these partitions can now be treated separately—they can be moved to different servers, put on different storage area networks (SANs), have different aggregation optimizations, and different storage modes. A standard example is that archived years will be stored in MOLAP mode—we don't really expect them to change at all, so they can be completely precalculated. We may keep the most recent closed-out year in HOLAP, since there will still be auditing and late records going in, but for the most part, it's established.

Finally, we keep the current year in ROLAP mode, since it is changing every time an order comes in. (If we're focusing on longer-term analytics, we may actually keep it in HOLAP.) As changes are made to the data source, the cube automatically detects those changes and they are cached into the relational store in SSAS. Calculations are then aggregated on the fly as required.

Star vs. Snowflake

One discussion you will often run into when discussing data mart architecture is whether to create a star or snowflake schema. This refers to the arrangement of fact and dimension tables in the schema used to build the cube, and it's often made more complicated than it needs to be. Very simply, a star schema is a schema where every dimension table is connected directly to a single fact table, as shown in Figure 3-18.

A snowflake schema, on the other hand is... everything else. Generally, you will see a "snowflake" when the dimension tables are normalized so they branch and/or are multiple levels deep, as shown in Figure 3-19. In this case, we have one dimension that uses three normalized tables (similar to the Product > Subcategory > Category tables in the AdventureWorks cube) and another dimension that has two supporting tables.

So when do you use which? The answer, as always, is "it depends." The first, most important factor is the intended use and intended tools. Some BI tools can only work with star schemas (the discontinued PerformancePoint planning engine was one example). Another factor will be your users and how heavily involved they will be and

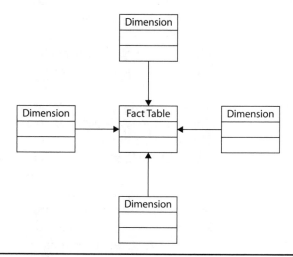

Figure 3-18 *A star schema*

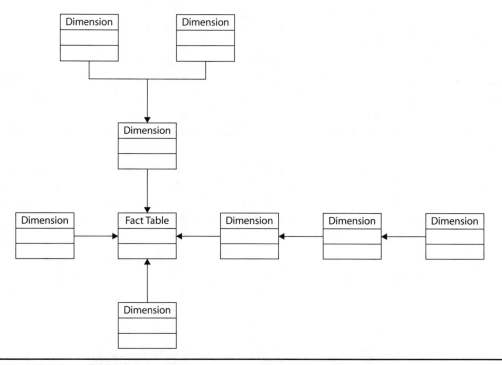

Figure 3-19   *A snowflake schema*

at what level of abstraction. If your users only ever interact with the dimension and measure group model presented by Analysis Services, then deciding between a star or snowflake schema may simply be a matter of what is easier to design and maintain.

You will also have to worry about the capability of the database engine running the data mart for Analysis Services. Converting to a star schema from a normalized database is a significant workload on the relational engine while sparing the Analysis Services engine the work necessary to convert a complex dimension table assembly into a dimension. On the other hand, sharing the load may make more sense.

Finally, if you have some rich hierarchies and a number of attributes, creating the star schema dimension tables may take a lot of storage for sparse data structures. A snowflake schema is closer to a normalized database perspective, and will be more efficient on space and maintenance. Ultimately, consider that you will have a normalized structure in the original data store and a dimensional structure in Analysis Services.

Writeback

Up to this point, every aspect of BI we've considered has been "read only." However, there is a powerful ability in SSAS to provide "what-if" analysis where an end user can change values in the cube and see what the resulting changes are. For example, if there is a cube with billable hours on a contract, a project manager may want to see how projected finish dates and margins change by hiring someone new, or perhaps by letting someone go.

You will need to enable writeback on the partition or partitions you'll be working with. In the Partitions tab of BIDS, right-click a partition and select Writeback Settings to open the Enable Writeback dialog, shown in Figure 3-20. This will create a new table on the server to store the settings that are written back by end users.

NOTE

Writing back data makes entries in the writeback table in the cube, but will not affect the underlying data source.

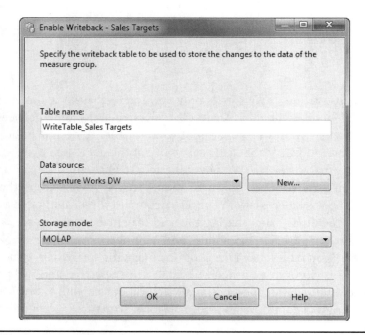

Figure 3-20   *Enabling writeback on a partition*

You cannot enable writeback on a partition unless all the measures in the measure group covered by that partition use SUM as their aggregate method. The big gotcha here is that when you create a cube with the BIDS wizard, it automatically creates a COUNT measure in each measure group.

When you write back a value to a higher level in the hierarchy (for example, changing a sales value for the calendar quarter), Analysis Services will promulgate those changes down the hierarchy. So, for example, if you change a sales amount for Q3 from zero to 120, then SSAS will also change August, September, and October to 40 each. This is called *spreading*.

The other major consideration in working with writeback measures is loading the server. When a user makes changes to a value in the front end and processes the changes, the value(s) are passed back to the Analysis Server, which will then try to determine what parts of the cube are affected by the posted changes. The problem is that in a measure that has a lot of dimensions associated with it, the server will have to evaluate *every single dimension* to identify any changes. Let's say you make a change in the Internet Sales measure and don't address the Geography dimension. Analysis Services will take the change and distribute it to each of the six countries, each of the states or provinces in each country, and each postal code for those states and provinces.

Now what if you didn't specify a member of the Products dimension as well? Then the value needs to be spread across the combination of Geography and Products down the hierarchy. You can see how this type of geometric expansion can quickly bring a server to its knees. The solution as a user is to ensure that every dimension you're dealing with is at the *leaf level*—the lowest level of the hierarchy. As an architect, this leads to the idea of creating measure groups specifically for writeback/what-if analysis that have fewer dimensions and map in fewer of the hierarchies and levels. For example, if you need to bring in the Geography dimension, you probably only want the Country level, and definitely don't want the Postal Code level.

We'll look more closely at writeback and what-if analysis when we cover Excel in the next chapter.

SSAS Front Ends

To wrap up this chapter, we want to give a quick overview of the types of front ends that can consume Analysis Services data. This is just a quick tour—we'll dig more deeply into each of them later in the book. There are significant ties between the products as well—PerformancePoint can present Excel Services workbooks and Reporting Services reports as reports on dashboards, and PerformancePoint scorecards can be published to Reporting Services.

Excel

Excel is, of course, the primary presentation layer for dimensional data, as shown in Figure 3-21. And as each iteration of Excel adds improved end-user functionality, it will continue in this role. The BI 2010 wave, with PowerPivot, Excel Web Apps, and a huge investment in business intelligence, truly augments Excel as an end-user application, but also puts it in the spotlight as an editing platform for server-based BI.

Excel as a simple desktop client can connect to Analysis Services, read cubes, and provide the data in pivot table or pivot chart format. One significant shortcoming in Excel pivot charts is that they are bound to pivot tables—there is very little editing you can do in the chart itself. Although they work well enough within a workbook, when you start looking at charts for online use, you will quickly get frustrated with Excel charts and should look at Reporting Services.

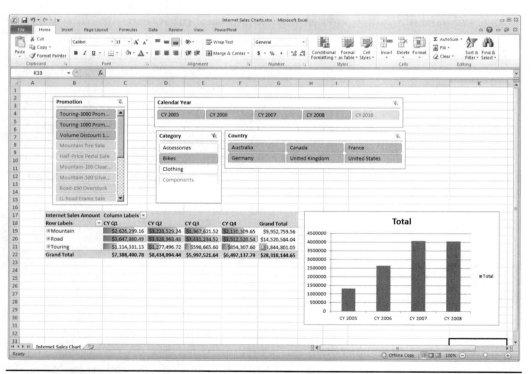

Figure 3-21 *Excel showing SSAS data*

NOTE

If you are a veteran of Office Web Components, remember that they have been deprecated in Office and are not "in the box" with Office 2010. They are still available as a free download from Microsoft.com, but if you don't have a pressing need for them, please don't use them. First of all, the web display is via an ActiveX component, which means that the component must be installed on every desktop. Second, while the web components are decent enough on their own, there is no extensibility whatsoever for them—when you run into a limit, you're stuck.

Excel is also the front end for Excel Services, a SharePoint application service that allows publishing workbooks to SharePoint. From there, the workbooks can be integrated with SharePoint content, viewed in a read-only format through Excel Services, viewed interactively through Excel Web Apps, or consumed in PerformancePoint dashboards.

SharePoint

Apart from hosting PerformancePoint Services, PowerPivot, and Excel Services, SharePoint also has KPI lists, which provide a lightweight method of consuming Analysis Services data and KPIs for publication on SharePoint sites. Figure 3-22 shows a single KPI from a SharePoint KPI list. Setting up a KPI in SharePoint is very, very easy—simply a matter of selecting the KPI from Analysis Services. However, SharePoint KPIs are also very limited in how much they can be customized. If you are used to *creating* KPIs, do not approach a SharePoint KPI list with this mindset—think of it in terms of simply *reporting* KPIs.

If you are looking for more robust customization in KPIs, you want to look at PerformancePoint Services.

PerformancePoint Services

PerformancePoint Services is targeted towards performance-based display of Analysis Services data, primarily scorecards and dashboards. PPS is centered on design of the key performance indicator, either by importing one from Analysis Services or creating

New ▾ Actions ▾ Settings ▾			View:	Status List ▾
Indicator	Goal	Value	Status	
Acquisition Cost	80	85	●	
Complaints	5	4.2	△	
Customer Volume	125,000	127,000	●	
Repeat Business	75	72	△	

Figure 3-22   *A SharePoint KPI list*

it in the PerformancePoint Dashboard Designer. You then use the KPIs to assemble a scorecard, and can host the scorecard in a dashboard, as shown in Figure 3-23, which can also host PerformancePoint-specific analytic reports, Excel Services charts and graphs, and Reporting Services reports. You can also embed slicers in the dashboard to enable filtering the entire dashboard on specific criteria.

While the data reported on in PerformancePoint does not have to be in Analysis Services, using a cube as the underlying data store lends itself to cleaner design, and will also enable a number of performance management scenarios (such as writeback for what-if scenarios).

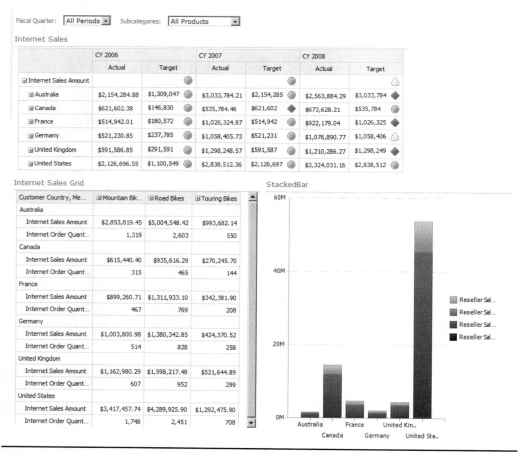

Figure 3-23   *A PerformancePoint Services dashboard in SharePoint*

Reporting Services

Reporting Services was introduced in 2003 as an add-on to SQL Server 2000. Since then, it has matured immensely and enjoyed massive support as an enterprise reporting tool. SQL Server Reporting Services is a web-based reporting engine. It does not require SharePoint for reporting, but SSRS reports can be integrated with SharePoint. Most notably, the data being reported on does not have to be in SQL Server. Figure 3-24 shows a report rendered in SQL Server Reporting Services.

Of course, in this specific instance, what we're looking at is using SSRS as a front end for SQL Server Analysis Services. One of the features introduced in SSRS 2008 that makes this even more compelling is the *Tablix* report designer. Previously, reports had to be either tables or matrixes. Tablix combines the best of both worlds, allowing table-type subreports in a matrix-style chart. SSRS 2008 also overhauled the graphing

Country	State Province	Internet Sales Amount		Tax	Trend
Australia	New South Wales	Category	Sales		
		Accessories	$59,839		
		Bikes	$3,843,862	$314,759	
		Clothing	$30,786		
	Queensland	Category	Sales		
		Accessories	$31,556		
		Bikes	$1,942,683	$159,073	
		Clothing	$14,177		
	South Australia	Category	Sales		
		Accessories	$8,838		
		Bikes	$605,056	$49,460	
		Clothing	$4,362		
	Tasmania	Category	Sales		
		Accessories	$4,041		
		Bikes	$233,197	$19,195	
		Clothing	$2,700		
	Victoria	Category	Sales		
		Accessories	$34,417		
		Bikes	$2,227,253	$182,392	
		Clothing	$18,236		
Canada	Alberta	Category	Sales		
		Accessories	$414		
		Bikes	$21,828	$1,797	
		Clothing	$225		
	British Columbia	Category	Sales		
		Accessories	$102,926		
		Bikes	$1,799,474	$156,427	
		Clothing	$52,939		
	Ontario	Category	Sales		
				$3	

Figure 3-24 *SQL Server Reporting Services report*

engine, providing exceptionally powerful graphs, new graphing types, and a much easier-to-use interface, as shown in Figure 3-25.

SSRS is intended generally to be an IT-driven enterprise reporting solution. However, there is an ad hoc report builder client application that can also create and publish SSRS reports.

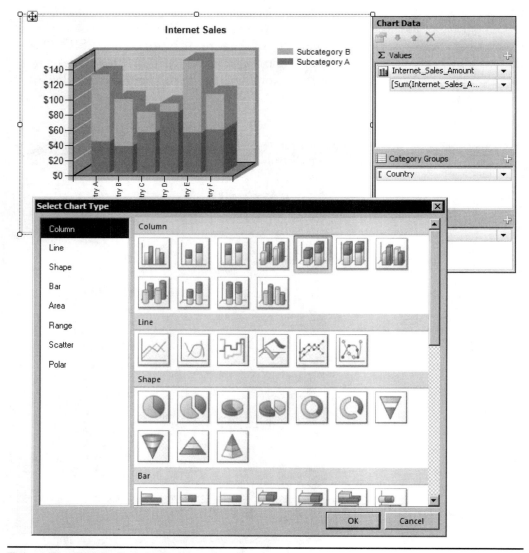

Figure 3-25   *SQL Server Reporting Services graph*

Report Builder

SQL Server Reporting Services 2005 shipped with a client-side report builder. However, it was fairly clunky, and since it depended on purpose-built report models, it didn't see much use. SSRS 2008 improved the Report Builder immensely, enabling it to work natively off data sources, adding Tablix and the new graphing engine, and making it much easier to use. SSRS 2008 R2 includes Report Builder 3.0, shown in Figure 3-26, which refines the improvements in 2.0 and adds a lot more functionality.

Again, Report Builder enables an end user to connect to an Analysis Services cube, create a report with charts and graphs from that data, and publish it for public consumption. This broadly expands our ability to provide analytic information from Analysis Services.

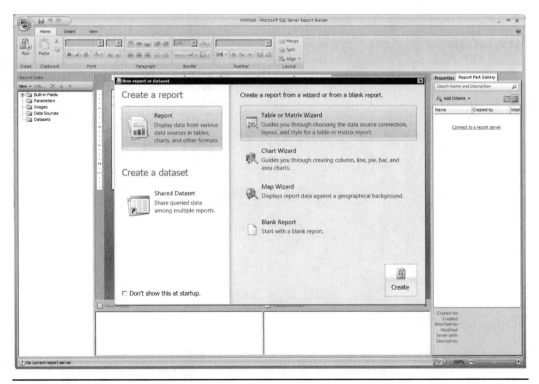

Figure 3-26   *SQL Server Report Builder 3.0*

Code

Despite the robust array of client tools available, there will be times when you need access to dimensional analytic data from a custom application. Analysis Services has a rich object model, referred to as the Analysis Management Objects (AMO) library. This managed code library provides an object model that will feel similar to someone who's worked with cubes in BIDS—databases, cubes and dimensions, members, etc.

From the data side, queries against Analysis Services use a query language called MDX (MultiDimensional eXpressions), which is just enough like SQL to really drive you nuts while learning it. Queries are made against a web service using XML/A, which is an industry standard. The query language can be executed against a connection, just like you are used to with standard SQL queries, and it will return an ADOMD.Cellset object, which is a collection of cells representing the results of the query (think in terms of a multidimensional recordset). You can then traverse the cellset to do what you need to with it.

Summary

This chapter provided a quick overview of Analysis Services—hopefully enough to help you understand the value of creating a multidimensional store for aggregating business data, especially complex structured data from multiple sources. In the next chapter, we'll take a look at our first, best client for SSAS—Excel (and Excel Services).

Chapter 4

Excel and Excel Services

In This Chapter

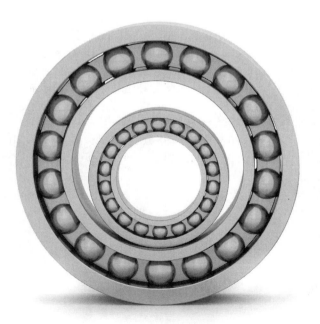

S ince its introduction in the mid-1980s, Excel has grown to be a powerful tool on any analyst's desktop. While the user interface remains the familiar landscape of rows and columns, the tools and capabilities at the fingertips of an Excel user have turned it into such a powerful analytic tool that, as evidenced by the problem of "spreadmarts," it can essentially run the company. Starting with Excel 2003, a major part of life in Excel became the ability to query directly against data sources instead of copying and pasting from another database query tool.

With Excel 2007 and SharePoint 2007, Excel moved on to the server. SharePoint 2007 offered Excel Services, which enabled analysts to publish Excel workbooks to SharePoint, run heavyweight Excel workbooks on the server, and users could view (read-only) Excel worksheets in a web browser without having Excel installed. Excel 2007 like its predecessor Excel 2003 also provided a native capability to connect to SQL Server Analysis Services, and could run pivot tables and pivot charts off SSAS cubes.

With the Office 2010 wave, Excel is pumped up yet again. In addition to significant improvements in native analysis capabilities, the Analysis Services interface is beefed up yet again, and most significant is the introduction of PowerPivot, which puts an instance of Analysis Services on the desktop with Excel as its front end. Excel Services has also gotten a booster shot—a lot of rough edges from the previous ("v1") incarnation have been smoothed out, but there is also a web-based read/write version of Excel, referred to as the "Excel Web App."

So let's take a look at the new Excel.

Excel as an Analysis Tool

We want to start with a quick exercise to review some basic functionality in Excel. Most of this was introduced in Excel 2007, but if you're still on 2003, or haven't investigated these features, they're worth knowing. We're going to grab a data set in Excel format, format it as a table, add some conditional formatting, and create a basic bar chart.

We're going to use the Excel worksheet entitled "DeathData.xls"—this is a collection of statistics for population and death rates by cause of death for the 50 states in the United States. If you open the file you'll see a standard table-type layout for Excel, as shown in Figure 4-1. It's a list of states with the FIPS code for each state and the death rates per 100,000 resident population in 1998.

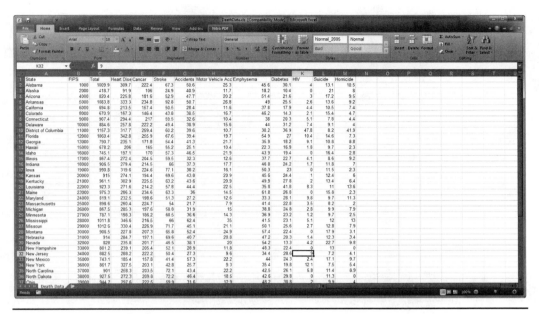

Figure 4-1   *Excel sample data*

NOTE

Although the data was extracted from the U.S. Census website, we make no guarantees regarding the data. So please don't use this spreadsheet for a research paper on death rates.

So first let's take advantage of Excel's table formatting feature, which was introduced in Excel 2007.

Exercise 4-1: Excel Table Formatting

1. Click cell A1, and then click the Format As Table drop-down button in the ribbon:

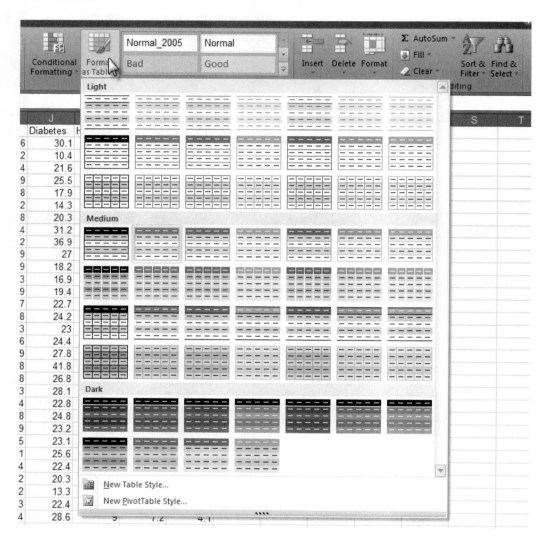

2. Select one of the table formats.

3. You will see the Format As Table dialog, which allows you to select a data range. Note that the range of values for your table has been automatically selected. Leave My Table Has Headers selected and click OK.

4. Note the table has been formatted with the style you selected.

5. Ensure that the Excel window is shorter than the data set, and scroll down. Note that the table headers replace the column headers instead of scrolling off the page, as shown here:

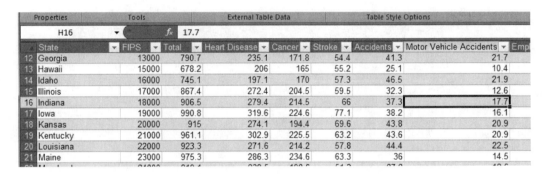

	Properties		Tools			External Table Data				Table Style Options		
	H16	▼		f_x	17.7							
	State ▼	FIPS ▼	Total ▼	Heart Disease ▼	Cancer ▼	Stroke ▼	Accidents ▼	Motor Vehicle Accidents ▼	Emp
12	Georgia	13000	790.7	235.1	171.8	54.4	41.3	21.7	
13	Hawaii	15000	678.2	206	165	55.2	25.1	10.4	
14	Idaho	16000	745.1	197.1	170	57.3	46.5	21.9	
15	Illinois	17000	867.4	272.4	204.5	59.5	32.3	12.6	
16	Indiana	18000	906.5	279.4	214.5	66	37.3	17.7	
17	Iowa	19000	990.8	319.6	224.6	77.1	38.2	16.1	
18	Kansas	20000	915	274.1	194.4	69.6	43.8	20.9	
19	Kentucky	21000	961.1	302.9	225.5	63.2	43.6	20.9	
20	Louisiana	22000	923.3	271.6	214.2	57.8	44.4	22.5	
21	Maine	23000	975.3	286.3	234.6	63.3	36	14.5	

6. Click the Filter button next to the Heart Disease header. Note the sorting and filtering features available, as shown:

fx	17.7								

C	D	E	F	G	H	I	J	K
Total ▾	Heart Disease ▾	Cancer ▾	Stroke ▾	Accidents ▾	Motor Vehicle Acciden ▾	Emphysema ▾	Diabetes ▾	HIV
1009.9	309				25.3	45.6	30.1	
418.7	9				11.7	18.2	10.4	
820.4	225				20.2	51.4	21.6	
1083.8	333				26.8	49	25.5	
694.8	213				11.6	37.8	17.9	
670.9	167				16.7	46.2	14.3	
907.4	294				10.4	38	20.3	
884.6	257					44	31.2	
1157.3	317					30.2	36.9	4
1060.4	342					54.9	27	1
790.7	235					35.9	18.2	
678.2	2					22.3	16.9	
745.1	197					43.9	19.4	
867.4	272					37.7	22.7	
906.5	279					46.8	24.2	
990.8	319					50.3	23	
915	274					45.6	24.4	
961.1	302					49.9	27.8	
923.3	271					35.8	41.8	
975.3	286					61.8	26.8	
819.1	232					33.3	28.1	
898.6	260					41.4	22.8	
867.5	285				15	38.8	24.8	
787.1	198				14.3	36.9	23.2	
1011.8	346				35	41.5	23.1	
1012.6	330				21.1	50.1	25.6	
906.5	227				24.9	57.4	22.4	
914	284.1	157.1	65.0	46.7	20.8	47.2	20.3	
828	235.8	201.7	46.5	38.1	20	54.2	13.3	

Menu overlay:
- ⊿↓ Sort Smallest to Largest
- ⊿↓ Sort Largest to Smallest
- Sort by Color ▸
- ⊠ Clear Filter From "Heart Disease"
- Filter by Color ▸
- Number Filters ▸
  - Equals...
  - Does Not Equal...
  - Greater Than...
  - Greater Than Or Equal To...
  - Less Than...
  - Less Than Or Equal To...
  - Between...
  - Top 10...
  - Above Average
  - Below Average
  - Custom Filter...
- Search 🔍
  - ☑ (Select All)
  - ☑ 91.9
  - ☑ 137.2
  - ☑ 167.3
  - ☑ 185.4
  - ☑ 197.1
  - ☑ 198.3
  - ☑ 202.4
  - ☑ 206
  - ☑ 213.5
  - ☑ 216.5
  - ☑ 218.5
  - ☑ 222.1
  - ☑ 225.8
  - ☑ 227.8
  - [OK] [Cancel]

7. Select Number Filters and then Top 10 to open the AutoFilter dialog.
8. Click the OK button to filter the table to show the ten states with the highest incidence of heart disease. Note that the table header now has a small filter icon on it, as shown:

9. Click the button again, and select Clear Filter From "Heart Disease" to restore the table.
10. Click in the table to ensure that the Design tab of the ribbon is visible, and click that tab.
11. In the Table Style Options section, select the Total Row option. Scroll to the bottom of the table to see the total row.

12. Only the far-right column is totaled; if you click in a cell under another row, you'll see a drop-down prompt—click the down arrow to see the options for adding a total for that column.

13. Let's create a calculated column to show all accidental causes of death—click in cell N6 (outside the table).

14. Type an equal sign (=), and then click in cell G6 (Accidents). Note that Excel has filled in the column name as opposed to a cell value.

15. Type a plus sign (+), then click in cell H6 (Motor Vehicle Accidents), and then press the ENTER key.

16. Note that Excel has filled in the entire column with the same relative formula.

17. Save the workbook; we'll use it again in the next exercise.

That is just some basic analysis, but if you're an Excel geek who hasn't used 2007 yet, you should already see some of the power under the hood. When Excel creates the table, it also creates a system of identifiers for the table, which you can use in formulas. The table name defaults to Table1, Table2, Table3, etc., but can be changed on the Design tab under Table Tools to the far right of the ribbon. The table name refers to the entire range of cells within the table, with the exception of the header and total rows, and the header can be used to refer to the column of the table, with the exception of the header and total rows.

So, for example, in the table we used in Exercise 4-1, you can use the *structured specifier* Table1[Cancer] to refer to the column of numbers (excluding the total) under the Cancer header, and it will operate just like a range definition in Excel. The following special item specifiers are also defined:

- ▶ **#All** The entire table, including header rows and totals
- ▶ **#Data** The same as the table name
- ▶ **#Headers** The header row
- ▶ **#Totals** Just the total row, if there is one

Conditional Formatting

Excel has had conditional formatting since Excel 97. However, even though this tool was pretty powerful, it was buried under a few menus, required writing a few arcane formulas to get working, and often involved trial and error to get the appearance you were looking for. In Excel 2007, conditional formatting got an overhaul, making it much easier to find, but also making it more "discoverable"—the layout makes it much easier to apply some basic, very functional conditional formatting, but also leads the user to more powerful conditional formatting capabilities.

About the "Ribbon"

If you're new to the ribbon (also called the "fluent UI"), please take some time to get used to it. The ribbon was born when the developers on the Office team discovered that 80 percent of all feature requests were already in the product; they were just difficult to find. So the goal behind the ribbon is to make functionality more accessible, and also to minimize the number of clicks necessary to find things. Microsoft also took the "ribbon overhaul" as an opportunity to normalize the UI across all of Office.

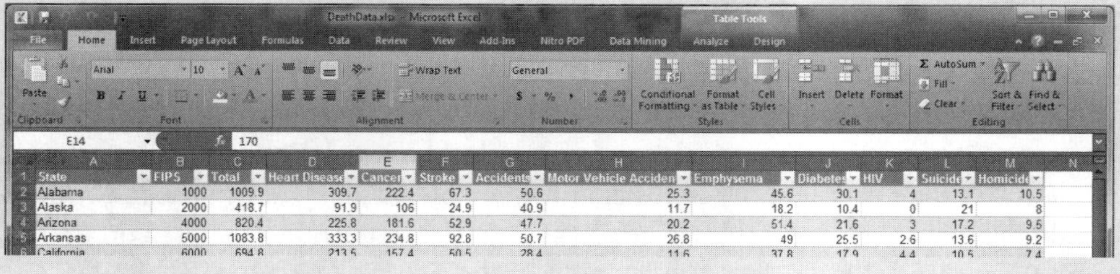

Conditional formatting is a powerful tool in that it adds readability to what could just be a sheet full of numbers. Figure 4-2 shows some conditional formatting features added to our Death Data spreadsheet. It may be a bit tough to make out in grayscale, but the Total column has highlighting on the top ten and bottom ten values, making the extremes easy to pick out visually. The Heart Disease column has data bars applied,

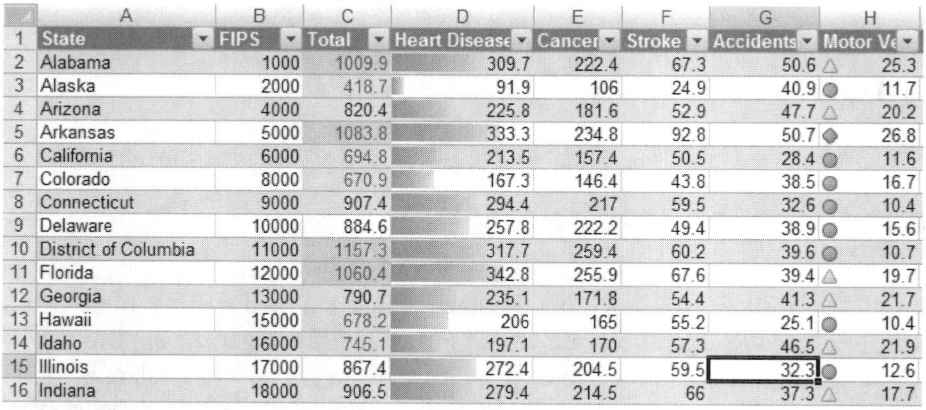

	A	B	C	D	E	F	G	H
1	State	FIPS	Total	Heart Disease	Cancer	Stroke	Accidents	Motor Ve
2	Alabama	1000	1009.9	309.7	222.4	67.3	50.6	25.3
3	Alaska	2000	418.7	91.9	106	24.9	40.9	11.7
4	Arizona	4000	820.4	225.8	181.6	52.9	47.7	20.2
5	Arkansas	5000	1083.8	333.3	234.8	92.8	50.7	26.8
6	California	6000	694.8	213.5	157.4	50.5	28.4	11.6
7	Colorado	8000	670.9	167.3	146.4	43.8	38.5	16.7
8	Connecticut	9000	907.4	294.4	217	59.5	32.6	10.4
9	Delaware	10000	884.6	257.8	222.2	49.4	38.9	15.6
10	District of Columbia	11000	1157.3	317.7	259.4	60.2	39.6	10.7
11	Florida	12000	1060.4	342.8	255.9	67.6	39.4	19.7
12	Georgia	13000	790.7	235.1	171.8	54.4	41.3	21.7
13	Hawaii	15000	678.2	206	165	55.2	25.1	10.4
14	Idaho	16000	745.1	197.1	170	57.3	46.5	21.9
15	Illinois	17000	867.4	272.4	204.5	59.5	32.3	12.6
16	Indiana	18000	906.5	279.4	214.5	66	37.3	17.7

Figure 4-2   *Illuminating data with conditional formatting*

which give a visual representation of the relative values shown in the column. (More on data bars in the next section.) Finally, the Motor Vehicle Deaths column on the far right has an icon set applied—green circles, yellow triangles, and red diamonds (insert "Lucky Charms" joke here).

Data Bars in 2007 and 2010

The data bars have an interesting history, short though it is. They were introduced with Excel 2007, and were a favorite feature to demo. However, over time, many people noticed a problem with the way they displayed. Figure 4-3 shows data bars in Excel 2007.

It looks pretty handy, until you start to look closer. The maximum value is near the center: 15,000. The minimum value is the first value: 10,500. But looking at the data bars, and especially that top value of 15,000, leads us to think the minimum value is small—perhaps less than 100—instead of seeing the reality—that the minimum value is two-thirds of the maximum. This is because Excel 2007 data bars set the range of the cell width between the minimum and maximum values. This can also have the effect of magnifying what are actually very small differences. Consider the data bars shown in Figure 4-4. The minimum and maximum values are less than 1 percent apart, but the data bars make it look like the maximum value dwarfs the minimum.

An additional challenge is that the gradient on the data bars could often make it difficult to make real comparisons. In Excel 2010, these challenges are addressed. The spans from Figures 4-3 and 4-4 are shown in Excel 2010 in Figure 4-5.

The selection from Figure 4-3 is on the left, formatted with a gradient data bar. Note that the values now look proportional and visually communicate the difference in value. Also the gradient now has a solid border instead of fading into the background, making it easier to differentiate the edges of the bars. We formatted the block on the right (the same numbers as in Figure 4-4) with solid data bars—an easily selectable option if you don't want gradients at all. Note how the difference between them is now imperceptible. (If you want the more relative scale similar to Excel 2007, you can still customize the data range.)

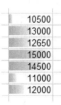

Figure 4-3   *Data bars in Excel 2007*

1000000
1000100
1000200
1000900
1000200
1000400

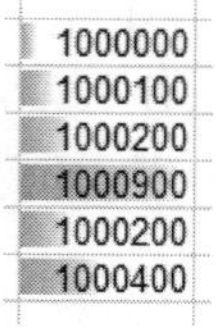

Figure 4-4 *Data bars showing a small difference*

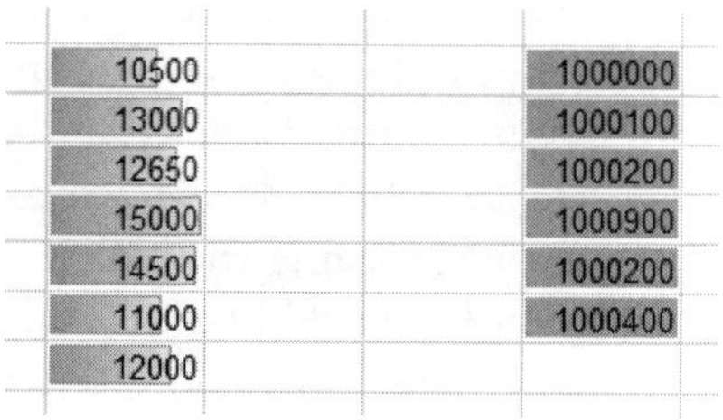
10500
13000
12650
15000
14500
11000
12000
1000000
1000100
1000200
1000900
1000200
1000400

Figure 4-5 *Data bars in Excel 2010*

Pivot Tables

Let's take a look at using Excel as a front-end tool for analyzing data. Starting with Excel 2007, the new wizard made it incredibly easier to pull data into Excel. The Data tab on the ribbon, shown in Figure 4-6, provides one-click access to a number of data sources. (From Web is very cool—enter a URL for a webpage, and it will show the page with tags on each of the tables on the page to import.) If you select a tabular data source, you will have the option to import data as a table, pivot table, or pivot chart. If you select Analysis Services, you will only have the Pivot Table and Pivot Chart options.

Creating a pivot table in Excel from an Analysis Services data source is intuitive. When you connect to a cube, Excel will present you with a PivotTable Field List task pane, as shown in Figure 4-7. At the very top is a drop-down list that allows you to filter the fields in the list to specific topics, similar to a dynamic perspective selector. The top panel lists the measures, KPIs, and dimensions in the cube you've selected. Hierarchies are shown as expandable, and will display the attributes in the hierarchy underneath, but you have to drag the entire hierarchy down to the table design areas.

Under the Field list are four areas for designing the pivot table. The Report Filter area will insert any dimension added as a filter selector above the pivot table. The Column Labels and Row Labels areas will add those dimensions to the appropriate parts of the pivot table. If you remember in Chapter 3 we talked about natural hierarchies—this is

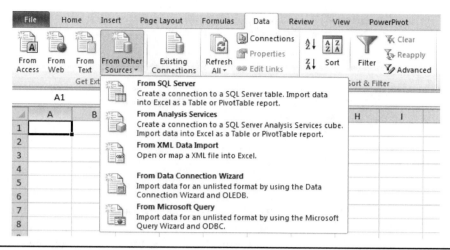

Figure 4-6   *The Data tab on the Excel 2010 ribbon*

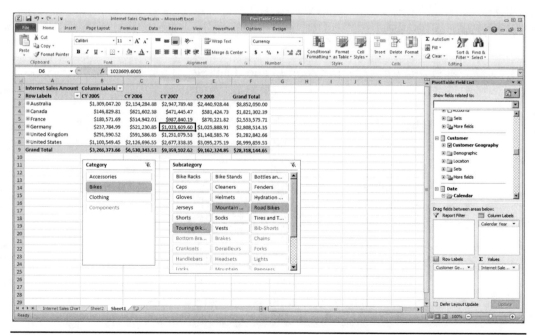

Figure 4-7   *Pivot table in Excel*

⊟ **Canada**	**$146,829.81**	**$621,602.38**
Canadian Dollar	$146,829.81	$459,801.97
US Dollar		$161,800.41
⊟ **France**	**$180,571.69**	**$514,942.01**
French Franc	$180,571.69	
US Dollar		$514,942.01
⊟ **Germany**	**$237,784.99**	**$521,230.85**
Deutsche Mark	$237,784.99	
US Dollar		$521,230.85

Figure 4-8   *An "unnatural" hierarchy*

where you can create "unnatural hierarchies." By dragging successive dimensions or attributes to a display area, you will create a hierarchy, such as shown in Figure 4-8, where we have a hierarchy of Customer Country followed by Source Currency, resulting in sales being broken down by the purchaser's currency under each nation.

Now that we've seen some of the basics of creating a pivot table, let's create a pivot table in Excel.

Exercise 4-2: Creating a Pivot Table

1. Open Excel 2010.
2. Select the Data tab in the ribbon.
3. Click the From Other Sources button and then select From Analysis Services as shown here:

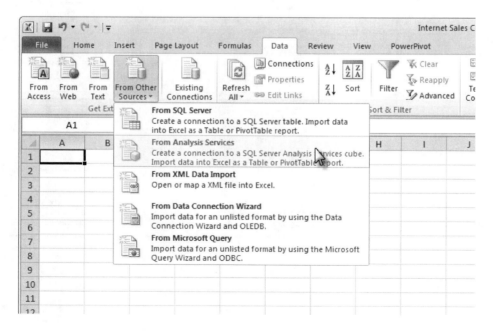

4. This opens the Data Connection Wizard. On the first page, enter the server name and then click Next.

5. On the Select Database And Table page, select the database you want to connect to. This will show a list of cubes and perspectives in the database, as shown:

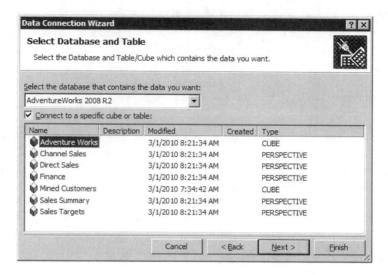

6. Select the Adventure Works cube, and then click the Next button.

7. On the final page, accept the defaults and click the Finish button.

8. On the Import Data dialog, select PivotTable Report and click OK.

9. You'll now have the Pivot Table designer, the Field List in the task pane to the right, and the PivotTable Tools tabs on the ribbon.

10. Drag the Internet Sales Amount measure to the Values pane.

11. Scroll down to Customer, Location, and drag the Country field to the Row Labels pane.

12. Now, scroll down to Date, Calendar, and drag Date.Calendar field to the Column Labels pane.

You should now have a table that looks similar to the illustration shown here:

	A	B	C	D	E	F
1	Internet Sales Amount	Column Labels ▼				
2	Row Labels ▼	CY 2005	CY 2006	CY 2007	CY 2008	Grand Total
3	Australia	$1,309,047.20	$2,154,284.88	$3,033,784.21	$2,563,884.29	$9,061,000.58
4	Canada	$146,829.81	$621,602.38	$535,784.46	$673,628.21	$1,977,844.86
5	France	$180,571.69	$514,942.01	$1,026,324.97	$922,179.04	$2,644,017.71
6	Germany	$237,784.99	$521,230.85	$1,058,405.73	$1,076,890.77	$2,894,312.34
7	United Kingdom	$291,590.52	$591,586.85	$1,298,248.57	$1,210,286.27	$3,391,712.21
8	United States	$1,100,549.45	$2,126,696.55	$2,838,512.36	$3,324,031.16	$9,389,789.51
9	Grand Total	$3,266,373.66	$6,530,343.53	$9,791,060.30	$9,770,899.74	$29,358,677.22

Thanks to the work invested in building the AdventureWorks cubes, you can create a table of sales data broken down by country and year in fewer than a dozen steps. With conditional formatting, you can add significant usability by highlighting numbers of interest, outlying values, or relative weights.

This table was easy to read, but what if we were interested in a subset of the data? If we're looking at U.S. states, or even U.S. cities, the data quickly scrolls off the page and becomes difficult to evaluate visually. Analysis Services provides various ways of grouping members of a dimension in named sets, making it easier to reuse collections of items you use frequently.

NOTE

There are two types of named sets: static and dynamic. Static named sets are established groups of items, like having a set of "Southeastern States" that contains Florida, Georgia, South Carolina, and Alabama. Dynamic named sets are created based on data—top ten sellers, bottom 10 percent of performers, etc. Prior to Excel 2010, Excel didn't handle dynamic named sets very well because of the way it created the MDX query behind the scenes. This problem is fixed in Excel 2010.

Unfortunately, named sets had to be created in the cube, which isn't helpful if you're an analyst who has to create sets of items on an ongoing basis—if you're creating a set every week or more, you can't ask IT to write the MDX to create the set and reprocess the cube every time. Luckily, now you don't have to.

Excel 2010 gives users the ability to create their own named sets. Found under the Fields, Items, & Sets button on the PivotTable Tools/Options tab in the ribbon, you can create and manage sets of items. Figure 4-9 shows the designer for creating a set in Excel. The designer has some limitations—the set must be created based on the current hierarchy in the rows or columns of the pivot table, and it's created as a hierarchy. So in the example shown in Figure 4-9, this set will always be displayed as Country – State – City. In addition, the set won't have a filter option—it's all or nothing for the members in the set.

New Set (Gemini AdventureWorks 2008 R2 Adventure Works)

Set name: Major Cities

Display folder (optional):

Add Row ✕ Delete Row Copy Row ▲ ▼

Country	State-Province	City
United States	California	Los Angeles
United States	New York	New York
United States	Georgia	Atlanta
United States	Washington	Seattle
United States	Texas	Dallas
United States	Illinois	Chicago

☑ Display items from different levels in separate fields
☑ Replace the fields currently in the row area with the new set

Edit MDX...

OK   Cancel

Figure 4-9 *Creating a named set in Excel*

NOTE

User-created sets will only work for OLAP-based pivot tables.

Two more new features in Excel 2010 are sparklines and slicers. Sparklines are small graphs designed to give a quick contextual idea of a relative performance measure. Figure 4-10 shows sparklines in the far-right column on our pivot table from Exercise 4-2. These graphs are plotted for the four points in the table, and give a quick

Internet Sales Amount	Column Labels				
Row Labels	CY 2005	CY 2006	CY 2007	CY 2008	Grand Total
Australia	$1,309,047.20	$2,154,284.88	$3,033,784.21	$2,563,884.29	$9,061,000.58
Canada	$146,829.81	$621,602.38	$535,784.46	$673,628.21	$1,977,844.86
France	$180,571.69	$514,942.01	$1,026,324.97	$922,179.04	$2,644,017.71
Germany	$237,784.99	$521,230.85	$1,058,405.73	$1,076,890.77	$2,894,312.34
United Kingdom	$291,590.52	$591,586.85	$1,298,248.57	$1,210,286.27	$3,391,712.21
United States	$1,100,549.45	$2,126,696.55	$2,838,512.36	$3,324,031.16	$9,389,789.51
Grand Total	$3,266,373.66	$6,530,343.53	$9,791,060.30	$9,770,899.74	$29,358,677.22

Figure 4-10 *Sparklines on a pivot table*

indication of the performance over time. Similar to data bars, the default settings on sparklines define the axis values for each graph, and may be a bit misleading, depending on how they are used. However, there are options to change the axis to be fixed for all sparklines in a series, if you desire.

Slicers are custom filters that you can add to a pivot table that enable users to quickly apply filters to a table. What makes slicers really compelling are the way they can be used together. Figure 4-11 shows a pivot table with two slicers—one for Product Categories, one for Promotion Type. Note that in the Promotion Type slicer at the top, the two last promotions are faded out, indicating there is no data in the pivot table under those promotions.

But if we select a product category, say Bikes, as shown in Figure 4-12, note two things. First, the Excess Inventory promotion is now grayed out, indicating that there is no data in the table for that promotion. And second, the other three categories still have bold text but no background fill, indicating that there is data in the table for those categories, but they are not selected. With this functionality, the slicers themselves are

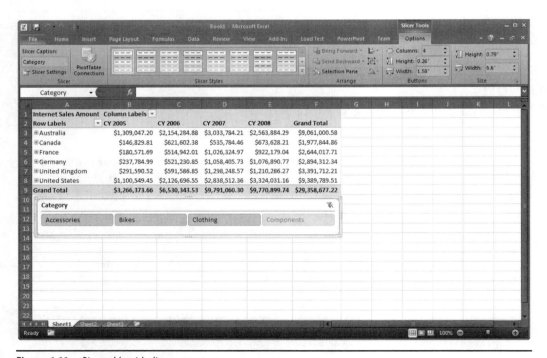

Figure 4-11   *Pivot table with slicers*

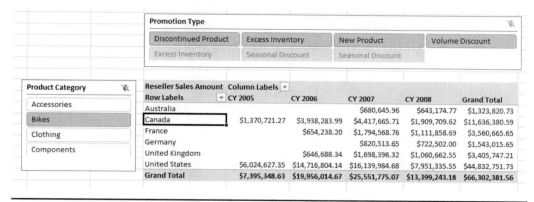

Figure 4-12 *Pivot table with a slicer selected*

indicators as much as filters—they can make it easy to discover things about the data you might not otherwise be aware of.

NOTE

Slicers are only compatible with Excel 2010.

Let's go ahead and add a slicer to the pivot table we created in Exercise 4-2.

Exercise 4-3: Add a Slicer to a Pivot Table

1. Open the pivot table you created in Exercise 4-2.
2. Click in the pivot table to enable the pivot table tabs in the ribbon.
3. Select Options.
4. Click the Insert Slicer button and then select Insert Slicer.

5. From the Insert Slicers dialog, select Category under Product, as shown next:

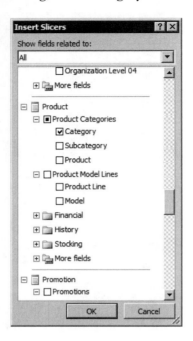

6. Click the OK button. You should have a slicer added to your workbook, with the four categories arranged vertically.
7. Select the slicer to enable the Slicer Tools tab in the ribbon, and click Options.
8. To the right (you may have to scroll over), change Columns to 4.

9. Resize the slicer to make room for the buttons to be arranged horizontally, as shown:

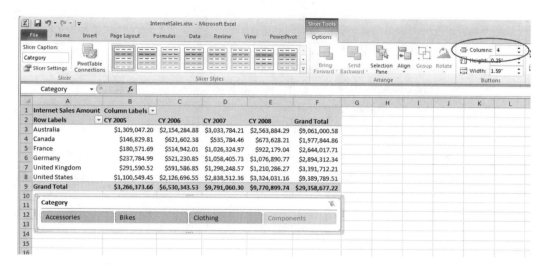

10. Now you can click each of the categories to filter the pivot table. Click the small filter icon in the top-right area of the slicer to clear all selections (no filter).

11. Save the workbook.

Writeback

An incredible capability in SQL Server Analysis Services is the ability to actually change the data that's displayed. This is referred to as *writeback*. Essentially, it enables an end user to edit a value that is in the cube without affecting the underlying data source. This is generally used for projections and what-if scenarios.

For example, consider the pivot table in Figure 4-13. This shows sales quotas broken down by quarter. The manager, Stephen Jiang, is considering third-quarter quotas and

Sales Amount Quota	Column Labels						
	CY 2008					CY 2008 Total	Grand Total
	H1 CY 2008		H1 CY 2008 Total	H2 CY 2008	H2 CY 2008 Total		
Row Labels	Q1 CY 2008	Q2 CY 2008		Q3 CY 2008			
Ken J. Sánchez	$5,573,000.00	$7,047,000.00	$12,620,000.00			$12,620,000.00	$12,620,000.00
Brian S. Welcker	$5,573,000.00	$7,047,000.00	$12,620,000.00			$12,620,000.00	$12,620,000.00
Stephen Y. Jiang	$5,573,000.00	$7,047,000.00	$12,620,000.00			$12,620,000.00	$12,620,000.00
David R. Campbell	$234,000.00	$403,000.00	$637,000.00			$637,000.00	$637,000.00
Garrett R. Vargas	$280,000.00	$390,000.00	$670,000.00			$670,000.00	$670,000.00
Jillian Carson	$714,000.00	$947,000.00	$1,661,000.00			$1,661,000.00	$1,661,000.00
José Edvaldo. Saraiva	$569,000.00	$830,000.00	$1,399,000.00			$1,399,000.00	$1,399,000.00
Linda C. Mitchell	$894,000.00	$1,124,000.00	$2,018,000.00			$2,018,000.00	$2,018,000.00
Michael G. Blythe	$849,000.00	$869,000.00	$1,718,000.00			$1,718,000.00	$1,718,000.00
Pamela O. Ansman-Wolfe	$343,000.00	$390,000.00	$733,000.00			$733,000.00	$733,000.00
Shu K. Ito	$614,000.00	$724,000.00	$1,338,000.00			$1,338,000.00	$1,338,000.00
Tete A. Mensa-Annan	$454,000.00	$497,000.00	$951,000.00			$951,000.00	$951,000.00
Tsvi Michael. Reiter	$538,000.00	$686,000.00	$1,224,000.00			$1,224,000.00	$1,224,000.00
Grand Total	$5,573,000.00	$7,047,000.00	$12,620,000.00			$12,620,000.00	$12,620,000.00

Figure 4-13   *Pivot table showing sales quotas*

what the effect might be on his overall year. By enabling what-if scenarios, he can actually enter the numbers in the pivot table and look at the results, as shown in Figure 4-14.

After Stephen makes his edits, he can run the calculations in the pivot table without affecting the back-end data source (everyone else who connects to the cube sees the original data). This way, he can try different numbers and see what works. Once he's happy with it, he can publish the numbers back to the cube, at which point other users will see the edits. That means Stephen's boss can ask his subordinates to submit projections into the cube, and he can view all the submitted forecasts directly in a pivot table.

Sales Amount Quota	Column Labels						
	CY 2008					CY 2008 Total	Grand Total
	H1 CY 2008		H1 CY 2008 Total	H2 CY 2008	H2 CY 2008 Total		
Row Labels	Q1 CY 2008	Q2 CY 2008		Q3 CY 2008			
Ken J. Sánchez	$5,573,000.00	$7,047,000.00	$12,620,000.00			$12,620,000.00	$12,620,000.00
Brian S. Welcker	$5,573,000.00	$7,047,000.00	$12,620,000.00			$12,620,000.00	$12,620,000.00
Stephen Y. Jiang	$5,573,000.00	$7,047,000.00	$12,620,000.00			$12,620,000.00	$12,620,000.00
David R. Campbell	$234,000.00	$403,000.00	$637,000.00	$500,000.00		$637,000.00	$637,000.00
Garrett R. Vargas	$280,000.00	$390,000.00	$670,000.00	$400,000.00		$670,000.00	$670,000.00
Jillian Carson	$714,000.00	$947,000.00	$1,661,000.00	$1,100,000.00		$1,661,000.00	$1,661,000.00
José Edvaldo. Saraiva	$569,000.00	$830,000.00	$1,399,000.00	$1,000,000.00		$1,399,000.00	$1,399,000.00
Linda C. Mitchell	$894,000.00	$1,124,000.00	$2,018,000.00	$1,300,000.00		$2,018,000.00	$2,018,000.00
Michael G. Blythe	$849,000.00	$869,000.00	$1,718,000.00	$1,000,000.00		$1,718,000.00	$1,718,000.00
Pamela O. Ansman-Wolfe	$343,000.00	$390,000.00	$733,000.00	$500,000.00		$733,000.00	$733,000.00
Shu K. Ito	$614,000.00	$724,000.00	$1,338,000.00	$800,000.00		$1,338,000.00	$1,338,000.00
Tete A. Mensa-Annan	$454,000.00	$497,000.00	$951,000.00	$600,000.00		$951,000.00	$951,000.00
Tsvi Michael. Reiter	$538,000.00	$686,000.00	$1,224,000.00	$750,000.00		$1,224,000.00	$1,224,000.00
Grand Total	$5,573,000.00	$7,047,000.00	$12,620,000.00			$12,620,000.00	$12,620,000.00

Figure 4-14   *Pivot table with edited values*

When you enable writeback on a cube partition, Analysis Services creates a table in the data source you indicate. This table holds the deltas for writeback values—if a value is 50 and you change it to 75, the table will have a value of 25. Then the values are simply summed in when queries are run against the cube. For this reason, currently you can only enable writeback on partitions whose measure groups only use SUM as an aggregate function. If you're having problems enabling writeback on a partition, check to see if you used the cube wizard, with which you can easily create a COUNT measure without noticing.

NOTE

To clear out the writeback values, currently you have to either set the partition back to read-only or go into the database and delete the records representing the writeback; there is no easy way to do it from Excel.

Let us make a final note about scalability and writeback. When you write back, you are actually entering what are referred to as "leaf-level" values. This means each individual cell represents the lowest level you can drill to in a cube—a single member is selected *on every dimension associated with the measure.* Analysis Services writeback does support writing back at nonleaf-level values. For example, if you wanted to change a value for a product subcategory that had five products, Analysis Services would allocate the value—divide it by five and write that result to each cell.

If you wanted to write a value to that subcategory for the United States, SSAS would have to divide the number by 250 (five products times 50 states). Now consider that the dimensions in AdventureWorks go down to the individual day, individual ZIP codes, even individual customers. If you don't select a member from every dimension, the calculations can quickly consume all the memory on even large servers. For this reason, you may want to create a measure group specifically for what-if scenarios, such as the Sales Targets measure group in AdventureWorks.

Now that we have a firm grasp on the capabilities of Excel as an analysis client, let's look at some of the functionality added with SharePoint 2010 and Excel Services.

Excel Services

Excel Services was introduced with SharePoint 2007 Enterprise Edition. This server-based Excel engine targets three main scenarios:

▶ **Publishing spreadsheets to a thin client**   Often, when power users create a useful spreadsheet, they need to be able to share it with a broad audience, but that audience has no business requirement for editing the spreadsheet. In addition, you can't always be sure everyone in the audience will have Excel (or the right version) available. With Excel Services, it's possible to publish a spreadsheet to SharePoint, and end users can open the spreadsheet in a browser to view it without needing Excel.

► **Analytic reporting** This is generally a subset of the previous scenario, but an important one. With the increased emphasis on connecting to external data sources in Excel 2007, Excel Services enables publishing a spreadsheet to SharePoint and displaying it in a browser but with current data. In addition, the spreadsheet can keep some basic interactivity (opening hierarchies, basic parameterization).

► **Automating Excel on a server** For the extreme power users, Excel Services provides a way to run spreadsheets on a server.

In SharePoint 2010, Excel Services has really been overhauled. First of all, the display now uses AJAX to provide a smoother user experience when working with the workbook. Excel Services also supports a number of new features as the product group continues to work on making Excel Services more in line with the desktop client. These include

► Sparklines

► Conditional formatting (icon sets and data bars)

► Slicers

► PivotTable named sets

► Embedded images

In SharePoint 2007, if you uploaded a file with features unsupported by Excel Services, loading the file would simply fail. In SharePoint 2010, Excel Services will do its best to open and display the file, disabling features it doesn't support and showing a notification bar with those problems. (Some features can still block loading a workbook completely.)

The best way to understand Excel Services is simply to use it. If you have SharePoint 2010 handy, let's upload our pivot table workbook.

Exercise 4-4: Excel Services

1. Open the pivot table workbook from Exercise 4-3.
2. Click the File button to open Backstage.
3. Click Share.
4. Click Publish To Excel Services.

5. Click the Publish To Excel Services button, as shown here:

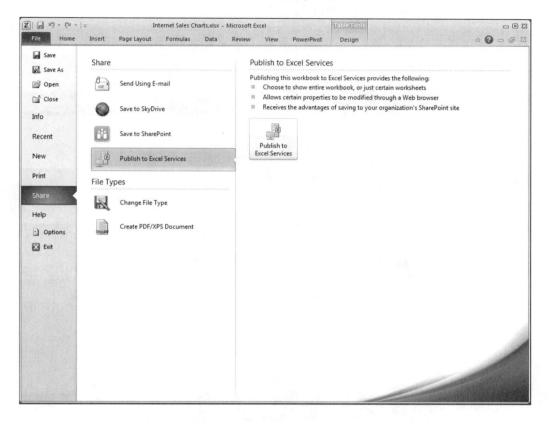

6. Once you click the button, you'll be presented with a Save As dialog. If it's not open to a document library on SharePoint, you can put in the URL for your SharePoint server (http://servername), and you should get a list of libraries on the site.

7. Select a library, name the document, ensure that Open In Excel Services is selected, and click Save.

8. Wait for the grinding to stop, and you should have a browser open with the pivot table and slicer showing, as shown:

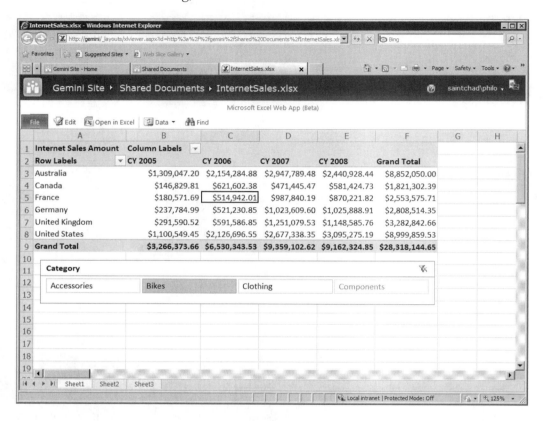

9. You can click the slicer, and it will dynamically filter the pivot table. You can also use the filter buttons next to the Column Labels and Row Labels areas.

10. Note the Data button in the menu bar—with this you can refresh the data from the data source at any time you choose.

Web Services

With respect to the third scenario noted earlier, a benefit to having Excel Services running on the server is that it can effectively make Excel available via web service to any application. One challenge developers have often had in the past is that an application would demand something that was incredibly easy to do in Excel, but hard to do in code. An option they would often resort to is installing Excel and automating it. Unfortunately, Microsoft does not support the automation of Office applications on a server, so this was an unsupported scenario.

With Excel Services, it's possible to access Excel via web services, so a developer can either make a call to Excel on its own, or they could set up a workbook designed for the application and use that via web services. The Excel Web Services have been significantly beefed up with SharePoint 2010, including the ability to edit cells and ranges, set parameters, and even fetch the image of a chart back via URL (to embed a snapshot of a chart into a webpage). Also, error handling has been revamped so that cell error values are the traditional "#VALUE!" string, and errors in processing throw a SOAP exception.

Excel Web Application

One of the major new changes in SharePoint 2010 is the addition of the Office Web Apps. With Excel Web Services, it occasionally seemed misleading because you could click in a cell and select it, but you couldn't edit it. If you look at the pivot table we uploaded to Excel Services, you'll notice something—a button next to the File tab that says "Edit" (if you have the Office Web Apps installed and enabled).

To edit the document we uploaded, we'll have to be sure that the instance of Excel we used is closed, and we'll have to check the document out in the document library. However, after that, if we edit the document, we'll have a ribbon and editing controls available in the browser. We can click in a cell and type a formula, clicking around the spreadsheet to pick up cell references. Typing an equal sign and the beginning of a function name brings up IntelliSense for the functions supported. Just like with Excel Services, sparklines, slicers, and conditional formatting will display properly, although you can't edit them in the browser.

Summary

Hopefully, now you have a strong appreciation for Excel as an analysis tool. We can pull data from various sources, create pivot tables and pivot charts, add dynamic filtering tools, and highlight the workbooks as necessary using conditional formatting. In addition, we can publish our workbooks to a SharePoint Server and have users view them without having Excel installed.

One thing we didn't do—is it possible to combine data from different data sources? What if we've got billing data in one database and personnel data in another? Can we create a table combining the data? Before Office 2010, there was no easy and scalable way to do this (lookup functions are limited). But Office 2010 and SQL Server 2008 R2 have added a new feature called PowerPivot that enables exactly that. Let's take a look.

Chapter 5

PowerPivot

In This Chapter

As the Microsoft business intelligence solution set evolved, an interesting gap developed. There is a robust data platform in SQL Server Analysis Services where IT professionals can create complex multidimensional data models using the Business Intelligence Development Studio. And, of course, there's the old standby ad hoc analysis tool that causes a lot of the problems we're trying to solve with enterprise BI: Excel. But there wasn't a tool to address the problem of spreadmarts.

Analysts were creating analytic models on their desktops, and IT pros were triaging what cubes they built to serve the organization. Since the OLAP heavy lifting couldn't keep up with the demands of the field, we had Excel spreadsheets driving the organization. Management was difficult, and auditing was almost impossible. And as Microsoft put more analytic capabilities into Excel and more powerful data modeling into SSAS, the gap grew.

Microsoft took a first step towards addressing this gap with the Planning Module of PerformancePoint. Unfortunately, the attempt to create a brand-new modeling tool was creating new problems instead of filling the gap. And so PowerPivot was born.

Introducing PowerPivot

PowerPivot is actually a solution integrating several technologies. The centerpiece is an instance of Analysis Services that runs on the server for SharePoint and on the desktop for Excel. The server-based instance is installed via the SSAS installer—there is now an option to install Analysis Services in "SharePoint integrated mode." This will set SSAS in *Vertipaq mode,* which is optimized to execute aggregations and queries in memory in response to calls from SharePoint.

NOTE

When Analysis Services is installed in Vertipaq mode, you cannot publish SSAS solutions from BIDS to it; it exists solely to respond to SharePoint. You can install a second instance of SSAS in native mode alongside for servicing standard OLAP cubes.

On the desktop, PowerPivot is installed as an add-in for Excel 2010. This installs a local instance of Analysis Services (again, in Vertipaq mode) for running PowerPivot models from Excel and answering queries. In this case, the Vertipaq engine runs in-process with Excel. When you think about the size of multidimensional stores, running queries and creating models and aggregations, it should be obvious that PowerPivot is going to be a heavy driver for 64-bit Excel (Office 2010 is available in x64).

NOTE

The biggest issue with 64-bit Office is that it can't run 32-bit add-ins. So if you are dependent on a specific add-in, be sure it is available for 64-bit before installing x64 Office. (PowerPivot for Excel is available in both 32-bit and 64-bit versions.)

Once you have installed PowerPivot for Excel, you'll have a PowerPivot tab in the ribbon, as shown in Figure 5-1. It doesn't seem like there's a lot here—ten new buttons, half of which are disabled when you first start up Excel. Most of these are for use once you've created a PowerPivot model, and we do that in the PowerPivot window, which is launched using the first button on the ribbon.

When you first launch it, the PowerPivot designer isn't much to look at, as shown in Figure 5-2. But this lowly interface provides a capability that has been in demand in Excel for ages—the ability to join data sets from disparate data sources. This window is a designer for creating data models by importing data. The first section on the Home tab is Get External Data—this allows you to import data from SQL Server, Analysis Services, Access, Excel spreadsheets, Reporting Services, Oracle, Teradata, SQL Azure, or XML data feeds. Yes, "import"—when you connect to a data source in PowerPivot, the data is imported into the data model for you to work with.

Before importing the data, the PowerPivot wizard gives the user the option to select which columns they want to import. For example, many of the AdventureWorks data sets have dozens of columns, many of which would be of no service in an analytic report. There might also be a BLOB or image field that you don't need to bother with. Also, the wizard provides a selector on each column.

Let's say you have a data set that covers all 50 states in the United States. However, you want to do analysis on just the states in the Northeast. Instead of pulling in 50 states' worth of data only to delete about four-fifths of it, if there's a column for the state name, you can simply browse and deselect those states you don't plan to analyze. Net result: Only about one-fifth of the data needs to be pulled down to your desktop.

Once imported, you will have a collection of data grids, as shown in Figure 5-3. The table works similarly to tables in Excel 2007 and 2010—drop-down tabs in the

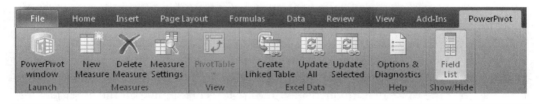

Figure 5-1   *The PowerPivot tab*

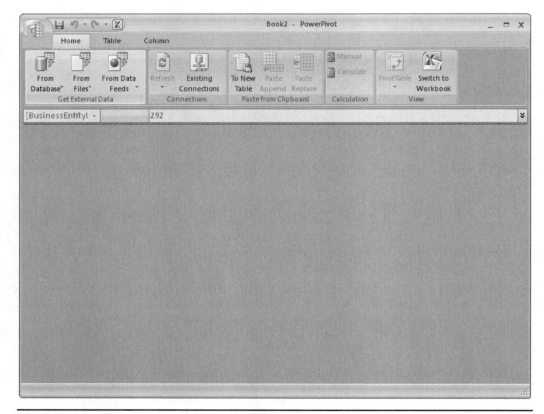

Figure 5-2 *The PowerPivot designer*

headers allow you to sort and filter the records based on various criteria. Right-clicking the header of a column gives you some column options, similar to Excel (including the ability to create a calculated column). What's new is the relationship icon, which you can see in the header for the Geography column of the table in Figure 5-3.

Note the tabs along the bottom of the window. Each tab represents a table that's been imported. The tables can be from one data source or several different data sources. Once imported, you can create relationships between the tables, provided they meet standard primary key/foreign key relationships. A *primary key* must be unique and non-null. For example, in a list of states, the state name could be a primary key. However, in a list of products and descriptions, you would not choose the product color or size as a primary key, since those values will be repeated. The best way to think of a primary key for a record is the value that uniquely identifies that record among all the other records.

A *foreign key* is a value that can be used to link to the primary key. For example, consider a table of states that has the state name and abbreviation, as well as other

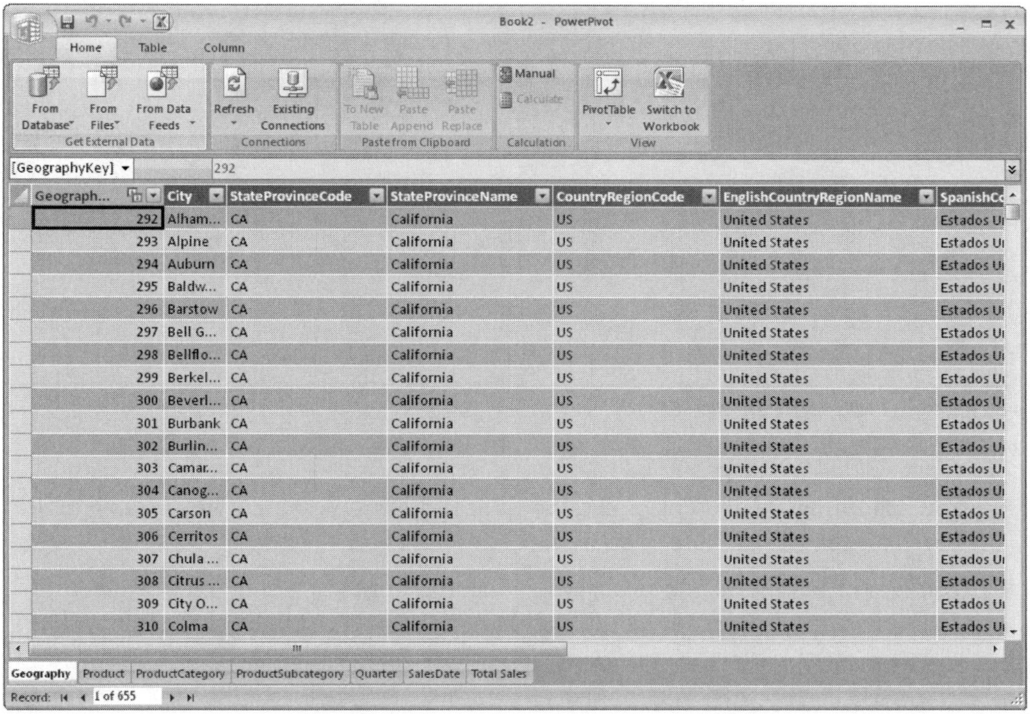

Figure 5-3   *PowerPivot with data loaded*

information about the state. We could assign the two-letter state abbreviation to be the primary key. Then, if we have a list of addresses where each address has a two-letter state abbreviation, we can make that abbreviation the foreign key and link it to the two-letter state abbreviation in the states table. This way, for each address, we can reference the states table to look up additional information about the state. Figure 5-4 shows this concept.

You can link from one table to another, but the following requirements apply:

▶ At least one column in each table must provide a unique identifier for each row.

▶ The data type must be the same in both columns.

▶ The matching columns do not have to have the same name.

▶ You can only have one relationship between two tables.

▶ Composite keys must be concatenated so that the relationship is between two single fields.

ID	Abbreviation	Name
	AL	ALABAMA
	AK	ALASKA
	AZ	ARIZONA
	AR	ARKANSAS
	CA	CALIFORNIA
	CO	COLORADO
	CT	CONNECTICUT
	DE	DELAWARE
	DC	DISTRICT OF COLUMBIA
	FL	FLORIDA
	GA	GEORGIA
	GU	GUAM
	HI	HAWAII
	ID	IDAHO
	IL	ILLINOIS
	IN	INDIANA
	IA	IOWA
	KS	KANSAS

390	Loveland	CO	US	United States	80537
391	Parker	CO	US	United States	80138
392	Westminster	CO	US	United States	80030
393	East Haven	CT	US	United States	6512
394	Farmington	CT	US	United States	6032
395	Hamden	CT	US	United States	6518
396	Milford	CT	US	United States	6460
397	New Haven	CT	US	United States	6510
398	Stamford	CT	US	United States	6901
399	Waterbury	CT	US	United States	6710
400	Westport	CT	US	United States	6880
401	Altamonte Springs	FL	US	United States	32701
402	Bradenton	FL	US	United States	34205

Figure 5-4 *Primary keys and foreign keys*

▶ You cannot have self-joins or circular joins (for example, an employee table that has manager/subordinate relationships).

▶ You do not have to have a primary key member for every foreign key value (columns with foreign key values that don't exist in the primary key table will be matched to a hidden "Unknown" member and displayed as such).

You can manage the relationships in your model by clicking the Manage Relationships button on the Table tab of the ribbon to show the Manage Relationships dialog, as shown in Figure 5-5. This will show the table and column of each end of every relationship in the PowerPivot model.

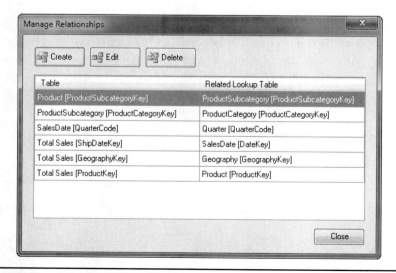

Figure 5-5 *Managing relationships in a PowerPivot model*

NOTE

If you've worked with Access or other major database solutions, you might be looking for a way to show an object-relational (or "OR") diagram. There isn't one in PowerPivot v1.

PowerPivot and Excel

There's one more aspect to PowerPivot that we'd like to point out before we move on to consuming our model—note the record count in Figure 5-6. Traditionally, versions of Excel up through Excel 2003 had a limit of 65,000 rows, which power analysts *always* ran up against. Excel 2007 took that limit out to more than one million rows. That limit remains in Excel 2010, until you install the PowerPivot add-in. The add-in removes the million-row limit, and the only limit becomes the memory limit on the workbook itself.

More important than the increased row limit is the responsiveness of the application. Once you've loaded a data set with millions of rows, the in-memory Analysis Server enables scrolling, manipulating, and filtering the data set with a smooth response. If you're used to working with large Excel spreadsheets, you may be used to trying to scroll and consistently getting the hourglass icon as the sheet loads and swaps. It's worth working through the exercise just to see how fluid the scrolling is on a huge data set.

Pivot Tables from PowerPivot

Once we've imported the data we need, we want to be able to use that data in Excel. On the Home tab in the PowerPivot ribbon is a button for inserting pivot tables into the Excel workbook you launched PowerPivot from, as shown in Figure 5-7. When you insert a pivot chart, PowerPivot/Excel automatically creates a new sheet for the pivot table data the chart will run from. You can always work with that sheet directly if you need to tweak a chart. (If you insert multiple charts—two or four from the drop-down button—then each chart will have its own sheet and pivot table.)

340	20020501	20020513
332	20020501	20020513
332	20020501	20020513

| Product | ProductCategory | ProductSubcategory | Quarter | SalesDate | Geo |

Record: ◀ ◀ 1 of 1,375,079 ▶ ▶

Figure 5-6   *Record count on a PowerPivot table*

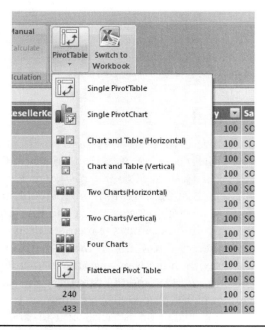

Figure 5-7   *Inserting pivot tables and pivot charts into Excel from PowerPivot*

Pivot tables from PowerPivot should look familiar, as shown in Figure 5-8 (this is one of the reasons PowerPivot is so awesome—familiar toolsets minimize training requirements!). When you click inside the pivot table, the task pane is visible on the right, with the tables and fields we've populated our behind-the-scenes model with. As we've done in the past, you can drag fields to the values, columns, rows, filters, or slicers area to get the appropriate changes to the pivot table.

NOTE

Unlike an Analysis Services cube, there is no differentiation in a PowerPivot designer between dimensions and measures—you can drag any column to any area and PowerPivot will do its best to create the table. So it's much easier to shoot yourself in the foot here.

If you want to return to the PowerPivot window, you can either check the taskbar for it (if you group your taskbar icons, it will group with Excel) or click the PowerPivot Window button on the PowerPivot tab of the ribbon in Excel. You can move back and forth between the PowerPivot designer and the workbook any number of times. To see the changes in the PowerPivot model after you've returned to Excel, simply click the Refresh All button on the Data tab in the ribbon. All right, let's give PowerPivot a try!

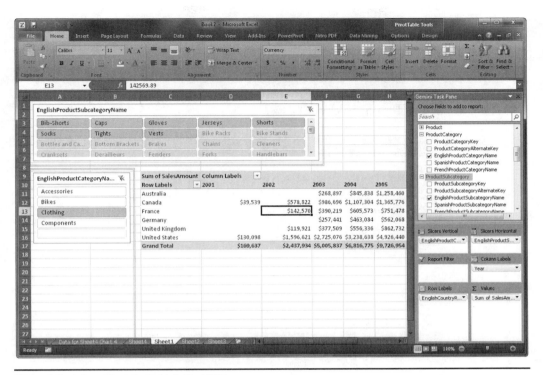

Figure 5-8   *PowerPivot pivot table in Excel 2010*

Exercise 5-1: PowerPivot

NOTE

This exercise uses the sample data from CodePlex, which you can download at http://powerpivotsampledata .codeplex.com. You want the PowerPivot Sample Data, not the Tutorial Sample Data.

1. Open Excel 2010.
2. Click the PowerPivot tab, and then click the PowerPivot Window Launch button.
3. In the PowerPivot window, click From Database and then From Access.
4. In the Table Import Wizard, name the connection **AdventureWorks**.
5. Click the Browse button.
6. Navigate to where you unzipped the samples; select the AW_CompanySales.accdb file, and click the Open button.
7. Click the Next button.

8. On the Choose How To Import The Data page, leave the default Select From A List Of Tables And Views To Choose The Data To Import selected, and click the Next button.

9. On the Select Tables And Views page, shown in the following illustration, select the Geography, Product, ProductCategory, ProductSubcategory, Quarter, SalesDate, and TotalSales check boxes.

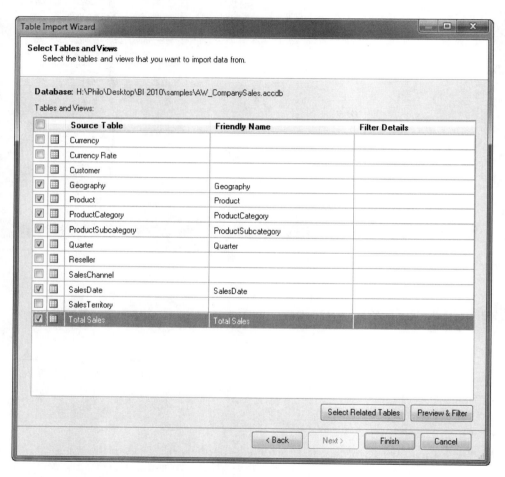

10. Select the Product table, and then click the Preview & Filter button.

11. Uncheck the columns for the foreign localization labels.

12. Click the down arrow in a column heading. Note that you can filter which records to import by unselecting various values. But we're going to bring everything in.

13. Click the OK button; note that now the Product table has "Applied filters" next to it.
14. Click the Finish button.
15. When the import is finished, it should look like the next illustration. Note that we've got almost 1.4 million rows in the Total Sales table!

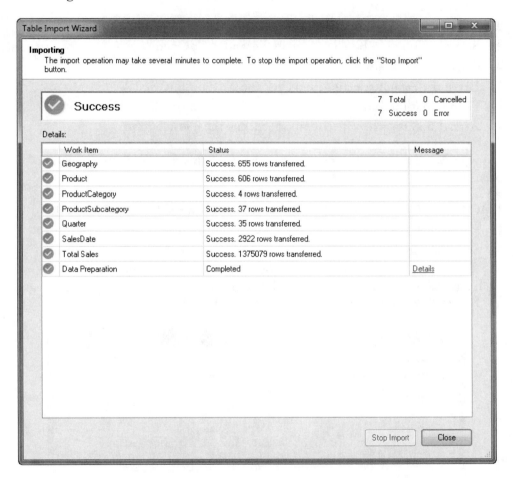

16. Click the Close button.
17. Note that we have the tables in PowerPivot now and that the relationships have been imported and re-created as well. Click the Total Sales tab at the bottom.
18. Scroll up and down the table; apply filters; sort the table. Note how responsive the application is.

Now we have some industry data we'd like to compare our sales data to. Let's import that.

1. In the ribbon in the PowerPivot designer, click the From Database button and select From Access.
2. Name this connection **IndustryData**, and click the Browse button.
3. Select the IndustryBikeSales.accdb file, and click Open.
4. Click the Next button.
5. Leave the default selection, and click the Next button.
6. Ensure that the IndustrySales table is selected, and click the Finish button.
7. After 1,368 rows have been imported, click the Close button.

Now we want to create the relationships between this table and our "dimension" tables.

1. Click the IndustrySales tab at the bottom to open the IndustrySales table.
2. Right-click the Country column.
3. Select Create Relationship.
4. In the Create Relationship dialog, the IndustrySales table and Country column should already be selected. Select Geography for the Related Lookup Table and EnglishCountryRegionName for the Related Lookup Column.

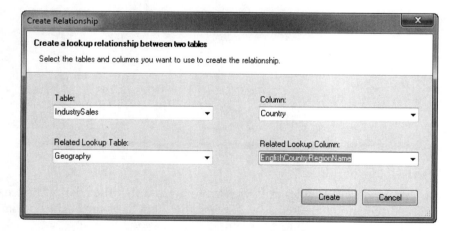

5. Click the Create button.

6. Whoops! You should get an error indicating that the relationship could not be created. Each of the tables we were trying to connect had multiple values for the country, so PowerPivot couldn't create a primary key/foreign key relationship.

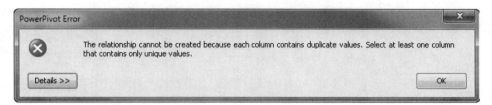

7. So what we need is a table that can act as the lookup source for the country codes in order to link these tables.

8. In the samples collection is an Excel document named Country.xslx—open that document now.

9. Highlight the table (CountryCode and CountryName) and copy it.

10. Switch to the PowerPivot designer and in the Paste From Clipboard section of the Home tab on the ribbon, click To New Table.

11. PowerPivot will open a Paste Preview dialog—verify that the data is correct and that Use First Row As Column Headers is selected. Click the OK button.

12. Now we have a country table. Note in the tab row at the bottom it's named "Table"—right-click the tab, select Rename, and name it **Countries**.

13. Now create a relationship between the CountryRegionCode in the Geography table and the CountryCode in the new Countries table.

14. Next, create a relationship between the Country column in the IndustrySales table and the CountryName column in the Countries table.

15. Also create the following relationships:

    ▶ IndustrySales/Quarter to Quarter/QuarterCode

    ▶ IndustrySales/Type of Bike to
        ProductSubcategory/EnglishProductSubcategoryName

16. Now click the PivotTable button, and select Chart And Table (Horizontal).

17. On the Insert Pivot dialog, select New Worksheet and click OK.

18. You should now have chart and table designers, as shown here:

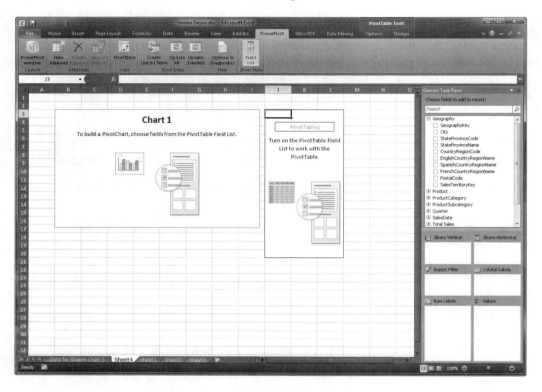

19. Click in the pivot table area on the worksheet, and then drag the OrderQuantity field from Total Sales and the Units field from IndustrySales to the Values area.

20. Drag the CountryName field from the Countries table to Row Labels, and drag the QuarterCode field from Quarters to the Column Labels.

21. Drag the EnglishProductCategoryName from ProductCategory to the Report Filter area. On the report, click the filter drop-down, and select Bikes to filter the sales report down to just bicycles.

22. Drag the EnglishProductSubcategoryName to the Slicers Vertical area to give us a way to slice the data by bicycle type.

23. You should now have a chart that shows industry sales vs. our company sales, as shown here:

EnglishPrc	Bikes	

EnglishProductSu...		Colum:								
Mountain Bikes		2001 Q4		2002 Q1		2002 Q2			2002 Q3	
Road Bikes	Row La	Sum of Ur	Sum of Or	Sum of Ur	Sum of Or	Sum of Units		Sum of OrderQuantity		Sum of Units
Touring Bikes	Australia	253121	1044	245990	979			249042	1006	2569:
Bib-Shorts	Canada	222057	4060	223627	3840			226403	4316	2335;
Bike Racks	France	885934	142	667976	188			676268	218	6976:
Bike Stands	Germany	1423823	206	1027162	209			1080997	285	106594
Bottles and Ca...	United Kir	664449	238	514344	244			520728	148	5372:
Bottom Brackets	United St:	5294315	15739	4360759	13606			4414892	15746	45547(
Brakes	Grand Tot	8743699	21429	7039858	19066			7168330	21719	73460(
Caps										
Chains										

24. Let's clean it up a bit. Right-click one of the values for "Sum of Units" in the chart to open the Value Field Settings dialog. Change the Custom name to **Industry Sales**.

25. Click the Number Format button, select Number, set Decimal Places to 0, and select the Use 1000 Separator check box.

26. Click OK and then OK again.

27. Similarly, change the Sum of OrderQuantity to **Company Sales**.

28. Finally, let's add data bars for a visual comparison—drag down the column for 2001 Q4 Industry Sales. Then click Conditional Formatting in the ribbon, select Data Bars, and select a color.

29. Do the same for Company Sales—you should see something like this:

EnglishProductCategoryName	Bikes				

	Column Labels				
	2001 Q4		2002 Q1		2002 Q2
Row Labels	Industry Sales	Company Sales	Industry Sales	Company Sales	Industry Sales
Australia	253,121	1,044	245,990	979	249,042
Canada	222,057	4,060	223,627	3,840	226,403
France	885,934	142	667,976	188	676,268
Germany	1,423,823	206	1,027,162	209	1,080,997
United Kingdom	664,449	238	514,344	244	520,728
United States	5,294,315	15,739	4,360,759	13,606	4,414,892
Grand Total	8,743,699	21,429	7,039,858	19,066	7,168,330

30. You can see at a glance that relatively speaking, the company's Canada sales outpace the industry, while European sales are lagging. You can select bike types from the slicer to view how each bicycle subcategory is doing as well.

31. Save the workbook.

In that exercise, you can see that it was straightforward to join an industry data source to our company sales data and analyze how the company sales are doing compared to the industry. In the past, this would have been, at best, a significant cut-and-paste job. However, the report is also dynamic—we can use slicers that filter *both* data sources on the fly.

This is just the beginning—we can also bring in manufacturing data from a different system and compare parts costs to sales trends. We could bring in QA reports to compare repair costs to profits. We can bring in customer satisfaction surveys from yet another system—compare customer satisfaction to repair costs and sales volumes.

As you saw with the Countries table, the biggest challenge in uniting data (as we discussed when talking about data warehouses) is finding a common field to connect them. On internal systems, it may be part numbers, nomenclature, catalog numbers, etc. When bringing in external data, we have to be critical about the cleanliness of the data we are bringing in. Are country names spelled correctly? Are demographic groups mapped to the ones we use? Are terms defined the same way? Note that our sales data has a SalesChannel column with "reseller" and "internet" while the Industry sales data has channel data of "retailer" and "web"—what if the two data sets define an Internet sale/web sale differently? You could end up comparing very different numbers.

PowerPivot for SharePoint

PowerPivot for SharePoint provides the server experience to complete the "BI for the masses" promise of PowerPivot. We started by designing a report in Excel that can unify data sources, display visual indicators for data, and help us in various types of analysis using the business data we have access to. However, it's still just a spreadsheet on our desktop. Are we still relegated to e-mailing this around to share it?

Not at all. PowerPivot for SharePoint allows us to publish a PowerPivot workbook to SharePoint where both the spreadsheet and the PowerPivot data can be consumed by other users. Similar to Excel Services, PowerPivot for SharePoint will provide a web-based view of our PowerPivot workbook objects. PowerPivot for SharePoint also provides an architecture for refreshing data in the underlying model so that the reports published in this manner are dynamic and can reflect real time or near real time.

The PowerPivot for SharePoint add-in installs on the SharePoint Server and provides the following features:

▶ **PowerPivot Gallery** A Silverlight-based gallery where users can share PowerPivot applications with others and visualize and interact with applications produced by others using Excel Services and Reporting Services.

▶ **PowerPivot Management Dashboard**   A management interface that helps SharePoint administrators monitor PowerPivot workbooks for usage and size. This helps to identify when a specific report suddenly gains a large amount of interest and viewers of the report spike. We can also identify whether increased user interest is likely to continue growing or is only a spike.

▶ **PowerPivot Web Service**   The "front-end" service that exposes PowerPivot data via XML/A to external applications such as Report Builder and Excel.

▶ **PowerPivot System Service**   The "back-end" service that manages the PowerPivot application database, load balancing, usage data collection, automatic data refresh, etc.

▶ **Analysis Services**   The Analysis Services server running the Vertipaq in-memory engine and integrated with SharePoint to load and manage the data within PowerPivot workbooks.

The PowerPivot Gallery in SharePoint, shown in Figure 5-9, is the users' primary point of interaction with PowerPivot. While it is a relatively standard document library

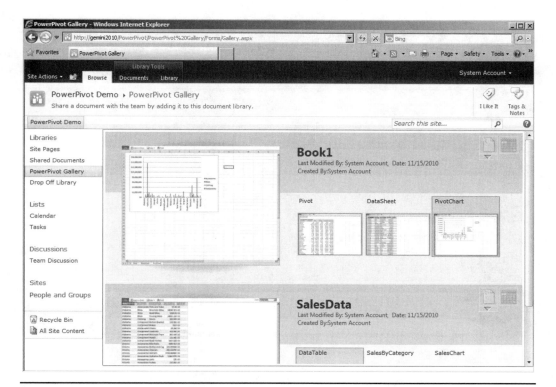

Figure 5-9   *The default view in a PowerPivot Gallery*

from the SharePoint perspective, the default view is a Silverlight web part that provides the thumbnail-style view of the published objects in the PowerPivot workbooks it contains. From this view, users can also create linked documents to the PowerPivot workbooks and manage their data refresh schedule.

Part of the PowerPivot integration is to provision sites and site templates with the web parts and content management to enable site owners to add a PowerPivot Report Gallery to their sites. They can also add a data feed library and will have the tools to manage data feed refresh schedules.

Let's publish our workbook to a PowerPivot Gallery. This is fairly straightforward, but an essential step for the final exercise.

Exercise 5-2: Publishing a PowerPivot Workbook

1. Open the workbook you created in Exercise 5-1.
2. Click the File tab in the top left to open the Backstage area.
3. Click Share on the left-hand pane.
4. Select "Publish to Excel Services."
5. Click the Publish To Excel Services button, as shown:

6. In the Save As dialog, enter the URL for the PowerPivot Gallery on your SharePoint Server (for example, http://server/PowerPivotGallery).

7. This will open a view to the PowerPivot Gallery, as shown here:

8. Click the Save button.

9. Once the upload is completed, a browser should pop open to the workbook in Excel Services. If you open the PowerPivot Gallery, at first you should see a generic icon with an hourglass. Once the thumbnails populate, you should either see the thumbnail or the same icon with a small red "X" icon.

This is reminiscent of Excel Services, except for the really sexy gallery view. However, the importance of what PowerPivot gives us will become apparent in our final exercise.

Management Dashboard

PowerPivot for SharePoint also installs a management dashboard to enable SharePoint administrators to keep an eye on the massive files and potential server loading involved with working with PowerPivot files. The dashboard can be found on the SharePoint Central Administration site under General Application Settings, as shown in Figure 5-10.

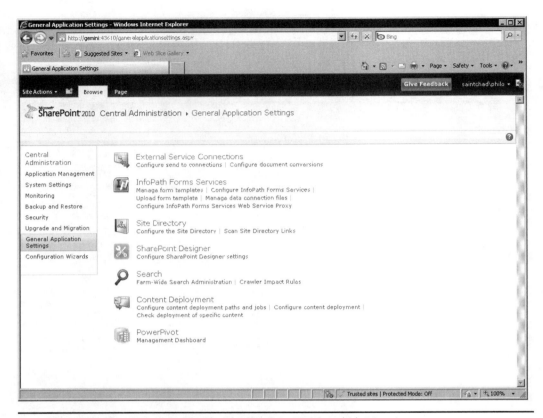

Figure 5-10   *PowerPivot Management Dashboard in SharePoint 2010 Central Administration*

The PowerPivot Management Dashboard is shown in Figure 5-11. The charts are Excel Web App charts showing server performance on top. The lower right is a SharePoint list that shows the PowerPivot workbooks loaded in the server. The most interesting part of the dashboard is the bubble chart in the lower right. The slider underneath it shows the chart from day to day over time. This allows the administrator to view how usage of PowerPivot workbooks is changing over time (looking for trends). The Management Dashboard is simply a SharePoint web part page, so it is completely configurable and extensible.

Before we finish up with PowerPivot, let's review the architecture of the application, as we feel it's important to understanding the bigger picture in BI land.

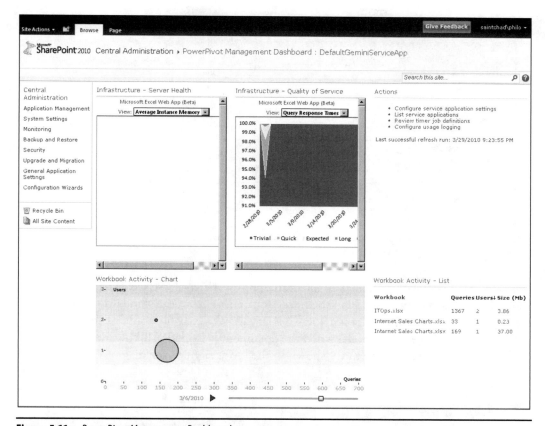

Figure 5-11 *PowerPivot Management Dashboard*

PowerPivot Architecture

As we mentioned earlier in the chapter, the fundamental architecture for PowerPivot is straightforward—essentially an instance of SQL Server Analysis Services integrated with SharePoint on the server side, and another instance integrated with Excel on the client side, as shown in Figure 5-12. Note that as of 2010, SharePoint can only be installed on a 64-bit architecture. To support PowerPivot, the SharePoint server must be on at least SQL Server 2005 SP3 (x64) as its repository.

NOTE

SQL Server 2008 and 2008 R2 are still available as 32-bit (x86) installations. However, PowerPivot on the server side is just plain 64-bit (x64), so it's a good idea when considering SharePoint as a business intelligence platform to just fix your mind in 64-bit terms.

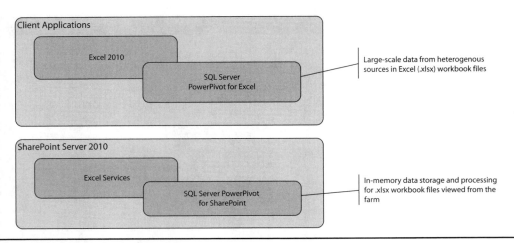

Figure 5-12 *Basic architecture for PowerPivot*

Figure 5-13 shows the detailed architecture for PowerPivot for Excel. The left-hand container represents the .xslx file in the file system. Aside from the standard file operations Excel performs on the file as shown, the XML part in the .xslx file contains the data used to populate the PowerPivot model when the document is loaded. All PowerPivot data is loaded into a data cache in memory, shown in the lower right of the diagram.

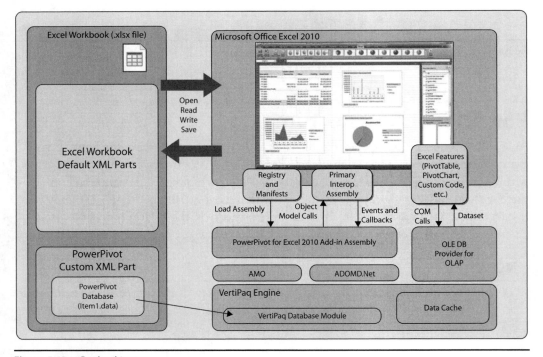

Figure 5-13 *Excel architecture*

The add-in assembly is then called by the Excel application to load the PowerPivot functionality (ribbon, designer, interoperability). The add-in assembly interoperates with the Vertipaq (SQL Server Analysis Services running in in-memory mode) engine via Analysis Management Objects (AMO) and ADOMD.Net (for multidimensional queries). Finally, of course, the objects in a workbook that display PowerPivot data make the necessary data calls to the Vertipaq engine via OLEDB for OLAP.

Figure 5-14 shows the architecture for PowerPivot for SharePoint, which we'll look at in the next section of this chapter. Again, the diagram is fairly self-explanatory.

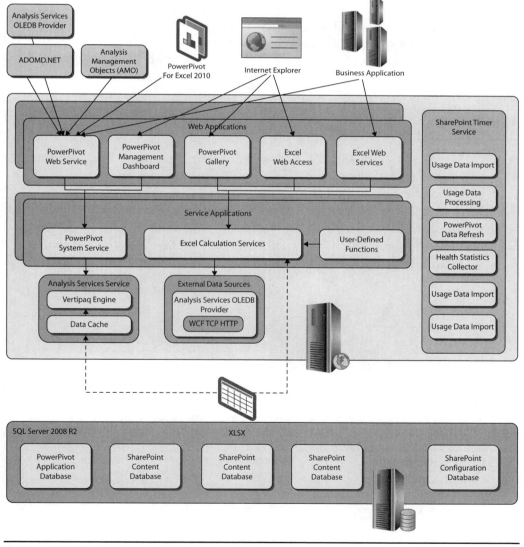

Figure 5-14   *SharePoint architecture*

The web applications, timer jobs, and PowerPivot System Service are installed by the PowerPivot for SharePoint add-in. The Analysis Services Service is installed via the SQL Server installer. (Remember that this instance of Analysis Services cannot be used for publishing cubes from BIDS.)

CAUTION

Due to integration concerns, don't shut down an SSAS instance in SharePoint integrated mode from the Services control panel; instead, manage it from the SharePoint administrative interface.

Also note the tight integration between Excel Services and PowerPivot once the PowerPivot add-in is installed. Excel Services can display workbooks with PowerPivot pivot tables and charts, but the Excel Web App can't be used to edit them. Since PowerPivot workbooks actually contain all the data in the PowerPivot model, they can get fairly large rather quickly. The PowerPivot System Service manages receiving published workbooks, and will block upload of any workbook larger than 4GB.

Integration with Excel Services

Because Excel Services and PowerPivot are so tightly integrated, there are considerations when introducing PowerPivot to a SharePoint farm. First and foremost—any SharePoint server with Excel Services but not PowerPivot will need to update the Analysis Services OLEDB provider to the latest version to enable connectivity with PowerPivot workbooks.

The PowerPivot web service is used when client applications access a PowerPivot workbook as a data source (we'll look at this at the end of the chapter). As shown in Figure 5-15, this web service bypasses SharePoint completely and connects directly to

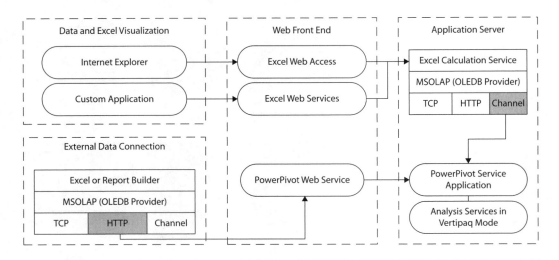

Figure 5-15   *Connecting to a PowerPivot workbook on SharePoint*

the PowerPivot Service and then Analysis Services in Vertipaq mode. On the other hand, if you open a PowerPivot workbook via Excel's File | Open command, the request is made to Excel Web Access, which delivers the workbook itself.

Figure 5-16 shows the sequence of events when a request is made from a browser to an .xlsx document, and how Excel Services and PowerPivot Services cooperate to render the workbook with its PowerPivot-driven content in place. Obviously, if there is no PowerPivot content in the workbook, then only Excel Services is involved in rendering the spreadsheet.

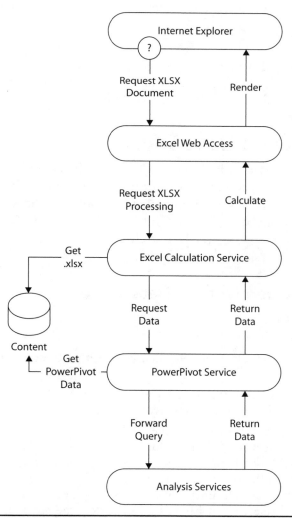

Figure 5-16 *Sequence diagram for a PowerPivot query*

A final note regarding setting up a PowerPivot library—configuring Excel Services–trusted locations. To ensure that PowerPivot runs properly, verify the settings in Excel Services for a trusted location as follows:

▶ Maximum Workbook Size: 2,000MB

▶ Maximum Chart or Image Size: 100MB

▶ Allow External Data: Trusted Data Connection Libraries And Embedded should be selected to allow data connections to be processed using published connection information and embedded connection strings within the workbook file.

▶ Warn On Data Refresh: Off

The final section of this chapter is what really excites us about PowerPivot—not just that our users can do this kind of analysis, but once those models are published, they can be accessed and look exactly like an OLAP cube.

PowerPivot as a Data Source

Once a PowerPivot workbook has been checked into SharePoint, the PowerPivot model is made available (permissions permitting) as a multidimensional data source via XML/A. This means that any application that can connect to SSAS can connect to a PowerPivot model. Connecting is as straightforward as selecting Analysis Services as a data source type, and then using the http:// URL of the PowerPivot workbook as the server address. This is easiest if we just try it.

Exercise 5-3: PowerPivot as a Data Source

1. Open Excel 2010.
2. Click the Data tab on the ribbon.
3. In the Get External Data section, click From Other Sources, and then click From Analysis Services.
4. Go to the SharePoint server where you uploaded the PowerPivot workbook from Exercise 5-2, and open the PowerPivot gallery.
5. This next part is tricky—you need the URL of the workbook. With the PowerPivot Gallery open, select the Library Tools/Library tab at the top, and then change the view to All Documents. Mouse over your document in this library and note the URL in the status bar—that is the URL you want to use. It should be similar to http://server/library/document.xslx. (For some bizarre reason, if you right-click and select Copy Shortcut on the document, you'll get a different URL that doesn't work.)

6. Switch back to Excel.

7. Enter the URL from step 5 in the Server Name box, and then click Next.

8. Excel will connect to your PowerPivot workbook and get a list of cubes, which will consist solely of a cube named "Sandbox." Select this and click Next.

9. Click Finish on the final page, select PivotTable Report on the Import Data dialog, and click OK.

10. Well, this should look familiar—a pivot table designer with our PowerPivot content! (Oddly enough, this designer understands what should be a measure and what should be a dimension...)

11. You can create a pivot table here and publish it to Excel Services.

Summary

The ramifications of the final exercise should be truly mind-altering. Anyone who can use Excel can now connect to multiple data sources and connect the data for analysis. Then they can take those models and publish them to SharePoint, and other users can use them as data sources. We've enabled the nontechnical user to create and publish Analysis Services cubes, to a degree. If you consider how "spreadmarts" are generally used and abused, it should seem straightforward that this technology can replace those file-based data sources with a server-based data source that is robust and scalable, and has a powerful management interface built in.

We've looked a lot at working with different types of data from various existing repositories. One thing we often need to do is provide for entering data or moving it into the places we want to work with it. Getting data into the system is the topic of Chapter 6.

Chapter 6

Getting Data In

In This Chapter

- ► **SQL Server Integration Services**
- ► **BizTalk Server**
- ► **InfoPath and Workflow**
- ► **StreamInsight**
- ► **SharePoint Lists**
- ► **Summary**

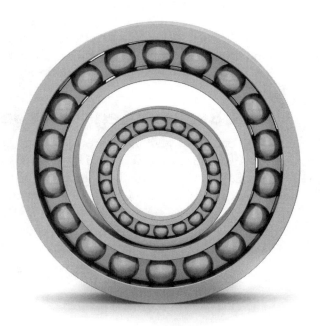

So far, we've talked a lot about analyzing data in databases, but to date, the data has already been in place. Business intelligence treatises often gloss over the idea that you have to get data *in* to the system to analyze and report on it. In this chapter, we're going to review some of the options you have to move data into the database or data warehouse.

We'll look at SQL Server Integration Services (SSIS), which is a SQL Server service that enables migrating data from one repository to another. SSIS is generally intended for bulk loading of data, as opposed to individual record or transactional operation. This differentiates it from BizTalk Server, which is a transactional integration engine. We'll discuss BizTalk Server briefly for completeness' sake, though we won't spend much time on it, as it's outside the scope of this book.

In the realm of human data entry, we'll cover InfoPath and InfoPath Services, which provides web-based data entry forms in SharePoint. With InfoPath, you can create rich client-based or web-based forms that integrate closely with SharePoint document libraries and workflow. We'll also talk a little bit about SharePoint workflow and the .Net workflow foundation (WF).

StreamInsight is a new platform that is part of SQL Server 2008 R2 designed to handle large-volume complex event processing (CEP). Targeted at scenarios where there are large volumes of data streaming from one or more sources, this service is optimized to load these streams into SQL Server, providing access to all the analytical tools we've been discussing over these huge volumes of data.

Finally, we'll take a quick look at an awesome new feature of SharePoint 2010—the External List. In Office 2007, creating a method to link to a table so that end users could create new records, find and edit existing records, or delete records could be done with InfoPath, but it was tricky and sometimes a bit kludgy. In SharePoint 2010, the new External List enables an administrator to essentially map a list to a database table, and it provides the SharePoint forms for entering new records and editing existing records. To us, this completes a significant omission in the Office BI suite.

SQL Server Integration Services

SQL Server Integration Services (SSIS) was introduced with SQL Server 2005 to replace Data Transformation Services (DTS). SSIS is an Enterprise "Extract, Transform, Load" (ETL) engine that is fundamentally designed to take data from one location, manipulate it as necessary, and load it into a second location. For example, you might design a package to pick up a comma-delimited file from an FTP server, parse through the data doing lookups to replace the values in one particular field with values from another data source, and finally load the data into an Oracle database.

That's right—neither end has to be SQL Server.

SSIS packages are created in the Business Intelligence Development Studio, which provides a drag-and-drop canvas for the various *tasks* provided in the toolbar. When you first create an SSIS project, you're left in the Control Flow canvas, shown in Figure 6-1. The tasks in the toolbox provide methods of running SQL Server packages, working with file systems, running data mining queries, etc. You might be a bit confused if you try to build an ETL flow, as there are no data sources or data destinations.

It turns out that the control flow, as the name indicates, is about tracing the actual flow of what the package is supposed to be doing. One of the tasks you can add is the *data flow task*. If you add one of those and double-click it, you'll be taken to the *Data Flow* canvas. And the toolbox here has data sources, data destinations, and tasks for transformations. (You can also switch back and forth between data flow and control flow using the tabs at the top of the canvas.)

NOTE

For a deep dive into SSIS, we highly recommend Microsoft SQL Server 2008 Integration Services Unleashed *(Sams, 2009) by Kirk Haselden. Kirk was one of the early product development managers on SSIS.*

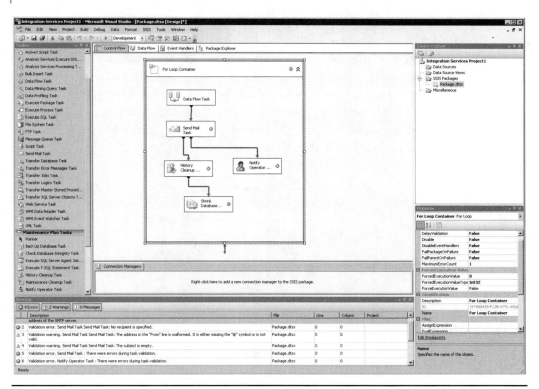

Figure 6-1   *SQL Server Integration Services Control Flow canvas in BIDS*

Samples/Tutorial

We've always felt the best exercises Microsoft ever put together are the SSIS tutorials. For a quick way to get up to speed on basic SSIS concepts, check out the samples, which you can download at http://go.microsoft.com/fwlink/?LinkId=87843.

The Integration Services tutorials are in the books online, so you can either find them via the help in any of the SQL Server client applications or find them online here: http://msdn.microsoft.com/en-us/library/ms167031.aspx.

Control Flow

The control flow, as we mentioned previously, consists of tasks and containers connected by the flow arrows defined by the tasks themselves. A container groups a collection of tasks together, either for ease of management or to provide some form of looping. For example, the ForEach Loop Container can be configured to loop through each file in a specific directory; you might use this to pull files from an FTP site or iterate through files that have been dropped in an incoming folder, and then archive them. Figure 6-2 shows a ForEach Loop Container with a data flow task inside.

Tasks are connected by selecting a task and dragging one of the arrows to another task. In the designer, green arrows are followed if the task is executed successfully; red arrows are in the event an exception is thrown. Some tasks can have multiple exit paths—only one will be shown until you connect it and select the task again, and then the second arrow will show, as in Figure 6-3. These follow-on paths will execute in parallel (there are exceptions in the data flow tasks).

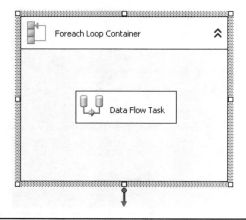

Figure 6-2 *ForEach Loop Container with a task*

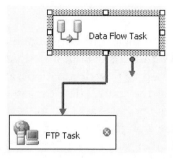

Figure 6-3   *Multiple exits from a task*

To configure a task, either double-click it or right-click and select Edit from the context menu. The configuration dialogs are all similar (by design, to make them more intuitive). Figure 6-4 shows the configuration dialog for a data mining task. The tabs on the dialog will enable you to select a mining model, build a query for it, and render the output, which can be piped to the next task.

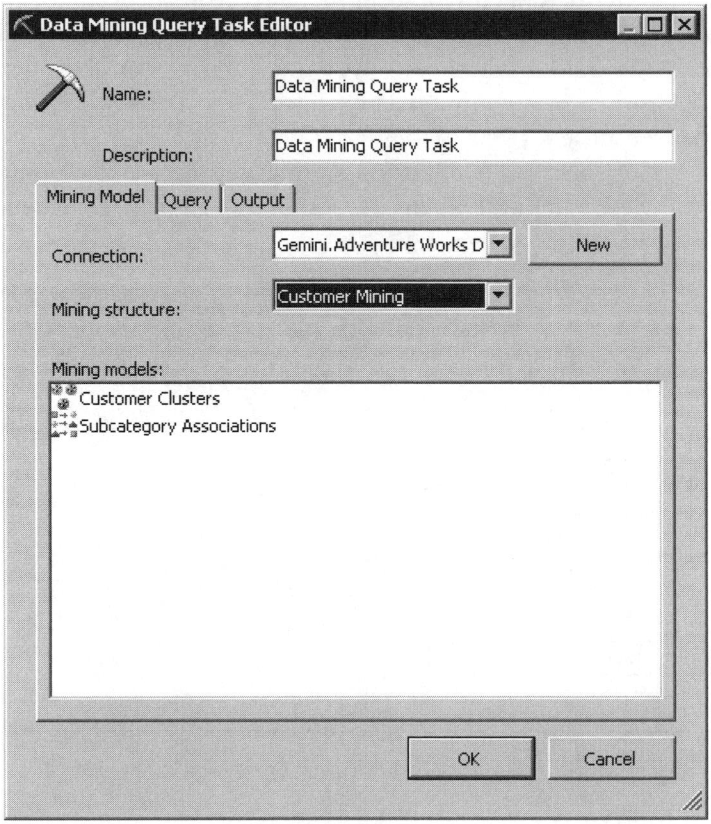

Figure 6-4   *Data mining configuration task*

Data Flow

When you add a data flow task to the control flow, double-clicking that data flow will open the data flow designer. Within the data flow designer you have a toolbox that has a collection of data flow sources, data flow destinations, and data flow transforms. This canvas operates the same way as the control flow canvas—drag tasks over and connect their outputs to direct the results of each task.

The transformation tasks are a pretty diverse set—the ability to change column values, perform lookups from other tables (thus "translating" terms that companies or departments may use differently), and perform different activities based on values or even the outputs of a specific transform. Figure 6-5 shows a conditional split task that uses custom formulas to route data to various destinations. Note the branch to the Fuzzy Lookup task is labeled with the Default Output, and we've just dragged a second output to the Percentage Sampling—the dialog shown allows you to select which of the remaining outputs to use.

This brings us to one overriding concept with Integration Services—if you think this way when working with SSIS, you'll be much happier. SSIS processes recordsets record by record. On occasion, it will seem that a record-processing operation requires processing column by column (end-user–generated Excel spreadsheets do this a lot). There's no native method to transpose rows and columns—your best bet is to, if possible, get the format of the input data changed. Alternatively, you can write a custom task to run the transpose for you.

In this quick tour, there are two last transformations we want to point out: Fuzzy Lookup and Slowly Changing Dimension. The Fuzzy Lookup transformation is a

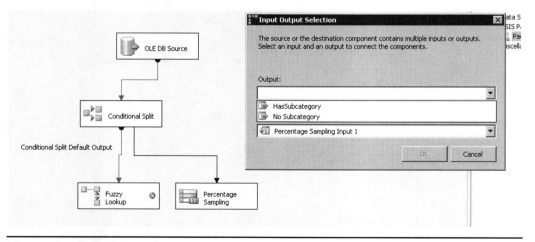

Figure 6-5   *A conditional split*

powerful tool to deal with hand-keyed data where there is a good possibility of typos, misspellings, and other minor mistakes. The Fuzzy Lookup takes the inbound data and compares it to an existing reference table (for example, the lookup table for a foreign key field). It then uses the data mining engine to perform a "best guess" match to the existing data. The output is the likely match and a confidence factor. You can then pipe the output into a conditional split and route the data records based on the lookup confidence factor, routing data records where the confidence factor is too low into a holding table for manual review.

Slowly changing dimensions are the bane of data warehouse developers—a dimension that we expect to change over time (for example, personnel or product models—remember the Pinto?). SSIS offers a Slowly Changing Dimension (SCD) transformation to handle the heavy lifting of working with data flows that feed into a slowly changing dimension in a data warehouse. The Slowly Changing Dimension transformation task is actually a wizard—drag it to the canvas, configure the input, and double-click it, and you'll get a wizard to configure the SCD workflow. After you select the fields that are static versus those that change and establish how to tell which record is active, the wizard will generate a data flow to process the incoming records and tag the existing records that are superseded, as shown in Figure 6-6.

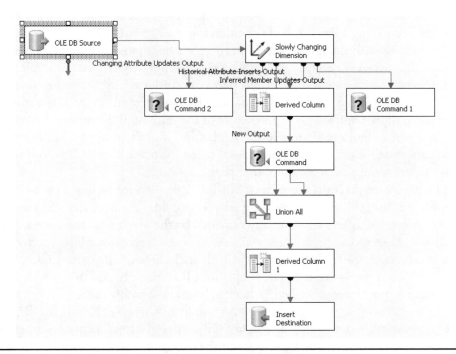

Figure 6-6   *Data flow generated by the Slowly Changing Dimension wizard*

If the data you are updating the dimension with might be unreliable, you can use a Fuzzy Lookup transform to clean it up before running it into the SCD flow. After changing the records in the data warehouse, the data flow can lead to an Analysis Services Processing Task to process the appropriate dimension and update the cube as necessary. (See how this all fits together?)

Integration Services is designed to work with batch processing of data. It's not meant for data flows where individual records need to be processed at a rapid pace. Transactional data processing is best handled by an Enterprise Application Integration (EAI) engine—let's talk about Microsoft BizTalk Server 2010.

BizTalk Server

BizTalk Server (BTS) was launched in 2000, primarily focused on message translation and transactions. The current version is BizTalk Server 2010 R2. BizTalk is focused on transactional processing of individual records. An example would be when you place an order at an online store—once your order is placed, the system will interact with the warehouse inventory system to verify that the item is in stock. If it's not in stock, the system will contact various vendors to see if they have the item in stock. If they do, and can ship it quickly, the system will place the order for the item and complete your order. On the other hand, if the item can't be shipped quickly, the retailer needs to contact you and see if you're willing to wait for a backorder, and act accordingly.

While working with the messaging from these various systems, it may be necessary to translate the messages received—BizTalk has a mapping engine that can pull a message apart, perform any manipulations necessary, and reassemble it. The BizTalk mapper is shown in Figure 6-7. The left-hand side shows the structure of the inbound document; the right-hand side is the structure of the outbound document. In between is a canvas where a developer can map the fields from input to output. On the trace lines you can see some small boxes—these are called "Functoids" and allow you to perform various actions on the data in that particular node.

Along with the connection framework, BizTalk is known for having a broad array of adapters for various business systems. The adapter provides connectivity and a standard document format. Adapters are generally provided by the vendor for the system they are connecting to. Dozens of adapters are available—some are free downloads; others are software products. Some of the adapters available include SAP (R/3 and ECC), Siebel, Oracle (database and eBusiness suite), PeopleSoft, JD Edwards, and others.

The ordering process we described earlier can be laid out in BizTalk as an *orchestration*. BizTalk orchestrations are designed in Visual Studio and are .Net based. The BizTalk 2010 R2 orchestration designer is in Visual Studio 2010. The orchestration designer is shown in Figure 6-8. The great thing about the designer is that orchestrations are

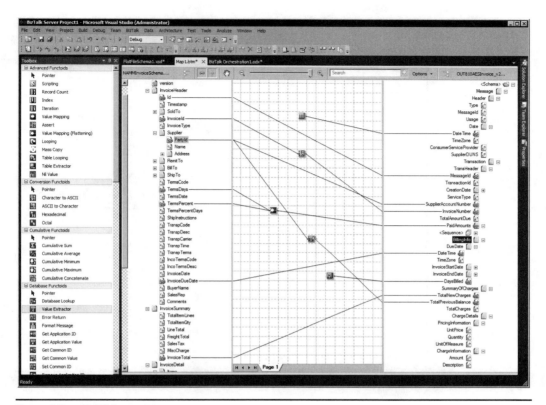

Figure 6-7   *BizTalk Server mapper*

laid out like flowcharts, making it easy for business users to verify the orchestration is designed properly.

Another feature of BizTalk Server is a Business Activity Monitoring (BAM) engine, which also installs a portal into SharePoint to enable IT staff to keep an eye on the business processes, find logjams, and make sure everything in the orchestrations are running smoothly. The portal is configurable with SharePoint web parts, which can show pivot tables, charts, and orchestration designs in a dashboard style to track performance.

BizTalk is a workhorse—when you have systems that process a lot of transactional data between business systems, often you will write code to perform the translations. Each piece of code is a liability—will it scale? Is it secure? Is it maintainable? BizTalk provides a secure, reliable platform to load all these translation engines into one place with a uniform interface and development paradigm.

Integration Services and BizTalk provide two different engines that can be used to automate loading data into a data warehouse or other BI repository. Our other significant concern is how to deal with manual data entry. Just about any company

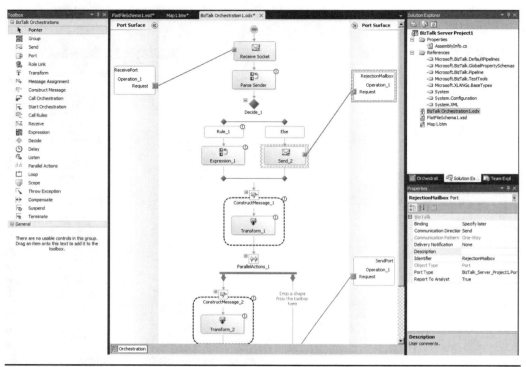

Figure 6-8   *Orchestration designer in Visual Studio*

will have at least one data source who is "the guy who walks around with a clipboard." Manual data entry is often a necessity, but entering data on paper and then transcribing it later doubles the opportunity for data entry errors. Let's look at SharePoint's electronic forms engine—InfoPath.

InfoPath and Workflow

InfoPath first shipped with Office 2003 as a stand-alone application for form design. A major limitation at that time was the requirement to have the full edition of InfoPath installed to fill in forms created in the software. Office 2007 eased that restriction by introducing InfoPath Forms Services in SharePoint—now InfoPath forms could be easily published as web-based forms without any additional form design effort.

InfoPath 2010 has two "entry points," as the product team calls them—a designer and a filler. When you install the InfoPath desktop application, shortcuts for each will be installed. The Designer shortcut opens InfoPath in design mode, while the Filler simply offers the "fill in a form" functionality with no design capabilities. As of this writing, there doesn't seem to be any way to install either "entry point" separately.

Electronic Forms

InfoPath is essentially an electronic forms designer. Probably the most important thing to understand when working with InfoPath is that the form *template* and the form *data* are two different things and are stored in different files. The form template is what you think of when you imagine a "blank form"—the structure and fields. The form data is just that—form data, without the form definition. We'll talk about the challenges this can provide in a bit.

In InfoPath, the form template is an .xsn file, which is an Office compressed file format containing the form definition. The form definition is mostly XML files—a manifest, an .xsd-compliant schema, sample data, form layout, rules, and embedded code in a compiled .Net DLL assembly. The form data is simply an XML file that uses the form schema as its schema definition. With that in mind, let's take a look at InfoPath.

InfoPath for Data Entry

When you first open InfoPath Designer, you are presented with options as to the various types of forms you can design, as shown in Figure 6-9. InfoPath provides a data structure for forms; then you are able to design layout on top of the data structure. As a result, hooking an InfoPath form to an existing data structure (for example, a database, XML schema, or web service) enables you to easily create a form layout that connects to that structure.

TIP

Although InfoPath has an option to connect directly to a database, we advise against it. The connection is limited to SQL Server and Access, and must connect directly to tables or views (not stored procedures). The security ramifications, as well as the tight coupling necessary to make this work, just make this route painful in the long run. (We wish the product group would either enable stored procedures and OLEDB or just get rid of the option, honestly.)

InfoPath is best used against SharePoint lists, web services, or generating XML for business systems that work with XML. If your organization is using Outlook 2007 or later and every desktop has InfoPath installed, e-mailing forms is also a great feature, as the recipient can fill out the form inside of Outlook and return it. As an editor, InfoPath is the tool you can use to modify the Document Information Panel in Office 2007 and 2010 applications, workflow forms in SharePoint 2010 workflows, and the forms for working with SharePoint 2010 External Lists.

The easiest way to wrap your head around InfoPath is simply to use it, so let's create a form.

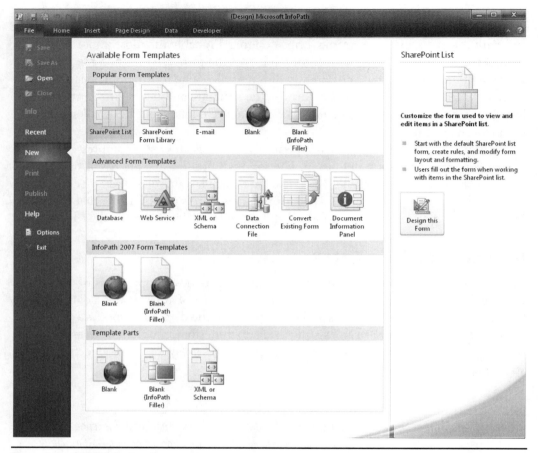

Figure 6-9 *InfoPath Designer*

Exercise 6-1: Creating an InfoPath Form

In this exercise we'll create a basic InfoPath form to understand the form layout and how the form data structure works.

1. Open InfoPath Designer.
2. If the Available Form Templates window isn't displayed, click File to open the application backstage, and then click New.

3. Select Blank and then click Design Form, as shown here:

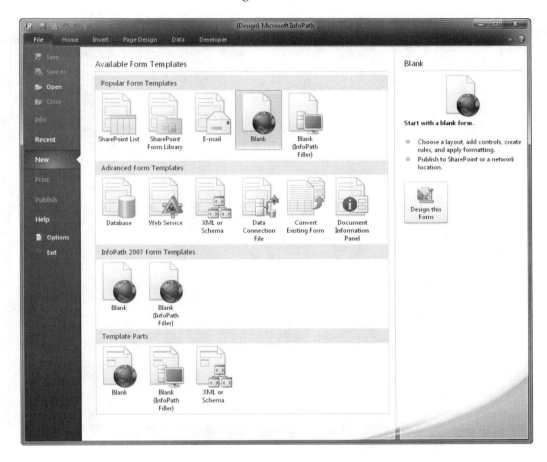

4. This will open a blank form canvas, as shown next. Note the fluent UI ("ribbon") interface.

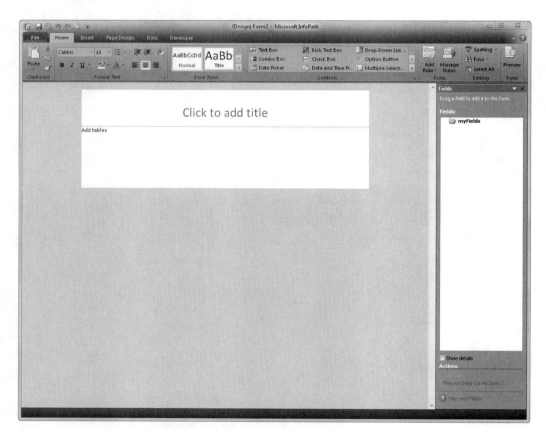

5. If you're used to InfoPath 2003 or 2007, the task pane is no longer "switchable"— the controls are in the ribbon (but can be expanded and docked); the View menu and page layout options are on the Page Design tab.

6. Click in the form area that says "Add tables." From the Controls pane of the ribbon, select the Section container (either click the down arrow to open the gallery, or click the expand icon in the lower right of the pane to open the Controls task pane).

7. This inserts a Section control into the form. Note the Fields task pane—it's added a folder named "group1." Click the Control Tools tab on the ribbon, and then change the control name to **Header** as shown in the next illustration.

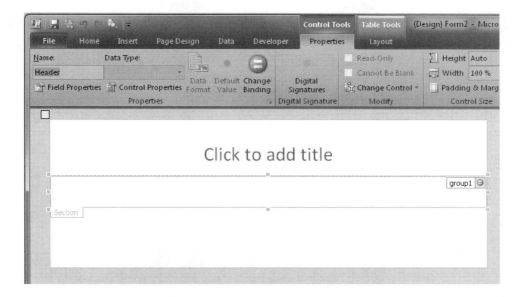

8. Click inside the Section control. For the header fields, we're going to insert a two-column layout, as shown here:

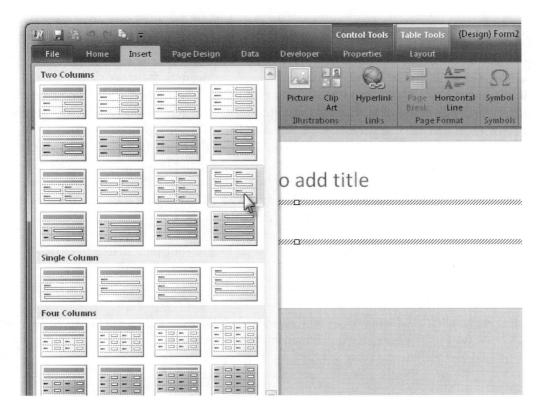

9. This inserts a table that you can use for the layout of the header fields in the form, as shown:

Click to add title

Add label and control	Add label and control
Add label and control	Add label and control
Add label and control	Add label and control

10. Click in the first cell. Type **Name** and then press ENTER. Click a Text Box control to insert a text box. (It is found in the Control pane of the home ribbon.)

11. On the Control Tools/Properties tab, change the name to **Name**. Note that the Name field is in the Header folder in the Fields task pane.

When you build an InfoPath form, the UI and the data source are bound together—think of the UI as a rendered view of the XML data source. (This is what InfoPath actually does—it uses XSL transforms to render the UI from the schema.) This can lead to some frustration if you're used to designing Windows forms, where the UI and data are totally separate. When this can really frustrate a form designer is when they are designing a form against an existing data source, which InfoPath will not allow you to edit.

To have controls that are not bound to data, you want to use the Calculated Value control, which will let you define the value using a combination of functions and script within the control (or you can set the value from code or rules). If you need data that is not bound to controls and you are working against an existing data source, add a new data source and add the control data nodes to that data source.

1. In the next cell, type **Date:** and click a Date Picker control. Rename the date picker to **Date**.

   We want to add a default value to this control so that whenever the form is opened, today's date is inserted.

2. Right-click the Date Picker control, and select Date Picker Properties to open the properties dialog. In the Default Value field, click the fx button to open the function dialog.

3. Click the Insert Function button to open the Insert Function dialog, shown in the following illustration. Select the Date category and then the Today function.

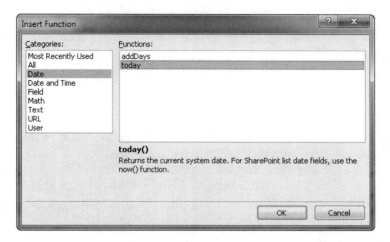

4. Click the OK button.
5. Click the OK button on the Insert Formula dialog.
6. Click the OK button on the Date Picker Properties dialog.
7. Drag across the next two cells to select them.
8. Select the Table Tools/Layout tab in the ribbon, and then click the Merge Cells button.
9. Click the Option Button control to insert an option button. You'll be prompted for the number of options—leave the default of 3 and click OK.
10. You'll have three option buttons inserted vertically as shown:

11. The option buttons are just laid out with carriage returns. Click after each button and press DELETE to bring them up to the same line. Add labels after each as shown here:

12. Change the name of the control to **InventoryType**. Selection of this field is not trivial. You will need to either select one of the options buttons, or select the field in the field list, right-click, and select Edit. Otherwise, by default, you will rename the header field, which is what gets selected if you click in the middle of the cell.

13. Click each button, and then click the Option Button Properties button in the ribbon. Change the value of each button to match the label.

14. Click after the Section control, and press ENTER to insert some space after the Section control.

15. Click in the empty space. From the Home ribbon, select the Repeating Table control to insert it, indicate five columns, and then click the OK button.

16. This will give you a repeating table, which has a fixed header and multiple data rows.

17. Add table headers and change the data field names as shown next:

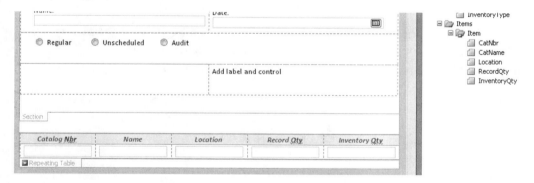

18. Select the RecordQty text box, and then on the Control Tools/Properties tab of the ribbon, change the Data Type field to Whole Number (Integer).

19. Do the same for the Inventory Qty text box.

20. Right-click the Repeating Table control, and select Repeating Table Properties.

21. Click the Display tab, select the Include Footer check box, and then click the OK button.

22. Click in the footer at the bottom of the Record Qty column, and insert a text box.

23. Name the text box **RecordTotal**, and change the data type to Whole Number.
24. Click the Field Properties button, and then click the fx button next to Default Value.
25. Click Insert Function, select Sum, and click the OK button.
26. Double-click the text that says "double click to insert field" as shown here:

27. In the Select A Field Or Group dialog that opens, open the Items group and then the Item group. Select RecordQty and click the OK button.
28. Click OK on the Insert Formula dialog.
29. Click OK on the Properties dialog.
30. Add another text box for the inventory total, and add the total formula in a similar way.
31. Now let's take a look at the form—on the Home tab, click the Preview button. Note the date is filled in by default and you can add rows to the table.
32. Enter values in the RecordQty and InventoryQty fields in the rows—note they're automatically totaled.
33. Close the preview.
34. Save the form template.

A really nice thing about InfoPath as a starting point is that once the form is designed, if you add some structure (such as the Header Section control), you can end up with an XML schema that defines the data. You can extract the XSD from the form template and use it to define the other aspects of a solution (BizTalk orchestrations, database structures, and other tools can derive structures from an existing schema).

Data Connections

InfoPath connects to other business systems through data connections. A form template can have multiple data connections for various reasons—posting data to the primary destination; reading data on loading; and also reading data for lookups, drop-down lists, etc. Click the Data tab in the ribbon to see the various options in working with data, as shown in Figure 6-10.

The data connections will enable you to build the connection to the appropriate data source—specify the tables and fields that you want to import or post to. Once the data connection is mapped, you can connect the fields as necessary to the data fields. Each data connection has settings as to whether data should be loaded when the form is loaded and if the data should be cached for use when the form is offline.

Two other features are on the Data tab—Rules and Submit Options. Rules are similar to "scripting" for InfoPath—you can put rules on controls, containers, views, and the form itself. Rules are created in InfoPath similar to how they are created in Outlook—a step-by-step wizard walks you through creating the rules as well as conditions on when the rule executes. A new feature called the Rule Inspector (shown in Figure 6-11) allows you to view all the rules in a form at once.

Normally, InfoPath forms operate simply by performing a file/save action. However, it's also possible to add a Submit functionality to a form. Submit will add a submit item to the ribbon of the InfoPath filler as well as a submit option in the Backstage. The person creating the form has the option whether or not to allow users to also save the XML file. With Submit enabled, you can add rules or code to the Submit button so that specific actions are taken when a user submits the form. This is also the only way to send form data to multiple targets (for example, saving to a file share and submitting to a web service connection).

InfoPath and SharePoint

When you fill out an InfoPath form created this way and save the form data, it's saved as an XML file, as we mentioned previously. Having structured form data by itself is valuable, but there's more we can do. If we publish the form to a SharePoint form library, then the form becomes a front end to a much more powerful data entry and reporting solution. With InfoPath associated with a SharePoint forms library, any user

Figure 6-10   *Data connections in InfoPath*

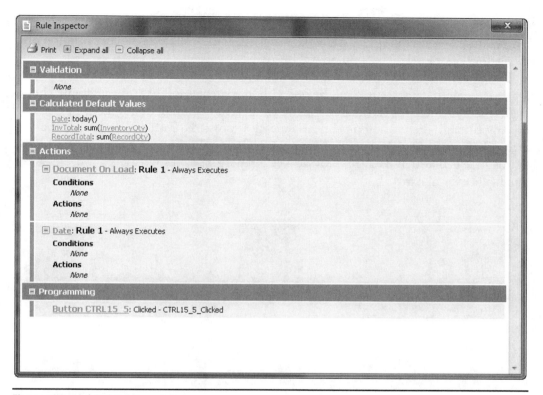

Figure 6-11   *InfoPath Rule Inspector*

who needs to fill out the form can simply click New on the library and the form will open in InfoPath; when they save their data, it will default to the form library.

With the form data posting to the form library, you have access to the SharePoint workflow engine. You can use form library views for lightweight reporting, as well as advanced business intelligence with PerformancePoint and reporting with SQL Server Reporting Services. In addition, SharePoint Enterprise offers InfoPath Form Services, which will take an InfoPath form template and display it in a browser so that users can fill in InfoPath forms without having InfoPath installed on their desktop. We'll look more at SharePoint integration in Chapter 8.

StreamInsight

StreamInsight debuted with SQL Server 2008 R2. StreamInsight is an engine and development framework to optimize complex event processing (CEP) applications. Consider an assembly line where you want to capture various environment readings from each operation several times per second. So a data package arrives full of temperatures, rotational speeds, state data, and other information from each station on the factory floor every few hundred milliseconds.

The StreamInsight platform is intended to provide a means of piping that data into a structured database in SQL Server with low latency and high throughput. The engine uses in-memory caching and incremental result computation to keep the data flowing through the loading pipeline as quickly as possible. The architecture for the StreamInsight engine is shown in Figure 6-12. Obviously, the reason we're interested in this here is that that data can provide a rich reporting data source for our business intelligence dashboards.

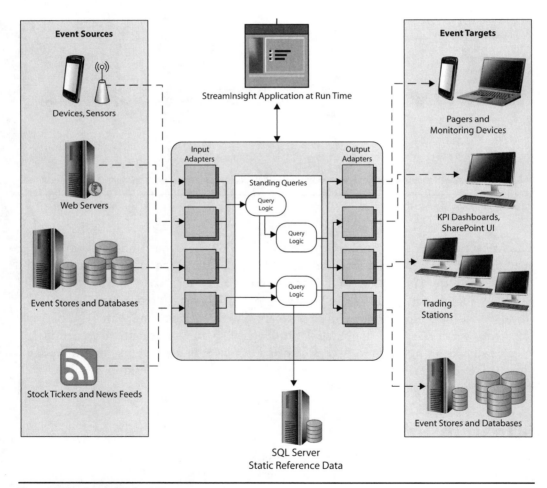

Figure 6-12 *StreamInsight architecture*

The major benefit of StreamInsight with respect to a Microsoft BI installation is that the query templates are written in LINQ and C#, and, of course, the repository is SQL Server. This provides our developers an easy way to start working with StreamInsight instead of having to start learning a whole new server engine.

The best starting point to learn more about StreamInsight is the SQL Server 2008 R2 pages at Microsoft.com: www.microsoft.com/sqlserver/2008/en/us/R2-complex-event.aspx.

From high-speed data loading, let's slow back down and look at human-paced data entry again.

SharePoint Lists

A significant gap in the Office platform with respect to databases was some way to easily provide CRUD (CReate, Update, Delete) capabilities for a database table. Normalized databases usually have a lot of small lookup tables, data tables, and other "administrative" tables that aren't strictly transactional, but do need to be maintained. An example would be the Product table in the AdventureWorks database, or an Employee table. While they don't change often, they do change.

In SharePoint 2003, you could have data tables that would display a read-only view of tables or views in SQL Server. SharePoint 2007 added the Business Data Connector (BCD), which improved connectivity to back-end business systems, but it was still read-only; we could view tables in business systems, but we couldn't edit them.

SharePoint 2010 adds Business Connectivity Services, which allows you to map a structured interface that SharePoint and Office 2010 can work with onto a number of business systems, and that interface can be read-write. So a Business Connectivity Services connector can be combined with a new SharePoint feature known as an External List and give us that full lifecycle maintenance of tables in databases we've been looking for.

To create an External List, you need to start with an External Content Type (ECT), which you create in SharePoint Designer. Once you open SharePoint Designer and open the SharePoint site you want to work with (we'll cover this in detail in Chapter 8), then you'll want to select the External Content Types object in the navigation pane on the left, as shown in Figure 6-13. The ribbon will then present the External Content Types tab, and you can select to create a new ECT.

NOTE

SharePoint Designer used to be a full-packaged product from Microsoft, but is now part of SharePoint licensing and doesn't cost extra.

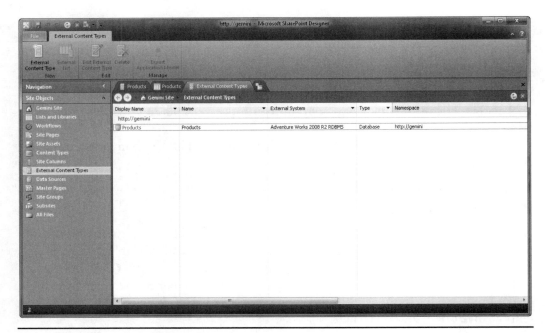

Figure 6-13 *Adding an External Content Type*

Once you create the External Content Type, you can connect it to an existing data connection or create a new one. Your options here are .Net Types, SQL Server, or a Windows Communication Foundation (WCF) Service. From there, you will be able to map entities and fields as necessary to create your content type associated with its data connection. After you have an External Content Type, you can create an External List based on it either from SharePoint Designer or from SharePoint itself.

From SharePoint you simply need to create a new list and then select the External List type, which gives you a standard list creation page, except that you can select the External Content Type at the bottom, as shown in Figure 6-14.

Once created, when you open the list, it will present a full list of the contents of the table you created the External Content Type from, as shown in Figure 6-15. This is a SharePoint list, so the view is sortable and filterable, and you can create additional views formatted in other ways. If you check the List Tools tab in the ribbon, you'll see that you have the full range of options with this list.

But the greatest feature of these External Lists is when you click an item and then edit it, as shown in Figure 6-16. We get a full editing form, including detection of Boolean fields, date/time fields, and field data types. This form can also be edited in InfoPath if you need a richer editing experience.

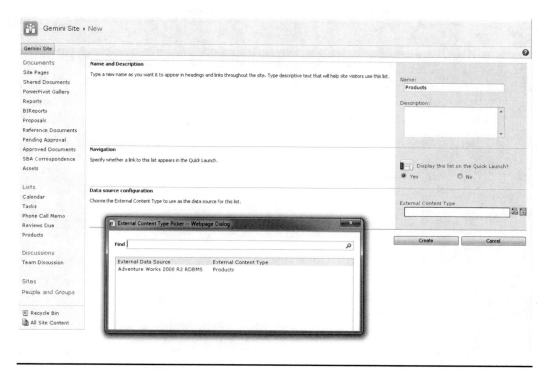

Figure 6-14 *Creating an External List*

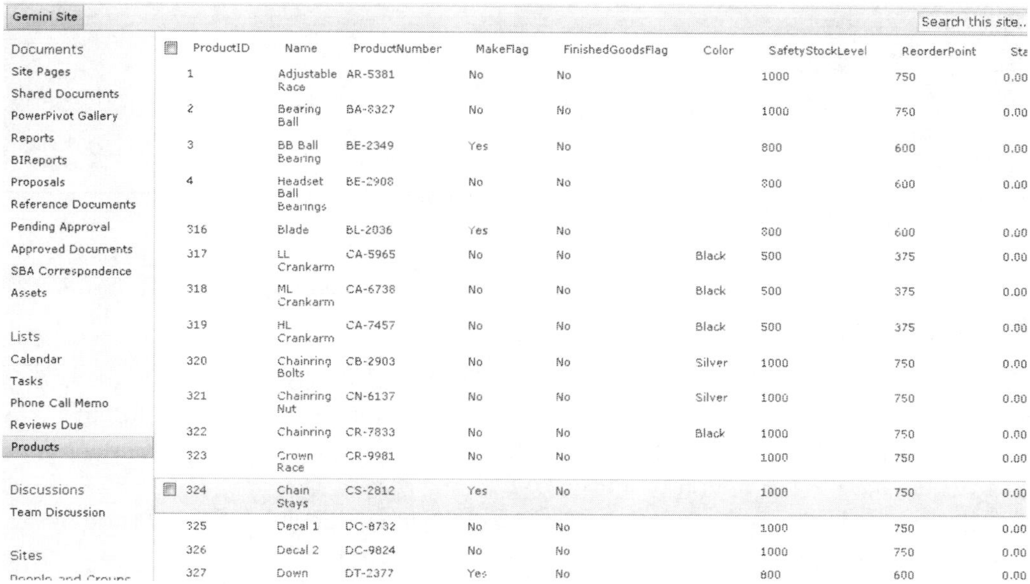

Figure 6-15 *Opening an External List*

Figure 6-16 *Editing a record in an external list*

Summary

We've covered a lot of different technologies here. The main goal has been to cover the ways that you can get data *in* to a business intelligence solution as part of a full lifecycle solution, instead of the standard approach that there's already a large storehouse of data and we just have to build on top of it.

In the next chapter we're going to look at SQL Server Reporting Services and how that can give us a powerful front end to our data, both from business systems and from our manual data entry such as the SharePoint lists we've seen here.

Chapter 7

SQL Server Reporting Services

In This Chapter

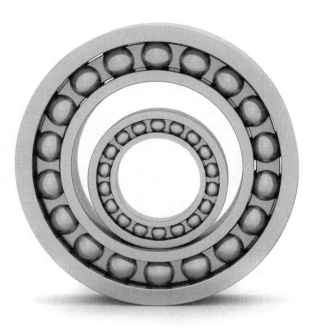

For a long time, "business intelligence" was actually enterprise reporting (where "report" in this sense refers to tables of data and the associated charts and graphs to show interrelationships). Before the 1980s, reports were printed on reams of green-bar paper, and were generally simply long tables of numbers produced from a business system. (If you wanted to combine data from different systems, you got a report from each.) Some exceptionally advanced systems could produce graphs on these reports, but they were very rudimentary.

Philip Russom, author of "21st Century Green Bar," *Intelligent Enterprise Magazine*, July 18, 2003, lists the rules of reporting in the green-bar era:

▶ When designing a report, include every number that any employee, consultant, partner, investor, or regulatory agent might ever need to see.

▶ When a report consumer requests a new report, don't create a new report. Instead, find a report similar to the request, add the requested information to that report, and add the requestor's name to the report's distribution list.

The net result was that reports were generally long, complex, and distributed sparingly. A colleague once remarked that in the era of green-bar reports, you could raise your status by getting your hands on one of the reports and leaving it visible on your desk.

With the advent and growth of relational databases, it became easier (somewhat) to create reports through queries that could be written by the average mortal. However, any form of graphing and charting was still just a pipe dream. Then a small company named Crystal Services looked for a reporting add-on for an accounting package. Finding none, they created Quik Reports for DOS in 1988. In 1992 they released Crystal Reports for Windows. Anyone who created reports in the 1990s knows where this story goes.

SQL Server Reporting Services was initially introduced in 2003 as an add-on for SQL Server 2000. A web-based reporting package, it allowed DBAs to create reports against any data source (not just SQL Server) using an add-in for Visual Studio. They could then publish the reports to a reporting server and deliver those reports through a browser, e-mail, web service, or various third-party applications.

Reporting Services 2005 introduced a report builder client that allowed users to create their own reports and publish them back to the server. The major problem was that they could only create reports against specialized Reporting Services report models, which were fairly complicated to create and had to be built for each data source.

With Reporting Services 2008, shown in Figure 7-1, Microsoft introduced integration with SharePoint—now reports could be managed via SharePoint libraries and retrieved by users from a new Reports Center. The goal here was to get away from having reports stashed in various locations on various servers, but rather introduce a

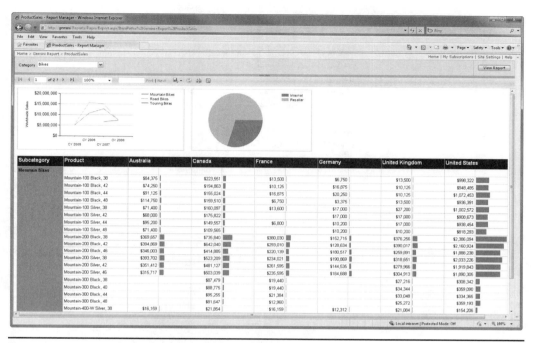

Figure 7-1   *A report in Reporting Services 2008 R2*

manner of centrally organizing enterprise reports. SSRS 2008 also saw the release of Report Builder 2.0, the end-user ad hoc reporting tool. Report Builder could now create reports directly from data sources without needing a report model built in advance.

Reporting Services 2008 R2 builds on the improvements. Report authors can now create and share "Report Parts"—think of reusable subreports. SharePoint integration has been improved, including the ability to use SharePoint lists as a data source. Reporting Services supports sparklines, data bars, and KPI indicator icons as well. The Report Manager interface has been overhauled, and Reporting Services now provides mapping capabilities to support the spatial functions introduced in SQL Server 2008 (we'll dig into mapping in Chapter 11). Finally, the Report Builder is now at version 3.0, and brings all these features forward for end users to leverage in ad hoc reports.

Creating Reports in BIDS

The primary tool for creating Reporting Services reports is the Business Intelligence Development Studio (BIDS). When you open BIDS, the New Project dialog has options to create a wizard-driven report project, to create an empty report project, or to create a reporting model for ad hoc reports, as shown in Figure 7-2. The Report Wizard

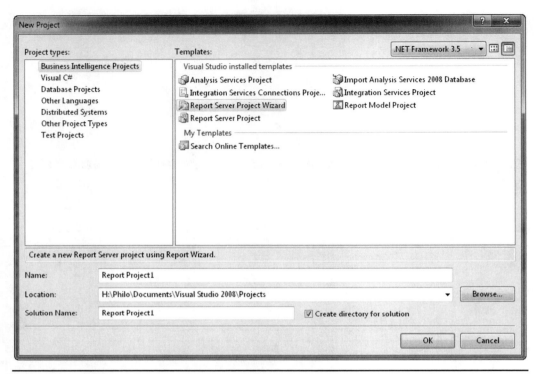

Figure 7-2   *Creating a report project in BIDS*

will walk you through the steps necessary to create a data source connection to the data you will be reporting on; create the data set from the data; or choose whether to create a table-style or matrix (pivot) type report, the layout, and some basic formatting.

To create a new report, you can right-click the Reports folder in the Solution Explorer and click Add New Report. This will open the Report Wizard, which will walk you through creating a data source, data set, and report. Let's give it a try.

Exercise 7-1: Creating a Report

1. Open BIDS. Create a new report project by selecting File | New | Project, and then select Report Server Project Wizard and click OK.
2. On the first page of the Report Wizard, click Next.
3. On the Select the Data Source page, the Share Data Source option is grayed out because there are no shared data sources in the project. Name the data source **AdventureWorksDB**, and then click the Edit button next to the Connection string area.

4. Enter the name of your database server (or localhost), and select the AdventureWorks2008R2 database, as shown in the following illustration. (This exercise can also work with the AdventureWorks 2008 sample database, but in that case, the relationship between Product and SalesOrderDetail has to be created manually.)

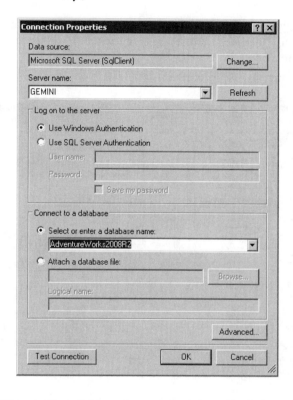

5. Select Make This A Shared Data Source, and then click the Next button.
6. Click the Query Builder button to open the query designer.
7. Right-click the top area in the query designer, and select Add Table.
8. Select the following tables:
   - ▶ ProductCategory
   - ▶ ProductSubcategory
   - ▶ Product
   - ▶ SalesOrderHeader
   - ▶ SalesOrderDetail
   - ▶ SalesTerritory

9. Click Close when you have selected them all.

10. Select the Name check box in the ProductCategory table. Enter **Category** in the Alias column (since we'll be adding two more columns titled "Name").

11. Select Name in the ProductSubcategory table, and make the alias Subcategory.

12. Select Name in the Product table, and add the alias Product.

13. Select OrderQty and LineTotal from the SalesOrderDetail table and the CountryRegionCode field from SalesTerritory. Add an alias of Country to the CountryRegionCode field.

14. The final designer should look like this:

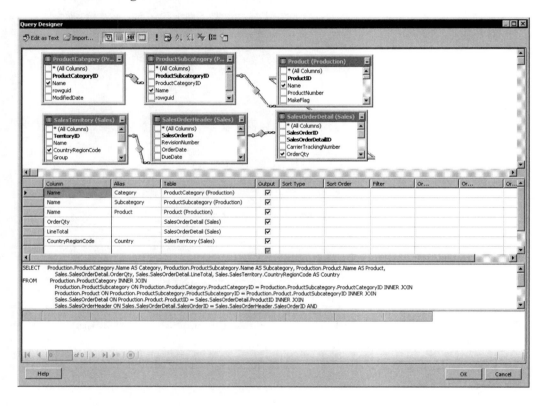

15. You can execute the query to see the results (there are 121,000 rows in the query).
16. Click the OK button when you're done.
17. On the Select The Report Type page, select Matrix and then click the Next button.
18. On the Design The Matrix page, move Category to the Page area, Country to Columns, Subcategory and Product to Rows, and OrderQty and LineTotal to Details. It should look like the following illustration when you're done:

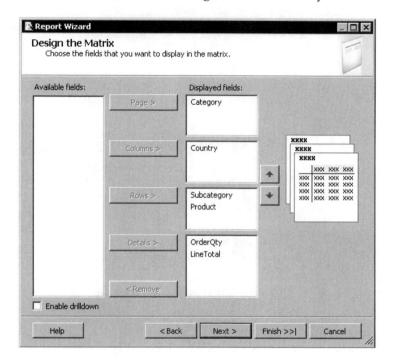

19. Click the Next button.
20. On the Choose The Matrix Style page, select any of the styles. Click the Next button.
21. On the Completing The Wizard page, name the report **Product Sales Report** and click the Finish button.

22. You'll end up with a report in the designer that looks like the illustration. If you click in the table area, the matrix frame will appear, as shown here:

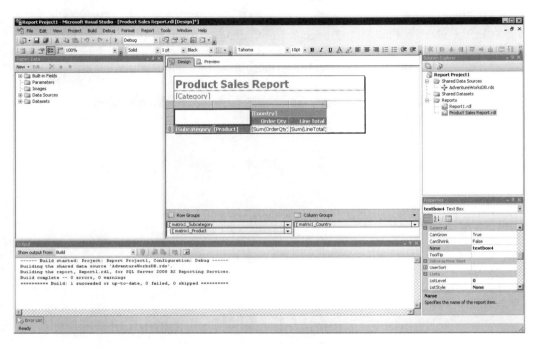

23. Click the Preview tab to render the report.
24. Note that the products are grouped by subcategory and that the order quantity and line total are repeated for each country.
25. Switch back to the Design tab.
26. Use the column header to enlarge the Subcategory and Product columns, as shown:

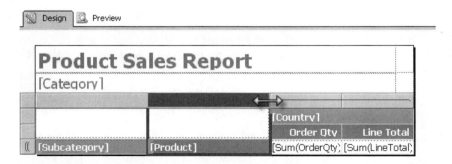

27. Right-click the [Sum(LineTotal)] text box and select Text Box Properties to open the properties dialog, shown next. Select the Number tab on the left.

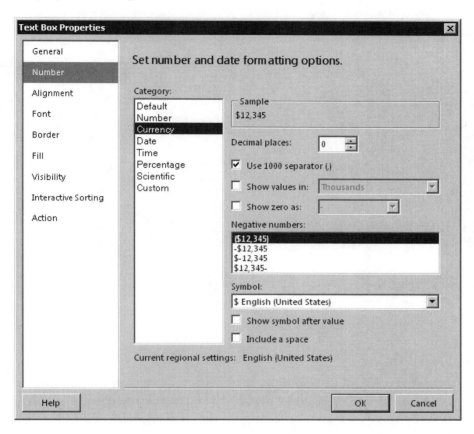

28. Select the Currency format. You may also want to set the decimal places to 0 and select the Use 1000 Separator (,) option.
29. Click the OK button.

30. Preview the report again. It should look like this:

Product Sales Report

Accessories

		AU		CA		DE		FR		GB	
		Order Qty	Line Total	Order Qty	Line Total	Order Qty	Line Total	Order Qty	Line Total	Order Qty	Line
Bike Racks	Hitch Rack - 4-Bike	223	$18,407	594	$44,576	246	$18,106	343	$24,427	268	$2(
Bike Stands	All-Purpose Bike Stand	65	$10,335	32	$5,088	20	$3,180	19	$3,021	28	$
Bottles and Cages	Mountain Bottle Cage	272	$2,717	362	$3,616	187	$1,868	167	$1,668	210	$
	Road Bottle Cage	509	$4,576	116	$1,043	176	$1,582	176	$1,582	229	$
	Water Bottle - 30 oz.	913	$4,314	1078	$4,383	677	$2,766	568	$2,371	679	$
Cleaners	Bike Wash - Dissolver	336	$2,286	594	$3,269	249	$1,379	281	$1,460	291	$
Fenders	Fender Set - Mountain	325	$7,144	400	$8,792	161	$3,539	102	$2,242	144	$
Helmets	Sport-100 Helmet, Black	528	$16,851	1285	$29,552	415	$11,646	499	$12,828	557	$1
	Sport-100 Helmet, Blue	544	$17,369	1241	$28,506	410	$11,235	519	$13,589	560	$1
	Sport-100 Helmet, Red	541	$17,628	1159	$27,309	412	$11,923	503	$13,616	545	$1
Hydration Packs	Hydration Pack - 70 oz.	304	$14,209	496	$18,527	259	$9,140	236	$8,829	261	$
Locks	Cable Lock			283	$4,210	1	$15	70	$1,050	49	
Pumps	Minipump			262	$3,135			90	$1,071	59	
Tires and Tubes	HL Mountain Tire	240	$8,400	277	$9,695	78	$2,730	65	$2,275	74	$
	HL Road Tire	167	$5,444	176	$5,738	37	$1,206	73	$2,380	62	$
	LL Mountain Tire	212	$5,298	139	$3,474	72	$1,799	55	$1,374	83	$
	LL Road Tire	204	$4,384	103	$2,213	153	$3,288	151	$3,245	147	$
	ML Mountain Tire	198	$5,938	226	$6,778	87	$2,609	91	$2,729	119	$
	ML Road Tire	285	$7,122	93	$2,324	89	$2,224	108	$2,699	117	$
	Mountain Tire Tube	514	$2,565	649	$3,239	188	$938	176	$878	239	$
	Patch Kit/8 Patches	674	$1,537	638	$1,340	311	$650	360	$755	381	
	Road Tire Tube	511	$2,039	303	$1,209	277	$1,105	293	$1,169	326	$
	Touring Tire	107	$3,102	92	$2,667	120	$3,479	165	$4,783	177	$
	Touring Tire Tube	195	$973	165	$823	185	$923	280	$1,397	301	$

31. Save everything.

Data Sources

The first step in creating a new report is to create the data source. You can either embed the data source in the report or create it as a shared data source in the project. For either type of data source, you need to select the type, the credentials, and the connection string for the source, as shown in Figure 7-3.

In R2, Reporting Services can query data from any of the following data sources:

► SQL Server Relational Database (including SQL Azure and SQL Server Parallel Data Warehousing Edition, both new in R2)

► SQL Server Analysis Services

► Oracle

► XML Web Services

► SharePoint Lists (new in R2)

► SAP NetWeaver BI

► Hyperion Essbase

► Teradata

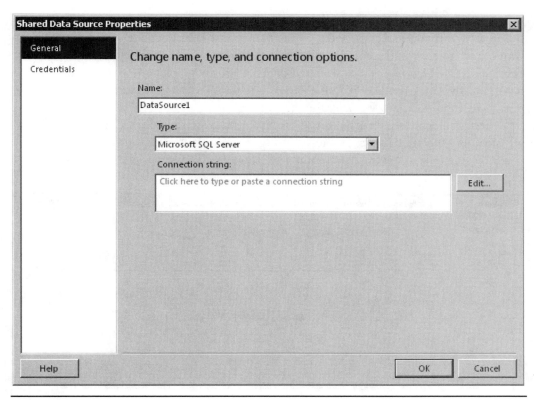

Figure 7-3   *Creating a shared data source*

For each data source, you need to indicate the credentials Reporting Services will use to connect. The options are fairly standard—anonymous (no credentials required for connecting), Windows integrated security, user name and password stored with the data connection, or Reporting Services can prompt the user running the report for their credentials to connect. With the final option, you can also specify the prompt shown the user when they have to enter their credentials.

Data Sets

Once you have one or more data connections defined, you need to create the data set(s) for your report. A data set is a query against a data source that returns a collection of columns and rows. The data set can be a result set from a relational database, a flattened result set from an XML data source, a flattened rowset from a multidimensional data source, a result set from a .Net Framework data provider, or data from a report model.

In Reporting Services 2008 and previous versions, data sets were always embedded in the report. If you had a set of data on which you wanted to create several reports, you would have to copy and paste the query text from one report to the next. In Reporting Services 2008 R2, you can create shared data sets in the project and then connect reports to them. This makes it much easier to reuse queries and ensure that multiple reports or subreports are showing the same thing.

When you create a data set, after selecting the data source, you will have to create or set the query for the data set, as shown in Figure 7-4. Depending on the data source, you'll be able to select from Text (enter a SQL query), Table (select a table name), or

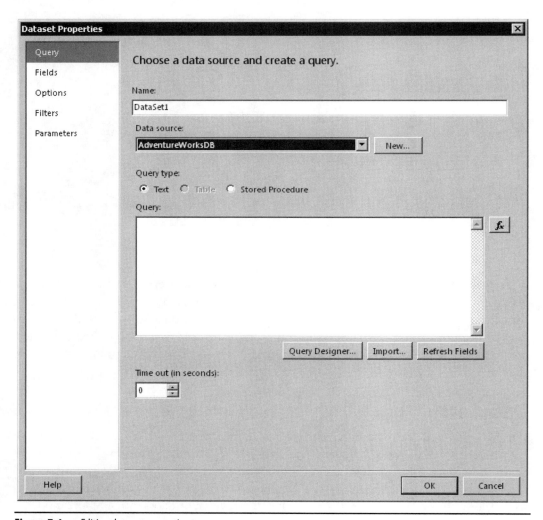

Figure 7-4   *Editing data set properties*

Stored Procedure (select a stored procedure from the data source). Even though the query type is Text, the important aspect is the query designer, which will make your life much easier.

There are several query designers, depending on the data source, although the ones you will see most often are the graphical and MDX query designers. The following sections discuss the query designers and the data connections they support.

Graphical (Relational) Query Designer

The graphical query designer is used for SQL Server data connections. The designer is shown in Figure 7-5. If you've ever used Microsoft Access, this should look familiar to you.

The top area in the designer is where you add tables from your database. Relationships in the database will be displayed automatically, but you can add joins in the designer by dragging one field to another. Select check boxes in the tables to display the columns

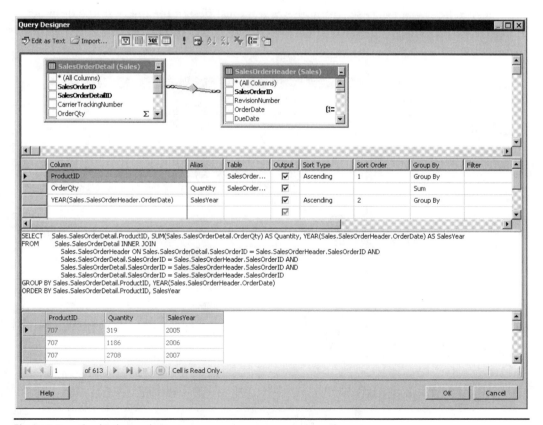

Figure 7-5   *Graphical query designer*

in the column list under the table canvas. In the column list, you can add an alias for columns, change the sort order and sort type, and add a column grouping (which can be toggled on or off in the toolbar).

Under the column list is the query text—you can view the query to ensure it's what you intended, and you can also edit the query directly; when you select out of the text editor, the designer will be updated if possible. The final area in the designer shows the results of the query. You can execute the query either with the Execute button [!] in the toolbar or by right-clicking the designer and selecting Execute SQL.

When you click OK on the designer, the query text will be pasted into the box on the data set properties dialog.

MDX Query Designer

One thing to note is that when you select an Analysis Services data source from the Dataset Properties dialog, the query text area is read-only. Because Reporting Services needs a specific style of data set from SSAS, you must design the query in the designer. The MDX query designer, shown in Figure 7-6, will look familiar after seeing Chapter 3.

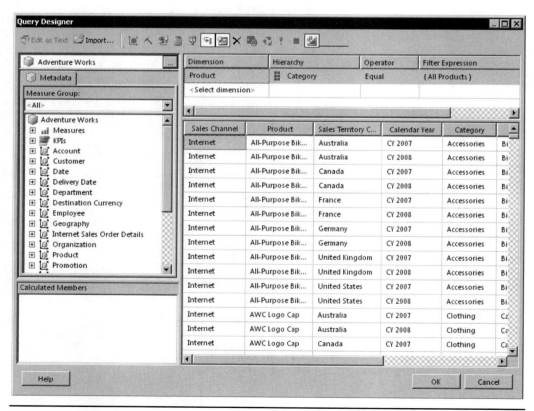

Figure 7-6   *MDX query designer*

And the query designer here works exactly as the browser did in the Cube Designer—you can drag over measures and hierarchies to create the flattened rowset necessary to fetch from Analysis Services. Drag hierarchy members to the Filter area above the output display to create filters. When you've finished creating the data set, click the OK button to return the query to the data set designer.

> **NOTE**
>
> *To create a filter parameter, drag the hierarchy member you want to filter on to the Filter area and then select the Parameter check box. You will probably have to scroll the window to the right to see it.*

SharePoint List Query Designer

A new feature in Reporting Services 2008 R2 is the ability to use SharePoint lists as a native data source. The data source needs to be pointed to a site root (wherever the lists .asmx web service can be found) and set to use Windows Integrated Authentication. Then the query designer will list all the lists in the SharePoint site, and you will be able to select the fields from a single list, as shown in Figure 7-7.

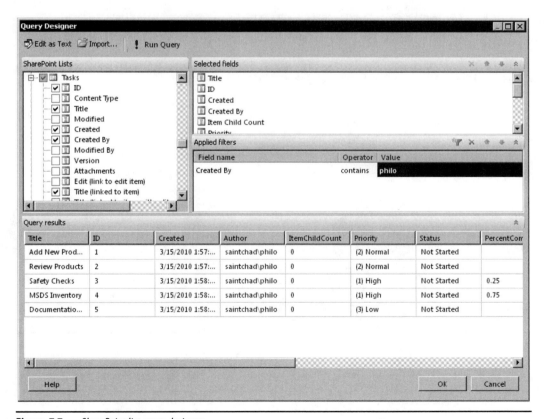

Figure 7-7 *SharePoint list query designer*

When you accept the query in the SharePoint query designer, it will paste the XML for the list query into the query text box on the data set properties dialog.

Text Query Designer

For any other relational data source, Reporting Services will provide a basic text query designer, as shown in Figure 7-8. This is simply a text editing area and a results pane to show the results of the query. You can also import any query from a *.sql or *.rdl file.

Other Query Designers

Reporting Services also has specific designers for SAP (NetWeaver BI) and Hyperion Essbase, both of which look and operate similarly to the MDX query designer. There's also a DMX-specific query designer for data mining queries—we'll take a look at that in Chapter 12.

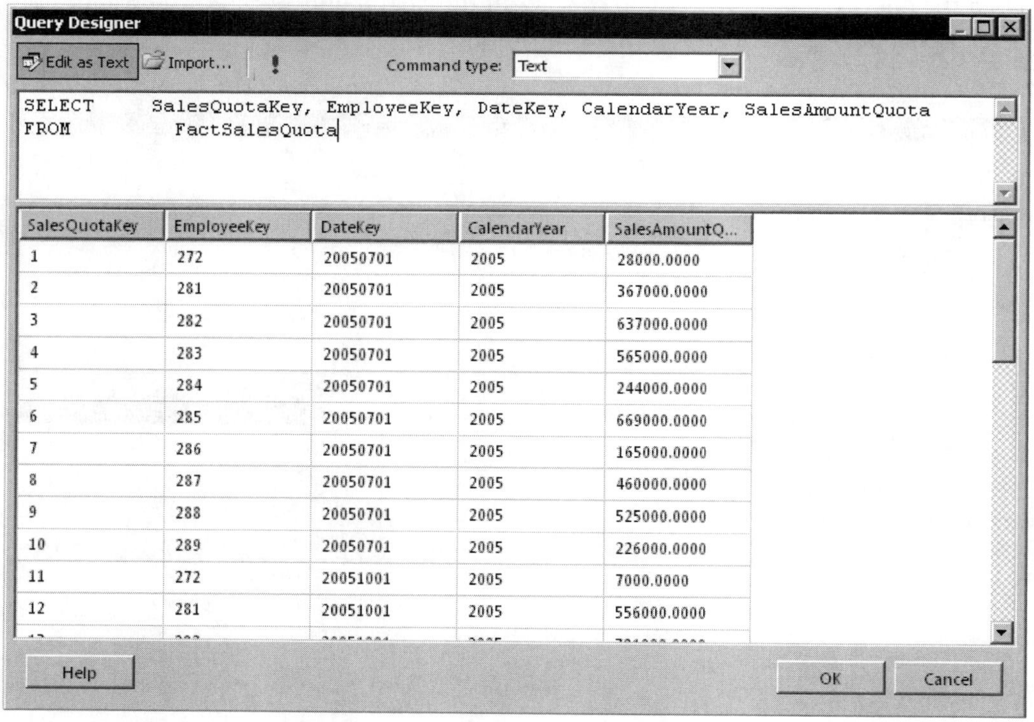

Figure 7-8   *Text query designer*

Report Design

Once you've created a data source and data set, it's time to design the report layout. We've already laid out a report in Exercise 7-1, but that's a simple report. To get the most use out of Reporting Services, you will want to design reports that provide an "at a glance" perspective on some area of the business you are reporting on. It seems to be counterproductive to use a platform like this and produce what is effectively the digital equivalent of a green-bar report!

Report design is pretty straightforward—drag-and-drop WYSIWYG. The databound elements are the Table, Matrix, and List (more on those in a moment), the Chart, Gauge, and Map. Each databound element can be connected to a single data set and then configured to display the data elements appropriately. The Textbox, Image, Data Bar, Sparkline, and Indicator controls are meant to be used within a databound element and bound to a field within the data set. The Sparkline control is actually just a specialized Chart control, and the Indicator is just a specialized Gauge control. Similarly, the Table, Matrix, and List controls are each a special kind of control that was introduced with Reporting Services 2008: Tablix.

Tablix

Before Reporting Services 2008, you had a choice of displaying data in either a table (rowset) or matrix (pivot table). These were great for introductory reports, but any kind of complexity quickly had a report developer writing code. Tablix is a component designed to answer these requirements, providing the flexibility to create a table or a matrix, embed one in the other, or create a multitude of various formats, as shown in Figure 7-9.

In this report, we've put a matrix (geography in rows, sales and tax measures in columns). However, we've added another table in the cell for the Internet sales amount and in that table created a breakdown of sales by category. In addition, we've added a data column to the right and put a sparkline control to show the sales trend by calendar year.

The key to working with a Tablix control is the design frame, shown in Figure 7-10. The two nested brackets in the left border indicate two nested groups. The bracket in the top border indicates one group. The group definitions can be seen in the grouping window at the bottom of the designer. If you want to work with groups (add nested groups, add or remove totals or subtotals, etc.), then you can manage that in the grouping window. Selecting the various components will display the grouping for those components (for example, selecting the nested table will show the grouping for that table).

Country	State Province	Internet Sales Amount		Tax	Trend
Australia	**New South Wales**	Category	Sales		
		Accessories	$59,839	$314,759	
		Bikes	$3,843,862		
		Clothing	$30,786		
	Queensland	Category	Sales		
		Accessories	$31,556	$159,073	
		Bikes	$1,942,683		
		Clothing	$14,177		
	South Australia	Category	Sales		
		Accessories	$8,838	$49,460	
		Bikes	$605,056		
		Clothing	$4,362		
	Tasmania	Category	Sales		
		Accessories	$4,041	$19,195	
		Bikes	$233,197		
		Clothing	$2,700		
	Victoria	Category	Sales		
		Accessories	$34,417	$182,392	
		Bikes	$2,227,253		
		Clothing	$18,236		
Canada	**Alberta**	Category	Sales		
		Accessories	$414	$1,797	
		Bikes	$21,828		
		Clothing	$225		
	British Columbia	Category	Sales		
		Accessories	$102,926	$156,427	
		Bikes	$1,799,474		
		Clothing	$52,939		
	Ontario	Category	Sales	$3	

Figure 7-9   *A Tablix report*

We created the Internet Sales Amount section by dragging another matrix control into the cell. Figure 7-11 shows the design frame around that table. Working with Tablix controls can take some getting used to, to understand the capabilities and limitations of the control. We also want to point out that the report shown in Figure 7-9 used an OLAP data source. In our experience, complex structures get much easier with dimensional data sources.

Country	State Province	Internet Sales Amount		Tax	Trend
[Country]	[State_Province]	Category	Sales	[Sum(Internet_Tax	
		[Category]	[Sum(Internet_Sales_/		

Figure 7-10   *Tablix designer*

Country	State Province			Tax	Trend
[Country]	[State_Province]	**Category**	**Sales**	[Sum(Internet_Tax	
		[Category]	[Sum(Internet_Sales_/		

Figure 7-11   *A matrix nested in a data cell*

Sparklines

The sparkline in the report in Figure 7-9 is, as we mentioned previously, simply a small specialized chart. When you add a sparkline to a report, you get a small designer, as shown in Figure 7-12. Populating the sparkline is then simply a matter of selecting the data fields to be used for the values (y-axis) and category groups (x-axis) of the chart. You can actually add a series group to show multiple sparklines, but in general, that will quickly make the report display confusing.

Multiple types of sparklines are available, as shown in Figure 7-13. Line and area sparklines are similar to what we've done so far. The column chart is best used for "win/loss" type charts as opposed to actually comparing values. The pie charts are fairly self-explanatory, and the range chart is probably usually too small to be of use, but it's available.

Sparklines are used to show multiple related values (generally a time series) for a single row of data. If we want an easy way to show comparative values across multiple rows of data, Reporting Services now has data bars, just like Excel.

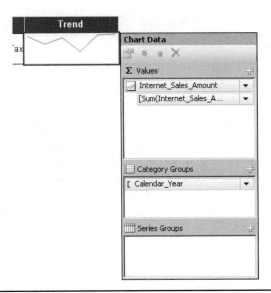

Figure 7-12   *Sparkline control and designer*

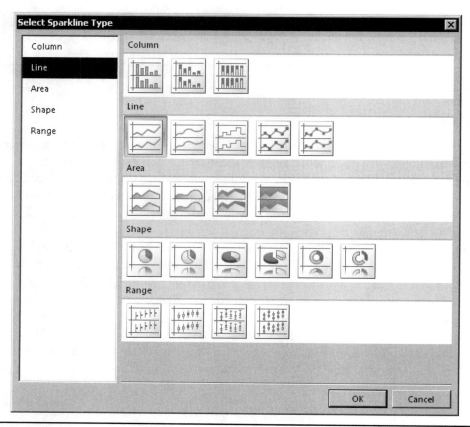

Figure 7-13 *Sparkline types*

Data Bars

You can see an example of data bars in a Reporting Services report in Figure 7-14. The setup for a data bar is similar to setting up a sparkline, and you can set more detailed properties through context menus on the data bar control. The data bars will be formatted across rows and columns in a matrix, and down rows in a table. The most important difference between SSRS and Excel data bars is that you can't overlay data bars in Reporting Services—they have to be in an adjacent cell to any values.

United Kingdom		United States	
$13,500		$998,322	
$10,125		$948,485	
$10,125		$1,072,453	
$13,500		$936,391	
$27,200		$1,002,572	
$17,000		$908,673	
$17,000		$938,454	
$10,200		$818,293	
$376,256		$2,386,094	
$390,017		$2,160,924	
$259,891		$1,888,238	
$318,651		$2,033,226	
$279,966		$1,919,843	
$304,913		$1,890,305	

Figure 7-14   *Data bars in a report*

Other Controls

We'll take a closer look at the Indicator control in Chapter 9 on scorecards. In Chapter 10, we'll dig into Reporting Services charts and graphs as we cover graphical data display across the Office 2010 suite.

Report Builder

As we mentioned in the introduction to the chapter, Report Builder was introduced with SQL Server Reporting Services 2005. At that time, users could only create reports from predesigned report models, which was a significant limitation. Report Builder 3.0, shown in Figure 7-15, will ship with SQL Server 2008 R2, and is essentially at feature parity with the report designer in BIDS.

Report Builder is a .Net "click once" application—it runs as an application on the desktop, but is installed from the Report Server the first time a user clicks the Report Builder button in Report Manager, shown in Figure 7-16. After a user clicks the button, they will be asked to verify installation of the application and then it will be downloaded (approximately 80MB), installed, and executed. Once it's installed, users can run Report Builder from the Windows Start menu.

Another new feature in Report Builder is the ability to create and share Report Parts. Report Parts are the configured components of a report—Tablix areas, charts, and

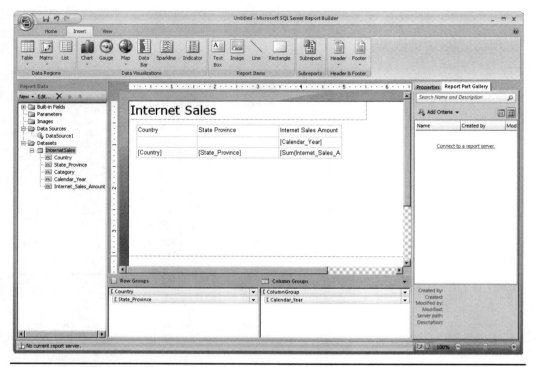

Figure 7-15 *Report Builder 3.0*

maps. You can publish Report Parts explicitly from Report Builder; when a report is published from BIDS, all the components in the report can be exported as Report Parts automatically. Report Parts can then be used in Report Builder in conjunction with shared data sources and shared data sets to create a new report or edit an existing one.

NOTE

As of SQL Server 2008 R2, there's no direct way to import Report Parts into a project in BIDS.

Once you've created a report in Report Builder, a user can simply execute it in the builder, view it, print the report, or export it to the standard output formats. Alternatively, if the user has permission, they can publish the report to a Reporting Server, where it will be just another report—users can view it, subscribe to it, edit it in BIDS, etc.

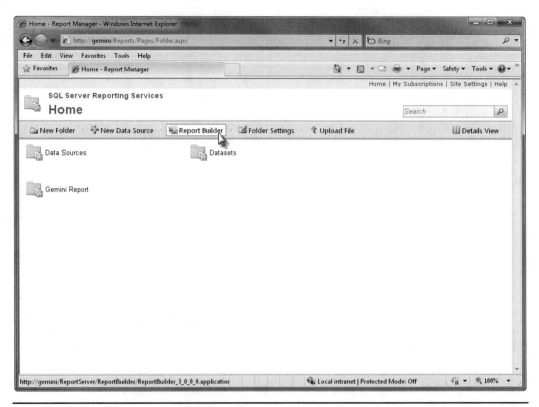

Figure 7-16   *Launching Report Builder from Report Manager*

Report Manager

We mentioned Report Manager—this is the web-based application where users interact with Reporting Services when SSRS is run in stand-alone or Native mode. Reporting Services can run in one of two modes: Native mode, which is as a stand-alone reporting server; or SharePoint integrated mode, which is as it sounds—the Reporting Services interface is all through SharePoint Server. Figure 7-17 shows the website that represents the home of Reporting Services when it's running in Native mode. Reports, data sets, and data sources are all stored in folders and accessible via the web interface (for users with appropriate permissions).

NOTE

Reporting Services 2008 and 2008 R2 run their own native http listener, separate from IIS. For more information about the listener, see http://msdn.microsoft.com/en-us/library/bb630409(SQL.105).aspx.

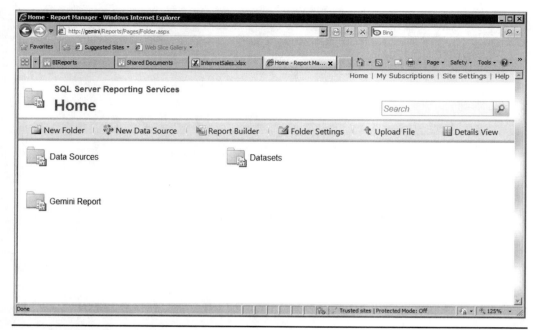

Figure 7-17 *Reporting Services Report Manager*

Selecting the Data Sources folder shows the data sources currently stored on the Report Server. If you mouse over a data source, you'll get a highlight with a context drop-down arrow, offering a context menu as shown in Figure 7-18. Note that you can generate a report model from here, or get a list of data sets and reports that are dependent on the data source. Either clicking the data source or selecting Manage from the context menu takes you to the Data Source Properties pages, if you have the appropriate permissions.

The Data Source Properties pages, shown in Figure 7-19, allow you to modify the connection string for the data source and the credentials. You can also access the dependent items and security pages from here. Note the credentials—in this case we're using Windows Integrated Security because we have all our services running on a single server. Remember that if you are running Reporting Services on a separate server from your data source, Windows Integrated Security credentials will not be passed from Reporting Services to the data source unless you have implemented Kerberos.

Properties for data sets are similar—you can change the data source, view dependent items, and manage security for the data set. Depending on the credentials scheme you're

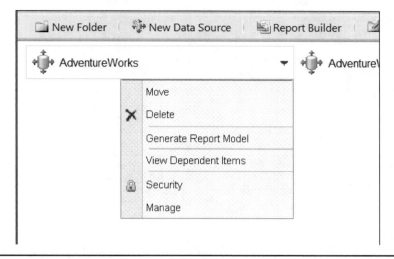

Figure 7-18   *Data source context menu*

using, you may also be able to cache the data set. This allows you to keep a data set in memory if it doesn't change that quickly or if the changes don't have major impact on a report. For example, a report showing quarterly sales across the country probably doesn't need to be updated hourly.

The properties for a report are, as you would expect, somewhat more robust, and shown in Figure 7-20. From Report Manager you can manage the report's data sets, data connections (if it has any—a report that only uses shared data sets may not), subscriptions, processing options (whether to use cached data or refresh data when the report is run), history, and so on.

SharePoint Integrated Mode

The other option for running Reporting Services was introduced in SQL Server Reporting Services 2005 SP2—SharePoint integrated mode. In SharePoint integrated mode, SSRS uses a SharePoint document library as the repository for report files, data connections, and data sets. Publishing reports from BIDS must be mapped to the appropriate SharePoint library and folders. Once configured, the report library gains the features of a SharePoint document library—metadata, versioning, access control, and workflow.

Configuration

The SSRS server is configured for SharePoint integrated mode in the Reporting Services Configuration Manager on the Database tab. You have to create a new configuration

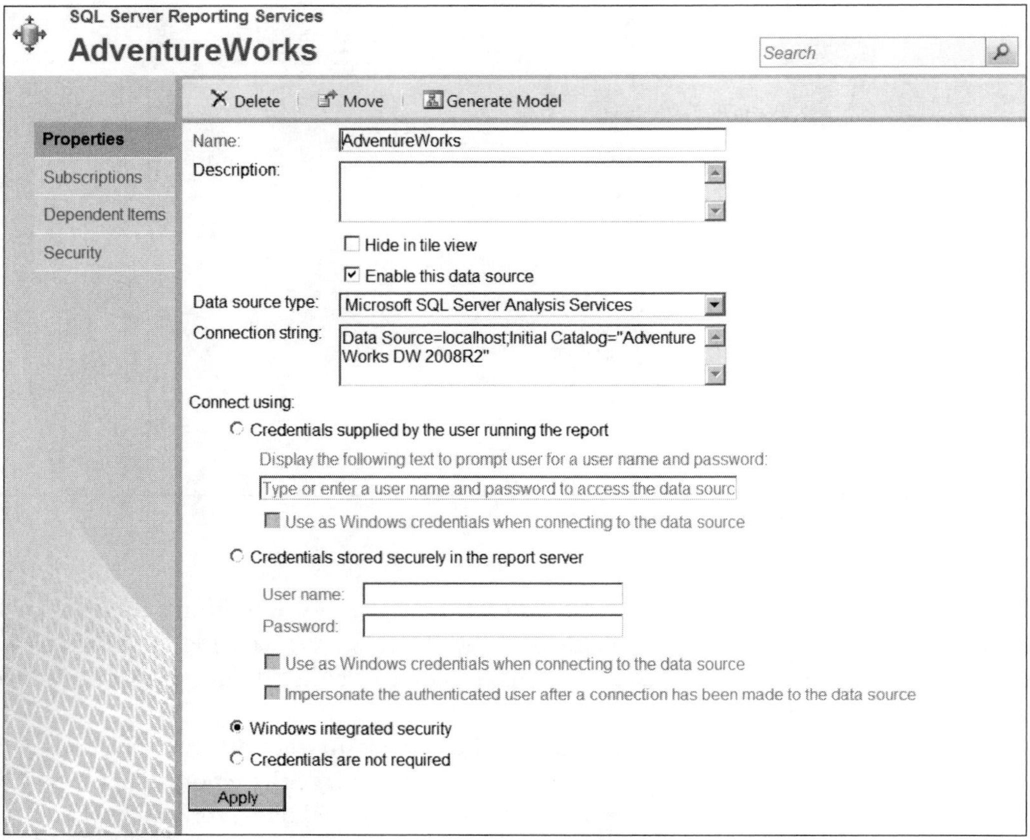

Figure 7-19 *Data source properties*

database, and in the database settings, select the mode, as shown in Figure 7-21. Once you have created a database of each type, you can switch back and forth by simply choosing the existing database instead of creating a new one each time.

NOTE

Once an SSRS 2008 instance was converted to SharePoint integrated mode, it wasn't possible to change it back to Native mode—you had to uninstall and reinstall SSRS. In Reporting Services 2008 R2, you can change the mode in either direction.

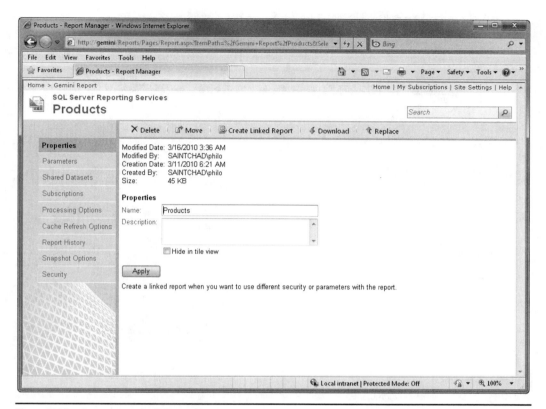

Figure 7-20   *Report properties in Report Manager*

After you've configured the Report Server, you'll need to configure SharePoint for Reporting Services integration. In previous versions of SharePoint, you had to download and install an add-in for the configuration; now it's simply a matter of making the appropriate configuration in Central Administration. For more information, see http://msdn.microsoft.com/en-us/library/bb326213(SQL.105).aspx.

Another feature of integrating Reporting Services with SharePoint is the ability to use a Report Viewer Web Part to display reports easily on SharePoint pages. You can also connect Web Parts to provide dynamic filtering based on selections in another Web Part.

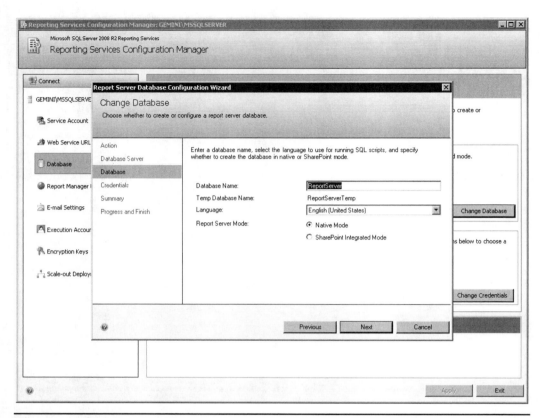

Figure 7-21   *Selecting SSRS Report Server mode*

Export Formats

Reports can be exported in a number of formats, as shown in Figure 7-22. The options here are pretty straightforward. Be sure you've configured your page size to suit the export format—if the report is wider than the page, it will cut off and wrap to intervening pages.

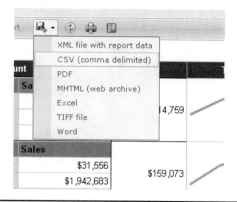

Figure 7-22   *Exporting reports*

Summary

This was a high-speed overview of SQL Server Reporting Services. We've tried to both introduce the platform and cover the 2008 R2–specific changes as thoroughly as possible, in this chapter and in Chapter 10 on charts, and Chapter 11 on mapping. If you want to dig deeper, we highly recommend *Microsoft SQL Server 2008 Reporting Services* by Brian Larson (McGraw-Hill, 2008). In the next chapter, we're going to start gluing together the pieces of business intelligence solutions that we've learned to date. Let's take a look at our platform, SharePoint Server 2010.

Chapter 8

SharePoint

In This Chapter

- ▶ **Business Intelligence Center**
- ▶ **SharePoint Dashboards**
- ▶ **Summary**

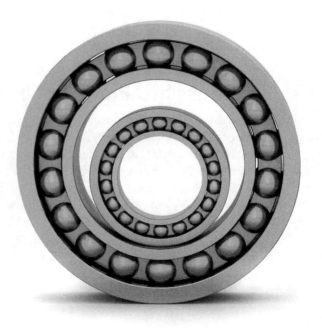

The business intelligence features in SharePoint 2010 easily accommodate the different levels of business intelligence maturity that exist in a typical organization. We like to think of SharePoint as having something for everyone because it facilitates sharing of information without requiring everyone to use a single tool or requiring all data to be in a cube. Whether one group uses an Analysis Services cube to support advanced slicing and dicing of data or another group manually updates a simple Excel workbook to measure progress towards a goal over time, information in all forms can be gathered into a central location and linked together in ways that support collaborative decision making. Meanwhile, each group can continue to work with their tool of choice and migrate later to tools with added functionality as their needs and business intelligence skills evolve.

Perhaps some of your users are still new to business intelligence. For this group, you can set up a simple but useful SharePoint site where they can input data directly into SharePoint using lists. Going a step further, they can maintain status lists manually as an easy way to share how well they are meeting specific objectives.

You probably have another group of users that rely heavily on Excel workbooks. SharePoint not only allows that group to publish workbooks to Excel Services for centralized access, but also to reuse the information in those workbooks in status lists and dashboards. The workbooks can also be a source for more advanced PerformancePoint scorecards and dashboards, accessible in SharePoint, as you'll learn in Chapter 9.

Maybe you also have a group that uses Reporting Services. SharePoint has a solution for these users, too. You can use SharePoint dashboards to combine lists and workbooks with reports from Reporting Services. As you'll see throughout this chapter, SharePoint gives you the flexibility to maintain analytical information in each user's tool of choice, yet bring together information from disparate applications in support of better, collaborative decision making.

Business Intelligence Center

An easy way to get started with business intelligence in SharePoint is to create a Business Intelligence Center site. Business Intelligence Center is a specialized site type in SharePoint 2010 that replaces the Report Center site type introduced in Microsoft Office SharePoint Server (MOSS) 2007. When you create a new instance of the site type, SharePoint automatically generates predefined pages, libraries, and more to help you get started right away. You can either use the Business Intelligence Center as a centralized storage location for all of your business intelligence reports, workbooks, diagrams, and other content or as a launching point for complex analytic applications.

At a minimum, you can use the built-in tools in SharePoint without making any changes. If necessary, you can modify the site by adding new content types, such as

Reporting Services reports and data sources, or adding pages with custom content but without writing any code. This simplicity hides the full power of SharePoint, which is also flexible and powerful enough for you to customize Business Intelligence Center to meet specific requirements with code-based SharePoint applications.

Before we explain more about working with document libraries and content types in the Business Intelligence Center, let's review the process for creating the site. If you don't already have a Business Intelligence Center available for use with the exercises in this chapter, you can add a SharePoint site to an existing site as long as you are designated as an owner of the site. Let's use this technique now to create a site for the business intelligence content that we'll create throughout this chapter.

Exercise 8-1: Creating a Business Intelligence Center Site

1. In your browser, open an existing SharePoint site for which you are a site owner.

2. Click the Site Actions button in the upper-left corner of the page to open the menu shown here:

3. On the Site Actions menu, click New Site.

The Create page for the new site provides a more user-friendly view of the available site templates than you see in Central Administration. The Create page also provides a description of the site to help you determine if the site type will meet your needs. The Business Intelligence Center template appears in the Data category, as shown in the following illustration, although you can see that its description is not as informative as other site descriptions. After you select the site type, you provide a title and a URL name for the site. SharePoint will display the title on the site's home page and in navigation links. The URL name can match the title, but typically, you provide a separate name that is shorter than the title and omits embedded spaces. SharePoint appends this URL name to the base URL for the SharePoint application and parent site. Users can then use the full URL to navigate directly to the new site without first navigating through the site collection.

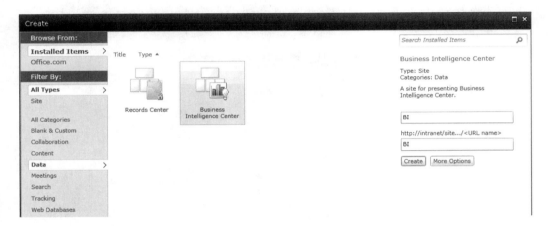

When you first create the Business Intelligence Center, the home page of the site (shown next) displays an information panel in the center of the screen and a Quick Launch panel for navigation on the left side of the screen.

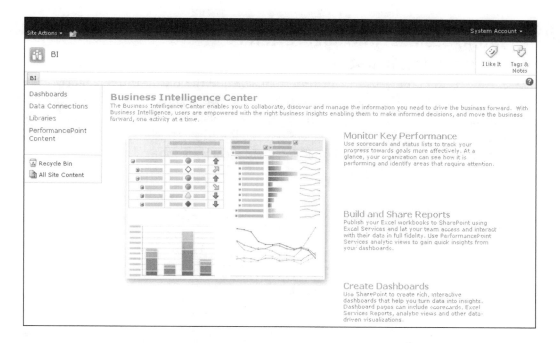

The center panel contains a specialized control called a Web Part. In this case, the Web Part is a container for content describing the features of the Business Intelligence Center site, but there are many other types of Web Parts that you can use in SharePoint, as you'll learn later in this chapter. The information about the features of the site might be useful when you first introduce SharePoint to your users, but later, you might consider customizing the contents of the center panel by editing the page and adding one or more Web Parts or by removing the existing Web Part. Working with this page is similar to working with a dashboard page, which you'll learn how to do later in this chapter.

Quick Launch

The Quick Launch panel contains links to other locations in the site, such as a document library or another site in the site collection (also known as a subsite), as you can see in the initial settings for the Business Intelligence Center shown in the previous illustration. In that site, for example, you can use the Dashboards link to open a document library containing only dashboard pages, or use the Data Connections link to open a document library containing only files that store information necessary for SharePoint to connect to data sources.

Creating Business Intelligence Center in Central Administration

If you're a SharePoint farm administrator, you can add the Business Intelligence Center site by creating a new site collection on the Application Management page in Central Administration. When you create a site collection, you must select a site template for the initial site in the collection. You'll find the Business Intelligence Center template on the Enterprise tab of site templates, as shown here:

Whether a link appears in the Quick Launch panel when you add new content to a site depends on site settings and whether you change the navigation option when you create the library. If a link gets added but you decide later that you want to remove it, just use the Site Actions menu and select Site Settings. On the Site Settings page, click the Navigation link in the Look And Feel group. As you can see in Figure 8-1, you can then access a tree view of the items in the Quick Launch panel in the Navigation Editing And Sorting section of the Navigation page, select the item to delete, and click the Delete button in the tree view's toolbar. Notice also that the toolbar contains buttons to rearrange items in the list, add items to the list, or edit the selected item by changing its URL, description, or audience properties.

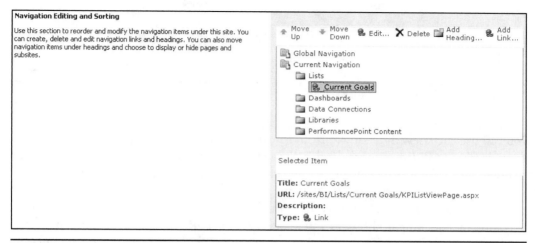

Figure 8-1 *Site navigation settings*

Document Libraries

The Quick Launch panel does not provide links to every document library available in Business Intelligence Center site. Instead, it includes only links to the document libraries you will likely access more frequently and a Libraries link to open a list of all available libraries (shown in Figure 8-2). And if you're interested in other content,

			Items	Last Modified
Document Libraries				
	Customized Reports	This Document library has the templates to create Web Analytics custom reports for this site collection	0	13 hours ago
	Dashboards	Contains Webpart pages, Web part pages with Status Lists and PerformancePoint deployed dashboards	1	83 minutes ago
	Data Connections	Contains ODC, UDC and PerformancePoint data connections	1	12 hours ago
	Documents	This system library was created by the Publishing feature to store documents that are used on pages in this site.	3	12 hours ago
	Form Templates	This library contains administrator-approved form templates that were activated to this site collection.	0	13 hours ago
	Images	This system library was created by the Publishing feature to store images that are used on pages in this site.	0	13 hours ago
	Pages	This system library was created by the Publishing feature to store pages that are created in this site.	5	85 minutes ago
	Site Collection Documents	This system library was created by the Publishing Resources feature to store documents that are used throughout the site collection.	0	13 hours ago
	Site Collection Images	This system library was created by the Publishing Resources feature to store images that are used throughout the site collection.	0	13 hours ago
	Style Library	Use the style library to store style sheets, such as CSS or XSL files. The style sheets in this gallery can be used by this site or any of its subsites.	41	88 minutes ago

Figure 8-2 *Business Intelligence Center document libraries*

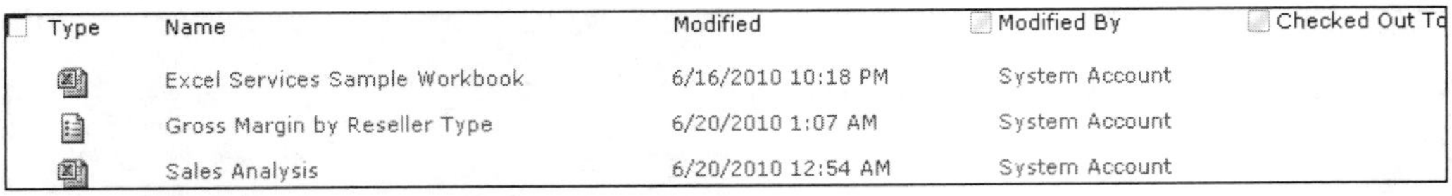

	Type	Name	Modified	Modified By	Checked Out To
		Excel Services Sample Workbook	6/16/2010 10:18 PM	System Account	
		Gross Margin by Reseller Type	6/20/2010 1:07 AM	System Account	
		Sales Analysis	6/20/2010 12:54 AM	System Account	

Figure 8-3   *Default view in a document library*

you can use the View drop-down list in the upper-right corner to view a specific content type or all site content. In this chapter, we'll focus on the following three types of document libraries—dashboards, data connections, and documents. You use the PerformancePoint Content library to store elements that you use to build scorecards and dashboards, which we'll discuss in more detail in the next chapter.

Think of a document library as a file drawer that you use for storing documents on SharePoint. Within a document library, you can use folders to separate documents into groups by subject matter, or you might use folders as a way to apply a common set of security permissions to a group of documents. Regardless of how you organize the document library, you can use it to store different types of documents, as shown in Figure 8-3. For example, when you publish an Excel workbook to SharePoint, you must specify a document library as the destination. Likewise, if you're running Reporting Services in SharePoint integrated mode, you can use the same document library to store reports.

When you open the document library in the browser, you see a list of the documents and folders it contains. The default view for the library displays each document with an icon to indicate its content type, the name of the document, the date and time of the last modification of the document, and the name of the user making the last modification. In addition, a user can check out a document for editing, in which case the document library view will also display the name of that user. When a document library contains a large number of documents, you might find it useful to sort the contents by one of the columns in this view.

In addition to saving a document to a library from within an application like Excel or Report Builder 3.0, you can upload documents directly from your hard drive or a network share. Let's try that now.

Exercise 8-2: Uploading Documents to a Document Library

1. On the home page of the Business Intelligence Center site, click the Libraries link in the Quick Launch panel.

2. In the Document Libraries list, click the Documents link.

3. Click the Add Document link, click the Browse button, navigate to the folder containing the files for this chapter, select Sales Analysis, click the Open button, and then click the Save button.

NOTE

If your SharePoint site is not running Reporting Services in SharePoint integrated mode, you can skip the next step.

4. Repeat the previous step to upload the "Gross Margin by Reseller Type" report.

NOTE

Both of these documents contain references to data connections that probably don't match your environment. Consequently, before you can view them in SharePoint, you'll need to fix their data connection references, which we'll show you how to do in the next exercise.

Data Connections Library

Data connections are a special file type that you use to store connection strings or information about data sources that SharePoint uses to locate and retrieve data in response to a user query. You store these data connections in a separate document library called the Data Connections library. Maintaining data connections separately from the documents dependent on them, such as workbooks, reports, and diagrams, allows you to make changes to server names or passwords in a single location rather than document by document.

In addition, as users build new workbooks or diagrams, they can retrieve a data connection from the library as long as they have the correct permissions to access and download the data connection files. That way, they don't need to know server names and other connection-related information. Instead, they can simply open the data connection file in Excel or Visio when they need to connect to an external data source and start building their document.

The default configuration of the Data Connections library supports PerformancePoint data sources, Office Data Connection (ODC) files, and Universal Data Connection (UDC) files. You use PerformancePoint data sources to describe connections used for key performance indicators (KPIs), scorecards, and dashboards. ODC files store connection strings for Excel workbooks and Visio Web drawings. Furthermore, if you create a status indicator that is based on an Analysis Services cube, you must first build an ODC file using either Excel or Visio, and then save the ODC file to the Data Connections library.

In the previous exercise, you uploaded documents to the Documents library. However, the Excel workbook requires you to store an ODC file in the Data Connections library. Similarly, the Reporting Services report depends on access to a Reporting Services Data Source (RSDS) file. In the next exercise, you'll learn how to work with these file types and the Data Connections library.

Work with Reporting Services Content Types

If you are running Reporting Services in SharePoint integrated mode, you can update the document libraries in Business Intelligence Center Reporting Services to recognize Reporting Services content types. To do this, open a document library, such as Documents or Data Connections, open the Library tab in the ribbon, and then click the Library Settings button on the ribbon. In the General Settings section, click the Advanced Settings link, select the Yes option to "Allow management of content types," and click OK to save the new setting. Back on the Document Library Settings page, in the Content Types section, click the Add From Existing Site Content Types link. In the Available Site Content Types list, scroll to locate the Reporting Services content types shown here:

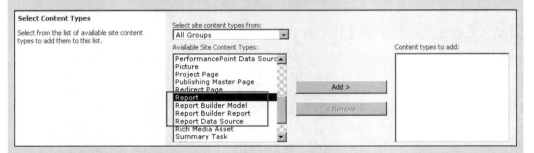

Select each content type that you want to add to the library, and click the "Add" button. For example, if you're adding content types to the Documents library, you might add only Report and Report Builder Report, but if you're adding content types to the Data Connections library, add Report Builder Model and Report Data Source. When you're finished, click the OK button.

Exercise 8-3: Working with Data Sources

1. In the Business Intelligence Center site, on the Documents page, point to Sales Analysis to display the drop-down menu (shown next), and then click Edit In Microsoft Excel.

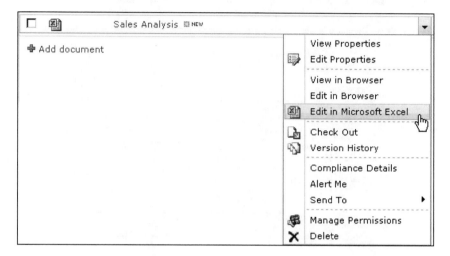

2. In the Open Document message box, click the OK button.
3. Select the Data tab in the ribbon, and click Connections.
4. In the Workbook Connections dialog box, click the Properties button.
5. In the Connection Properties dialog box, click the Definition tab.

6. Change the connection string to the correct values for your environment. For example, replace "(local)" with the correct server name for Analysis Services and replace "Adventure Works DW 2008R2" with the name of your sample database.

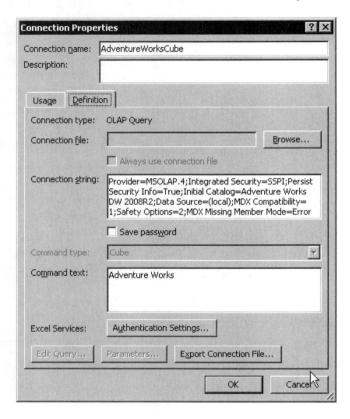

7. Click the Export Connection File button.

8. In the File Name box, type the URL for your Business Intelligence Center site, such as **http://servername/sites/BI**, and press ENTER. Double-click the Data Connections folder, and then click the Save button.

9. In the Web File Properties dialog box, change the Content Type to Office Data Connection File, and click the OK button.

10. In the Connection Properties dialog box, click the OK button, and then click the Close button in the Workbook Connections dialog box.

11. On the File menu, click Save to save the workbook to SharePoint with the updated connection, and then close Excel.

NOTE

If your SharePoint site is not running Reporting Services in SharePoint integrated mode, you can skip the remaining steps in this exercise.

12. Click the Data Connections link in the Quick Launch panel.

13. Click the Add New Item link, click the Browse button, navigate to the folder containing the files for this chapter, select AdventureWorksCubeReportSource. rsds, click the Open button, and then click the OK button.

14. In the Data Connections dialog box, click the Content Type drop-down list, select Report Data Source, and then click the Save button.

15. Point to the AdventureWorksCubeReportSource link, click the arrow to open the drop-down menu for the report data source, and then select Edit Data Source Definition, as shown here:

16. Change the connection string to the correct values for your environment. For example, replace "(local)" with the correct server name for Analysis Services and replace "Adventure Works DW 2008R2" with the name of your sample database. Click the OK button.

17. Next, click the Libraries link, click the Documents links, point to Gross Margin By Reseller Type to display the drop-down menu (shown next), and then click Edit In Report Builder.

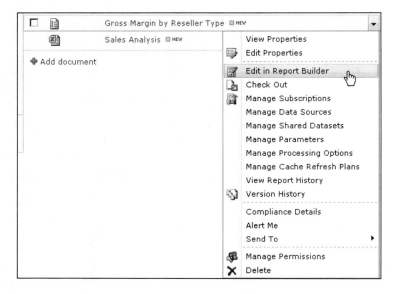

18. In the Report Data pane, expand the Data Sources folder, and then double-click DataSource1.

19. In the Data Source Properties dialog box, click the Browse button.

20. Navigate to the Data Connections Library in your Business Intelligence Center site, double-click Data Connections For PerformancePoint, and double-click AdventureWorksCubeReportSource.rsds.

21. In the Data Source Properties dialog box, click the OK button.

22. On the Report Builder menu, click Save As, verify the current location is the document library where you originally uploaded the report, and click the OK button. Now the report on SharePoint references the correct data source file in the Data Connections Library, which in turn properly defines the connection string to your Analysis Services database.

23. Close Report Builder.

Status Lists

A list is a SharePoint content type that provides a user-friendly way to manage small data sets without using a database. Although a full discussion of the benefits of a list is beyond the scope of this book, suffice it to say that a status list is a special type of

SharePoint list for which each item in the list—a status indicator—uses icons as a visual representation of the current state of one value—the indicator value—as compared to another value—the target value. Status lists were first introduced as KPI lists in MOSS 2007. Using a status list is a good first step towards establishing a common location for sharing performance indicators. When people can easily see how effectively the organization is performing (or not), they are more likely to make decisions that help improve performance indicators.

Consider the status list shown in Figure 8-4, where you can see that the structure of a status list is similar to the structure of a database table. Each status indicator in the list is analogous to a row in a table, and each field or column in the status indicator is like a table column. However, a list is a more flexible way to store status indicators than a table because you can base each status indicator on a different source of data and assign thresholds for the value ranges. The shape and color of the icons that display in the status list tell you whether the indicator value is currently in a good range, a warning range, or in a bad range, as determined by a set of rules that you specify for each status indicator.

Unlike other tools in the Microsoft business intelligence platform, you cannot create a status indicator with more than the three value ranges, nor can you use different colors or icons (although you can change the icon if you include the status list in a dashboard page). Despite these limitations, the status list is perfect for those situations when you need to track and share performance measurements in a simple way. However, if you need more advanced features for displaying indicators, you have the following options: conditional formatting in Excel, indicators in Reporting Services, or KPIs and scorecards in PerformancePoint Services.

SharePoint supports the following data sources for items in a status list:

▶   SharePoint list

▶   Excel Services workbook

▶   SQL Server Analysis Services cube

▶   Fixed value

Indicator	Goal	Value	Status
Tasks	10%	25%	△
Sales	$114,253,550.00	$80,450,596.98	◆
Gross Margin	0.12	11.43%	●➡
New Customers This Month	6	10	●

Figure 8-4   *Status list*

SharePoint List

A list item based on a SharePoint list uses a simple calculation to determine the current indicator value. This calculation can be a count of items in the list, a percentage of items in the list that meet specified criteria, or an aggregation of values in a column such as a sum or average. You then manually assign a goal value to status icons.

Let's assume that you have a list of tasks on your SharePoint site, as shown in Figure 8-5, and you want to monitor the percentage of high-priority items in the list that have not been started. You can create a new status indicator that references this list and defines the value calculation using the Priority and Status columns of the task list. Because your goal is to keep the percentage low, you should set the status icon rules to "Better values are lower" and then specify the threshold values that determine which icon displays in the status list.

For example, your goal might be to have fewer than 10 percent of the tasks meet the criteria, in which case you assign 10 to the green icon. You might then assign a higher value, such as 30, to the yellow icon to establish another threshold. SharePoint will then flag the list item with a red icon if the percentage of high-priority unstarted tasks is greater than 30 percent.

Excel Services

If people are already using Excel workbooks to track organizational progress against goals, why not move those tracking workbooks to SharePoint and then display the value-to-target comparisons by using a status indicator? All you need to do is supply the URL for the workbook and cell addresses for the indicator value and the thresholds for the warning and goal values, as shown in Figure 8-6. By using an Excel workbook, you can base each value on cells that contain either a constant value or a complex formula. Furthermore, when the workbook data changes on the SharePoint site, the corresponding status indicator also updates.

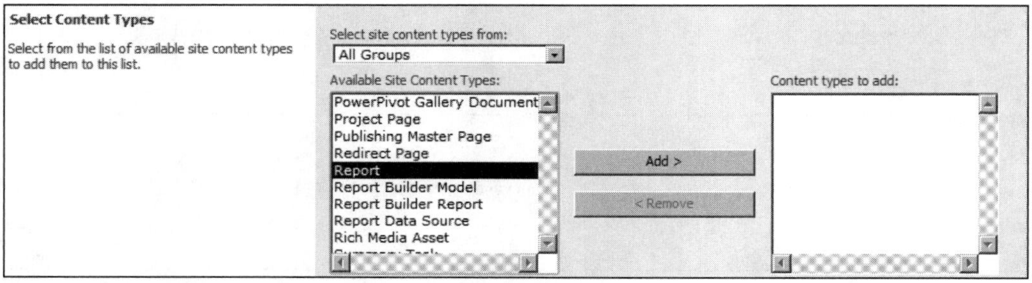

Figure 8-5   *Task list source for status indicator*

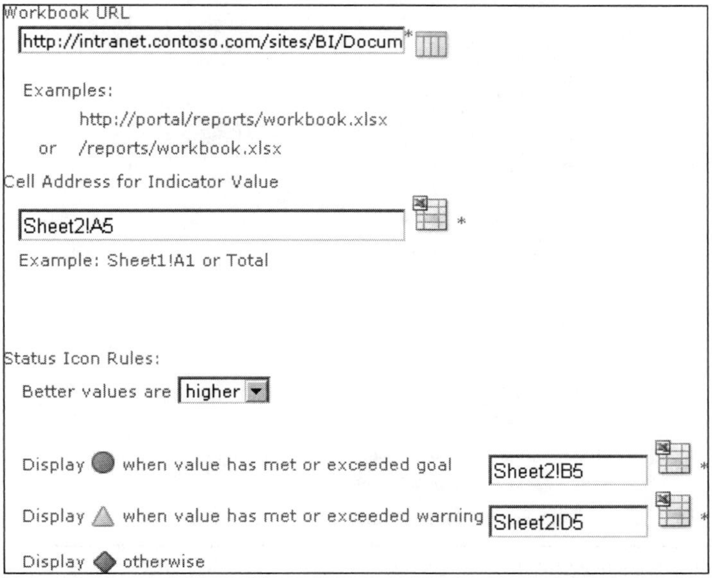

Figure 8-6   *Excel-based status indicators*

SQL Server Analysis Services

If you have an Analysis Services cube that contains KPI definitions, you can add an ODC file for that cube to the Data Connections library and then create a SharePoint status indicator to expose the KPI in the status list, as shown in Figure 8-7. By storing business logic for indicators in Analysis Services, you have consistent KPI calculations available at all times, whether users access them in a status list, in an Excel pivot table, a Reporting Services report, a PerformancePoint Services scorecard, or any client application that can query a cube. In addition, you can use much more complex logic to create KPIs in Analysis Services that isn't possible if you use any of the other source types for a status indicator. Last, you can apply filters in a SharePoint dashboard to a status indicator only when that indicator is based on Analysis Services.

Fixed Value

Some indicators are so simple that no calculation is required, nor is it necessary to track an indicator in a list, Excel workbook, or cube. Maybe you keep a running count of new customers for the month on a whiteboard in your office, and everyone knows the goal. A better way to share this information, especially for people who are unable to stop by your office regularly, is to create a status indicator that you manually update as needed, such as the one shown in Figure 8-8.

Now let's see how to create a status list.

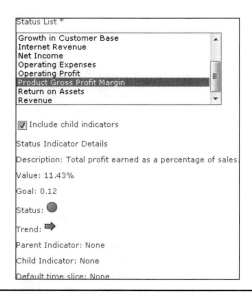

Figure 8-7   *Status indicator based on Analysis Services*

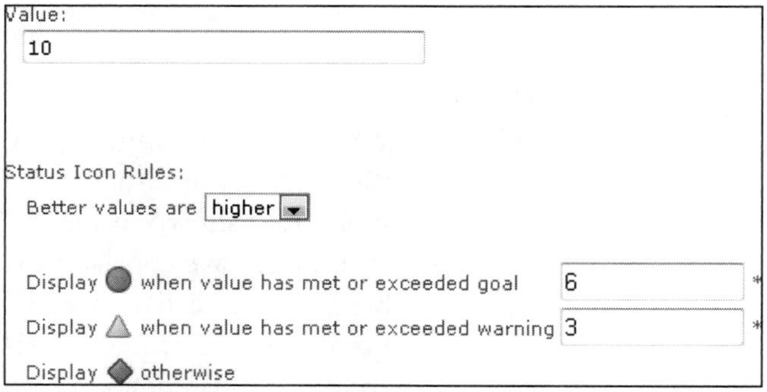

Figure 8-8   *Fixed value status indicator*

Exercise 8-4: Creating a Status List

1. Open the Business Intelligence Center site in Internet Explorer.
2. Click the Libraries link.
3. Click the Create button, select List in the Filter By list, and then select Status List.
4. In the Name box (above the Create button), type **Current Goals**, and click the Create button. Two new links appear in the Quick Launch panel—a link to lists for the new content type added to the site and a link to the Current Goals lists.

5. Click the Current Goals link in the Quick Launch panel. The list is currently empty. You use the toolbar to add items to the list.

6. Click the arrow button to the right of New, as shown next, and select SQL Server Analysis Services Based Status Indicator.

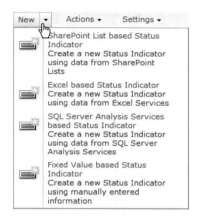

7. Click the Browse button to the right of the Data Connection box. Open Data Connections, and select the ODC file that you published in Exercise 8-3. Click the OK button.

8. In the Status List, select Product Gross Profit Margin.

9. In the Name box, type **Gross Margin**.

   In addition to configuring the rules for each status indicator, there are optional settings that you can specify for each status indicator, as shown in Figure 8-9. First, you can supply a URL to a page that contains more information about

Figure 8-9 *Optional settings for a status indicator*

a status indicator. This page might be on your SharePoint site, but it can be located anywhere that your users can access by using a URL. For example, you could create a page that provides a detailed explanation of how the indicator value, goal value, and warning value are assigned or calculated, the frequency with which these values are updated when applicable, and the people to contact for more information about the status indicator.

Second, you can choose between two options for update rules. By default, the indicator value updates for every viewer. This really means that the source for the status indicator will be checked each time you refresh the page that contains the indicator. As an alternative, you can require the user to manually update the indicator when viewing it in the status list or in a dashboard page. That is, when the user views the indicator in either of these locations, the indicator will display the value as of its last update and will not change its value unless the user purposely selects the option to update the indicator.

10. Click the OK button.

SharePoint Dashboards

A dashboard is a useful way to provide the user with a quick overview of multiple types of information that is important to the user for day-to-day decision making. A common way to use a dashboard is to review current conditions to determine whether action should be taken or further analysis is necessary. Just as status indicators let you know at a glance whether the situation is good or bad, a well-designed dashboard should communicate the current state at a glance and provide links to additional information if the user wants to view the underlying details. You might personalize a dashboard for each user, or provide a dashboard for different levels of the organizational hierarchy.

SharePoint 2010 continues support for the dashboard that was first introduced in MOSS 2007. For more advanced visualizations and more interactive components, including scorecards, you can use PerformancePoint Services, which we'll cover in the next chapter. In the remainder of this chapter, we'll explore the dashboard features available in SharePoint independently from PerformancePoint services.

Dashboard Pages

A dashboard is another name for a Web Part page, which is a webpage on your SharePoint site that displays multiple types of information on the same page, but in separate, configurable sections of the dashboard known as Web Parts. If you've ever used gadgets in iGoogle, content in My Yahoo!, or modules in My MSN, you've worked with objects that are similar to Web Parts. SharePoint 2010 maintains a gallery of many different types of Web Parts to display specific content, such as a status list or an Excel workbook. You can also update the gallery with custom Web Parts developed by third-party vendors or by an in-house developer.

To add a dashboard page to a site, you need to have the Add And Customize Pages permission. If you are a member of a group that has Full Control or Designer permission levels, you have this permission already. Otherwise, you will need to have a site administrator grant you permission before you can develop a dashboard.

Exercise 8-5: Creating a Dashboard Page

1. Click the Dashboards link in the Quick Launch panel.
2. Select the Documents tab on the ribbon.
3. Select the arrow next to New Document, and then click Web Part Page, as shown:

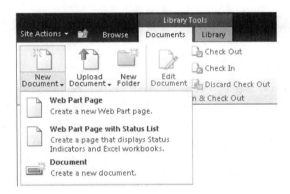

4. In the Name box, type **Reseller Sales**.
5. Review the available layout templates, and make a selection. You can see a preview of each layout when you click the template name in the list. We chose Header, Left Column, Body.

6. In the Document Library drop-down list, select Dashboards, and then click the Create button. An empty dashboard page displays in your browser, as shown next, and includes an outline of each Web Part zone.

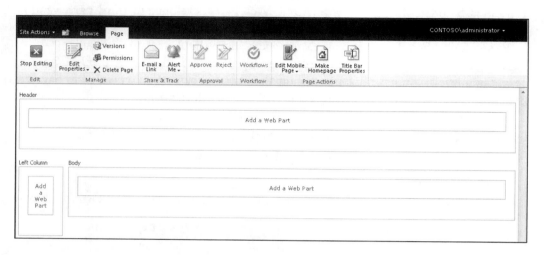

Status List Web Parts

If you already have a status list in your site (which you do if you successfully completed Exercise 8-4), you can easily add the status list to your dashboard. If you find that you need to add more indicators to the status list, you can add them right within the Web Part, but only if you enable the Display Edit Toolbar In View Mode option in the Web Part configuration. Other items that you can configure for the Web Part include the title of the Web Part, its height and width, and the type of icon that displays for the current value.

Exercise 8-6: Configuring a Status List Web Part

1. In the Header section, click the Add A Web Part link.
2. In the Categories pane, select the Business Data folder, as shown here:

3. In the Web Parts pane, select Status List, and then click the Add button.
4. In the Status List Web Part, click the Open The Tool Pane link, as shown:

5. Click the Browse button to the right of the Indicator List box, as you can see here:

6. In the Asset list on the left, select Current Goals. Click the OK button.
7. In the tool pane, select the Display Multiple Indicators Columns check box.
8. In the Status Indicator drop-down list, select Gross Margin.
9. In the Column Or Dimension drop-down list, select Product.
10. In the Hierarchy drop-down list, select Category.
11. Click the filter button for the Members To Display list, select the Accessories and Bikes check boxes, and click the OK button.
12. In the tool pane, click the OK button to view the status list in the dashboard, as shown here:

Reporting Services Web Parts

When you want precise control over the appearance of information in your dashboard, you should create a report in Reporting Services and then embed the report in the dashboard by using the Report Viewer Web Part. If you are running Reporting Services in SharePoint integrated mode, the Report Viewer Web Part installs automatically when you activate Reporting Services for the site collection. When you configure this Web Part, you can override default parameter values manually or by connecting a filter. You can also specify which buttons appear on the Report Viewer toolbar to control the type of interactivity available to the user. For example, you can prevent the user from exporting or printing the report.

NOTE

If your SharePoint site is not running Reporting Services in SharePoint integrated mode, you can skip this exercise.

Exercise 8-7: Configuring a Reporting Services Web Part

1. In the Left Column section, click the Add A Web Part link.
2. In the Categories pane, select the SQL Server Reporting folder, and then click the Add button.
3. In the Report Viewer Web Part, click the Click Here To Open The Tool Pane link.
4. You might need to scroll up in the browser window to view the tool pane. Click the button to the right of the Report box.
5. Navigate to the documents library containing the report (example: http:// servername/sites/BI/Documents), select the Gross Margin By Reseller Type report, and click the OK button.
6. In the tool pane, expand the View section, and then clear the Autogenerate Web Part Title check box.
7. Clear the Show Page Navigation Controls, Show Back Button, and Show Find Controls check boxes. Eliminating these items from the report viewer header reduces the horizontal width requirement for the Web Part.
8. In the Prompt Area drop-down list, select Collapsed.

9. Expand the Parameters section, and click the Load Parameters button. You can override the report default for any or all parameters that appear in the report.

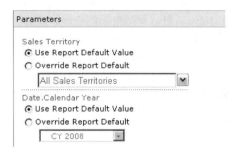

10. Clear the Show Page Navigation Controls, Show Back Button, and Show Find Controls check boxes.
11. Expand the Appearance section, and change the title to **Gross Margin by Reseller Type**.
12. In the Height area, set the Height property to 240 pixels.
13. In the Width area, select Yes and set the value to 450 pixels.
14. Click the OK button.

Chart Web Parts

You can use the new Chart Web Part to retrieve data from a source and then display the results in chart form. When you create a new Chart Web Part, you start by specifying the data source, which can be data from another Web Part on the same dashboard page or data from a SharePoint list, a Business Data Catalog, or Excel Services. Use the Chart Web Part when you don't have—or don't want to use—Reporting Services or PerformancePoint Services to display charts.

In this exercise, we'll focus more on the Web Part configuration. In Chapter 10, you can learn more about the data visualization features of the Chart Web Part.

Exercise 8-8: Configuring a Chart Web Part

1. In the Left Column section, click the Add A Web Part link.
2. In the Categories pane, select the Business Data folder, select Chart Web Part, and then click the Add button.
3. In the Chart Web Part, click the Data & Appearance link.
4. On the Data Connection Wizard page, click the Connect Chart To Data link.

5. On Step 1: Choose A Data Source, select the Connect To Excel Services option, and click the Next button.

6. On Step 2: Connect To Data From Excel Services, in the Excel Workbook Path box, type the path to the workbook, which will be similar to this: http://intranet/ sites/BI/Documents/Sales Analysis.xlsx.

7. In the Range Name box, QuotavsSales!$A$2:$C$5. Click the Next button.

8. On Step 3: Retrieve And Filter Data, you see a preview of the data, as shown in the following illustration. You can apply a filter in this step if you need to focus the data visualization results on a few key resources. Click the Next button.

Row Labels	Sales Amount	Sales Amount Quota
Europe	19800577.0623	23077600
North America	79353361.1796	85676000
Pacific	10655335.9611	2332300

Preview: First **3** of **3** records.

9. On Step 4: Bind Chart To Data, expand the Series Properties section and type **Sales** in the Series Name box, as you can see here:

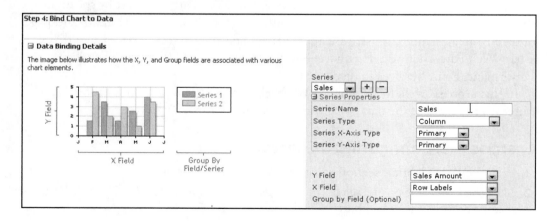

10. Click the plus sign next to the Series drop-down list, replace the Series Name value with Quota, and then select Sales Amount Quota in the Y Field drop-down list, as shown:

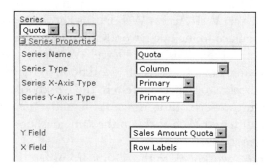

11. Click the Finish button. Your chart is now complete. You can use the Advanced Properties link to explore the charting capabilities even more, but we'll save our discussion of the chart details for Chapter 10.

12. When you point to the Web Part's title bar, the drop-down arrow appears in the upper-right corner of the Web Part. Click the arrow to display the Web Part menu, shown next, and then click Edit Web Part to open the tool pane.

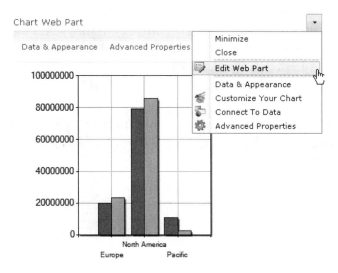

13. In the Appearance section, change the title to **Quota vs Sales**.

14. Change the Height property to 400.

15. Click the OK button.

Excel Web Access Web Parts

As you learned in Chapter 4, you can publish Excel workbooks to a SharePoint site that anyone (with permissions) can then view directly in a browser using the Excel Web Application. The Excel Web Access Web Part is another version of the Excel Web Application that you use to include a workbook into a dashboard page. Although you can display an entire workbook using the Excel Web Access Web Part, you should generally aim for displaying small sections of a workbook in the Web Part. You can go so far as to restrict the display to a specific item in the workbook, such as a chart or a pivot table. Or you can use a viewer drop-down list to allow the user to switch between items. You can also use different Web Parts on the same dashboard page to display different items in the workbook.

Let's add a chart from a workbook to the dashboard page.

Exercise 8-9: Configuring an Excel Web Access Web Part

1. In the Body section of the dashboard, click the Add A Web Part link.
2. In the Categories pane, select the Business Data folder, select Excel Web Access, and then click the Add button.
3. In the newly added part, click the Click Here To Open The Tool Pane link.
4. Click the button to the right of the Workbook box.
5. In the Asset list on the left, select Documents and then select Sales Analysis. Click the OK button.
6. In the Named Item box, type **Chart 1**.
7. Clear the Autogenerate Web Part Title and Named Item Drop-down List check boxes.
8. Expand the Appearance section, and change the title to **Sales Analysis**.
9. Click the OK button. A portion of the workbook now displays in the dashboard, as shown next:

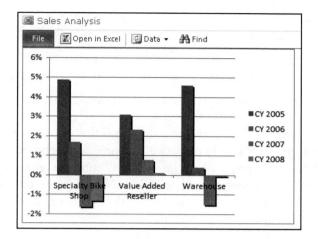

Filters

The display of multiple items on a dashboard page can be useful. However, the addition of a filter to the dashboard page provides multiple perspectives of your data with relatively little effort. As you create a filter, you first must decide how to prompt the user to supply a value. Will the user type in a value directly, which we don't recommend, or will you provide the user with a list from which the user can select one or more values? If you provide a list, where does this list come from? The answer to these questions determines which Filter Web Part that you should use. You can choose from the following filter types:

- ▶ Choice, which requires you to supply a list of values manually
- ▶ Current User, which passes properties associated with the current user to connected Web Parts
- ▶ Date, which allows the user to use a calendar control to select a date
- ▶ Page Field, which passes information about the current page to connected Web Parts
- ▶ Query String (URL), which passes a query string in the URL to connected Web Parts

► SharePoint List, which allows the user to select one or more values from an existing SharePoint list

► SQL Server Analysis Services, which allows the user to select one or more values from a list generated from a dimension and hierarchy that you specify

► Text, which allows the user to type a value that passes to connected Web Parts

When the user makes a selection, you need to send this value to one or more Web Parts. The Web Part must be able to consume the value as-is. For example, if you use the SQL Server Analysis Services filter, the user's selection passes to connected Web Parts in its MDX unique name format. But if that Web Part uses data from a SQL Server database, it has no way to translate the MDX unique name format into a value that the database engine understands how to use as a filter.

To help you better understand what that means, let's use an Analysis Services filter correctly in the following exercise. That is, we'll connect it to Web Parts that are able to accept the MDX unique name.

Exercise 8-10: Adding a Filter

1. In the dashboard's Body section, click the Add A Web Part link.

2. In the Categories pane, select the Filters folder.

3. Select SQL Server Analysis Services Filter, and then click the Add button. At this point, the filter appears above the Excel Web Access Web Part, but we want to move it to a lower section of the dashboard. You can either drag the Web Part by its title bar to a position below the Excel Web Access Web Part, or you can change a property in the tool pane, which we'll do later in this exercise.

4. In the Filter Web Part, click the Open The Tool Pane link.

5. Change the filter name to **Sales Territory**.

Notice in the next illustration that the ODC for the status list appears automatically because we started the development of this dashboard with a status list that was already associated with an ODC.

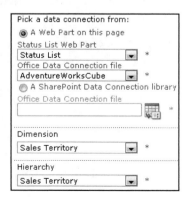

6. In the Dimension drop-down list, select Sales Territory.

7. In the Hierarchy drop-down list, select Sales Territory.

8. Expand the Advanced Filter Options section.

9. In the Default Value box, type **[Sales Territory].[Sales Territory].[All Sales Territories]**.

10. Expand the Layout section, and change the Zone Index value to move it below the Excel Web Access Web Part.

11. Click the OK button to complete the filter configuration. Notice in the following illustration that the filter is sending values to Status List, but when we look closer in a moment, we'll see that it's sending Status Indicator Value instead of sending filter values.

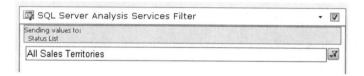

12. Click the arrow in the top-right corner of the Filter Web Part, point to Connections, point to Send Status Indicator Value To, and click Status List. Click the OK button to confirm removal of the connection.

13. Now let's add the correct connection. Click the arrow in the top-right corner of the Filter Web Part, point to Connections, point to Send Filter Values To, and click Status List. If you have pop-ups blocked in your browser, you will need to allow the pop-up to continue.

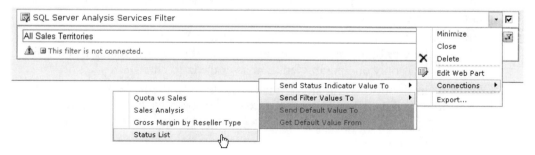

14. In the Configure Connection dialog box, select [Sales Territory].[Sales Territory] in the Filtered Parameter drop-down list (as shown next), and then click the Finish button.

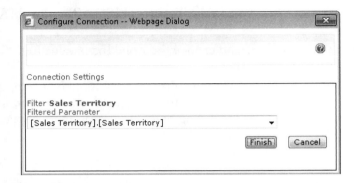

15. Notice the status bar in the Status List indicates a filter has been applied.

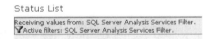

16. Click the arrow in the top-right corner of the Filter Web Part, point to Connections, point to Send Filter Values To, and click Gross Margin By Reseller Type. There is only one parameter in this report, so with nothing here to change, let's click the Finish button. This step connects the filter to the Report Viewer Web Part.

17. Click the arrow in the top-right corner of the Filter Web Part, point to Connections, point to Send Filter Values To, and click Sales Analysis.

18. In the Connection Type drop-down list, select Get Values For Multiple P, and then click the Configure button to open the second tab in the dialog box. Again, because there is only one parameter, there is nothing to change.

19. Click the Finish button. This step connects the filter to the Excel Web Access Web Part. If prompted with a warning about external queries, click the Yes button.

20. Click the Stop Editing button in the ribbon. Now all Web Parts except the Chart Web Part are connected to the filter.

21. Click the Filter icon in the Filter Web Part, clear the All Sales Territories check box, select Europe, and click the OK button to view the filtered results, as shown next.

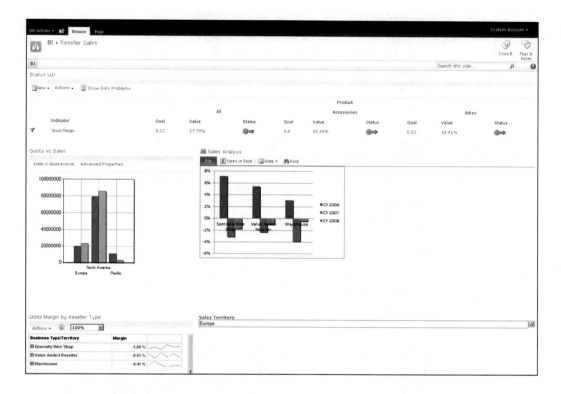

Your dashboard now contains four different types of Web Parts that display business intelligence information and one Filter Web Part for modifying the contents of three of those Web Parts. You can continue adding as many Web Parts as necessary to communicate important information about your business. Keep in mind that you're not limited to displaying data from databases here. Feel free to add text-based content, images, issues lists, or other types of content. For now, you might be thinking this dashboard page could use another Web Part in the bottom-right area to balance it out. We'll fill that gap by using a Web Part for a scorecard that we'll create in the next chapter.

Summary

Now that you've seen how to integrate different business intelligence tools in this chapter, you might be overwhelmed by the number of options that you have for displaying information and key performance indicators. Although there is some overlap between the tools, the main differences among the tools are the data sources that each supports, the amount of control that you have over the appearance and layout of the data, and the

Tool	Supported Data Sources	Appearance and Layout Control	Reusability
Status List	Analysis Services Excel Services Fixed value SharePoint list	Low	Status List SharePoint Dashboard
Reporting Services	Analysis Services Hyperion Essbase OLE DB/ODBC Oracle SAP NetWeaver BI SharePoint List SQL Server Teradata XML	High	Report SharePoint Dashboard PerformancePoint Dashboard
Chart Web Part	Business Data Catalog Excel Services SharePoint List Web Part	Medium	SharePoint Dashboard
Excel Services	Analysis Services OLE DB/ODBC SQL Server XML	Medium	Excel Web Access SharePoint Dashboard PerformancePoint Dashboard

Table 8-1   *Business Intelligence Tool Comparison*

reusability of information that you prepare in the tool. Table 8-1 summarizes the tools we described in this chapter according to these criteria.

This chapter introduced you to the key business intelligence features available in SharePoint 2010. If you take advantage of these features along with the other collaboration and content management features of SharePoint, which are too extensive to cover in this chapter, you can help people better integrate business intelligence into their daily activities, and isn't that a worthy goal? In this chapter, we focused on dashboard functionality without regard for design principles. If you'd like to learn more on this topic, we recommend *Information Dashboard Design: The Effective Visual Communication of Data* by Stephen Few (O'Reilly Media, 2006). In the next chapter, we'll explore the dashboard and scorecard features available in PerformancePoint Services that provide more advanced capabilities than we discovered in this chapter.

Chapter 9

Scorecards and Dashboards

In This Chapter

- ▶ PerformancePoint Services
- ▶ Building Scorecards
- ▶ PerformancePoint Reports
- ▶ Building Dashboards
- ▶ Summary

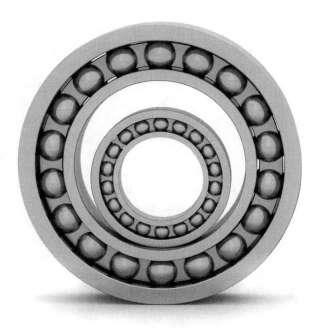

The SharePoint features that we explored in the previous chapters make it easy to put together a basic dashboard from components that were created for other purposes. With more planning, you can create scorecards and more advanced dashboards by using PerformancePoint Services. Even if you don't need a scorecard or a dashboard, you might consider creating some of the PerformancePoint report types, which you can view independently of a dashboard, to support more interactive analysis than you can provide with Excel workbooks or Reporting Services reports.

PerformancePoint Services

PerformancePoint Services runs as a service application in SharePoint 2010. It was designed for a SharePoint administrator to configure the service on the SharePoint farm, and then for power users to create PerformancePoint content types that can be combined later into either scorecards or dashboards. Dashboard Designer is the tool they use to create these content types, which they then store and secure in SharePoint.

PerformancePoint Content Types

Some PerformancePoint content types are directly accessible by users, while other content types serve in a supporting role. The three user-facing content types are scorecards, dashboards, and analytic reports. PerformancePoint dashboards are similar to SharePoint dashboards in the way that they allow you to combine multiple items on the same page. You can embed scorecards and analytical reports in PerformancePoint dashboards and SharePoint dashboards, or you can view them as stand-alone reports in the PerformancePoint Content list. The other content types include data sources, indicators, KPIs, filters, and other nonanalytic reports.

Before we continue, let's clarify some terminology. A *content type* is a term that describes the content that you store in SharePoint lists and libraries. SharePoint allows you to define metadata for each content type, establish workflows by content type, and create new items based on a template for the content type. An *item* is the instantiation of a content type, which you create by using the Dashboard Designer and then store in SharePoint lists and libraries, as shown in Table 9-1.

The advantage of storing PerformancePoint content in lists and libraries is the ability to leverage SharePoint features. For example, you can use a single security model to limit access to PerformancePoint items. You can also take advantage of the ability to check items in and out. Finally, versioning is enabled by default, so you can easily revert back to a prior version of an item when the need arises.

Figure 9-1 shows the relationship between PerformancePoint content types in the construction of a dashboard. Notice that you use data sources to create almost every content type except an indicator and two report types. To create a KPI, you must first create a data source and an indicator (or use a built-in indicator). An *indicator* in

SharePoint Location	Content Type
Dashboards document library	Dashboard (published)
Data Connections document library	Data Source
PerformancePoint Content list	Dashboard (unpublished) Filter Indicator KPI Reports Scorecard

Table 9-1   *Storage Locations in SharePoint by PerformancePoint Content Type*

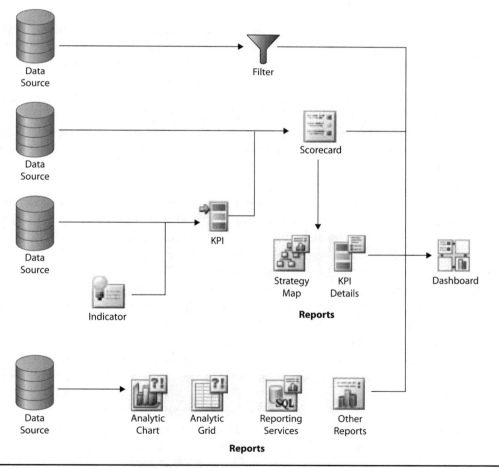

Figure 9-1   *Relationships between PerformancePoint content types*

PerformancePoint Services is an image, such as a flag, a traffic light, or a gauge. When you assign an indicator to a KPI, you specify the rules that determine how the indicator displays, such as a red flag for a low score or a green flag for a high score. You use KPIs to create a scorecard, which in turn has its own dependency on data sources so that you can display KPIs for selected dimension members. KPI Details and Strategy Maps use a data source indirectly because they are based on a scorecard. You also use a data source to create a filter, which is an optional content type that works much like the filter introduced in the previous chapter, to modify the information that displays in a dashboard. In addition, each type of report requires a data source, except the two we already mentioned. After creating filters, scorecards, and reports, you link all items together in a dashboard.

Dashboard Designer

Dashboard Designer is the application that you use to create a variety of content types needed for scorecards and dashboards. It integrates with SharePoint by storing content in lists and document libraries and by accessing content from these locations for reuse by other dashboard authors. You can use it to quickly build one or more items, or you can use it to create and manage a workspace file when you want to save item definitions to your local computer. A workspace file is analogous to a project file in BIDS or Visual Studio; it's simply a container for related items, but you're not required to save it if you want to work on items one at a time. You might consider using a workspace file when you have a lot of items that you're using to build a complex scorecard or dashboard and require an extended period to complete your work.

You can start Dashboard Designer from the first page of Business Intelligence Center if the default home page is still in place. Just navigate to the Business Intelligence Center, point to Monitor Key Performance, click Start Using PerformancePoint Services, and then click the Run Dashboard Designer button. As an alternative, Dashboard Designer launches automatically when you use the New Document option in the Data Connections library or the New Item option in the PerformancePoint Content list, as shown in Figure 9-2. Or you can double-click an existing PerformancePoint item in the Data Connections library or PerformancePoint Content list.

When you start Dashboard Designer, it creates an empty workspace file. Below the ribbon, you see the Workspace Browser pane on the left and a center pane to the right. The user interface in the center pane changes when you select a different item in the Workspace Browser.

In a new workspace, you can select only category items, Data Connections, or PerformancePoint Content. If you have already saved PerformancePoint items to SharePoint, you can see a list of those items when you click a category item, as shown in Figure 9-3. You can add a SharePoint item to your workspace file by double-clicking

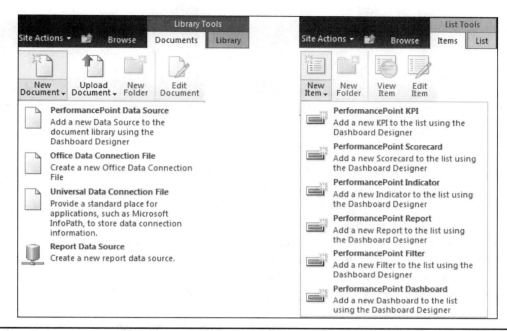

Figure 9-2   *Creating new PerformancePoint items*

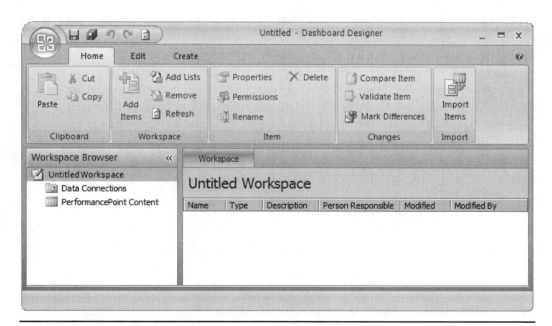

Figure 9-3   *List of published items in Dashboard Designer*

Figure 9-4 *Create tab of Dashboard Designer ribbon*

the item in the list. If you click the Workspace tab in the center pane, you can view a list of all items that are part of the current workspace file, whether you imported those items from SharePoint or created them for the current workspace. As you import or create items, they appear in the Workspace Browser beneath their respective categories.

To create new items, you use the Create tab of the ribbon, shown in Figure 9-4. You must first select a category in the Workspace Browser to activate the applicable buttons in the ribbon. If you select Data Connections, Data Source is the only available button, but when you select PerformancePoint Content, all buttons except Data Source are available.

As you work on items in Dashboard Designer, a pencil symbol appears with the item's icon in the Workspace Browser, as you can see in Figure 9-5. This symbol provides you with a visual cue that the item currently exists only in your workspace and is not yet saved to SharePoint. You can press CTRL-S to save it, click the Save icon in the Quick Access toolbar above the ribbon, or click the File button in the upper-left corner of the application window to access commands to save your work.

The Details pane appears to the right of the center pane whenever you select an item in the Workspace Browser. When you select a data source, a KPI, an indicator, or a filter, the Details pane provides a list of related items. For example, the Details pane for a KPI, shown in Figure 9-6, displays the data source and indicator that are part of the KPI definition and the scorecard that includes the KPI. Other content types, such as analytic reports, scorecards, and dashboards, use the Details pane to display items that you can use to design the current item, as you'll see when you perform the exercises later in this chapter.

We need to make one final point about Dashboard Designer before we move on to a closer look at PerformancePoint content types. As you view items that have been saved previously to SharePoint or save items as you work in Dashboard Designer, you can use

Figure 9-5 *The pencil symbol indicates an unsaved item.*

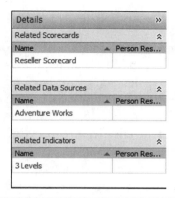

Figure 9-6   *Details pane for a KPI*

only one site collection at a time. More specifically, the same site collection from which you launched Dashboard Designer is the location for the SharePoint lists and libraries that you access during your design session. If you need to use content from a different site collection, click the Add Lists button on the Home tab of the ribbon, and you can then use the Workspace Browser to locate items in the added lists. To change the target site collection of items that you save, click the File button, click the Designer Options button, click the Server tab in the Options dialog box, and change the SharePoint URL to the URL for the alternate site collection.

Building Scorecards

As we explained in Chapter 1, a scorecard is a special type of report that you use to compare actual values to target values, much like the status list in SharePoint. However, the scorecard has more advanced features to allow the viewer to drill down into greater detail and access analytic tools for slicing and dicing the data. Not only does a scorecard support more interactivity, but it also allows you to access a broader variety of data sources than the status list. Furthermore, you can use a different data source for an actual value than you use for a target value. This feature is particularly useful when you have an Analysis Services cube available for actual values, but the target values are available only in an Excel workbook.

To build a scorecard in the Dashboard Designer, you must first create at least one data source and one KPI. The KPI itself requires a data source and an indicator that you create or select from a built-in collection. Once you have all the base items ready, you can assemble the scorecard by arranging the KPIs with dimension members in a layout of rows and columns. You must add the scorecard to a dashboard to enable users to view it.

Data Sources

Data sources are the foundation for most of the items that you create for PerformancePoint Services. KPIs, scorecards, reports, and filters all require a data source. Unlike other reporting or analytics tools with which you might be familiar, the data source definition is much more than the location and authentication information that PerformancePoint Services uses to connect to a data source. More specifically, the data source includes properties used for the Time Intelligence feature in PerformancePoint Services. Time Intelligence allows you to support time-based analysis for points in time, which you might use to compare one quarter to a previous quarter. You can also use Time Intelligence for date ranges, which you might use to display values for a cumulative period, like year-to-date, or a set of periods, like the previous ten days.

Using the data source workspace in Dashboard Designer, you configure connection settings, data source settings, and Time Intelligence. If you're working with one of the tabular data sources—that is, a data source other than Analysis Services—you must specify column definitions. Let's take a look at each of these configuration settings separately.

Connection Settings

As you might expect, the connection settings depend on the type of data source that you're configuring. Table 9-2 describes the information required to configure the connection settings by data source type.

Data Source Type	Connection Settings
Analysis Services	Server name, database name, cube name or Connection string
Excel Services	SharePoint site, document library, workbook, named item (optional), parameter value (if applicable)
Excel Workbook	File name, if importing data
SharePoint List	SharePoint site, SharePoint site list, list
SQL Server Table	Server name, database name, table name or Connection string

Table 9-2   *Data Source Connection Setting Requirements*

Analysis Services is the best data source type to use with PerformancePoint Services overall, especially when you're working with data that is larger than 10,000 rows, because an Analysis Services cube is optimized for fast query performance. You can also use a PowerPivot workbook just as you would use an Analysis Services cube, except that you use a connection string rather than selecting connection settings from drop-down lists. A connection string for a PowerPivot workbook might look something like this:

> Provider=MSOLAP;Data Source=http://intranet/PowerPivot Gallery/ myWorkbook.xlsx

where you use the workbook's URL as the data source. Accessing data in a PowerPivot workbook might give you better performance than you might experience if you try to access data directly from the other available data source types.

When you use one of the other available data source types, PerformancePoint Services aggregates the data into a structure that is similar to a cube, but this simulated cube won't give you the same performance optimizations that already are built into Analysis Services. Although your next best option is to use data in a SQL Server table or view, you might find that users are managing small data sets independently of the IT department by using SharePoint lists or workbooks published to Excel Services. Fortunately, you can easily make these data sources available to PerformancePoint Services. It's even possible to simply import data from an Excel workbook that's not stored in Excel Services or to create data and store it in an internal Excel workbook solely for use in PerformancePoint Services.

Data Source Settings

Like the connection settings, the data source settings also depend on the type of data source. In general, all data source types require you to specify the authentication method and a refresh rate for the data source, but your options for these settings vary by data source type. Also, if you're using an Analysis Services data source, you must specify a formatting dimension.

Let's start with a review of the options for the authentication method.

▶ **Unattended Service Account**   The service application administrator for PerformancePoint Services configures this account on the SharePoint server to provide a single, low-privileged Windows login that connects to a data source on behalf of the current user. The unattended service account must have read permission for the data source. This option is the simplest authentication method to implement. Furthermore, users are more likely to benefit from caching.

► **Unattended Service Account And Add Authenticated User In The Connection String** This authentication method applies only to an Analysis Services data source. PerformancePoint Services connects to the defined cube using the unattended service account, but includes the user's name in the "CustomData" property in the connection string. You can then use the CustomData() function in an MDX expression to read the property value and apply security dynamically to a cell or a dimension. Although this option provides you with an alternative to Kerberos delegation when you need to restrict access to data by user, it does require you to spend more time configuring cell- and dimension-level security in the cube.

► **Per User Identity** This option sends the user's Windows credentials to the data source. This means you cannot use anonymous logins or forms authentication. Furthermore, this method of authentication works only under certain conditions. You can use it when you run SharePoint in a stand-alone mode and the data source is on the same machine, or when you configure Kerberos delegation or claims-based authentication on your SharePoint server and your data source is located on a separate server. Using Per User Identity is necessary when you want to restrict the data by user, but it requires more effort to implement correctly in a multiserver environment. Moreover, caching might be less effective because each user sees different data and the cache mechanism is unable to share query results across multiple users.

Another data source setting relates to caching. Analysis Services and SharePoint List data sources refer to this setting as the cache lifetime, whereas Excel Services and SQL Server refer to it instead as the refresh interval. (Because you maintain the Excel Workbook data source strictly within Dashboard Designer, there is no cache-related setting for this data source type.) The default setting for caching is ten minutes, which should be adequate for most situations. If a cache does not exist or has expired when a user views one of the user-facing content types, the applicable queries execute and the results are stored in cache to speed up requests for the same data at a later time. Changes to the underlying data in a SharePoint list, Excel Services, or SQL Server are only visible to the user after the cache expires and PerformancePoint Services queries the data source again. On the other hand, processing an Analysis Services cube expires the cache. However, processing typically occurs on a daily basis, or sometimes less frequently, so you might consider extending the cache lifetime for this data source type for better performance.

Time Intelligence

Scorecards and dashboards often include a time element. In other words, you use these types of reports to compare one time period to another time period or to show values for a specific data range. But remember one of the advantages of using PerformancePoint Services is the ability to use different data sources to display results in these reports. You need a way to handle time consistently across multiple data sources. Fortunately, PerformancePoint Services uses Time Intelligence as a type of lingua franca that allows you to easily describe what you need to display without the hassle of writing code in each data source's native language.

This process is different among Analysis Services and the other data sources. With Analysis Services, you select a hierarchy in a date dimension (which Dashboard Designer refers to as a Time Dimension). You then select a member from this dimension to represent the first day of a year, which would be January 1 of a specific year if the Time Dimension is a calendar year hierarchy, or the fiscal year start date if the Time Dimension is a fiscal year hierarchy. Alternatively, you could choose a starting month or quarter as the reference member if your cube does not use Day at the most granular level. Because you have this flexibility in granularity, you must specify a hierarchy level for the selected reference member. Your next step is to use a Date Picker control to select the date that corresponds to the reference member. Last, you associate each level in the dimension's hierarchy to a Time Aggregation label that PerformancePoint Services uses to conform time across data sources. You can see an example of the Time Intelligence settings for an Analysis Services data source in Figure 9-7.

For other data source types, Dashboard Designer detects the date columns and displays these columns as a list of Time Dimensions. If you don't see any date columns, you will need to specify a TimeDimension column on the View tab, which we'll explain shortly. You must select a column in this list as the Master column and then select the levels of time that you want to use for Time Intelligence, such as Day, Month, or Year, as shown in Figure 9-8. You must also specify the Fiscal Start Month to align the first day of the year across data sources.

Column Definitions

PerformancePoint Services uses column definitions to generate the equivalent of a cube structure for tabular data sources. To access the column definitions, select a tabular data source in the Workspace Browser, and then click the View tab in the center pane. Dashboard Designer displays the columns in the data source and assigns default

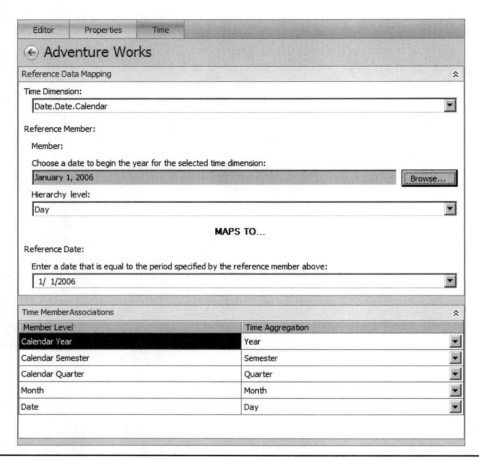

Figure 9-7   *Analysis Services Time Intelligence settings*

properties to each column, which you can view by clicking a column. To make it easier to understand the structure of the data so that you can correct the column definition properties where necessary, you can click the Preview Data button to display a subset of the data, as shown in Figure 9-9.

For each column, you specify a column name that displays when you work with the data source and a column unique name that PerformancePoint Services uses internally. You can generally leave those values as you find them without a problem, but to get proper results from the data source, you must check the column type of each column and change the remaining properties as needed according to Table 9-3.

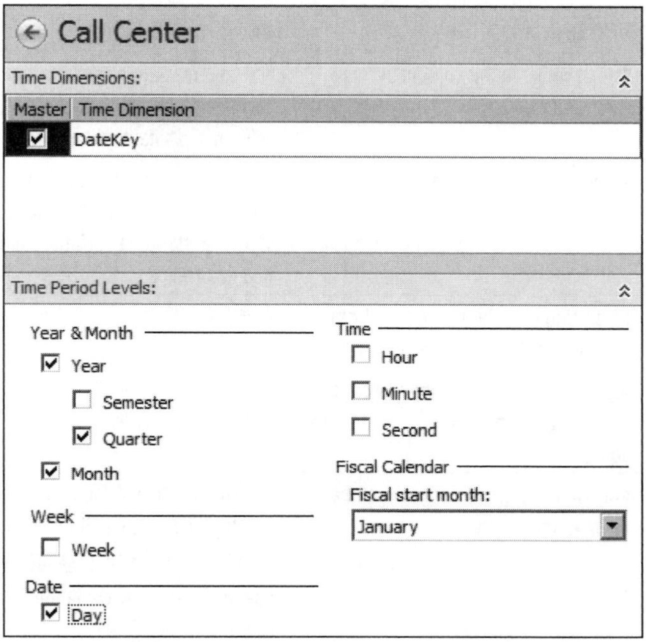

Figure 9-8   *Time Intelligence settings for a tabular data source*

Because Analysis Services is our best option as a data source in PerformancePoint Services, we'll create a data source based on the sample AdventureWorks cube from Chapter 3. We'll be able to use this same data source for a KPI, a scorecard, an analytic chart, and a filter that we'll build in other exercises in this chapter.

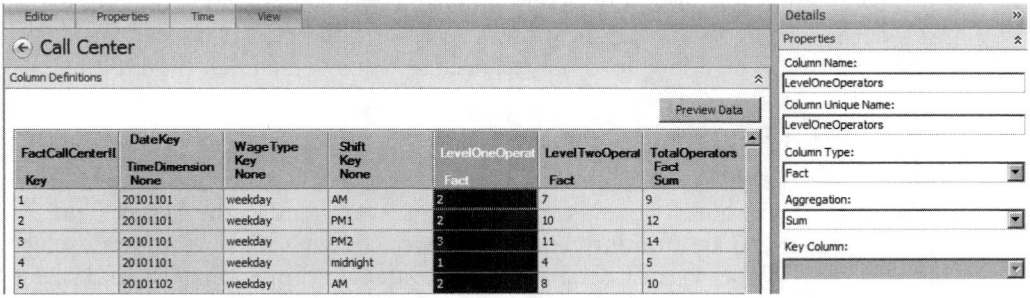

Figure 9-9   *Column definitions for a tabular data source*

Column Type	Description	Additional Settings
Dimension	Distinct values in this column become dimension members	Key Column: Select a column that uniquely identifies each member if the data source contains both a key column and a name column for a dimension
Fact	Values in this column aggregate like a measure in a cube	Aggregation: Specify one of the following aggregation functions: average, count, maximum, minimum, none, statistical standard deviation, sum, statistical variance, first occurrence
Ignore	This setting excludes the column from processing by PerformancePoint Services	
Key	Values in this column uniquely identify each record or dimension member in the source	
TimeDimension	Values in this column become members of the Time Dimension	Key Column: If applicable, specify a column to uniquely identify each member if the data source contains both a key column and a name column for the Time Dimension Use the Time tab to configure Time Intelligence for this column

Table 9-3   *Column Types for Tabular Data Sources*

Exercise 9-1: Creating a Data Source

1. In your browser, open the Business Intelligence Center site that you used in Chapter 8, and then click the Data Connections link in the Quick Launch panel.

2. On the Documents tab in the ribbon, click the arrow icon next to New Document, and then click PerformancePoint Data Source to launch the Dashboard Designer. If Dashboard Designer has not yet installed, this "click-once" application will download from the SharePoint server and install permanently on your computer, just like the Report Builder application that we introduced in Chapter 7. Updates to the application will download only as needed when you launch the Dashboard Designer.

3. In the Select A Data Source Template dialog box, select Analysis Services, and click the OK button.

4. In the New Data Source workspace, type your server name in the Server field (or **localhost** if you are running Analysis Services on your local computer), select the AdventureWorks sample database in the Database drop-down list, and select the AdventureWorks cube in the Cube drop-down list.

5. Click the Properties tab in the New Data Source workspace, and type **AdventureWorks** in the Name field.

6. Click the Time tab, and then select Date.Date.Calendar in the Time Dimension drop-down list.

7. Click the Browse button, expand All Periods, expand CY 2006, expand H1 CY 2006, expand Q1 CY 2006, expand January 2006, select January 1, 2006, and click the OK button.

8. In the Hierarchy Level drop-down list, select Day.

9. In the Reference Date drop-down list, click the year in the date picker header, click the left arrow button until the year is 2006, click Jan, and then click 1 to set the date to 1/1/2006.

10. In the Time Member Associations section, set the values in each Time Aggregation drop-down list to match Figure 9-7.

11. Click the File button in the upper-left corner, and then click Save Item as shown here. When you save the data source, the Dashboard Designer saves it as a new item in the Data Connections library in your SharePoint site.

At this point, you could save the data source as part of a workspace or close Dashboard Designer. We'll assume that you'll leave the application open to continue with subsequent exercises in this chapter. If you decide to save the workspace instead, you can launch Dashboard Designer and open the saved workspace to continue with the next exercise.

Indicators

Although an indicator appears as a single item in the Workspace Browser, it's really a collection of graphical images, static text, and fill colors that you later associate with scores when you assign the indicator to a KPI. As you'll see later when we discuss KPIs in more detail, a *score* is the result of the comparison between an actual and a target value.

Dashboard Designer includes many predefined indicators, which you can use "as is" or modify to better meet your needs. Alternatively, you can start with a blank indicator, add custom images (using BMP, GIF, JPG, or PNG formats), and set the text and fill properties manually. In Figure 9-10, you can see several examples of the built-in indicators available. From left to right, the figure shows cylinders, a bar, a gauge, and two different kinds of stoplights.

In addition to deciding the visual characteristics of an indicator, you must decide whether to use a standard or centered indicator. When you use a standard indicator, the target is either at the high end or low end of a range of values. For example, when you have a sales quota as a target, you might display an indicator that shows actual sales as a percentage of the sales quota, with 0 at the low end of the value range and 100 at the high end.

Another way to display a result is to use a centered indicator in which the target is in the middle. In that case, the indicator shows how far away from the center the actual is. This type of indicator is useful when a value that is much higher or much lower than the target is undesirable, such as the variance in the actual length of a product as compared to the product specifications in manufacturing.

You define the visual characteristics of an indicator—that is, the image, text, and colors—separately for each level. An indicator can have from two to ten levels. These levels will eventually correspond to specific ranges for KPI scores. That way, you can use the same indicator with multiple KPIs that use different value ranges for their scores. Figure 9-11 shows the default settings for a standard indicator with three levels.

Figure 9-10   *Examples of indicators*

Level	Display Name	Image	Text Color	Background Color
No Data	No Data	✗	▨	▨
Level 1 (Worst)	Off Target	✗	▨	▪
Level 2	Slightly Off Target	!	▨	☐
Level 3 (Best)	On Target	✔	▨	☐

Figure 9-11   *Standard indicator with three levels*

Next, we'll add an indicator to the workspace that we started in the previous exercise. We'll also customize the display name for each level of the indicator.

Exercise 9-2: Creating an Indicator

1. If PerformancePoint Content already displays in the Workspace Browser, you can skip this step. On the Home tab of the ribbon in Dashboard Designer, click Add Lists, and then click PerformancePoint Content.

2. On the Create tab in the ribbon, click Indicator.

3. In the Category list, select Miscellaneous, select Check A – Small in the Template section as shown, and then click the OK button.

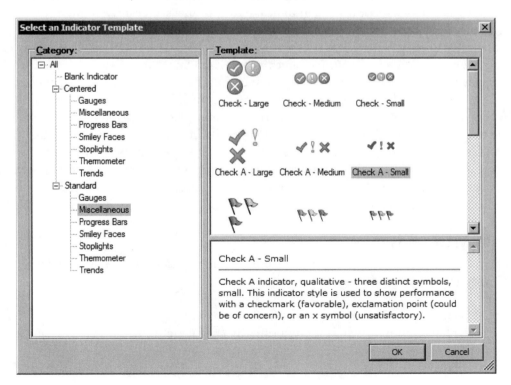

4. In the Workspace Browser, right-click New Indicator, click Rename, and then type a name for the indicator, such as **CheckA**.

5. If you want to change any of the Image, Text Color, or Background Color properties, double-click the cell intersection of the property and level that you want to change. For now, let's change the Display Name properties by changing Off Target to Need Action, Slightly Off Target to Watch, and On Target to Satisfactory as shown here:

Level	Display Name	Image	Text Color	Background Color
No Data	No Data	✖		
Level 1 (Worst)	Need Action	✖		
Level 2	Watch	!		
Level 3 (Best)	Satisfactory	✔		

6. On the Quick Access toolbar above the ribbon, click Save.

KPIs

A KPI is an item that you use exclusively in a scorecard. The KPI calculates a score representing the difference between an actual and a target value, and then presents this score either as raw data or using a graphical indicator in a scorecard. An interesting capability with PerformancePoint KPIs is the ability to use one data source for the actual value and a different data source for the target. Also, each KPI can have both multiple actual values and multiple target values. Each target value has a Compare To property that you use to associate it with a specific actual value for calculating the score.

You can create KPIs manually or import them from an Analysis Services cube. When you create a KPI manually, you start by defining the data mappings for actual and target values, which are also known as *metrics*. Each metric has formatting and calculation properties that you must also configure to properly display KPIs in a scorecard. In addition to these basic settings, each target value requires a scoring pattern for each indicator level. The target's scoring pattern affects how PerformancePoint Services calculates the score and displays the results.

Data Mappings

There are three possible types of data mappings that you can configure for a metric: fixed value, data source, or calculated metric.

▶ **Fixed value**   Selecting a fixed value allows you to enter a specific value for the metric definition, which is useful primarily for a target value that rarely changes and is not readily available from another data source.

▶ **Data source**   Using a data source mapping is the most common selection, and is relatively straightforward to implement. You simply select one of the data sources in your workspace and then select a measure available in that data source, such as a measure if your data source is a cube, as shown in Figure 9-12, or a fact column if you are using a tabular data source. You can also filter by dimension or by using Time Intelligence.

If you're using an Analysis Services data source, you can choose to map the data source to an MDX tuple formula instead of a cube measure. For example, if you have a target value that is based on a 5 percent increase in sales from the previous period, you can use the following formula:

```
([Measures].[Reseller Sales Amount],[Date].[Calendar Year].
PrevMember) * 1.05
```

▶ **Calculated metric**   As we just explained, you can create complex metrics using an MDX tuple formula with an Analysis Services data source, but your formula requires all data to exist in a cube. What if some of your data resides elsewhere? That's where the calculated metric comes in handy. You can create a calculation that operates on values from multiple data sources, even if those data sources are different data source types.

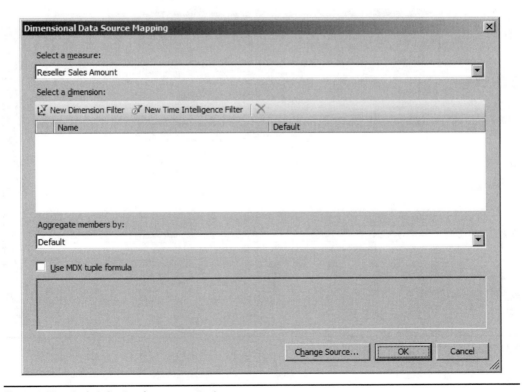

Figure 9-12   *Analysis Services data source mapping*

You start with a blank template for your calculation, or use one of several built-in templates, shown in Figure 9-13. After making a template selection, you map values in each data source to a name that you then use in a formula. For example, to find a simple ratio between two values using the formula Value1/Value2, you assign Value1 to a measure in the first data source and Value2 to a measure in the second data source. It's that simple.

Scoring Pattern

By now, you know that a KPI uses an indicator to display a score calculated from the KPI's metrics and that an indicator has multiple levels to indicate different conditions for the KPI from bad to good at a point in time. A *band* represents the range of score values that you associate with each level, and a *threshold* is the value at which the KPI switches to a new band and displays the version of the indicator assigned to that band. Collectively, the set of bands and thresholds are known as a *scoring pattern*.

Configuration of the scoring pattern begins by defining how the threshold values change from band to band. For standard indicator types, you choose Increasing Is Better when the target is a high value and an actual value that is below the target but

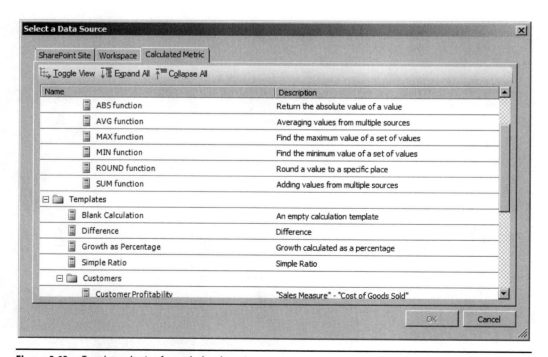

Figure 9-13 *Template selection for a calculated metric*

increasing in value is considered to be improving. For the opposition situation, you choose Decreasing Is Better when the target is a low value and the actual value starts higher than the target but decreases as the situation improves. You use Closer To Target Is Better for centered indicator types.

After selecting the indicator direction, your next step is to specify a banding method. Use Table 9-4 to understand the configuration steps for each banding method.

Now that we have a data source and indicator ready, we can create a KPI that compares the Reseller Sales Amount measure to the Sales Amount Quotas measure in the sample cube.

Exercise 9-3: Creating a KPI

1. On the Create tab in the ribbon, click KPI.
2. In the Select A KPI Template dialog box, select Blank KPI and then click the OK button.
3. In the Workspace Browser, type a name like **Sales Targets** for the KPI.
4. In the Editor, on the Actual row, click the link in the Data Mappings column as shown here:

Name	Compare To	Number	Indicators	Data Mappings	Calculation
Actual		(Default)		1 (Fixed values)	Default
Target	Actual	(Default)	◆ △ ●	1 (Fixed values)	Default

5. In the Fixed Values Data Source Mapping dialog box, click the Change Source button.

Banding Method	Configuration	Result
Band by Actual Values	Specify a best and worst value and threshold values for each level for comparison to the raw actual value	Maps the actual value to the applicable band
Band by Normalized Values	Specify worst value and adjust threshold values for each level as percentages	Maps the ratio (Actual – Worst) / (Target – Worst) to the applicable band
Band by Stated Scores	Specify a data source mapping to a measure that resolves to –1 at worst and 1 at best and ratios for threshold values in between	Maps the query result to the applicable band

Table 9-4 *KPI Banding Methods*

6. In the Select A Data Source dialog box, select the AdventureWorks data source, and then click the OK button.

7. In the Dimensional Data Mapping dialog box, select Reseller Sales Amount in the Measure drop-down list, and then click the OK button.

8. Because in a later exercise we'll combine this KPI with another KPI imported from the AdventureWorks cube, we need to rename the metrics in this KPI. In the Name column, replace Actual with Value.

9. Next, we'll repeat the process for the target value. Click the link in the Data Mappings column on the Target row.

10. In the Fixed Values Data Source Mapping dialog box, click the Change Source button.

11. In the Select A Data Source dialog box, select the AdventureWorks data source, and then click the OK button.

12. In the Dimensional Data Mapping dialog box, select Sales Amount Quota in the Measure drop-down list, and then click the OK button.

13. Rename the target metric by replacing Target with **Goal and Status**.

14. The Dashboard Designer assigns a default indicator to the target and establishes thresholds for each indicator level as the actual value's percentage of the target. Let's first change the indicator. Click the Set Scoring Pattern And Indicator button.

15. The first page of the Edit Banding Settings wizard lets you select a scoring pattern, such as Increasing Is Better, and a banding method. Let's accept the default settings, and click the Next button.

16. On the Select An Indicator page of the wizard, you can choose indicators from the PerformancePoint Content library on your SharePoint site, from the workspace if you have created indicators that you have not yet published to SharePoint, or from a list of the built-in indicators. Click the Workspace tab, select the CheckA indicator that you created in the previous exercise, and then click the Next button.

17. On the Specify The Worst Value page, keep the default value of 0, and click the Finish button.

18. Now let's change the threshold values to set Threshold 2 at 85% and Threshold 1 at 50%, as shown in the following illustration. Just type **85** and **50** in the respective fields to change the values, or use the sliders to the right of the threshold fields. These settings will apply the green check indicator when the actual value is 85 percent of the target or higher, the yellow exclamation point

indicator when the actual value is between 50 percent and 85 percent of the target, and the red X indicator when the actual value is 50 percent or lower of the target.

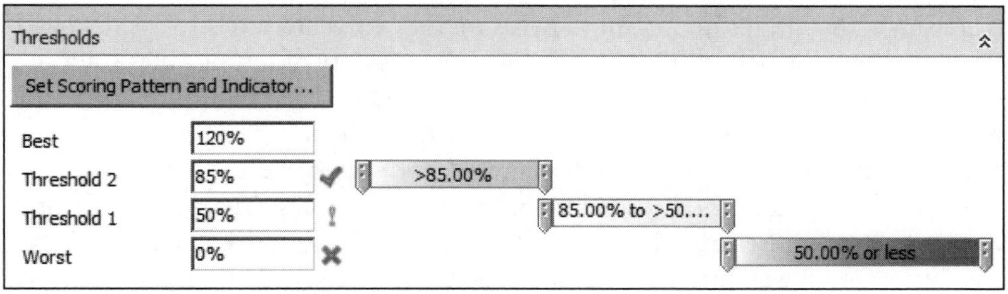

19. Save the item to SharePoint.

Scorecards

There are two ways to create a scorecard. You can start with a blank scorecard and use the editor to manually add items that you've already created. Or you can use the Scorecard Wizard to step through the process. In the latter case, as long as you have at least one data source created, you're all set, because you can create KPIs as you step through the wizard. Using the wizard is an easy way to jumpstart the scorecard design process and, of course, you can make changes to it later.

When you use the Scorecard Wizard, you start by selecting a template, which sets the data source for the default dimensions and other data-related items in the Details pane that you use to design the scorecard. The steps through the Scorecard Wizard depend on the template that you select.

If you select the Analysis Services template, your next step is to select a data source, and then you must choose whether to create KPIs from measures in the cube or to import KPI definitions that already exist in the cube. Ideally, you should maintain KPIs in the cube because they are then available for use in any front-end tool that a user has available to query a cube. If you decide to create a KPI from a measure, you first select an existing measure as the actual metric, then select another existing measure as the target value, and then specify a banding method, as you can see in Figure 9-14. Another option is to choose a KPI that you have in the PerformancePoint Content library.

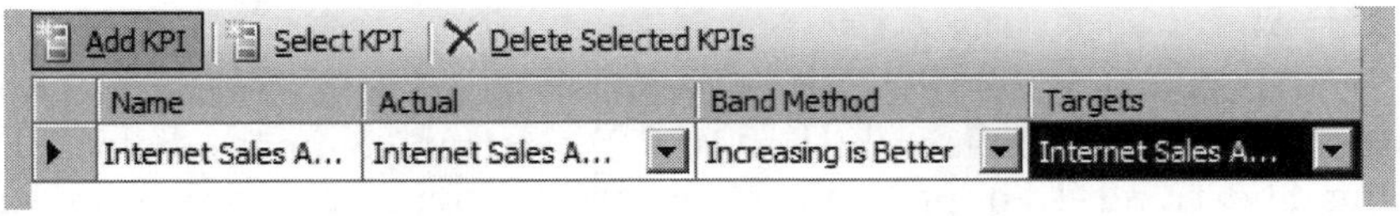

Figure 9-14 *Adding a KPI from a cube by using the Scorecard Wizard*

When you finish the wizard, the Details pane contains all the items in your workspace that you can use in your scorecard design. As you add items to the scorecard, you can use the Update button on the Edit tab of the ribbon to populate the scorecard with data as a preview, although it's important to be aware that the scorecard displays data without filtering it by time period. The Edit tab also has a variety of settings that you can use to enhance the appearance of your scorecard, such as font style, color, and indentation, and to configure settings for the scorecard view, such as interactive features to allow, scorecard and scorecard toolbar elements to display, tool, and status filters.

In the Settings group on the Edit tab, you can access KPI, Metric, and Member Settings. The KPI Settings dialog box allows you to change a KPI's name and assign it a weight for use in weighted average calculations. The Metric Settings dialog box prompts only for a new name if you select an actual metric in the scorecard. However, if you first select a target metric, you have the option not only to change the metric's name, but also to configure how the indicator displays, how scoring rolls up in a scorecard with multiple levels, and how to score the variance between the actual and target metrics. Last, the Member Settings dialog box lets you configure whether to allow dynamic expansion of members and allow the user to drill down within a hierarchy.

Now let's put together all the items we've created thus far into a scorecard.

Exercise 9-4: Creating a Scorecard

1. On the Create tab in the ribbon, click Scorecard.

2. In the Select A Scorecard Template dialog box, select Analysis Services. Make sure the Use Wizards To Create Scorecards check box is selected, and then click the OK button.

3. On the Select A Data Source page of the Create An Analysis Services Scorecard Wizard, select the AdventureWorks data source, and then click the Next button.

4. On the Select A KPI Source page of the wizard, select the Import SQL Server Analysis Services KPIs option, and click the Next button.

5. On the Select KPIs To Import page, select the Product Gross Profit Margin check box, and click the Next button.

6. Click the Next button two more times to accept the default settings (that is, no measure filters and no member columns), and then click the Finish button on the Locations page of the wizard. The Dashboard Designer will save the KPIs to the PerformancePoint Content list unless you first choose a different location on this page.

7. In the Workspace Browser, type a name for the scorecard, **Reseller Scorecard**. The scorecard now displays the KPI with the default columns—Value, Goal and Status, and Trend. To improve the appearance of the scorecard metrics, you can change the formatting of Value and Goal.

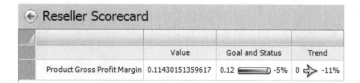

8. Click the new KPI that now appears in the Workspace Browser, Product Gross Profit Margin, and then click the Default link in the Number Format column on the Value row.

9. In the Format Numbers dialog box, select Percentage in the Format drop-down list as shown next, and then click the OK button. Repeat these steps to set the number format for Goal and Status to percentage.

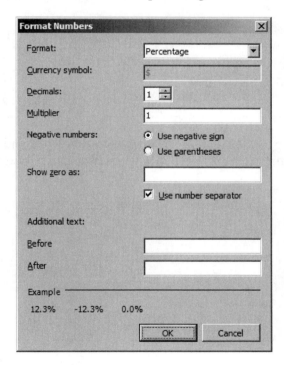

Incidentally, you can change the KPI definition in the Dashboard Designer as needed without changing the KPI in the cube. That might not be a good idea if you want to promote consistency between tools, but now you know that it's possible to override the cube if the need ever arises.

10. Save the KPI.

11. Let's add another KPI to the scorecard. In the Workspace Browser, click Reseller Scorecard.

12. In the Details pane, expand KPIs, expand PerformancePoint Content, and then drag Sales Targets to the scorecard. When you position your mouse over the lower part of the cell containing Product Gross Profit Margin, a blue line displays along the bottom edge of the cell to indicate the location for a new cell when you release the mouse button. You can add cells to the right, the left, or above the current cell, as shown here:

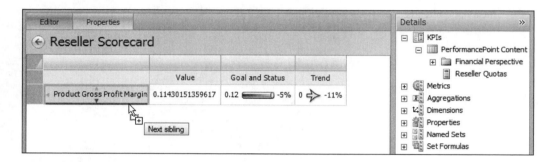

13. In the Details pane, expand Dimensions, expand Product, and then drag Categories to the right edge of the Product Gross Profit Margin cell as shown next.

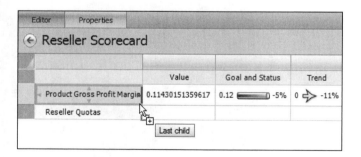

14. In the Select Members dialog box, shown in the following illustration, right-click All Products, point to Autoselect Members, and then select Select Children. Click the OK button.

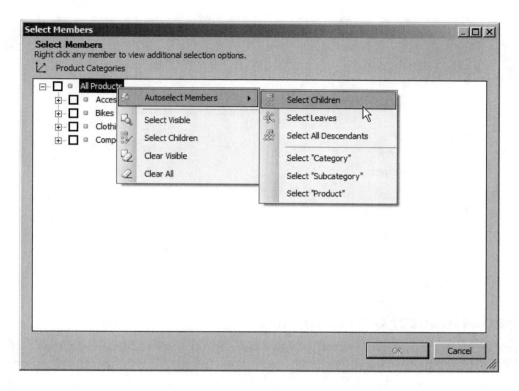

15. In the Details pane, expand Employee, and drag Employees to the right edge of Reseller Quotas. In the Select Members dialog box, expand All Employees, expand Ken J. Sanchez, right-click Brian S. Welcker, point to Autoselect Members, and then select Select Children. Click the OK button.

16. Although the wizard updates the scorecard with values upon completion, any subsequent changes to the scorecard require you to perform a manual refresh to retrieve the values from the respective data sources and calculate the scores.

On the Edit tab of the ribbon, click the Update button to preview the scorecard, as shown here:

Reseller Scorecard	Value	Goal and Status		Trend	
⊟ Product Gross Profit Margin		▭		⇨	
⊞ Accessories	49.9%	40.0%	▭ 25%	0 ⇨	-50%
⊞ Bikes	11.1%	12.0%	▭ -7%	0 ⇨	-11%
⊞ Clothing	17.4%	20.0%	▭ -13%	0 ⇨	-17%
⊞ Components	8.8%	10.0%	▭ -12%	0 ⇨	-9%
⊟ Reseller Quotas	$80,450,596.98	$114,253,550.00	! -30%		
⊞ Amy E. Alberts	$15,535,946.26	$24,202,000.00	! -36%		
⊞ Stephen Y. Jiang	$63,320,315.35	$87,336,050.00	! -27%		
⊞ Syed E. Abbas	$1,594,335.38	$2,715,500.00	! -41%		

17. Save the scorecard to SharePoint.

PerformancePoint Web Parts

In the previous chapter, you learned how to build a SharePoint dashboard using Web Parts. When an administrator activates PerformancePoint Services, a set of PerformancePoint Web Parts (shown in Figure 9-15) is available for you to use in a SharePoint dashboard. For example, after you create a scorecard, you can display that scorecard in a SharePoint dashboard by using the PerformancePoint Scorecard Web Part. You can also display PerformancePoint reports in a dashboard and use PerformancePoint filters with many different types of Web Parts, not just those available for PerformancePoint content. The PerformancePoint Stack Selector is a special Web Part that allows you to switch between multiple items that you place in the same location.

Let's add the scorecard that you created in the previous exercise to the SharePoint dashboard that you created in the previous chapter and then explore some of the interactive features of the scorecard.

Figure 9-15   *PerformancePoint Web Parts*

Exercise 9-5: Adding a Scorecard to a SharePoint Dashboard

1. In the Business Intelligence Center site, click the Dashboards link, and then click the Reseller Sales link.

2. On the Page tab of the ribbon, click the Edit Page button.

3. In the Body zone on the right, click the Add A Web Part link.

4. In the Categories list, select PerformancePoint, click PerformancePoint Scorecard, and then click the Add button.

5. In the PerformancePoint Scorecard Web Part, click the Click Here To Open The Tool Pane link.

6. In the tool pane, click the Browse link to the right of the Location box.

7. In the Select An Asset dialog box, click PerformancePoint Content in the left pane, click Reseller Scorecard, and then click the OK button.

8. In the Title box, type **Reseller Sales**, and then click the OK button.

9. Click the Stop Editing button in the ribbon.

10. Now let's do some exploring. In the scorecard, expand Bikes, right-click the cell at the intersection of Touring Bikes and Value, and click Comments.

11. If comments were already associated with this cell, you would see them in the Comments dialog box that displays. Click the Add Comment link.

12. In the Title box, type **Need Action Plan**.

13. In the Comment box, type **This value is too far below target and requires action**.

14. Click the Save button, and then click the Close button. Notice the small triangle that denotes the comment that you just entered.

Reseller Sales	Value	Goal and Status		Trend	
⊟Product Gross Profit Margin		▭		⇨	
⊞Accessories	49.9%	40.0%	▭ 25%	0 ⇨	-50%
⊟Bikes	11.1%	12.0%	▭ -7%	0 ⇨	-11%
⊞Mountain Bikes	16.3%	12.0%	▭ 36%	0 ⇨	-16%
⊞Road Bikes	9.9%	12.0%	▭ -17%	0 ⇨	-10%
⊞Touring Bikes	1.5%	12.0%	▭ -87%	0 ⇨	-2%
⊞Clothing	17.4%	20.0%	▭ -13%	0 ⇨	-17%
⊞Components	8.8%	10.0%	▭ -12%	0 ⇨	-9%
⊟Reseller Quotas	$80,450,596.98	$114,253,550.00	!	-30%	
⊞Amy E. Alberts	$15,535,946.26	$24,202,000.00	!	-36%	
⊞Stephen Y. Jiang	$63,320,315.35	$87,336,050.00	!	-27%	
⊞Syed E. Abbas	$1,594,335.38	$2,715,500.00	!	-41%	

15. Right-click the cell intersection at Goal And Status and Syed E. Abbas, and click Show Details.

Export to Excel				Page 1 of 1 ▷ ▷ All
Employee	Sales Territory Region	Calendar Quarter	Sales Amount Quota	
Lynn N. Tsoflias	Australia	Q3 CY 2007	478000	
Lynn N. Tsoflias	Australia	Q4 CY 2007	389000	
Lynn N. Tsoflias	Australia	Q1 CY 2008	399000	
Lynn N. Tsoflias	Australia	Q2 CY 2008	421000	
Syed E. Abbas	NA	Q3 CY 2007	132000	
Syed E. Abbas	NA	Q4 CY 2007	40000	
Syed E. Abbas	NA	Q1 CY 2008	7000	
Syed E. Abbas	NA	Q2 CY 2008	26000	

16. Close the Show Details window.

Decomposition Tree

The Decomposition Tree is a supplemental data visualization tool that you open
in SharePoint as an alternative to using drill-down features in scorecards, analytic
grids, or analytic charts. Unlike other PerformancePoint items, you don't design the
Decomposition Tree in Dashboard Designer. In fact, you don't design it at all. You
simply open it by right-clicking a scorecard cell or a value in an analytic report, but only
if you have Microsoft Silverlight 3 (or higher) installed on your computer.

When you first open the Decomposition Tree, you can see how the value that you
selected breaks down by dimension members. The bar chart structure of the report
allows you to easily compare the percentage contribution and ranking of each member,
which sort by default in decreasing order, as shown in Figure 9-16. This arrangement
of members highlights the largest contributors to the selected value. Each bar is a node
in the tree that you can expand to drill down to view another level of detail within the
same hierarchy, if a lower level exists, or a separate dimension. This ability to change the
drill path at any node is a feature unique to the Decomposition Tree.

The best way to understand how the Decomposition Tree works is to try it out. Let's
use the scorecard that we added to the SharePoint dashboard in the previous exercise as
our starting point.

Exercise 9-6: Exploring the Decomposition Tree

1. In the scorecard, right-click the cell intersection at Value and Stephen Y. Jiang,
   and click Decomposition Tree.

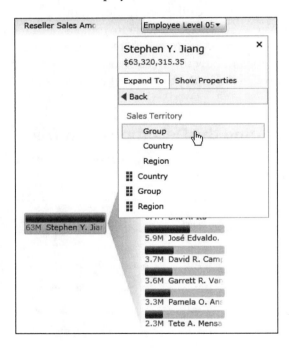

Figure 9-16 *Decomposition Tree*

2. In the Decomposition Tree window, click Stephen Y. Jiang, click Sales Territory in the information box that displays, as shown next, and then click Group.

3. Point to North America, and then click the plus symbol to its left.

4. Click United States, click Product in the information box, and then click Category (at the top of the Categories hierarchy). At any level of decomposition, you can switch to a different dimension.

5.   Point to Bikes and note the information that displays, as shown here:

6.   In the Category drop-down menu above the Decomposition Tree, click Show
      Grid. You are now viewing an analytic grid, a report type about which we'll
      explain more later in this chapter. Notice that you can also change the sort order
      or show a chart of the categories data instead of a grid.

7.   Notice the buttons available in the toolbar to change the view to a chart or to
      filter empty rows or columns. Right-click a value and click Decomposition Tree
      to switch back to the original report type.

PerformancePoint Reports

PerformancePoint features are not limited to displaying KPIs. You can design a
variety of reports in Dashboard Designer to include in a PerformancePoint dashboard,
although you can also view several of these report types as stand-alone reports in the
PerformancePoint Content library. Any report type can also appear in a SharePoint
dashboard when you use a PerformancePoint Report Web Part. There are eight
different report types that you can create in PerformancePoint, which we have grouped
by category as shown in Table 9-5.

Analytic Reports

While exploring the Decomposition Tree in the previous exercise, you got a sneak
preview of the analytical grid, just one of the several PerformancePoint report
types that you can design. Closely related to the analytical grid is the analytic chart.

Report Category	Report Type	Usage
Analytic Reports	Analytic Chart	Interactive exploration of Analysis Services data in chart form
	Analytic Grid	Interactive exploration of Analysis Services data in grid form
Dashboard Reports	Excel Services	Drill down, filtering, and sorting PivotTable data or static display of data from other sources
	Reporting Services	Precise layout of data in a report with full support of Reporting Services interactivity features
	ProClarity Analytics Server Page	ProClarity View of Analysis Services data from ProClarity Analytics Server
	Web Page	Link to intranet page or application with web interface
Scorecard Reports	KPI Details	Descriptive information about a selected scorecard cell, including scoring pattern, threshold values by band, and custom properties
	Strategy Map	Visio diagram with shapes representing relationships between KPIs in a scorecard

Table 9-5   *PerformancePoint Reports*

The Decomposition Tree, analytic grid, and analytic chart all have their origins in the ProClarity product acquired by Microsoft in 2006. These three report types provide a higher degree of interactivity than a report that you develop with Reporting Services, but you have less control over their appearance. That's because their primary purpose is to support analysis and exploration of your data. These reports also require Analysis Services as a data source.

Let's create an analytic chart in preparation for designing a dashboard later in this chapter. We'll design this chart to compare gross margin percent by product category and by reseller type as a starting point for deeper analysis.

Exercise 9-7: Creating an Analytic Chart

1. In Dashboard Designer, on the Create tab in the ribbon, click Analytic Chart.
2. In the Create An Analytic Chart Report dialog box, select the AdventureWorks data source, and then click the Finish button.
3. In the Workspace Browser, rename the report **Margin by Category**.
4. In the Details pane, expand Measures, and then drag Reseller Gross Profit Margin to the Background pane in the report designer.
5. In the Details pane, expand Dimensions, expand Product, and then drag Categories to the Bottom Axis pane where it displays as Product Categories.

6. Right-click Product Categories, click Select Members, and then clear the Default Member (All Products) check box. In a chart, it's rarely useful to have the top level of a hierarchy display in the chart.

7. Right-click All Products, point to Autoselect Members, click Select Children, and then click the OK button.

8. In the Details pane, expand Reseller and drag Type to the Series pane in the report designer.

9. Right-click Reseller Type, click Select Members, and clear the Default Member (All Resellers) check box.

10. Right-click All Resellers, point to Autoselect Members, click Select Children, and then click the OK button.

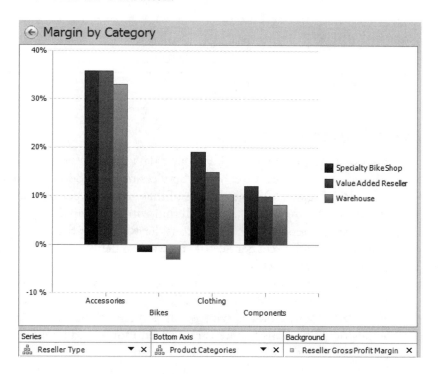

11. Save the report.

Now that you know how to design an analytical chart, you have the basic knowledge necessary to design an analytic grid. Instead of working with Bottom Axis and Series, as you do in the analytical chart, you work with Columns and Rows respectively. Alternatively, you can start with a chart and switch to a grid, as shown in Figure 9-17, or vice versa.

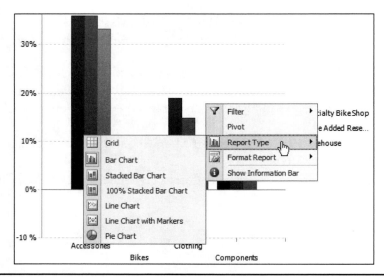

Figure 9-17 *Switching to an alternate analytic report type*

Dashboard Reports

If you are less interested in interactivity, or if you have data in sources other than Analysis Services, you can configure a Reporting Services or Excel Services report for use as a PerformancePoint report. Of course, both of these report types have interactive features, too, but not to the same extent that you'll find with the analytic reports. When deciding which of these two report types to use, consider Reporting Services if you need a pixel-perfect layout and Excel Services if you want to deliver drill-down and filtering capabilities with minimal effort.

If you're running a ProClarity Analytics Server in your environment, you can present a ProClarity view as a report in a dashboard page. Several of the ProClarity reports are available natively in PerformancePoint Services, such as the Analytic Chart, Analytic Grid, and Decomposition Tree. This feature is more useful for providing other types of reports, such as the Perspective View or Performance Map.

A more generic report type is the Web Page. This report is simply a viewer for a URL that you provide. It's a good option for linking to a page in your intranet, or for integrating third-party reporting tools that have a Web interface.

Exercise 9-8: Configuring an Excel Services Report

1. In Dashboard Designer, on the Create tab in the ribbon, click Other Reports.
2. In the Workspace Browser, rename the report **Sales Analysis**.

3. In the Report Settings section of the report editor, type the URL for your SharePoint site, select Documents in the Document Library drop-down list, and then select Sales Analysis.xlsx in the Excel Workbook drop-down list.

4. In the Workbook Parameters section, type **[Sales Territory].[Sales Territory] .[All Sales Territories]** in the Value field.

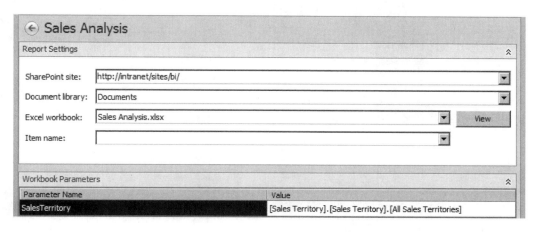

5. Save the report configuration.

Scorecard Reports

To enhance the summary information that a scorecard provides about performance, you can create two different types of reports that you link together with a scorecard on a dashboard page—KPI Details and Strategy Map. You create these reports in Dashboard Designer and then link them to a scorecard in a dashboard page.

You can use a KPI Details report to do what its name implies—provide details about a KPI. When you click a scorecard cell, the KPI Details report displays the selected KPI's description, information about its scoring pattern, threshold values by band, and custom properties. We'll see how this report works later when we build a dashboard.

The Strategy Map report requires you to create a Visio diagram first. You can create the diagram using Microsoft Visio 2007 or Microsoft Visio 2010 and then import it into the Strategy Map Editor in Dashboard Designer. Alternatively, you can open a Visio stencil file (if you have Visio installed on your computer) and develop the diagram within the editor. Once you have your diagram ready, you select a shape and then click the Connect Shape button in the editor to open the scorecard and select a KPI to a shape in the diagram, as shown in Figure 9-18.

Let's prepare a KPI Details report to accompany the scorecard report that we'll be adding to a dashboard in a later exercise.

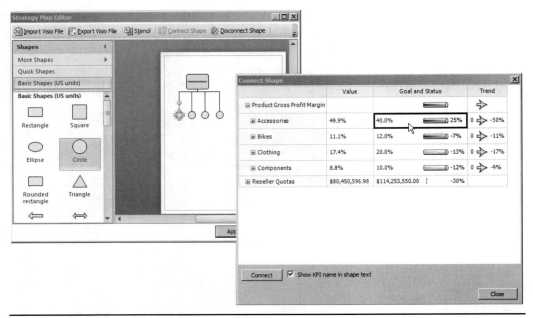

Figure 9-18 *Connecting a KPI to a Strategy Map shape*

Exercise 9-9: Configuring a KPI Details Report

1. In Dashboard Designer, on the Create tab in the ribbon, click KPI Details.
2. In the Workspace Browser, rename the report **KPI Details**.
3. Select the Show Score check box.
4. Save the report.

Building Dashboards

A PerformancePoint dashboard is similar to a SharePoint dashboard, but it has some distinguishing characteristics that might make it a better option for displaying performance-related information on a single page. Like a SharePoint dashboard, the PerformancePoint dashboard has multiple configurable zones. However, instead of adding Web Parts to a zone, you add an item from the PerformancePoint Content list. In fact, you're limited to using only PerformancePoint items in this type of dashboard, whereas a SharePoint dashboard can combine PerformancePoint items with other content types. On the other hand, a PerformancePoint dashboard has more advanced filtering options and is not restricted to a single page. When you finish designing a dashboard, you must deploy it to SharePoint to make it available to users.

Filters

Before we start building a dashboard, let's explore the PerformancePoint filter. If you're familiar with PerformancePoint Server 2007, you'll discover that the filter item is much improved over the prior version. Previously, you had to build a filter into the dashboard, but now you create it just like any other PerformancePoint item and reuse it in as many different dashboards as necessary. Furthermore, it's compatible with SharePoint Web Parts, so you can really get a lot of usage out of it. Of course, if you connect a PerformancePoint filter to a SharePoint Web Part or a PerformancePoint dashboard item, the connected item must use data that includes the dimension used by the filter.

When you create a filter, you must first decide on the display method that you want to use. You can display values in either a list or tree view for single-value selections, or a multiselect tree view for multiple value selections, as shown in Figure 9-19.

Next, you must decide how to populate the list of values for the filter. You can choose from the following filter templates:

Template	Data Source	Description
Custom Table	Tabular	Select key column/name column pair
MDX Query	Analysis Services	Provide an MDX set expression
Member Selection	Analysis Services Tabular Fixed Values	Select dimension, members, and default member
Named Set	Analysis Services	Select named set from cube
Time Intelligence	Analysis Services Tabular Fixed Values	Define a formula for each list member
Time Intelligence Connection Formula	Analysis Services Tabular Fixed Values	Nothing to configure—user selects from date picker

Let's create two filters—one for year using the Time Intelligence template and another for sales territories using the Member Selection template.

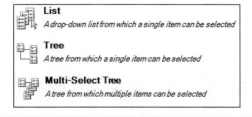

Figure 9-19   *Filter display methods*

Exercise 9-10: Creating a Filter

1. In Dashboard Designer, on the Create tab of the ribbon, click Filter and select Time Intelligence.

2. On the Select A Data Source page of the wizard, click the Add Data Source button, select AdventureWorks, and then click the OK button. Click the Next button.

3. On the Enter Time Formula page, click the Add Formula button.

4. In the Formula column, you need to create a formula that resolves to a year that exists in the AdventureWorks cube. If you were working with your own cube with current dates, you could use Year as the formula. However, because the latest year with data in the AdventureWorks cube is 2008, you need to create a formula that resolves to that year. For example, if the current year is 2010, use the formula Year-2 and enter a display name, **Year 2008**.

5. Add another formula for 2007, such as Year-3, and provide a display name.

6. You can test the formulas by clicking the Preview button, as shown in the following illustration. When the formula is valid, you will see the results of the formula in the Members column.

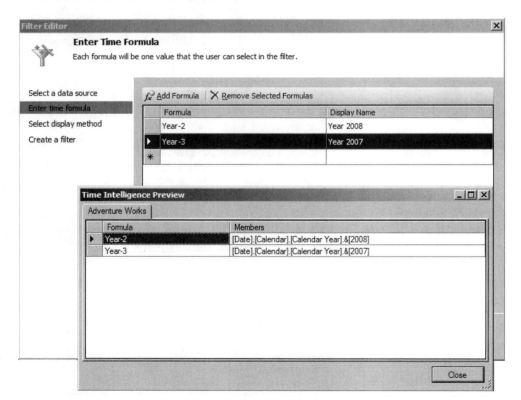

7. Click the Close button to return to the wizard, and then click the Next button.

8. On the Select Display Method page, select List, and click the Finish button.

9. In the Workspace Browser, right-click the filter, click Rename, and type **Year**.

10. Let's continue with the next filter. On the Create tab of the ribbon, click Filter and select Member Selection.

11. On the Select A Data Source page of the wizard, select AdventureWorks, click the OK button, and then click the Next button.

12. On the Select Members page, click the Select Dimension button. In the Select Dimension dialog box, select Sales Territory.Sales Territory, and click the OK button.

13. Click the Select Members button, select Default Member (All Sales Territories).

14. Right-click All Sales Territories, point to Autoselect Members, select Select All Descendants, click the OK button, and then click the Next button.

15. On the Select Display Method button, select Tree and click the Finish button.

16. In the Workspace Browser, right-click the newly added filter, click Rename, and type **Sales Territories**.

17. Save each filter.

Dashboards

After you have built all the PerformancePoint items that you want to display in the dashboard, you're ready to pick a layout and position items on the page. Remember that you can create multiple pages for your dashboard. Also, if you add filters to the dashboard, you must create a connection between the filter and the items that you want to filter.

At last, we're ready to build our dashboard using all the items we've created in the previous exercises in this chapter.

Exercise 9-11: Creating a Dashboard

1. In Dashboard Designer, on the Create tab of the ribbon, click Dashboard.

2. In the Select A Dashboard Page Template dialog box, select the 2 Columns layout and click the OK button.

3. In the Pages section, replace Page 1 with KPIs.

4. In the Details pane, expand Filters, expand PerformancePoint Content, and drag Year to the left column of the Dashboard Content section.

5. In the Details pane, expand Scorecards, expand PerformancePoint Content, and then drag Reseller Scorecard to the left column of Dashboard Content below the filter. As you move your cursor into the left column zone, a blue line appears

at the insertion point for the item. Release the mouse button when the blue line appears where you want the scorecard to appear.

6. Drag Sales Territories from the Details pane to the right column.

7. In the Details pane, expand Reports, expand PerformancePoint Content, and drag KPI Details into the right column of Dashboard Content below the Sales Territories filter.

8. Now you're ready to link the filters to the scorecard. When you move your cursor over the Year filter, the item expands to display the various items you can use to link to another part. Drag Member Unique Name from the Year filter to the section in the scorecard labeled Drop Fields To Create Connections, as shown here:

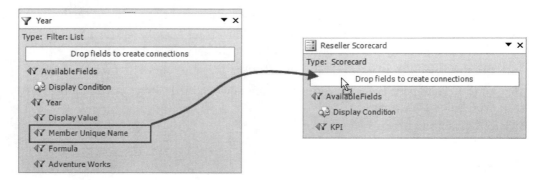

9. When you drop the field, the Connection dialog box displays with the correct default values showing that the source value, Member Unique Name, will connect to the Page axis of the scorecard, which is the equivalent of a background filter. Click the OK button.

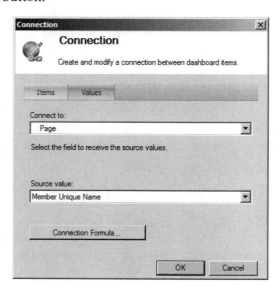

10. Drag Member Unique Name from the Sales Territories filter to the connections zone of the Reseller Scorecard.

11. Next, drag KPI from the Reseller Scorecard to KPI Details.

12. In the Connection dialog box, select Cell:Context in the Source Value drop-down list, and then click the OK button.

13. In the Pages section of the dashboard editor, click the New Page button.

14. In the Select A Dashboard Page Template dialog box, select 2 Columns, and then click the OK button.

15. Name the page **Reports**.

16. Add the Sales Territories filter and the Margin By Category report to the Left Column zone.

17. Drag the Sales Analysis report to the Right Column zone.

18. Now connect the Sales Territory filter to the Margin By Category report, and click the OK button in the Connections dialog box. The filter connects to measure, which will filter the values in the chart.

19. Next, connect the filter to the Sales Analysis report.

20. In the Connections dialog box, select Sales Territory in the Connect To drop-down list, and then click the OK button.

21. In the Workspace Browser, rename the dashboard **Sales Dashboard**.

22. Save the dashboard.

Dashboard Deployment

When you save a dashboard in Dashboard Designer, the item saves to the PerformancePoint Content list, but is unavailable for viewing by users. To make it available, you must deploy the dashboard to SharePoint. When you deploy the dashboard, Dashboard Designer creates a folder in the Dashboards library and stores each page of the dashboard as a separate document in the folder.

Exercise 9-12: Deploying a Dashboard to SharePoint

1. In the Workspace Browser in Dashboard Designer, right-click Sales Dashboard, and then click Deploy To SharePoint.

2. In the Deploy To dialog box, select Dashboards, and then click the OK button.

3. In the Year drop-down list, select Year 2007.

4. Click the All Sales Territories link, expand All Sales Territories, and click Europe.

5. Click the cell at the intersection of Accessories and Goal And Status, and then notice the information that displays in the Reseller Quotas KPI Details report to the right.

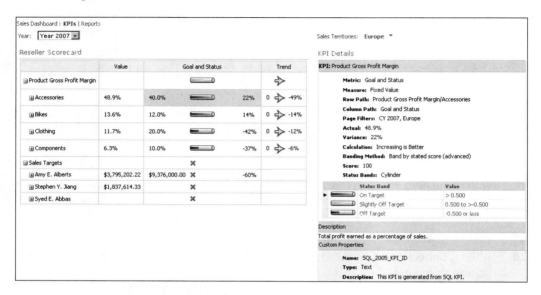

6. Click a cell in the Trend column and then a cell related to the Reseller Quotas to view the different types of details associated with different metrics and KPIs

7. Click the Reports link at the top of the page.

8. Notice that the dashboard retains the filter value from the KPIs page. Change the filter to Pacific.

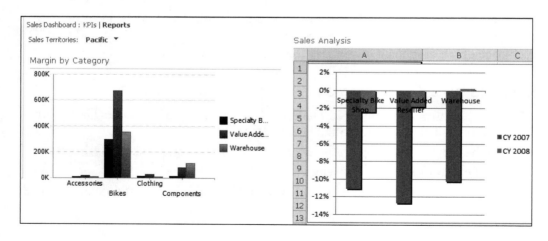

Summary

In this chapter, you explored the main features of PerformancePoint Services. At one end of the spectrum, you can use PerformancePoint Services to display KPIs in a scorecard. At the other end of the spectrum, you can combine scorecards with analytic reports in dashboards.

If all you need to do is display KPIs to users, do you really need to use PerformancePoint Services, or can you use a different tool instead? The answer depends on what data sources you have available for KPIs, how you want to display KPIs, and how much additional information users need. It's likely that a tool that works well for one business intelligence solution might not be the best choice in another solution, or even that multiple tools are necessary. Consider the pros and cons of each tool when selecting a KPI for your solution, as summarized in Table 9-6.

Tool	Pros	Cons
Analysis Services	Centralization of business rules	Knowledge of MDX required
	Consumable in Excel, Reporting Services, SharePoint List, and PerformancePoint Services, and any third-party tool that can consume Analysis Services data	Data must be stored in Analysis Services
Excel Services	Easy creation of KPIs using Excel formulas and conditional formatting	Limited control over appearance of KPIs
	Able to derive actual value for KPI formula from different data source than target value	Inability to roll up multiple KPIs to derive an overall score
	Easy access to KPIs from Analysis Services	No built-in mechanism for linking to KPI details
	PivotTable interactivity with KPIs from Analysis Services	
Reporting Services	Ability to develop KPIs from sources other than Analysis Services	More advanced skills required to develop custom KPIS
	Unlimited choice of images for KPIs	Inability to use images from Analysis Services KPIs
	Complete control over layout and behavior of KPIs	
	Actions support link to another report with KPI details	Separate development effort to display KPI details
		Manual development of formulas to roll up multiple KPIs to an overall score

Table 9-6   *KPI Support* (continued)

Tool	Pros	Cons
SharePoint List	Easy creation of KPI list	Limited sources for KPIs
	Ability to link to additional information about KPIs	Limitation of three value ranges and basic set of icons and colors
PerformancePoint Services	Centralization of KPIs	Enterprise Edition required
	Variety of images available for indicators, including support for custom images	KPIs not consumable in other BI tools
	Ability to derive actual value for KPI formula from different data source than target value	
	Multiple actual and target values supported	
	Support for both simple and complex calculations of KPI scores	
	Scorecard supports rollup of multiple KPIs to derive an overall score, drill features, and optional link to details or strategy map	

Table 9-6   *KPI Support*

Of course, PerformancePoint Services can do more than display KPIs. If you use Analysis Services as a data source, the combination of PerformancePoint scorecards with analytic reports in dashboards is a really great interactive solution for analyzing data in a web browser. And if you have Reporting Services and Excel Services reports available, you can extend their usefulness by including them in a PerformancePoint dashboard. The design possibilities really are limitless. But all these options for data visualization might be confusing you more than helping you come up with a plan for building a business intelligence solution. In the next chapter, we'll look more closely at the charting capabilities across the various tools to help you make the best selection for your needs.

Chapter 10

Charts and Graphs

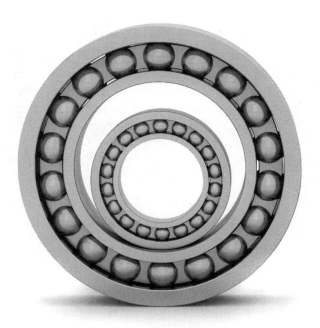

The use of charts and graphs is a great way to summarize large volumes of data so that viewers can detect relationships, patterns, or trends that might otherwise remain obscured in row after row of raw data. What would you say if someone asked you to explain the difference between a chart and a graph? Don't worry if you struggle for an answer. Not many people are clear on the difference, and some people use each term to mean the opposite of what you might expect.

If you check a dictionary, you'll find a graph is commonly defined as a diagram of the relationship between two sets of numbers represented as coordinates or points on a horizontal and vertical axis, and might include a line that connects the points sequentially, whereas a chart is more broadly defined as an illustration of quantitative relationships. In this context, a graph is merely a type of chart. On the other hand, another definition for a chart is a tabular layout of data. It's no wonder that people get confused. However, when comparing data visualization capabilities among business intelligence tools, you'll likely find reference only to charts. For that reason, we'll refer to charts throughout this chapter in reference to both charts and graphs.

Whether a chart effectively communicates meaningful information depends on the type of quantitative relationship that you want to show, the capabilities of your charting tool, and the techniques that you use to develop the chart. We'll start this chapter by reviewing the quantitative relationships that are commonly represented in charts. Then we'll consider the pros and cons of the charting tools available in Office and SQL Server. As we explore each tool, we'll also look at specific techniques for chart development. Armed with this information, you can make an informed decision about which tool to use the next time you need to create a chart.

Working with Quantitative Data

When you develop a chart to display quantitative data, your objective is to help the viewer understand the relationships between values. Although there are dozens of chart types across the Microsoft BI stack from which you can choose, you'll find that certain chart types are better for displaying particular types of relationships than others. Most charts in business intelligence solutions focus on depicting the following six types of data relationships:

- ▶ Time series
- ▶ Category comparison
- ▶ Ratios

- ▶ Variance
- ▶ Correlation
- ▶ Distribution

Time Series

Business users are constantly comparing how data changes over time. For example, a chart might compare values for this month to last month or monitor how values are trending from period to period over an extended range of time, as shown in Figure 10-1. To help users visualize these changes, you use a time series relationship, often in the form of a line chart, which displays data chronologically from left to right.

Category Comparison

Not only do users compare data over time, but they also compare categories of data. Categories are simply groups of people, places, or things. A column chart, as shown in Figure 10-2, helps users easily determine whether one category is higher or lower than the others. A horizontal bar chart is another useful type of chart for category comparisons. You might consider arranging the categories in ranked order to facilitate the comparison.

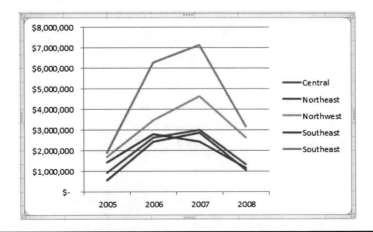

Figure 10-1   *Line chart for time series*

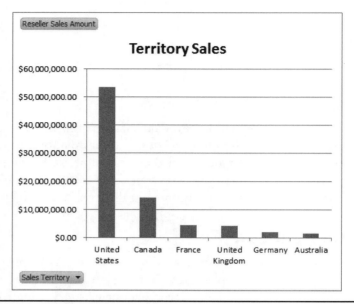

Figure 10-2 *Column chart for category comparison*

Ratios

When you need to communicate both an overall value and a breakdown of that value by category, you need a chart type that displays relationships among ratios, such as the stacked chart shown in Figure 10-3. Another popular option for displaying ratios is

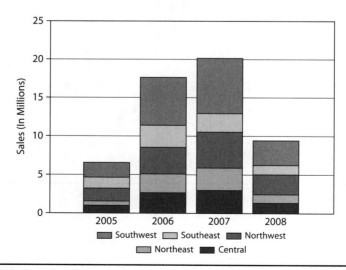

Figure 10-3 *Stacked column chart for ratios*

a pie chart. These types of charts work best when you have a small number of categories contributing to the overall value and users need to see only the relative contributions of the categories. If greater precision of each category's contribution is necessary, consider using a clustered column chart to separate each category.

Variance

Sometimes, the variance, or deviation, of a final value from a base value is more important than the final value itself. For these scenarios, you display the variance as a percentage of the base value in a chart. A base value might be a budget amount or a target value. When you use a column chart, you might use color to differentiate between values that are below target from values that are above target, as shown in Figure 10-4.

Correlations

Another useful type of chart is one that depicts the correlation relationship between two values, although it's used less frequently than the other types we've discussed so far. Unlike a column chart in which there is one category axis (the horizontal axis) and one value axis (the vertical axis), a chart for correlations has two value axes to plot the pairs of values. The scatter chart shown in Figure 10-5 illustrates the correlation between the gross margin percentage and the average unit price of products—the lower the unit price, the higher the gross margin.

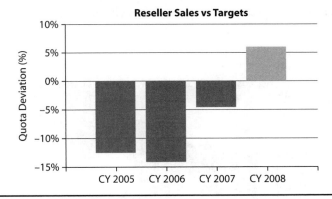

Figure 10-4   *Column chart for variance*

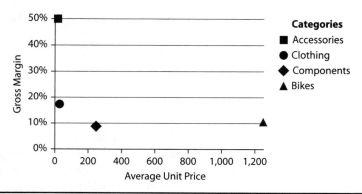

Figure 10-5   *Scatter chart for correlations*

Distribution

A distribution relationship shows how a count of items in a set breaks out across a range of values. The horizontal axis displays this range from lowest to highest value, and then each column in the chart represents a count for the designated value. For example, in Figure 10-6, each column represents the number of cars owned for a set of customers, with 0 as the lowest number of cars and 4 as the highest value. The height of each column indicates the number of customers associated with the respective number of cars. When you have a wider range of values, such as you might have for yearly income, each column can represent a discrete range, like "0 to $20,000," rather than a distinct number like 0. Instead of using a column chart, you can use a line chart to display the distribution as a curve.

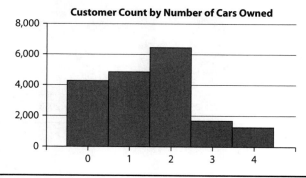

Figure 10-6   *Distribution*

Excel

Now that we've explained the types of charts that you'll build for your business intelligence solutions, let's consider how well each tool supports our ability to develop them, starting with Excel. In this section, we'll review the supported data sources and important points about working with charts in Excel. For more in-depth information about working with charts in Excel, we recommend *Charts and Graphs: Microsoft Excel 2010* by Bill Jelen (Que, 2010).

Excel Data Sources

You can create a chart from data that you manually enter into the spreadsheet or that you import from any data source that Excel supports. As a reminder, Excel can retrieve relational data from Access or SQL Server, tabular data from a website or a text file, multidimensional data from Analysis Services, or hierarchical data from an XML file. You can access relational data from other sources by using either an OLE DB connection or ODBC.

Keep in mind that you can manipulate the data in the spreadsheet before developing your chart, as long as you're not using Analysis Services data. For example, you might need to add formulas to calculate deviations or sort the data for ranking in a category comparison. If you're using Analysis Services as a source for a deviation chart, you must first create a calculated member in the cube because a PivotChart relies exclusively on data in the cube.

Excel Charts

In Chapter 4, we introduced two of Excel's chart features: sparklines and data bars. In this chapter, we'll focus on the standard chart and PivotChart. You can use any range of cells as the source data for a standard chart, whereas a PivotChart requires you to connect to Analysis Services, use PowerPivot data in the workbook, or convert an existing range of cells into a pivot table.

Let's start with a review of the process to create a standard chart. Use the Insert tab of the ribbon (shown in Figure 10-7) to select the type of chart you want from a gallery. For a complete reference of available chart types in Excel, refer to the Appendix. You can always switch to a different chart type later if your original selection doesn't suit your requirements.

Figure 10-7   *Insert tab of Excel ribbon*

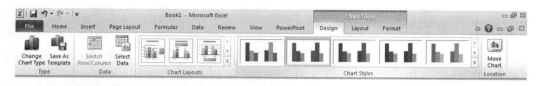

Figure 10-8   *Design tab under Chart Tools on the ribbon*

After inserting the chart, you have access to the Design, Layout, and Format tabs under Chart Tools on the ribbon, as shown in Figure 10-8, but only when you select the chart in the worksheet. It's easier to work with the tools on these tabs when you display data in the chart.

The Design tab includes a Select Data button that opens the Select Data Source dialog box, as shown in Figure 10-9. Here you provide the range of cells to include in your chart and designate which cells to use for the chart series and which cells to use for the category axis. If you have a large, complex data set, this part of the chart development process can be tedious.

If your data set for the chart is small, you'll find that your chart is reasonably well formatted by default. Using any of the Chart Tools options, you can make a change to your chart and see the effect immediately. If you don't like it, you can use the Undo button to reverse the change.

As with most Microsoft products, there is more than one way to accomplish a task. On the ribbon, you can use the Layout and Format tabs under Chart Tools to fine-tune the appearance of chart elements. If you prefer to use a context menu, you can right-click an element on the chart to access its properties.

Using Excel, you can create a chart for any of the six data relationships that we described at the beginning of this chapter. To get a basic introduction to charts in

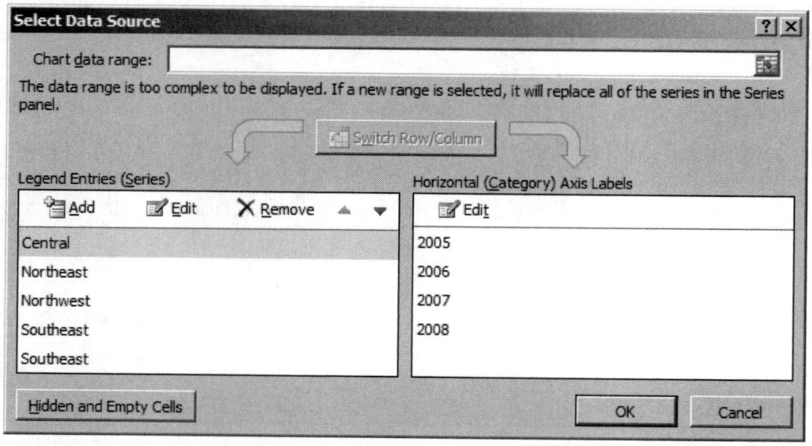

Figure 10-9   *Data range, series, and category selection for a chart*

Excel, let's create a time series chart to display not only sales data across multiple years, but also to display sales separately by product category. We'll use a table in an existing workbook to get started quickly. The data in the table originally comes from the AdventureWorksDW2008R2 database.

Exercise 10-1: Creating an Excel Chart

1. Open the Sales workbook.
2. On the Insert tab of the ribbon, in the Charts group, click the Line button, and then click the Line chart type in the 2D Line group (the first button in the group) as shown here:

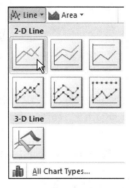

3. Drag the chart to move it next to the table so that its top-left edge is between columns D and E on row 1 as shown:

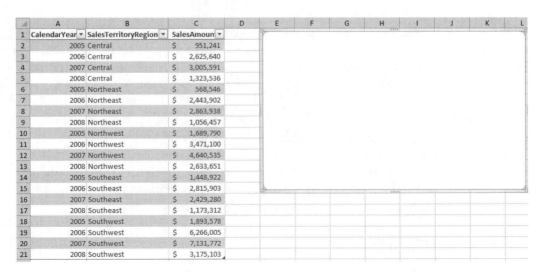

	CalendarYear	SalesTerritoryRegion	SalesAmoun
1	CalendarYear	SalesTerritoryRegion	SalesAmoun
2	2005	Central	$ 951,241
3	2006	Central	$ 2,625,640
4	2007	Central	$ 3,005,591
5	2008	Central	$ 1,323,536
6	2005	Northeast	$ 568,546
7	2006	Northeast	$ 2,443,902
8	2007	Northeast	$ 2,863,938
9	2008	Northeast	$ 1,056,457
10	2005	Northwest	$ 1,689,790
11	2006	Northwest	$ 3,471,100
12	2007	Northwest	$ 4,640,535
13	2008	Northwest	$ 2,633,651
14	2005	Southeast	$ 1,448,922
15	2006	Southeast	$ 2,815,903
16	2007	Southeast	$ 2,429,280
17	2008	Southeast	$ 1,173,312
18	2005	Southwest	$ 1,893,578
19	2006	Southwest	$ 6,266,005
20	2007	Southwest	$ 7,131,772
21	2008	Southwest	$ 3,175,103

4. On the Chart Tools – Design tab of the ribbon, click the Select Data button.

5. Click cell A2 in the worksheet and then, while pressing the SHIFT key, click cell C21 to select the table; press the TAB key to update the dialog box with your selection.

6. In the Legend Entries (Series) section of the dialog box, click the Add button.

7. In the workbook, click cell B2 to update the Series Name box.

8. Clear the expression in the Series Values box, select the range of cells from C2 to C5, and then click the OK button.

9. In the Legend Entries (Series) section of the dialog box, click the Add button for each series shown in the following table and provide the respective expressions for Series Name and Series Values:

Series Label	Series Name	Series Values
Northeast	=Sheet1!$B$6	=Sheet1!$C$6:$C$9
Northwest	=Sheet1!$B$10	=Sheet1!$C$10:$C$13
Southeast	=Sheet1!$B$14	=Sheet1!$C$14:$C$17
Southwest	=Sheet1!$B$18	=Sheet1!$C$18:$C$21

10. In the Horizontal (Category) Axis Labels section of the dialog box, click the Edit button.

11. In the workbook, highlight cells A2 to A5 to update the Axis Label Range box, and then click the OK button.

12. Leave this workbook open for the next exercise.

You can see the final version of the time series chart in Figure 10-10, which enables us to clearly see trends over time by sales territory. Before we move on to other charts in this chapter, we'd like to point out that Excel applies the formatting of value ranges in the source data to the vertical axis. Other tools are not as helpful with regard to formatting.

Also, although this chart provides a useful visual summary of the data, it doesn't provide a way to explore the underlying data or to change perspective. Furthermore, if we get more data for the years between 2008 and the present year, we'll have to manually update the workbook and reset the data selection for the chart to include the additional data. Therefore, you should use a standard Excel chart only for scenarios that don't require interactivity and that don't require a data refresh.

Excel PivotCharts

Now let's move on to the PivotChart feature. If your data is in a table, a range, or an external data source like Analysis Services, you can transform it into a pivot table, which

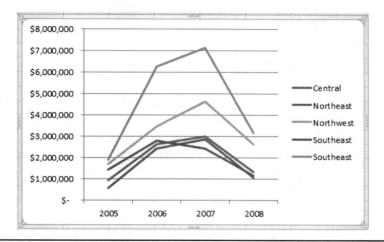

Figure 10-10 *Line chart in Excel*

in turn becomes the source for a PivotChart. A PivotChart can also use PowerPivot data as a source.

Unlike the process to create a standard chart, you use the Insert tab of the ribbon to create a PivotChart. Just click the PivotChart option on the PivotTable button, as shown in Figure 10-11, and specify where to find the source data and where to place the new chart in the workbook. You then select the value, series, and category fields to display in the chart.

By default, Excel creates the PivotChart as a column chart. However, you can easily change to a different chart type by using the tabs under PivotChart Tools on the ribbon. PivotChart Tools closely resembles Chart Tools, but includes an Analyze tab that you use to work with slicers and the PivotTable Field list.

Let's add a PivotChart to the Sales workbook to learn how to construct a category comparison chart. We'll connect to the cube that you deployed to Analysis Services in Chapter 3 to retrieve sales data that we can use to compare one sales territory to another. We'll also rank the sales territories in descending order from highest to lowest sales volume.

Figure 10-11 *Inserting a PivotChart*

Exercise 10-2: Creating an Excel PivotChart

1. In the Sales workbook, click the Sheet2 tab.
2. On the Data tab of the ribbon, click the From Other Sources button, and then click From Analysis Services.
3. In the Server Name box of the Data Connection Wizard, type the name of the Analysis Services server, such as **localhost**, and click the Next button.
4. In the drop-down list, select the AdventureWorks sample database, select AdventureWorks if necessary, click the Next button, and then click the Finish button.
5. In the Import Data dialog box, select the PivotChart And PivotTable Report option, and then click the OK button.
6. On the Insert tab of the ribbon, in the Tables group, click the PivotTable button, and then click PivotChart.
7. In the Create PivotTable with PivotChart dialog box, select the Use An External Data Source option, and click the Choose Connection button.
8. In the PivotTable Field list, select Reseller Sales Amount in the Reseller Sales measure group, scroll to a location near the bottom of the list, and select Sales Territory.

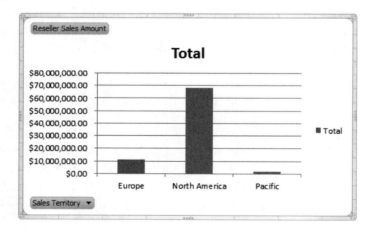

9. Select the sales territory cells (A2 to A4), right-click one of the cells, click Expand/Collapse, and then click Expand Entire Field as shown here:

10. Right-click one of the cells containing a country, such as A4, and click Show/Hide Fields, and then clear Group from the list of selected fields.

11. Right-click A4 again, click Sort, and then click More Sort Options.

12. Select Descending (Z To A) By, select Reseller Sales Amount in the drop-down list, and then click the OK button.

13. Click the chart, position the cursor along the bottom edge until it changes to display an arrow at each end of the cursor, and then drag the edge of the chart downward to expand the chart by about five rows.

14. Click Total in the legend, and then press the DELETE key to eliminate the legend, because one item in the series doesn't require a legend.

15. Right-click Total above the chart, click Edit Text, and replace Total with **Territory Sales**.

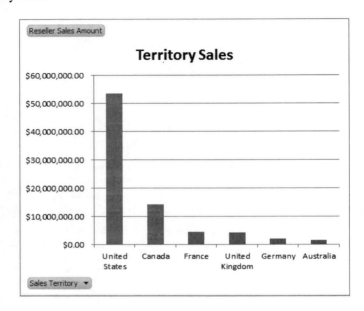

16. Before closing this workbook, save it to the Documents library in the Business Intelligence Center in SharePoint that you created in Chapter 8 so that you can use it as a data source in the next exercise.

An Excel pivot chart in a business intelligence solution is useful for analysis of large data sets when you base it on Analysis Services (or PowerPivot data), because the chart can take advantage of faster query processing than other data sources can provide. If you plan to display the pivot chart to users in a dashboard, you can provide some interactivity by adding a workbook parameter for the pivot table to which the pivot chart belongs and then assigning the value of a dashboard filter to the workbook parameter. Also, if you include the pivot table in the dashboard, changes made by the user to the pivot table to drill down or up also affect the pivot chart, but only if you can view both items in the same Web Part. Lastly, the pivot chart based on Analysis Services will display current data with no additional steps required, unlike the Excel chart, which requires you to find a way to update the chart's data source.

SharePoint Chart Web Part

We introduced the SharePoint Chart Web Part in Chapter 8. In that chapter, we provided an exercise that demonstrates how to create a time series chart, but there's much more that you can do with this Web Part. On the one hand, the number of data sources that you can use with your chart is limited. On the other hand, despite its apparent simplicity, the Chart Web Part is highly configurable and offers some unique chart types that make it worthwhile to explore as an option when you're building a SharePoint dashboard.

Chart Web Part Data Sources

The Chart Web Part in SharePoint's Enterprise Edition is useful as a quick way to set up a chart without publishing workbooks or reports to a document library. It's also an easy way to chart data that might not be easy to get into Excel or Reporting Services, such as data from another Web Part in your dashboard, as long as that Web Part is capable of sharing data through a Web Part connection. Check out the Web Parts in the Lists and Libraries category of the Web Parts gallery to discover which Web Parts you can use.

Here's a complete list of supported data sources for the Chart Web Part:

▶ SharePoint Web Part

▶ SharePoint list

▶ Excel Services workbook

▶ Business Data Catalog

Chart Web Part

The Chart Web Part is the only built-in option you have for presenting data in chart form in SharePoint if you're not using Reporting Services or Excel Services. It uses a wizard interface to simplify the process of creating a chart, as you learned in Chapter 8, but also provides access to an interface for configuring the Web Part's many properties when you need to create a more sophisticated chart layout. After you add the Chart Web Part to a dashboard page, two links appear above the default chart layout: Data & Appearance and Advanced Properties. The Data & Appearance link leads you to a page listing available wizards, one of which is the Chart Appearance Wizard, which is a three-step process of selecting a chart type, setting properties that affect the chart's overall appearance, and configuring individual chart elements. If you prefer to go straight to the individual properties of each chart element, use the Advanced Properties link instead.

If you use the Chart Appearance Wizard to configure your chart, you'll find a substantial array of choices on the chart type selection page. But if you look more closely, you'll notice that many chart types are slight variations of common chart types that you'll find in Excel and Reporting Services. For example, you'll find Clustered

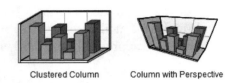

Clustered Column   Column with Perspective

Figure 10-12 *Separate chart type selections for 3-D column layout*

Column and Column With Perspective as two separate chart types, as shown in Figure 10-12, whereas Excel and Reporting Services let you select only one chart type, 3-D Column, and then you can change properties to adjust the perspective. Refer to the Appendix to discover the chart types that are unique to the Chart Web Part.

Let's take some time to explore both the Chart Appearance Wizard and Advanced Properties pages as we create a ratios chart to display the contribution of each sales territory to overall sales by year. We'll use the workbook that you published to SharePoint in the previous exercise as our data source.

Exercise 10-3: Creating a SharePoint Chart Web Part

1. In your browser, open the Reseller Sales dashboard that you created in Chapter 8.
2. On the Page tab of the ribbon, click Edit Page.
3. Click any Add A Web Part link.
4. In the Categories pane, select the Business Data folder, select Chart Web Part, and then click the Add button.
5. In the Chart Web Part, click the Data & Appearance link.
6. On the Data Connection Wizard page, click the Connect Chart To Data link.
7. On Step 1: Choose A Data Source, select the Connect To Excel Services option, and click the Next button.
8. On Step 2: Connect To Data From Excel Services, in the Excel Workbook Path box, type the path to the Sales workbook, such as **http://<servername>/sites/BI/Documents/Sales.xlsx**.
9. In the Range Name box, type the following range: **Sheet1!A1:C21**.
10. Click the Next button twice.
11. In the Y Field drop-down list, select SalesAmount.
12. In the X Field drop-down list, select CalendarYear.
13. In the Group By Field drop-down list, select SalesTerritoryRegion.

14. Click the Finish button to view the newly added Chart Web Part, shown here:

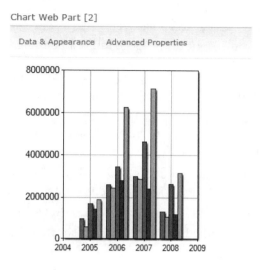

15. Click the Data & Appearance link in the Web Part.
16. Click the Customize Your Chart link.
17. In the Chart Templates list, select Stacked Column, as shown in the illustration, and then click the Next button.

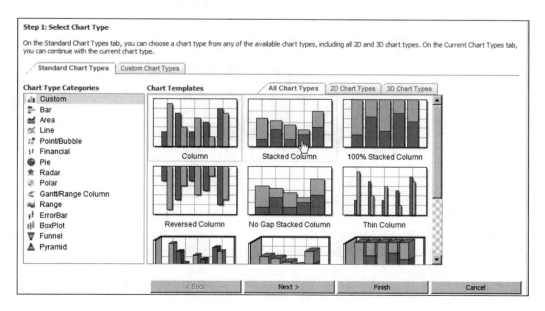

18. On the Step 2 page, change the theme to Green Blue, change the chart width to 400px, and then click the Next button.

19. On the Step 3 page, select the Show Legend check box.

20. Click the button to the right of the Legend Font box, change the font size to 6 pt, and click the OK button.

21. Click the arrow to the right of the box below the Legend Font box, type **040404** in the # box to set the font color to black, and then click the OK button.

22. In the Style drop-down list, select Row, and then, in the set of radio buttons for Position, click the center button in the bottommost row.

23. Click the Axes And Grid Lines tab.

24. In the X-Axis section, clear the Show Major Grid Lines check box.

25. In the Y-Axis section, select the Show Axis Title check box.

26. In the Title box, type the following string: **Sales (in Millions)**.

27. In the Format box, type the following string to shorten the axis labels: **#,0,,**

28. Click the Finish button.

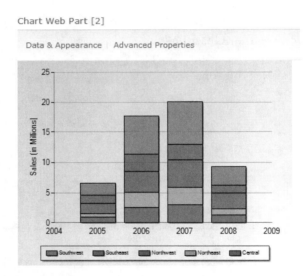

29. Now click the Advanced Properties link.

30. In the Back Color drop-down list, select Transparent.

31. In the Select An Element list on the left side of the browser, click Chart Areas.

32. Set the ShadowColor properties to Transparent.

33. In the Axis Menu drop-down list above the properties list, select X Axis, and then in the LabelStyle section, change the IsEndLabelVisible property to False.

34. In the Select An Element list, click Legends, and then set the BorderDashStyle property to NotSet and the ShadowColor property to Transparent.

35. Click the Finish button to view the final version of the chart, as shown:

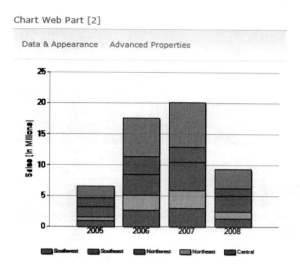

One of the features of the Chart Web Part that differentiates it from Excel is the ability to add hyperlinks and tooltips to provide interactivity in the SharePoint dashboard. On Step 3 of the Chart Appearance Wizard, you can access a set of properties for each data series in the chart, as shown in Figure 10-13.

Figure 10-13 *Hyperlinks and tooltips properties for Chart Web Part*

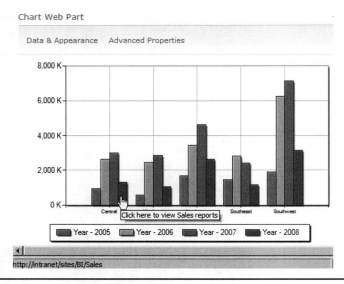

Figure 10-14 *Viewing a hyperlink and tooltip in a chart*

The series hyperlink and tooltip in a column chart activate when you click a column for that series in the chart. Notice the URL in the status bar and the tooltip above the chart in Figure 10-14 when we hover over the chart. The legend hyperlink and tooltip appear when you hover over the legend marker or the legend label, if you include a legend in the chart. Similarly, the label hyperlink and tooltip properties require you to display data labels on the chart.

If you configure the chart with multiple series, you can have a different set of hyperlinks and tooltips for each data series, but you must configure these values manually. Be aware that these are static settings, and will vary only by series. If you need dynamic hyperlinks and tooltips that understand the context of the cursor position (such as sales in the Central region for year 2008 in the example above), then you should instead use Reporting Services for charting.

Reporting Services

In both SQL Server 2000 and SQL Server 2005, the charting capabilities of Reporting Services were relatively basic with regard to managing the look and feel of charts. In SQL Server 2008 and continuing in SQL Server 2008 R2, Microsoft implemented more advanced controls purchased from Dundas. These new controls provide a wider range of chart types from which to choose and give you access to many more properties for each chart element.

The ability to create charts as Report Parts gives you more reusability options than the other charting tools that we consider in this chapter. You can literally build a chart once and reuse it many times in multiple Reporting Services reports, which in turn you can use in both SharePoint and PerformancePoint dashboards. Furthermore, the number of data sources that Reporting Services supports (described in Chapter 7) is the most extensive of all the charting tools across the suite. The steps to build a chart are the same whether you use Business Intelligence Development Studio (BIDS) or Report Builder 3.0, although Report Builder 3.0 has a Chart Wizard that you can use for simple charts or to lay the foundation for more complex charts.

Chart Wizard

The Chart Wizard in Report Builder 3.0 limits you to the following basic chart types: column, line, pie, bar, and area. You can optionally specify whether the chart should present the data as stacked or 100 percent stacked if the chart type supports that layout. Unless you have a simple chart, you'll probably have much more work ahead to format the chart properly. You'll need to switch between design mode and preview mode frequently to see the effect of changing chart properties, but Report Builder caches the report data (much like BIDS), so you'll be able to switch between modes fairly quickly.

In the next exercise, we'll use the Chart Wizard to create a variance report that compares sales to target values. We'll use the AdventureWorks cube as a data source. Although the cube doesn't include a calculation for variance, we can easily add an expression to the report to derive the variance. To make the report more flexible, we'll add a parameter that allows the user to view variance for all employees or for a specific employee.

Exercise 10-4: Using the Report Builder Chart Wizard

1. Launch Report Builder.

NOTE

If you're running a Native mode server, you can click the Report Builder button on the toolbar in Report Manager. If you're running a SharePoint integrated mode report server, you can click New Document | Report Builder Report on the ribbon of a document library for which Report Builder has been enabled. You can also install Report Builder locally.

2. Start the Chart Wizard in the Getting Started dialog box. If you've previously disabled that dialog box, you can launch the wizard from the Insert Chart button on the Insert tab of the ribbon.

3. On the Choose A Dataset page, click the Next button to accept the default to create a new data set.

4. On the Choose A Connection To A Data Source page, click the New button.

5. In the Data Source Properties dialog box, select Microsoft SQL Server Analysis Services in the Select Connection Type drop-down list.

6. Click the Build button.

7. In the Connection Properties dialog box, type your server name (or localhost) in the Server Name box and select the sample AdventureWorks database in the database drop-down list.

8. Click the OK button twice, and then click the Next button.

9. On the Design A Query page of the wizard, expand Measures, expand Reseller Sales, and drag Reseller Sales Amount to the center pane labeled "Drag levels or measures here to add to the query," as shown here:

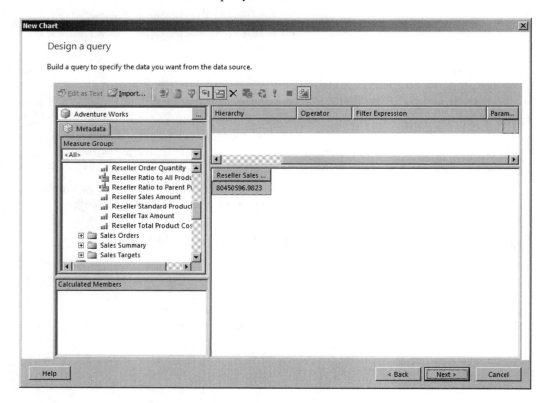

10. Expand Sales Targets, and drag Sales Amount Quota to the center pane to the right of Reseller Sales Amount.

11. Expand Date, expand Calendar, and drag Date.Calendar Year to the center pane to complete the query, as you see in this illustration.

Calendar Year	Reseller Sales A...	Sales Amount Q...
CY 2005	8065435.3053	9513000
CY 2006	24144429.654	29009000
CY 2007	32202669.4252	38782000
CY 2008	16038062.5978	18410000

12. In the filter pane in the top right of the query designer, scroll to the left if necessary, and select Employee in the Dimension drop-down list.

13. Select Employees in the Hierarchy drop-down list, select All Employees in the Filter Expression drop-down list, and select the Parameter check box.

14. Click the Next button.

15. On the Choose A Chart Type page, select Column, and then click the Next button.

16. On the Arrange Chart Fields page, drag Reseller_Sales_Amount to the Values list, drag Calendar_Year to the Categories list (as shown next), and then click the Next button.

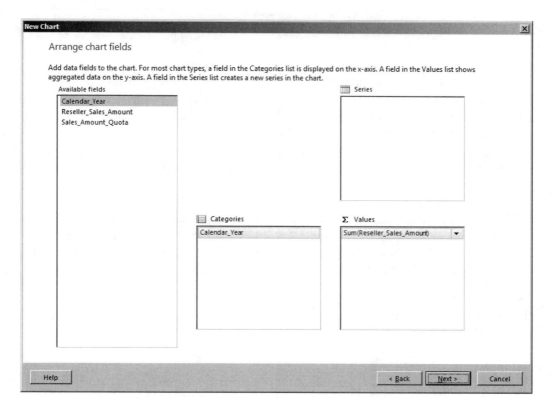

17. On the Choose A Style page, select Generic, and then click the Finish button.
18. Resize the chart to approximately 5 inches wide and 3.5 inches tall.
19. Click the chart to display the Chart Data pane to the right of the chart, as shown:

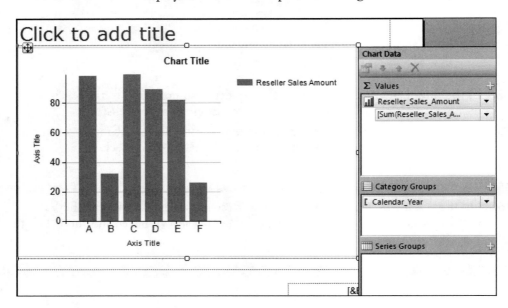

20. Click the arrow to the right of [Sum(Reseller_Sales_Amount)], and click Expression.
21. Modify the expression to compute the percentage difference between the sales amount and the sales quota as follows:

```
=(Sum(Fields!Reseller_Sales_Amount.Value)-Sum(Fields!Sales_Amount_
Quota.Value))/Sum(Fields!Sales_Amount_Quota.Value)
```

NOTE

An alternate approach to calculating variance would be to add a calculated member in the query designer for the data set. An even better approach would be to add a variance calculation to the cube to have it available to all charting, reporting, and analytical tools.

22. Click the OK button.
23. Click the Run button in the ribbon to preview the chart, which should now look like the chart in this illustration.

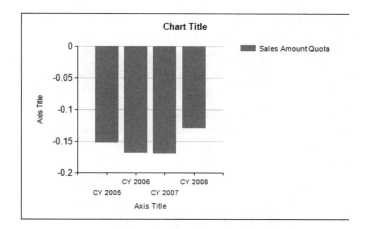

24. Click the Design button in the ribbon to return to the design mode.
25. Click the Axis Title label to the left of the y-axis (the vertical axis) twice to edit the text, and replace the title with the following text: **Quota Deviation (%)**.
26. Right-click any of the values on the y-axis, and click Vertical Axis Properties.
27. In the Vertical Axis Properties dialog box, click Number, click Percentage in the Category list, change Decimal Places to 0, and click the OK button.
28. Right-click the Axis Title label below the x-axis (the horizontal axis), and clear the Show Axis Title selection.
29. Right-click the legend to the right of the chart, and click Delete Legend.
30. Double-click the chart title, and replace the text with the following text: **Reseller Sales vs Targets**.
31. Click the chart twice to display the Chart Data pane, select <Expr>, and click the Properties button in the Chart Data pane's toolbar.
32. In the Series Properties dialog box, click Fill, and click the expression button to the right of the color button.
33. Change the expression as follows to set the fill to red whenever the deviation is below 0:

```
=iif((Sum(Fields!Reseller_Sales_Amount.Value)-Sum(Fields!Sales_Amount_Quota
.Value))/Sum(Fields!Sales_Amount_Quota.Value)<0, "Red", "Automatic")
```

34. Click the OK button twice.
35. Click the Run button to preview the report.

36. In the Employees drop-down list, select David R. Campbell, and then click the View Report button to test the report, shown here:

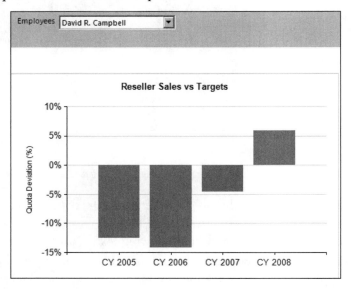

37. Save the report.

Charting Correlated Quantitative Values in Reporting Services

As you saw in the previous exercise, the Chart Wizard is a good way to start a report, but you often must continue refining the chart by working with chart control properties to adjust the appearance of the chart. For example, if you need to create a correlation chart, the Chart Wizard isn't any help, as scatter charts aren't available as an option. Therefore, you build this type of report by working directly with the chart control and manually configuring the two quantitative values in the series.

Let's try the direct approach by using the Chart Data pane to configure a scatter chart that plots the correlation between gross margin percentage values and average unit price by product category. We'll use the AdventureWorks cube as a data source for this chart.

NOTE

Although we'll be using Report Builder for this exercise, the steps related to working with the chart control are the same when you use BIDS.

Exercise 10-5: Creating a Scatter Chart

1. In Report Builder 3.0, create a new report.
2. In the Report Data pane, click New and then click Data Source.
3. In the Data Source Properties dialog box, select the Use A Connection Embedded In My Report option, select Microsoft SQL Server Analysis Services in the Connection Type drop-down list, and then click the Build button.
4. Use the Connection Properties dialog box to create a connection to the AdventureWorks sample database, and then click the OK button twice to close all dialog boxes.
5. Next, click New in the Report Data pane, but this time click Dataset.
6. In the Dataset Properties dialog box, select the Use A Dataset Embedded In My Report option, select your newly added data source in the drop-down list, and then click the Query Designer button.
7. Drag the following items to the center pane: Category (from the Products dimension), Average Unit Price, and Gross Profit Margin (both from the Sales Summary folder in the Measures dimension).
8. Click the OK button twice.
9. On the Insert tab of the ribbon, click Chart, and then click Insert Chart.
10. Position the cursor in the upper-left corner of the report body.
11. In the Select Chart Type dialog box, click Scatter in the list on the left, click the Scatter chart type as shown next, and then click the OK button.

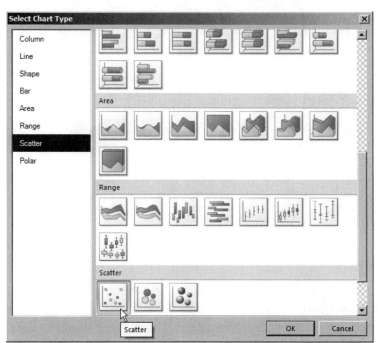

12. Resize the chart to about 5 inches wide and 2 inches high.

13. Click the chart to display the Chart Data pane, click the Add Field button (the plus sign) in the Values section as shown here, and then click Gross_Profit_Margin to set the value to the vertical axis.

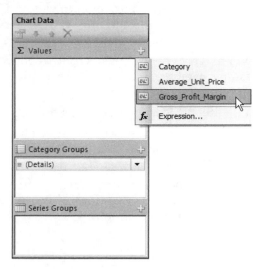

14. Because you selected a scatter chart type, you now need to assign a value to the horizontal axis by clicking the arrow for the X Value item in the Chart Data pane and clicking Average_Unit_Price as shown:

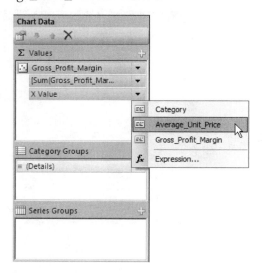

15. Now let's group the series data values by category by clicking the Add Field button for the Series Group section and selecting Category.

NOTE

By setting Category as a series group, we are configuring the chart to display a different marker for each category. Because our data set has only four rows of data, one for each category, we'll see four markers for the four values in this chart. If the data set was more granular, we would see multiple values per marker. Using a series group is not required; it merely allows you to see the complete set of values as a collection of subsets differentiated by marker (or color, if you prefer).

16. Delete the chart title, change the vertical axis title to **Gross Margin**, and change the horizontal axis title to **Average Unit Price**.

17. Right-click the legend, select Show Legend Title, and then change the legend title to **Categories**.

18. Change the vertical axis properties to display values using the percentage format with zero decimal places.

19. Set the interval properties for the horizontal axis properties by changing Minimum to 0 and Interval to 200, as shown here:

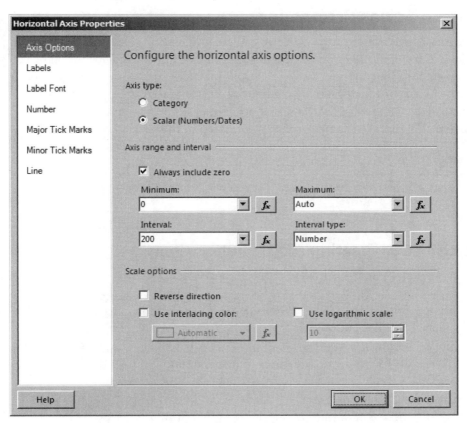

20. Click any point in the chart, right-click the point, and click Series Properties.

21. In the Series Properties dialog box, click Markers in the list, change Marker Size to 10pt, and then click the OK button.

22. Preview the report, which should now resemble this illustration:

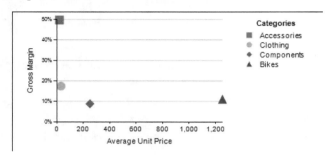

23. Keep the report open for the next exercise.

Custom Series Properties

There are many different ways that you can create a distribution chart in Reporting Services. You can either build a standard column chart to show distribution by category or use a smooth line chart to show a distribution curve. You can also transform a column chart into a histogram by configuring custom properties for the chart series. Let's create a chart to display the distribution of customers by number of cars owned. We'll add this chart to the report that you created in the previous exercise.

NOTE

The custom series properties are also available if you use BIDS to create your chart.

Exercise 10-6: Creating a Distribution Chart

1. In Report Builder, click New in the Report Data pane, and then click Dataset.

2. In the Dataset Properties dialog box, select the Use A Dataset Embedded In My Report option, select a data source in the drop-down list, and then click the Query Designer button.

3. Drag the following items to the center pane: Customer Count (from the Internet Customers folder in the Measures dimension) and Number of Cars Owned (from the Demographics folder in the Customer dimension).

4. Click the OK button twice.

5. On the Insert tab of the ribbon, click Chart and then click Insert Chart.

6. Position the cursor in the report body below the scatter chart.

7. In the Select Chart Type dialog box, click the default chart type, Column, and click the OK button.

8. In the Chart Data pane, add Customer_Count to the Values section, and add Number_of_Cars_Owned to the Category Groups section.

9. Delete the legend title and both axis titles from the chart.

10. Change the chart title to **Customer Count by Number of Cars Owned**.

11. Change the number format of the vertical axis to number with 0 decimal places and enable the 1000 separator.

12. Open the Horizontal Axis Properties dialog box, and select the Hide First And Last Labels Along This Axis check box on the Labels page.

13. If the Properties pane is not already open, select the Properties check box on the View tab of the ribbon.

14. Click any column in the chart again to display the Customer properties in the Properties pane.

15. Change the Color property to Silver.

16. Expand CustomAttributes and change the PointWidth property to 1.

NOTE

If you want to create a histogram chart, you must set the ShowColumnAs property to Histogram, and then set either HistogramSegmentIntervalNumber or HistogramSegmentIntervalWidth. Optionally, you can set the HistogramShowPercentOnSecondaryYAxis property if you want to include percentages with distribution frequency. A histogram chart requires more detailed data than we're using in this exercise. For example, you would need to include customer-level detail in the data set to produce a customer histogram.

17. Preview the report to view the distribution chart, which should appear similar to the chart shown here:

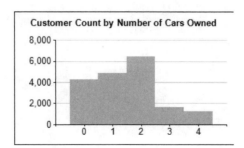

18. Save the report.

Other Controls

In addition to the chart control, Reporting Services includes a control for a map, data bar, sparkline, indicator, and gauge. We'll show you how to work with the map control in the next chapter, and we already explained data bars and sparklines in Chapter 7. What's left to discuss? The indicator and the gauge.

Indicator

During our discussion of PerformancePoint Services in the previous chapter, we showed you how to build a scorecard from KPIs. If you prefer not to implement PerformancePoint Services in your SharePoint farm, you can still develop a scorecard by using Reporting Services instead. In Reporting Services, a scorecard is a table or matrix that includes a column to which you add the indicator control. You configure the indicator control much like a chart control, but access a Gauge pane instead of a Chart Data pane. After assigning an expression to the control, you configure its Value and State properties, shown in Figure 10-15, much like the scoring pattern definition in PerformancePoint Services.

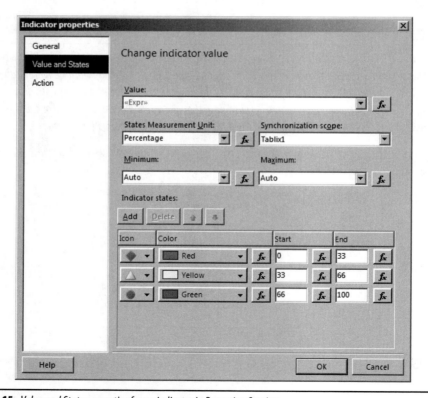

Figure 10-15 *Value and State properties for an indicator in Reporting Services*

Calendar Year	Reseller Sales Amount	Sales Amount Quota	Variance	
CY 2005	$8,065,435	$9,513,000	-15.22 %	△
CY 2006	$24,144,430	$29,009,000	-16.77 %	◆
CY 2007	$32,202,669	$38,782,000	-16.96 %	◆
CY 2008	$16,038,063	$18,410,000	-12.88 %	●

Figure 10-16 *A table containing indicators*

Using indicators in a table, as shown in Figure 10-16, is an alternative to the variance report that we developed in the last exercise.

Gauge

A gauge is a special type of chart that combines both a value and a target value. If that sounds like a key performance indicator, you're right. In fact, gauges are included in the indicator library in PerformancePoint Services, but the gauge is a distinct report item type in Reporting Services. It can have the shape of a radial gauge, similar to the fuel gauge in many cars or a utility meter, or it can have a linear shape like a thermometer. Keep in mind that it's easy to overwhelm users with too many gauges, and it's even possible to obscure the meaning of data relationships by using a gauge. If you can use a chart to show important data relationships, a chart is often the more effective data visualization option.

That said, if you really must use a gauge, try the new bullet graph gauge, shown in Figure 10-17. In this example, we configured two linear pointers for this gauge.

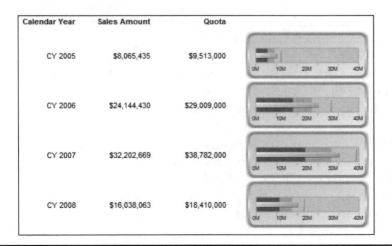

Figure 10-17 *Bullet graph*

The first linear pointer displays the position of sales amount along a scale using a bar, and the second linear pointer displays quota along the same scale using a vertical marker. We set a fixed scale length of 40,000,000 for all gauges in this report to better compare the changes in sales and quotas from year to year. A scale can have ranges with different colors to indicate scoring bands. In this example, we configured three separate ranges to represent values of 50 percent of quota and lower, values between 50 percent and 75 percent of quota, and values above 75 percent of quota.

PerformancePoint Services

The last tool to review is the Analytic Chart, which we introduced in the previous chapter. The Analytic Chart has limited charting functionality, which means you won't be able to produce all six of the data relationships that we discussed at the beginning of this chapter. However, because the Analytic Chart is much more interactive than any of the other charting tools, your primary objective as a chart developer is to establish a starting point for user analysis. Whatever you create, a user will change!

Basic Structure

The Analytic Chart is unique among the charting tools provided in the suite for several reasons. First, it's the only one that supports a single data source—specifically, Analysis Services. Second, it's the only tool that fully supports the user's exploration of the data in the cube with filtering, drill-down, and pivot capabilities. Although you could replicate the drill-down capability to some extent with Reporting Services by using actions, you would have to build a lot of reports to match the built-in capability of the Analytic Chart. The third distinctive difference in the Analytic Chart is the limited chart types—bar chart (called a column chart in all other tools), line chart, and pie chart. Fourth, you don't have any control over the colors, fonts, or any other appearance of any chart element.

Creating an Analytic Chart is straightforward. A Details pane, like the one shown in Figure 10-18, lists the measures, dimensions, and hierarchies that you use to define the structure of the chart. You drag fields from the Details pane to the Series, Bottom Axis, or Background boxes along the bottom of the designer. The Analytic Chart displays items in the Series box as bars or lines according to the value scale that applies to the measure that you select and uses items in the Bottom Axis box to group categories along the horizontal axis. The Background box operates as a filter on the values that display in the chart. It's perfectly fine to place multiple items in each box, except you can only include one measure at a time in the Background box.

Typically, you include the measure that you want to use for chart values in the Background box. If you omit it, the Analytic Chart uses the default measure for the

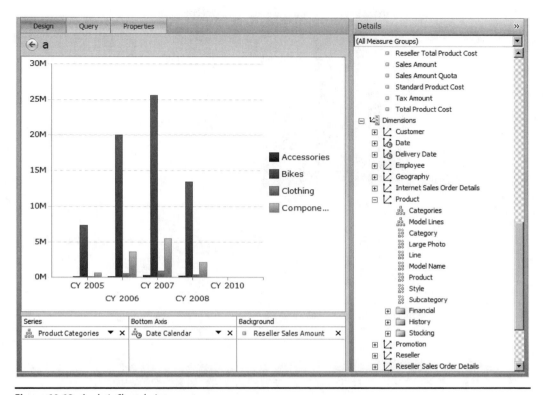

Figure 10-18 *Analytic Chart designer*

cube, which might not be your intent. You could put multiple measures in the Bottom Axis or the Series box to compare measures by category, but if the scales are different, the chart might be difficult to read. On the other hand, you can automatically generate a line chart with a bar chart by using both a percentage measure and a value measure, as shown in Figure 10-19.

When you place dimensions or hierarchies in the Series and Bottom Axis boxes, the chart displays the All member by default (unless you've defined a default member for the dimension in the cube design). To select a specific member or set of members, click the drop-down arrow of the item to open the Select Members dialog box, shown in Figure 10-20. You can use the Autoselect Members list to choose members dynamically. That is, as new members are added to the dimension over time, they appear automatically in the chart with no action required on your part. If you want to show specific members, regardless of future additions to the dimension, you can expand each node in the hierarchy and select the check box for each member that you want to include. Be sure to clear the All member if you don't want to see it in your chart.

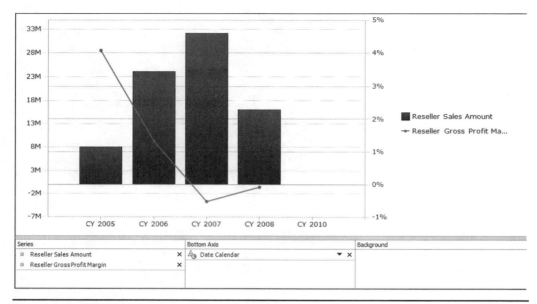

Figure 10-19 *Combination of percentage measure and value measure*

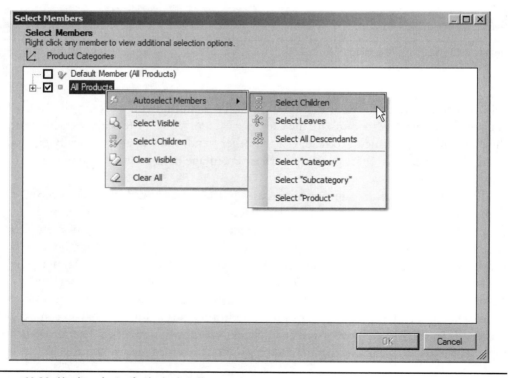

Figure 10-20 *Member selection for the Analytic Chart*

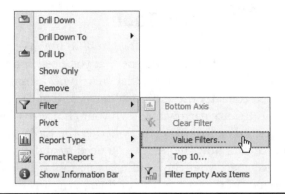

Figure 10-21 *Filter options for axis or legend members*

Filters

Besides setting up the basic structure of the chart to help users start analyzing cube data, you can also apply filters to members in the Series box or the Bottom Axis box. To do this, you right-click a label in the legend or along the horizontal axis, click Filter, and then select the Top 10 or Value Filters option, as shown in Figure 10-21. When you apply a value filter, the chart displays only those members and the corresponding measure values that meet the criteria that you specify, such as "Reseller Sales Amount is greater than 10,000,000."

A Top 10 filter is more complex, and more than its name implies. You can use it to create a subset of members that are ranked the highest according to your criteria or the lowest using a Top or Bottom filter, respectively. The number indicates the comparison value, such as the count, cumulative sum, or cumulative percentage, that determines whether a chart includes a dimension member.

Summary

We provided a lot of information in this chapter about the tools that you can use to produce charts. We explained how to get started creating a chart in each tool, highlighted key features, and warned about potential issues you might encounter with a particular tool. In addition, we provided a high-level review of techniques for developing charts, but there is so much more to learn. One of our favorite resources for effective design techniques for tables and charts is Edward Tufte's *The Visual Display of Quantitative Information, Second Edition* (Graphics Press, 2001). Another highly recommended resource is Stephen Few's *Show Me the Numbers* (Analytics Press, 2004). Incidentally, the idea of a bullet graph was developed by Few.

How to Choose a Charting Tool

Are you still stumped about how to choose which tool to use? We recommend that you start by thinking about the particular chart type that you need and use the table in the Appendix to determine which tools support that chart type. If multiple tools support the same chart type, then consider the additional features that each tool provides.

If you're still having difficulty narrowing down your choice to a single tool, consider how you're going to access data for the report, whether the tool you want to use supports that data source, and how frequently you need to update data. For example, if you're creating a variance chart, your choice of charting tool will determine whether you must calculate the variance in the source data or if you can provide an expression in the chart to calculate the result at runtime.

Lastly, consider how users will want to work with charts. Will they just glance at a chart to derive information quickly? If so, spend as little effort as possible building the chart by using the SharePoint Chart Web Part. Or will they want to seamlessly transition from viewing a report to performing an in-depth analysis of the underlying data? In that case, the Analytic Chart is a better choice. On the other hand, if users wind up importing data into Excel, you might simplify the process for them by storing charts in Excel Services whenever possible.

Do users need any of the following features: pixel-perfect layout or dynamic behavior in parameters, or complex expressions? For precision in appearance or behavior, use Reporting Services. It's also the best option for creating reusable charts.

Speaking of Reporting Services, we'll devote the next chapter to a discussion about maps. As you'll see, a map wizard makes it easy to set up a simple map. Yet the map control is loaded with properties for complex visualizations of spatial data, whether that data is geographic or a set of coordinates that describes boundaries of shapes that you can use to produce less conventional maps.

Chapter 11

Maps

In This Chapter

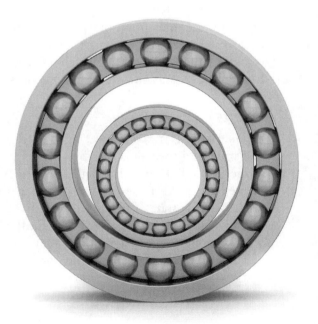

Traditionally, charting has been the method of choice for visually communicating patterns and relationships in data. Often, charts display these patterns and relationships across time, but viewing this type of information across space can be just as useful and enlightening. In the latest version of Reporting Services, you now have the ability to present data in the form of a map. Your map can represent a geographic location or even something simpler, like a floor plan, or it could show routes between locations. You can also superimpose colors and shapes onto your map to use for comparing analytical data by location. For example, you could use color to illustrate the population density or other demographic information for selected geographic areas.

In this chapter, we'll explore the new map feature in Reporting Services. We'll start by explaining how to use the Map Wizard to build the foundation for a map. Then we'll show you how to work with map layers to combine multiple data sets on the same map and how to configure map component properties to fine-tune the appearance of your map.

Introducing Maps

Before you start building a map, you need to have spatial data that Reporting Services can render in the form of a map. You can use built-in spatial data sources for creating maps of locations in the United States, or you can provide data using one of the other spatial data sources that Reporting Services supports.

Spatial Data Types

There are three types of spatial data that you can use in Reporting Services—points, lines, and polygons. You can use a SQL Server 2008 (or higher) database to store spatial data in a Geography or Geometry column and then use Common Language Runtime (CLR) methods to derive points, lines, or polygons for a Reporting Services data set. Let's take a look at how Reporting Services renders each spatial data type.

Points

A point is an (X,Y) coordinate representing a location at the street level or city level that you can display on a map by using a marker, such as a circle, a pushpin, or other image. If you link analytical data to a point, you can change the color or size of the marker. Figure 11-1 shows a map of points that shows the location of AdventureWorks resellers in the state of Nevada, using color to show sales volume, with the lighter colors for the lowest sales and darker colors for the highest sales. By themselves, however, the points don't convey enough information about location.

To put the sales data by customer location into context, you have two options. The first option is to add another layer to the map to show a polygon, or lines representing

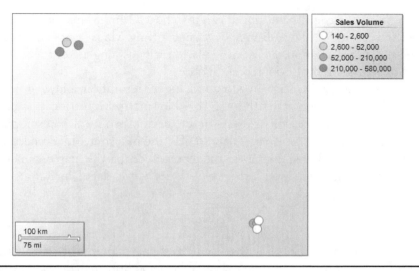

Figure 11-1   *Point data to map locations for AdventureWorks resellers*

the geographical boundaries of Nevada. We'll explain more about polygons shortly, but first, let's look at the second option. Instead of a polygon, you can use a Bing Maps tile layer to provide a background for you automatically, as shown in Figure 11-2. To build the Bing Maps layer, Reporting Services can analyze the spatial locations in your

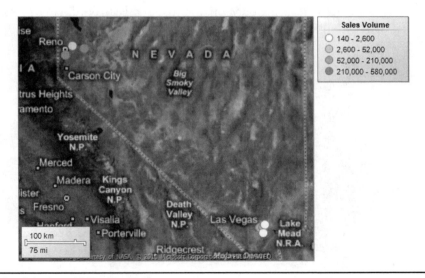

Figure 11-2   *Point data with Bing Maps layer*

map to determine the coordinates that it can match to a Bing Maps tile at the same zoom level and resolution. The advantage of using a Bing Maps layer is that you can include point data for locations all over the world easily, as long as your report server is configured to access the Bing Maps Web Service.

The Bing Maps layer also lets you zoom to a higher resolution, allowing you to see more detail. Figure 11-3 shows another type of point map with the location of each fictional reseller relative to major roadways and to each other. A salesperson planning to visit each reseller could use this spatial data to plan the best route. If you need to display more detail, you could add parameters to the report to center the map on a particular location and adjust the zoom level further to see street-level detail, including directional indicators for one-way streets.

Lines

Another type of spatial data is a line that connects a pair of points or coordinates. Lines are useful for showing routes between points. When you link analytical data to lines, you can use the data to vary the color or width of lines. Just as with points, you'll need a background for the lines to provide spatial context, either by adding a polygon layer or a Bing Maps layer. In Figure 11-4, you can see route information for a shipment sent from Alaska to an AdventureWorks reseller in Nevada.

Polygons

You can create a polygon object from a set of four or more coordinates that define the boundaries of a closed area. In a polygon, the first and last coordinates in the set

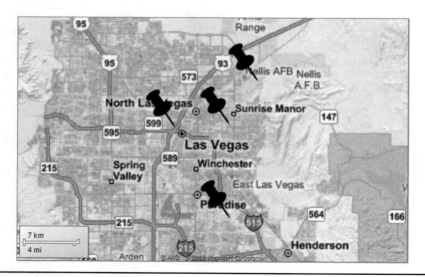

Figure 11-3 *Higher-resolution Bing Maps layer*

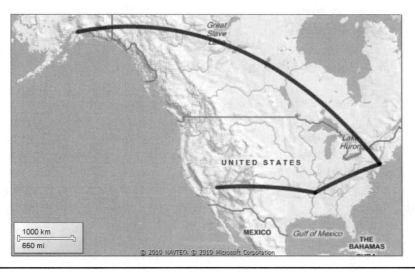

Figure 11-4   *Line data to map shipment route*

are identical. In effect, a polygon is a series of lines that start and end at the same location. Figure 11-5 shows a map based on two polygons for the states of Nevada and California. Keep in mind that a polygon can represent an area unrelated to geography, such as the shop floor plan in the AdventureWorks manufacturing plant.

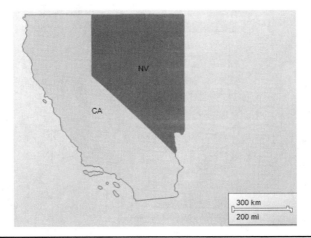

Figure 11-5   *Map of polygon objects*

Spatial Data Sources

Now that you know what type of data you can map in Reporting Services, how can you provide that data to Reporting Services? You can use three data sources:

► **Data embedded in a report** To help you get started quickly with maps, if your spatial data is based in the United States, the Reporting Services installation adds a collection of reports in the Program Files\Microsoft Visual Studio 9.0\ Common7\IDE\PrivateAssemblies\MapGallery folder. These reports use polygon objects created from TIGER/Line Shapefiles, available free from the United States Census Bureau. Three of the reports provide alternate views of the United States, and the remaining reports display county boundaries by state. For example, one of the reports shows the counties in the state of Washington, as you can see in Figure 11-6.

NOTE

Because political boundaries in other countries might be subject to change, Microsoft made the decision to include only the United States in this report collection. If you want to develop maps for other countries, you can create reports based on polygon objects for each country and save them to this folder to add items to the Map Gallery. You'll need to do this on each report developer's computer. Another option is to save a country map as a report part; then Report Builder users can use the map in other reports. However, users who author reports using BIDS cannot use the Report Part Gallery.

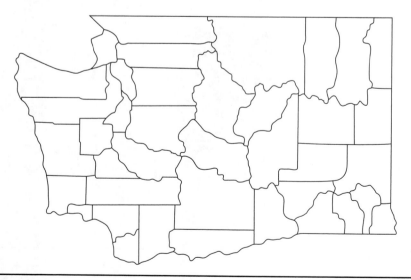

Figure 11-6 *Map Gallery report for the state of Washington*

▶ **ESRI shapefile** The Environmental Systems Research Institute (ESRI) developed a spatial data format for points, lines, and polygons called a shapefile that is commonly used in geographic information systems. When you specify a shapefile as a source for your map, you reference an SHP file, which describes the geographic or geometric shape, but you will also need to store the corresponding DBF file available in the same folder as the SHP file.

▶ **SQL Server spatial data** SQL Server 2008 introduced the SQLGeometry and SQLGeography data types, which you can use to describe points, lines, or polygons for your map. When you create the map, you specify a data set that includes a spatial data column for one of these three object types. Each row in the data set becomes a separate map element. For example, if your data set contains point data, the map displays each row as a separate point.

NOTE

Fortunately for our purposes in this chapter, we have access to spatial data in the AdventureWorks2008R2 sample database. If you need to geocode your own data, consider the options presented by Ed Katibah in his blog post, "Address Geocoding with SQL Server 2008 Spatial" at http://blogs.msdn.com/b/edkatibah/archive/2009/03/10/address-geocoding-with-sql-server-2008-spatial.aspx.

Creating a Map

There are two ways to create a map in Reporting Services, whether you use Business Intelligence Development Studio or Report Builder 3.0. By far, the easier way is to use the Map Wizard. The alternative is to add a map control to the report layout and then manually add layers and configure the properties of each component.

Whichever method you choose to create the map, the process is much the same. You start by selecting the source of the spatial data. As we explained in the previous section of this chapter, you can select a report from the Map Gallery, use an ESRI shapefile, or create a data set from a query that returns spatial data.

One of the choices you must make is whether to embed the spatial data in the report or to retrieve the data from the source each time the report executes. If you embed data in the report, the size of the RDL file will be much larger, but the time required by the report server to render the report will be less. You should choose the embedded data option if your spatial data is static, which is typical of points that represent fixed locations or polygons that represent geographic boundaries. Another benefit of using embedded data is the ability to view the spatial data in both the design and preview modes. Conversely, if you retrieve the spatial data at runtime, you will have a smaller RDL file to maintain on the report server, but the report will require more time to process. This latter option is better suited for a report that relies on parameters to filter the data or to configure a report item's properties based on a user's selection at runtime.

> **NOTE**
>
> *If you decide to use a shapefile as a data source for your map but you don't want to embed the data in your report, you must upload the shapefile and its corresponding DBF file to your report server. You can then reference the shapefile from its location on the report server.*

When creating the map from spatial data, you can adjust the map view options to focus on a particular area of interest. If you're using the Map Wizard, you can make this change on the second step of the Map Wizard, shown in Figure 11-7. This page includes a slider to adjust the zoom level and four directional arrow buttons to change the center point of the map. If you miss the step while working through the wizard, you have similar controls in the Map Layers pane that appears when you click twice on the map in design mode.

After providing the spatial data source and setting the map view options, your next step is to specify what type of map you want to create. The set of choices from which

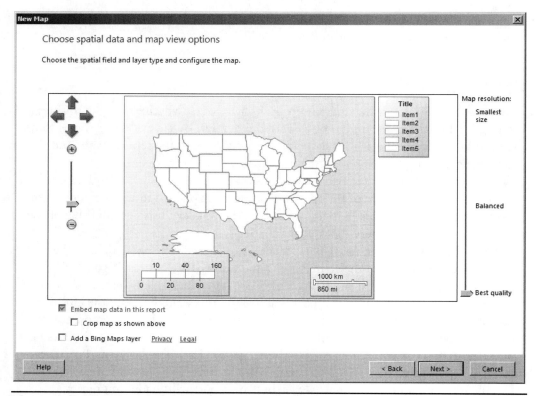

Figure 11-7 *Setting spatial data and map view options in the wizard*

Style	Usage	Example
Basic marker map	Display locations using a single marker type without a link to analytical data	
Bubble marker map	Display locations using a bubble as a marker and varying the size of the bubbles according to a single value in the analytical data set (e.g., sales volume)	
Analytical marker map	Display locations using a marker style, size, and color that depend on multiple values in the analytical data set (e.g., sales volume, years in business, number of employees)	

Table 11-1   *Point Data Map Styles*

you can choose depends on the type of spatial data that you're using as a source for your map and whether you intend to link analytical data to your spatial data.

When you're using point data, you can choose from the map styles shown in Table 11-1.

When your spatial data is based on line objects, you can choose from the map styles shown in Table 11-2.

Last, when your map is based on polygon objects, you can choose from the map styles shown in Table 11-3.

Style	Usage	Example
Basic map	Display lines using a single color and line width without a link to analytical data	
Analytical map	Display lines using a color and line width that depend on multiple values in the analytical data set (e.g., on-time delivery and number of items shipped)	

Table 11-2   *Line Data Map Styles*

Style	Usage	Example
Basic map	Display polygons either using a single color or randomly assigned colors in a specified palette without a link to analytical data	
Color analytical map	Display polygons using colors that depend on a single value in the analytical data set (e.g., population count)	
Bubble map	Display bubbles at center point of polygons and vary the size of the bubbles according to a single value in the analytical data set (e.g., sales volume)	

Table 11-3   *Polygon Data Map Styles*

If you select a map type that requires an analytical data set, you must add another data set to your report that includes one or more fields that match fields in the spatial data set and uniquely identify a matching row in the spatial data set. For example, let's assume that your spatial data set includes a column containing a polygon object and a column that uniquely identifies the polygon, such as a state name. To display correctly in the rendered map, your analytical data set must also have a state name column, which you match to the state name column in the spatial data set. Take care to ensure that the matching fields in each data set have the same data type and formatting so that Reporting Services can properly link the two data sets during the rendering process.

Let's use the Map Wizard to create a map that uses color to illustrate the distribution of AdventureWorks resellers by state in the United States. We'll use the Map Gallery as the data source for the polygon shapes of the states.

Exercise 11-1: Using the Map Wizard

1. Open Report Builder 3.0.
2. If the Getting Started dialog box displays, click Map Wizard. Otherwise, launch the wizard from the Insert Map button of the ribbon.
3. In the New Map Wizard, on the Choose A Source Of Spatial Data page, keep the default selection of Map Gallery, select USA By State Inset, and click the Next button.
4. On the Choose Spatial Data And Map View Options page, click the Next button.

5. On the Choose Map Visualization page, select Color Analytical Map, and then click the Next button.

6. On the Choose The Analytical Dataset page, select the option to add a data set, and click the Next button.

7. On the Choose A Connection To A Data Source page, click the New button.

8. In the Data Source Properties dialog box, click the Build button.

9. In the Connection Properties dialog box, type your server name (or localhost) in the Server Name box, select the AdventureWorks2008R2 database, and then click the OK button twice.

10. On the Choose A Connection To A Data Source page, click the Next button.

11. On the Design A Query page, click the Import button, navigate to the folder for this chapter, select the ResellerByState.sql file, and click the Open button.

12. Click the Run button (the exclamation point) to test the query, and then click the Next button.

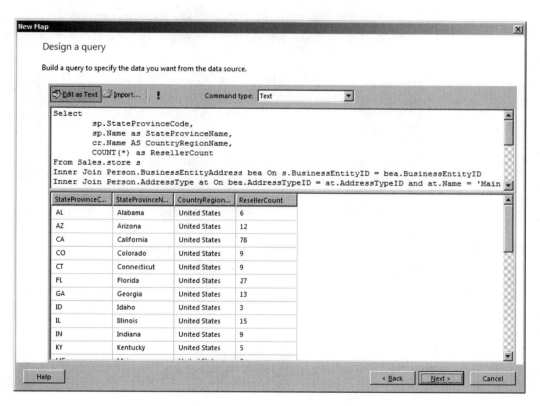

13. On the Specify The Match Fields For Spatial And Analytical Data page, select the Match Fields check box on the STATENAME row, select StateProvinceName in the Analytical Dataset Fields drop-down, and then click the Next button.

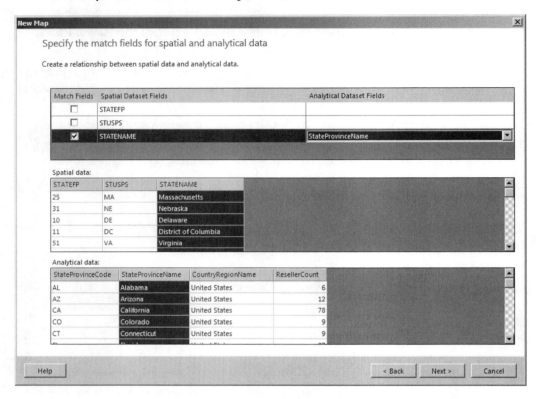

14. On the Choose Color Theme And Data Visualization page, select Generic in the Theme drop-down list.
15. Select [Sum(ResellerCount)] in the Field To Visualize drop-down list.
16. Select Light-Dark in the Color Rule drop-down list.

17. Select the Display Labels check box, select [Sum(ResellerCount)] in the Data
Field drop-down list, and then click the Finish button.

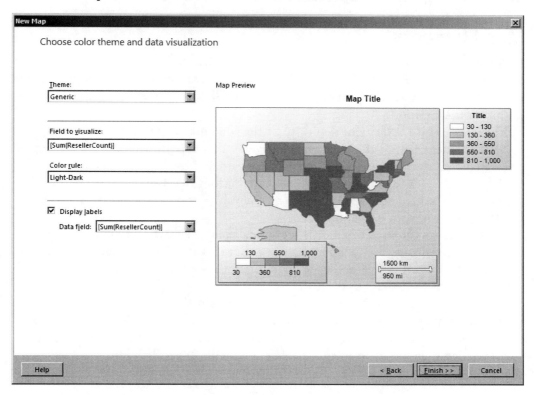

18. Click the Run button in the ribbon to preview the report.

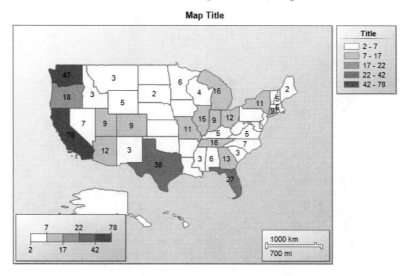

19. Click the Design button in the ribbon.
20. Save the report, and leave Report Builder open for the next exercise.

Map Elements

Although a map is a single report item in the report definition file, it consists of several elements, shown in Figure 11-8. Each element has its own set of properties that you can configure to enhance the appearance of your map. All of these elements are optional, except for the viewport.

The viewport is the element that displays the contents of your map. When you move the center point or change the zoom level of the map, you're changing properties associated with the viewport. Both the Map Wizard and the Map Layers pane (which we'll introduce in the next section) have buttons that you use to make these adjustments. For greater control, you can set the viewport properties directly in the Properties pane, shown in Figure 11-9.

By default, the color scale and distance scale display inside the viewport and the legend displays outside the viewport. You can relocate the color scale and distance scale to maximize the visible area in the viewport, or eliminate the scales altogether. Similarly, you can relocate the legend or delete it.

If you have multiple analytical data sets for your map, the color scale will display the colors-by-value range for each data set. The legend will also include the colors or markers for each data set, as applicable. However, you can create multiple legends for your map and then associate an analytical data set with a specific legend.

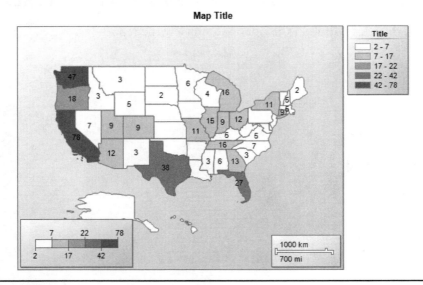

Figure 11-8   *Map elements*

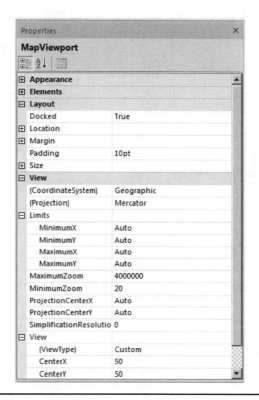

Figure 11-9   *Viewport properties*

Working with Map Layers

The viewport can display multiple map layers simultaneously. Each map layer has its own spatial data set, and optionally, an analytical data set. The type of spatial data that you associate with the map layer determines whether the new map layer is a point layer, a line layer, or a polygon layer. Figure 11-10 is an example of a map that has a polygon layer for state boundaries and a point layer to mark locations. Both layers have analytical data sets that the map uses to encode the polygons and points with color.

Adding a Map Layer

To add a new map layer, you can use a Layer Wizard and step through the process, much like you do when using the Map Wizard. As an alternative approach, you can use the Map Layers pane to add a new layer manually and then use the layer's context menus to access dialog boxes that help you set the layer's properties. Of course, you can

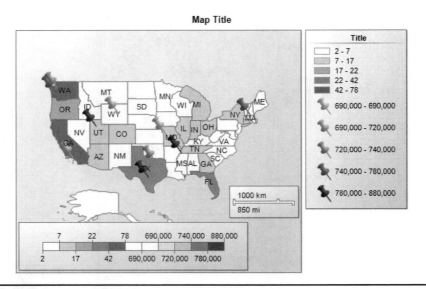

Figure 11-10 *Map with a polygon layer and a point layer*

also use the Properties pane to set property values for a selected layer, although you'll find it easier to use the dialog boxes when you're still learning how to work with maps.

When your map has multiple layers, you can control the order in which each layer renders by managing the sequence of layers from bottom to top in the Map Layers pane, shown in Figure 11-11. In this example, the point layer renders after the polygon layer. If the layers were reversed, with the polygon layer above the point layer, the point layer would not be visible because the polygon layer's position would obscure the point layer.

When you have multiple map layers, there are a few techniques that you can use to manage the appearance of your map. First, you can use the arrow buttons in the Map Layers toolbar to arrange the sequence of the layers so that point layers appear above line layers, which in turn appear above polygon layers. Another option is to select a layer

Figure 11-11 *Map layer sequence*

in the Map Layers pane and use the Properties button in the toolbar to set visibility properties, as shown in Figure 11-12. You can increase the percentage of transparency of a layer that is positioned above another layer to make the lower layer more visible when the map renders. A third option is to use the layer visibility options to show or hide the selected layer based on a minimum and maximum zoom level that you specify based on an expression. For example, you could add a report parameter that prompts the user to select the layers to display in the map and then reference that parameter in an expression for the layer visibility.

Let's add another layer to the map we created in the previous exercise. We'll create a point layer to highlight the location of the top ten resellers in the United States based on sales volume, and we'll use color codes for marking each location to help us compare the sales volume levels across this set of resellers. When we're finished, we'll be able to use the map not only to see the distribution of resellers across the United States, but also where the resellers that sell the most products for AdventureWorks are located and how much they sell.

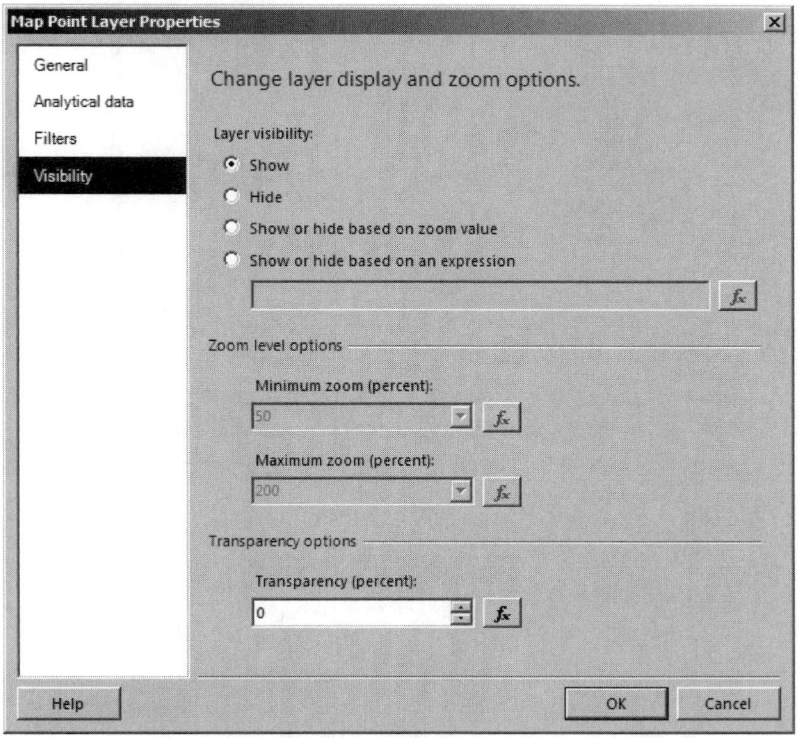

Figure 11-12 *Visibility properties for a point layer*

Exercise 11-2: Configuring a New Map Layer

1. In the report that you created in the previous exercise, right-click the Datasets folder in the Report Data pane, and click Add Dataset.

2. In the Dataset Properties dialog box, select Use A Dataset Embedded In My Report.

3. In the Data Source drop-down list, select the data source that you created in the previous exercise.

4. Click the Import button, navigate to the folder containing files for this chapter, select Top10ResellerLocations.sql, click the Open button, and then click the OK button to add DataSet2.

5. Repeat the previous four steps to import Top10Resellers.sql as DataSet3.

6. If the Map Layers pane is not visible, click the map twice to display it.

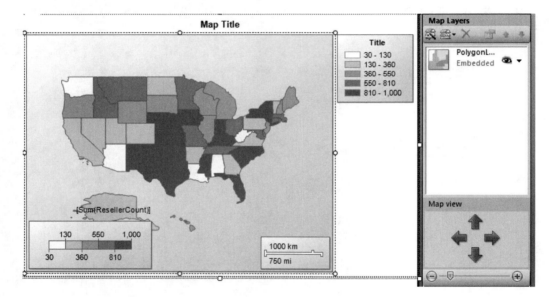

7. Click the Add Layer button in the Map Layers toolbar, and then click Point Layer.

8. Click the arrow icon to the right of the PointLayer1 label to display the context menu, and click Layer Data.

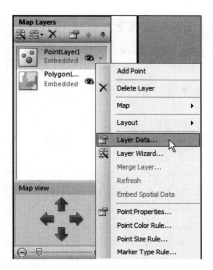

9. In the Map Point Layer Properties dialog box, select Spatial Field In A Dataset as the spatial data source, select Dataset2 in the Dataset Name drop-down list, and select SpatialLocation in the Spatial Field Name drop-down list.

10. Click Analytical Data in the left pane, and select Dataset3 in the Analytical Dataset drop-down list.

11. Click the Add button.

12. Select AccountNumber in the From Spatial Dataset drop-down list, select [ResellerAlternateKey] in the From Analytical Dataset drop-down list, and then click the OK button.

13. Preview the report to check your progress.

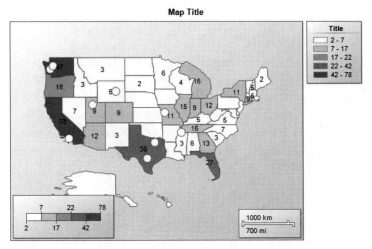

14. Save your report, and keep it open for the next exercise.

Configuring Map Element Properties

As with other report items that you can configure in Reporting Services, the map item and its elements each have a collection of properties that you can use to produce just the right appearance and behavior. There are properties that relate to the type of spatial data that you associate with a layer—point, line, or polygon. In addition, there are properties that determine how the map renders the analytical data—color, size, and marker type. In general, if you can select an element in the map, you'll find a set of properties for that element.

Along with all this flexibility comes the potential for confusion, because it is possible to set properties that conflict with one another. Reporting Services uses an order of precedence to determine which property value to apply in the case of conflict. First, if you add a custom point (which we'll explain how to do later in this chapter), the properties you configure for that point overrule all other properties. The properties that apply to analytical data rules—color, size, width, or marker type—are next in line. If neither of these conditions applies to a map element, then Reporting Services applies the properties that are configured for the spatial data. Last, the visibility and transparency properties of the layer apply.

Spatial Data Properties

For the spatial data in each layer, you can configure whether to label the data and what font type, size, and color to use for the labels. You can also add an action to allow the user to click an item, such as a polygon or a point, to open another report or link to a URL. Additional properties depend on the type of spatial data that you used to create the layer. You can configure a specific marker type and size to apply to all points in a layer or a default line width in a line layer.

Analytical Data Properties

The set of properties that control the appearance of analytical data depend on the spatial data in the layer. For a point layer, you can configure these properties to dynamically change the marker size or marker type, such as circle or pushpin, based on the value of a field in the analytical data set. Likewise, you can use an analytical data set field to change the line color or width in a line layer. A polygon layer can use analytical data only to change the polygon color, or, if you elect to show center points, the color, size, or marker type of each polygon's center point.

Color Rule

Whether you are configuring a color rule for a point, line, or polygon layer, you have similar choices. You select a data field from your analytical data set to use as the basis

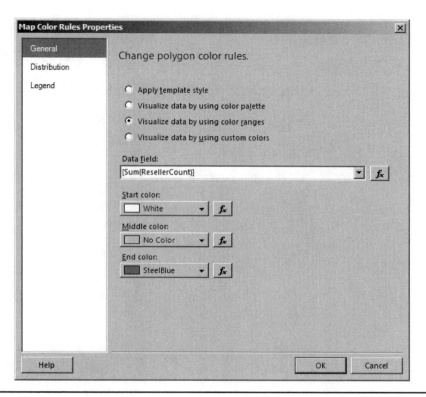

Figure 11-13 *Properties for color rules*

for the color rule, and then assign a set of colors to apply to the specified data field, as shown in Figure 11-13. The set of colors can be from a limited selection of color palettes; a range of colors for which you specify the start, middle, and end colors; or a set of custom colors if you need a wider range of colors. You might use color ranges when you want to use a particular spectrum of colors, and use the custom colors when you have specific color scale requirements.

The actual number of distinct colors that become the color scale for your analytical data depends on the way that you configure the distribution options, shown in Figure 11-14, for the color rules. Reporting Services assigns a distinct color to each subrange. You configure the number of subranges that you want to display for the current map layer, and optionally define the minimum and maximum values of the entire range by setting the Range Start and Range End values, which can be static or based on an expression.

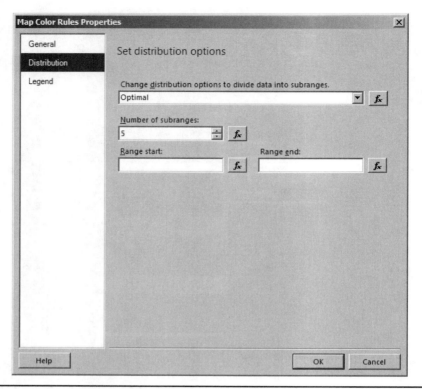

Figure 11-14 *Distribution options for color rules*

You can let Reporting Services allocate values to each subrange, or specify each subrange yourself by selecting one of the following distribution options:

▶ **Optimal**   This is the default distribution setting, which Reporting Services uses to create balanced subranges. If you have fewer than four data points, Reporting Services uses the equal distribution option. Otherwise, it uses an algorithm to find natural breaks in the data as boundaries for each subrange.

▶ **Equal interval**   Use this option when you want the span of values in each range to be identical. For example, with number of subranges set to 5 and minimum and maximum values set to 0 and 100, respectively, this option would produce the following ranges: 0–20, 20–40, 40–60, 60–80, and 80–100.

▶ **Equal distribution**   If you prefer to have the number of rows in your analytical data set distributed more or less evenly across the specified number of subranges, you should use this option. As an example, if you use this option to distribute the 35 records returned for the ResellersByState query (DataSet1) by reseller count, Reporting Services creates the following five subranges: 0–3, 3–6, 6–9, 9–15, and 15–100. Most of the subranges represent about eight records, with the others representing six records.

▶ **Custom**   For maximum control over the distribution, you can create as many subranges (called buckets in the dialog box) as you need and define the start and end values for each.

Legend formatting options are also part of the color rules properties, as shown in Figure 11-15. You can specify whether to include the current layer in the color scale and which legend to use when your map has multiple legends. You can also customize the legend text that describes the values for each subrange as shown in Table 11-4.

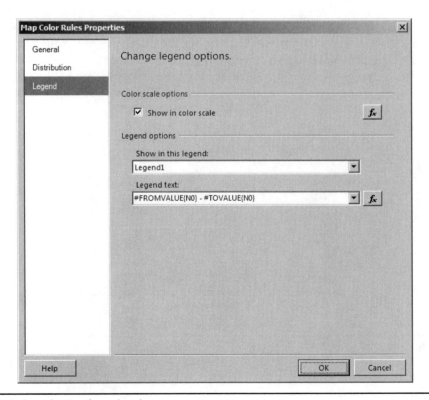

Figure 11-15 *Legend options for a color rule*

Format	Example
#FROMVALUE {C0}	$600,000
#FROMVALUE {C2}	$600,000.00
#TOVALUE	700000
#FROMVALUE{N0} - #TOVALUE{N0}	Note that this is the default format: 600,000 - 700,000

Table 11-4 *Custom Formats for Legend Text*

Custom Point

If you choose to embed spatial data in a layer, you can add a custom point to the same layer quite easily. You use the Add Point command on the layer's context menu, and then click any location on the map. After adding the point, you can configure data values and fine-tune the coordinates for the point in the Properties pane, shown in Figure 11-16. You can also right-click the point and click Embedded Point Properties to set the data values, but that dialog box does not give you access to the spatial values.

In the next exercise, we'll continue fine-tuning the map by configuring properties for various map elements. We'll assign the point layer to a second legend, add a tooltip to the point layer, change the distribution scales for each layer, format the legend, and add a tooltip to the point layer.

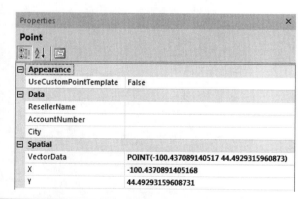

Figure 11-16 *Custom point properties*

Exercise 11-3: Working with Map Element Properties

1. Switch to design mode in your report, right-click the map, click Map, and click Add Legend.

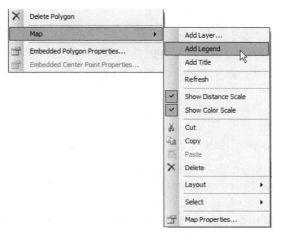

2. Right-click the new legend, and click Legend Properties.
3. In the Map Legend Properties dialog box, click the bottom position button in the right vertical column, and then click the OK button.

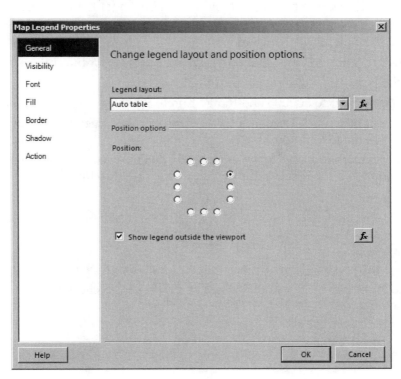

4. Open the PolygonLayer1 context menu, and select Polygon Color Rule.
5. In the left pane, click Distribution.
6. In the Distribution Options drop-down list, select Equal Interval.
7. Set the Number Of Subranges field to 4.
8. Set Range Start to 0 and Range End to 100, and then click the OK button.
9. Open the PointLayer1 context menu in your map, and select Point Properties.
10. In the Map Point Properties dialog box, type the following expression into the Tooltip box:

```
=Fields!ResellerName.Value + ", Sales: " + FormatCurrency(Fields!
ResellerSalesAmount.Value,0)
```

11. Select PushPin in the Marker Type drop-down list, and click the OK button.
12. Open the PointLayer1 context menu, and select Point Color Rule.
13. In the Map Color Rules Properties dialog box, select Visualize Data By Using Color Ranges.
14. In the Data Field drop-down list, select [Sum(ResellerSalesAmount)].
15. Click the Start Color button, and select White.
16. Click the Middle Color button, and select Light Green (at the bottom of the Green column).
17. Click the End Color button, and select Dark Green (at the top of the Green column).
18. In the left pane, click Distribution.
19. In the Distribution Options drop-down list, select Equal Interval.
20. Set the Number Of Subranges field to 3.
21. Set Range Start to 600000 and Range End to 900000.
22. In the left pane, click Legend, select Legend2 in the Legend drop-down list, and then click the OK button.
23. Click the title of Legend1 (the top legend), double-click the title to change to edit mode, and then replace the default title with **# Resellers**.

24. Repeat the previous step to change the Legend2 title to **Sales $**.
25. If the Properties pane is not open, select the Properties check box on the View tab of the ribbon.

26. Select the Legend1 item in the designer to display its properties in the Properties pane.

27. Scroll to the bottom to locate the Size property, expand Size, select False in the Auto drop-down list, change Height to 40, and change Width to 27.

28. Select the color scale in the map, and press the DELETE key to remove it from the map.

29. Click the map title, double-click the title to change to edit mode, and then replace the default title with **Resellers**.

30. Click the Run button on the Home tab of the ribbon.

31. Hover the cursor over one of the pushpins to view the tooltip.

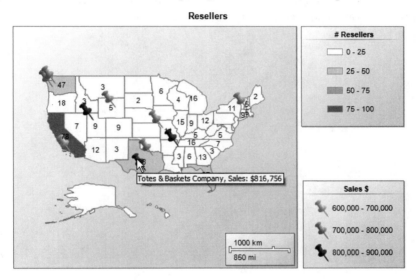

32. Save the report.

Summary

Hopefully, this chapter has whet your appetite for designing maps to display your own data. There are so many ways that you can use maps in a business intelligence solution. You could use a map simply to display the locations of your customers. You could create a map to aggregate information about your customer locations for the sales manager to use when deciding how to divide up sales territories among sales staff. Alternatively, you could create a detailed map of the roads in a particular area that a salesperson could use to determine the best route to follow to visit customers in a particular area. Adding multiple layers gives you the ability to overlay all sorts of analytical data on top of geographic regions using markers or bubbles. Probably the trickiest part of developing maps in Reporting Services is setting up data sets with spatial data. To learn more about spatial data in SQL Server, we recommend *Beginning Spatial with SQL Server 2008* by Alastair Aitchison (Apress, 2009).

In the last few chapters, we've reviewed several different ways to present data visually, from KPIs to charts to maps. Our next chapter shifts to a new topic, data mining. Whereas the data visualization tools that we have discussed thus far rely on the user to draw conclusions about patterns and relationships in the data, data mining takes another approach by automatically finding the patterns and relationships that users would have difficulty discovering themselves and then presenting the results. Sometimes the results can be presented in visual form, while other times the results are used as input for some other activity. You'll find out all about the possibilities in the next chapter!

Chapter 12

Data Mining

In This Chapter

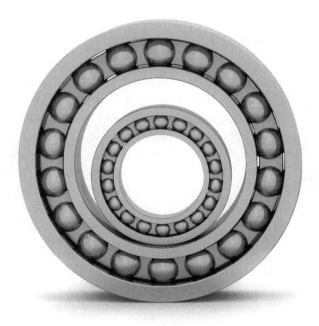

Business intelligence should help us solve the problem of being data rich and information poor. As much as we continue to implement business intelligence tools, which get better with each release, the volume of data that we're storing is outpacing our ability to understand the value of the information that it contains. The job of data mining is to help us sift through that information and uncover these patterns and relationships that would otherwise be difficult, if not impossible, to find.

The Microsoft BI suite supports two options for working with the Analysis Services data mining engine. One option requires you to install the Microsoft Data Mining Add-ins for Office, which provides a simple interface in Excel for a variety of data mining tasks. This desktop interface for data mining is well suited for an individual who needs to perform data mining with relatively small data sets in order to answer specific questions, but without a need to repeat the process regularly. Another option is to create an Analysis Services project to support scalable enterprise-class data mining projects requiring much larger data volumes and integration with other applications and business processes.

Introduction to Data Mining

Because data mining is still an unfamiliar subject to many people, let's start with an introduction to data mining concepts and processes. We'll also provide an overview of the goals of data mining to help you understand the business case for using it. Then we'll compare data mining to other tools and techniques often used for statistical analysis to help you better understand why you might want to incorporate data mining into your business intelligence solutions.

What Is Data Mining?

Data mining is one of those terms that people have seen used both in technical publications and newspaper articles, but rarely understand what it means unless they have direct experience with the technology. Perhaps you've heard it touted as the next best thing to solving all your business problems or vilified as an unethical invasion of your privacy. Like any technology, whether data mining is good or bad is dependent on the actions that people take as a result of using it, but that still doesn't help us understand what it is. Further compounding the problem of understanding data mining is the variety of ways that you can approach data mining and assortment of tools that you can use, even within the same data mining project. You see, data mining with the Microsoft BI suite isn't simply an application that you install. Instead, it's a process that you apply to data to extract meaningful patterns. That process is largely automated, but typically involves several manual tasks before you obtain the final results. We'll explain more about both the automated and manual activities in this process later in this chapter.

To perform the automated extraction of data patterns, you use a data mining *algorithm*. There are many different algorithms from which you can choose, and you might even use multiple algorithms in the same data mining project. Each algorithm applies a different technique to analyze the data in its quest for patterns. The output of an algorithm is a set of rules, or *data mining model,* that best describes the effect of changing one or more variables on another variable or set of variables. That's an abstract concept that will make more sense when we look at specific examples. Fortunately, you don't need an advanced mathematics degree to use an algorithm. You simply need to understand how to select the right algorithm for your business problem and how to prepare your data adequately for the selected algorithm, which we'll describe in more detail later in this chapter.

Goal of Data Mining

Data mining fits nicely into the collection of technologies that comprise business intelligence, because the key goal of data mining is to discover information that either helps you make money or save money. Finding interesting patterns in the data is merely a waste of time if the information is not actionable. The following list represents just a few common examples of business goals for which data mining is well suited:

▶ **Discover relationships**   The simplest type of data mining helps you understand relationships. Relationships can exist among events, products, or people, to name a few. A common type of data mining in this category is market basket analysis in which the data miner seeks to understand which products sell together. You can then use that knowledge to promote sales by placing these products in close proximity in a physical store or by seeding a recommendation engine for online shoppers.

▶ **Find outliers**   Another type of data mining looks for patterns to determine whether a new transaction or event corresponds to normal patterns. If you have enough data for an algorithm to define the rules for normal data, you can then apply these rules to new data to identify outliers. This type of data mining is often used to detect fraud. Perhaps you've received a telephone call from your bank to confirm a transaction that didn't match your typical purchasing patterns. In that case, the algorithm used by the bank identified an outlier that prompted the bank to take action to prevent a loss of money.

▶ **Improve processes**   Rather than use data mining to identify normal patterns as discrete events, you could use it to identify normal trends over time and thereby detect a shift away from normal trends. A manufacturer might use this type of data mining to monitor yields and output of machinery, and then take action to assess and repair machinery when the data begins to trend away from the norm.

Likewise, an IT department managing thousands of servers might use data mining to evaluate server logs to detect new patterns that might adversely affect server availability.

▶ **Make predictions** Data mining can also use historical data to predict future trends. A marketing department using predictive data mining can spend its budget more wisely by targeting customers who are likely to purchase a particular product. As another option, a sales manager might extrapolate historical sales to forecast future sales.

Data Mining Process

As we mentioned earlier, data mining is not limited to the software that you install. Data mining encompasses both the tools and the process. Cross Industry Standard Process for Data Mining, or CRISP-DM, is an industry-standard methodology that you can apply, regardless of the data mining tool that you decide to use. In this section, we'll review this methodology at a high level and then discuss how to apply CRISP-DM to Microsoft data mining.

Introducing CRISP-DM

CRISP-DM was originally released in 1999 by a consortium of commercial entities and data mining practitioners, and was updated in 2006. The CRISP-DM methodology consists of six phases, as shown in Figure 12-1. You can download a user guide that provides details about the methodology and step-by-step instructions from the CRISP-DM website (www.crisp-dm.org).

The first phase is the *Business Understanding* phase in which you communicate the goals of the project with the data mining team and clarify the business requirements. It's very important that you understand the project goals. For example, if your purpose is to develop a marketing campaign, your approach to the data mining project is quite different than it would be if your objective was to develop a forecast of sales for the next four quarters. Your project goals help you determine the type of data you need. The goals also identify the items you need to produce at the end of the project, such as a mailing list for a marketing campaign or a chart of sales forecasts that you can share with others. Also, by understanding the objective, you're better able to choose a data mining algorithm for the problem at hand.

The next phase is *Data Understanding*. This is your opportunity to survey the data, much like you do in a data warehouse project. In this phase, your time is spent determining what you already have, what's missing, and whether it's possible to obtain missing data in some other way. During this phase, you must also assess data quality and develop a strategy for resolving data quality issues. A considerable amount of time

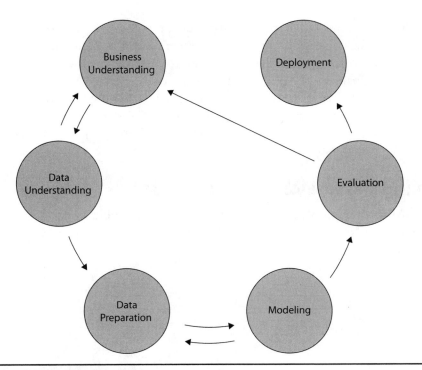

Figure 12-1   *CRISP-DM methodology phases*

will be spent in this phase, and could include a return to the Business Understanding phase to refine or adapt the project goals based on your findings during the Data Understanding phase.

The third phase is *Data Preparation*, which also will require significant time. During this phase, you perform the data cleansing and transformation tasks to address data quality issues and to structure the data for use with the selected modeling tool. You will likely return to this phase multiple times as you discover issues in the data during the next phase.

During the *Modeling* phase, you apply one or more algorithms to the prepared data. You might try the same algorithm multiple times using different parameter values to assess the result on the model. Or you might try various algorithms to produce multiple models, which you can compare for accuracy. Each algorithm might require a different data structure, or execution of the algorithm might reveal a problem in the data that requires intervention, so plan to revert back to the Data Preparation phase before you complete the Modeling phase.

After building a model, you move to the *Evaluation* phase. This is your opportunity to decide whether the data mining results are valid and useful, or whether you need to clean the data still more and go through the modeling process again. You also assess whether the business objectives are met, or whether new information uncovered by the Modeling phase alters the objectives. This phase is the critical point between starting a new iteration or finalizing the process and moving to the next phase.

The final phase is *Deployment*. In this phase, you organize the information developed from the data mining process and share it in a way that is useful. You might do something as simple as publish a report, or something more complex, like developing an application to incorporate the results into business processes.

Applying CRISP-DM to Microsoft BI

CRISP-DM is a methodology that works with any data mining tool. Let's see how we can take advantage of the Microsoft BI to work through these phases, as shown in Figure 12-2.

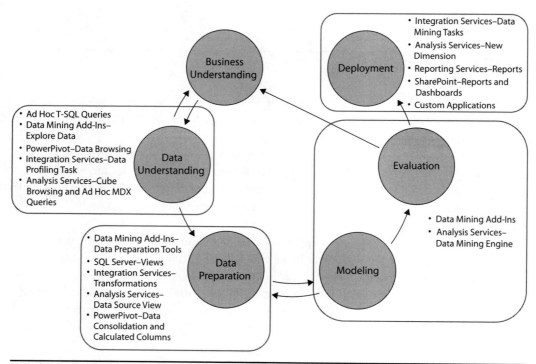

Figure 12-2   *CRISP-DM and Microsoft BI*

Business Understanding   An important task in the Business Understanding phase is to understand the category of your business problem—is it descriptive or predictive? You can use *descriptive data mining* to obtain statistical information about your data; find natural groupings in the data, which you can display in charts; or reveal relationships between variables. Whereas descriptive data mining is useful for understanding known data, *predictive data mining* uses known data to calculate potential results using statistical probabilities. You should rigorously test a predictive data mining model before taking action on its results. With the category of business problem in mind, you can then choose an applicable tool or algorithm. Table 12-1 lists the tools available in our data mining toolset for these two categories. Note that in Analysis Services, many algorithms are useful for both categories.

Data Understanding   The Business Understanding process guides the Data Understanding process by steering you toward the tools or algorithms that you can use to explore your data or use to predict values. With an understanding of those tools or algorithms, you can determine how much data you need to produce valid results and assess the quality of the data that you have. You can perform this assessment by running T-SQL queries against your SQL Server data, or by browsing an Analysis Services cube or PowerPivot data if your data is stored multidimensionally, but an ad hoc approach

Microsoft Product	Descriptive Problems	Predictive Problems
Table Analysis Tools (Data Mining Add-in for Excel)	Analyze Key Influencers Detect Categories Highlight Exceptions Shopping Basket Analysis Cluster Associate	Fill From Example Forecast Goal Seek What If Prediction Calculator Classify Estimate
Data Modeling Tools (Data Mining Add-in for Excel) and Analysis Services Project	Microsoft Association Rules Microsoft Clustering Microsoft Decision Trees Microsoft Naïve Bayes Microsoft Sequence Clustering	Microsoft Association Rules Microsoft Clustering Microsoft Decision Trees Microsoft Linear Regression Microsoft Logistic Regression Microsoft Naïve Bayes Microsoft Neural Network Microsoft Sequence Clustering Microsoft Time Series

Table 12-1   *Tools and Algorithms by Problem Type and Product*

to either of these data sources could be a tedious process. Instead, you could use the Explore Data option in the Data Mining Add-ins for small data sets, or you might consider using the Data Profiling Task in Integration Services for relational data. This task allows you to target one or more tables or views in a SQL Server database and generate an XML file that you can study using the Data Profile Viewer (found in the Microsoft SQL Server 2008 R2/Integration Services program group), as shown in Figure 12-3.

Data Preparation   During the Data Understanding phase, you take note of the changes necessary to put your data in working order for the modeling process. In the Data Preparation phase, you implement the noted changes. There are several transformations that are almost always necessary. For example, some data mining tools work better with numbers than with text or dates, so if there's a way to convert string and date values to numeric values, you should make the change. Also, the tools do a better job of finding patterns when any given variable (or column, as you probably think of this data when it's stored in a relational table) has a relatively small set of distinct values. That is, rather than keeping continuous values like ages or sales amounts, consider creating three to eight groups that organize the continuous values into ranges. Here is a list of common data cleansing activities:

▶ Group continuous data into buckets or normalize the data by converting values to ranges between 0 and 1 or between −1 and 1.

▶ Group a high number of distinct values into smaller sets of distinct values.

▶ Transform dates into periods of time, such as calculating an age from a birth date or number of years since a customer's first purchase calculated from the first purchase date, unless you're using a time series algorithm that requires dates.

▶ Avoid using multiple columns that contain similar information, such as both an age column and a birth date column.

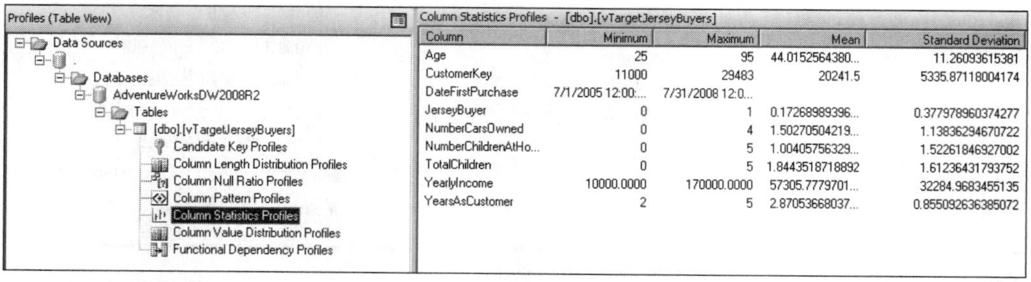

Figure 12-3   *Data Profile Viewer*

▶ Aggregate detail records into fewer derived attributes.

▶ Replace missing values with most common or average value, or remove rows with missing values.

▶ Eliminate unnecessary duplicate values.

▶ Remove outliers to avoid skewing the model.

▶ Normalize the distribution of data as much as possible.

The data preparation process is likely the most time-consuming part of the data mining process, and one that you will continually revisit. For a much more thorough discussion of all the factors you should consider and tasks to performn when preparing your data, we recommend *Data Preparation for Data Mining* by Dorian Pyle (Morgan Kaufmann, 1999). Despite the fact that this book was written more than a decade ago, the principles that Pyle espouses are still sound.

In the Microsoft BI suite, there are several ways that you can approach the data preparation process, depending on the volume of data that you want to mine, the cleanliness of the data, and the complexity of the preparation tasks that you need to perform. The following list provides examples in increasing order of complexity:

▶ Use the Data Preparation tools in the Data Mining Add-ins to identify and update outliers and to relabel categories.

▶ Use PowerPivot for Excel to consolidate data from multiple types of data sources (both relational and nonrelational), derive new values using calculated columns, aggregate detail records, and so on.

▶ Use SQL Server to consolidate multiple relational tables into a single view, perform date conversions, and group data into buckets. You can find an example of this technique in the vDMPrep view, which you can find in the AdventureWorksDW2008R2 database.

▶ Use Integration Services to consolidate large volumes of data from a variety of data sources and to perform complex transformations using repeatable processes.

Before we continue with the next phase, let's take a moment to explore how we might approach data preparation in SQL Server for a simple data mining problem. Assume that you're an analyst working for the marketing manager at AdventureWorks. The company has decided it has too many jerseys in inventory and has asked the marketing manager to launch a campaign to promote jersey sales. You decide to use data mining both to learn more about your customers, which you will share as reports for the marketing department, and to predict likely prospects, which you will provide to the marketing manager as a list of customers to contact for the promotion. As you survey your data, you find that you have the information you need in the data warehouse. All you need to do is create a view to prepare the data for use in your data mining project.

Exercise 12-1: Preparing Data in SQL Server

1. Open SQL Server Management Studio, and connect to the database engine.
2. On the File menu, point to Open, and click File.
3. Navigate to the folder for this chapter, select the vTargetJerseyBuyers.sql query file, and click the Open button.
4. Review the structure of the view script.

    First, notice that this view builds upon another view in the data warehouse, vDMPrep. Next, review the columns that the view returns. Not all columns will be used directly for data mining, but are required to produce the list of prospects, such as customer name and e-mail address. Take a look at the CASE statement, which assigns a flag to segregate buyers of jerseys from nonbuyers. Also, note the conversion of DateOfFirstPurchase to YearsAsCustomer.

5. In the toolbar, click the Execute button to add the view to the AdventureWorksDW2008R2 database.
6. Optionally, open the vDMPrep view to review its structure. To do this, in Object Explorer, expand AdventureWorksDW, expand the Views folder, right-click dbo.vDMPrep, point to Script View As, point to Create To, and click New Query Editor Window.

    The main goal of this view is to select only the columns that are considered to be most important to the analysis of Internet sales data. Note some of the data preparation techniques applied in this view include:

    ▶ Coalesce – to handle missing values

    ▶ Case statement – to transform BirthDate into an age

    ▶ Case statement – to group Yearly Income into a smaller set of distinct values

After we've collected the data and cleansed it, we need to split it into two groups, a training set and a testing set. This step isn't always required for the simple data mining tasks that you can do using Excel, but for more rigorous testing of your data, you should use this partitioning strategy with your data. In order to validate the results of the modeling, we need data to use for validation. So before we do the modeling, we carve off some of the data, which we designate as training data, and then we build the data mining model using the training set. During training, the data mining algorithm finds the patterns and defines the rules that describe those patterns. To find out how well the algorithm developed those rules, we have the test data, which usually, but not always, contains the data for which we know the answer. That way, we can see how well the model fits the data that we held back and thereby determine its accuracy before we commit to actions that rely on the model results.

We'll explore other data preparation tasks, as well as the remaining phases of the data mining methodology, in subsequent exercises. In general, other data preparation tasks include cleansing and partitioning the data. For example, in the next exercise in this chapter, you'll learn how to clean and separate a simple data set using the Data Mining Add-ins.

Data Mining Modeling

After preparing your data, you're ready to build the data mining model. During this phase, you give the data mining modeling tool access to the data and select an algorithm. If necessary, you can configure the algorithm's parameters to fine-tune the modeling behavior. All of the available algorithms were developed by Microsoft Research for you to use, whether you're processing models with the Data Mining Add-ins (unless otherwise noted) or an Analysis Services project.

Microsoft Association Rules   The Microsoft Association Rules algorithm searches for patterns that reveal the frequency of combinations of items in a data set. This type of algorithm is popular for market basket analysis, which describes which products are often purchased as a group. It also calculates the probability that the purchase of one product will result in the purchase of another product.

Microsoft Clustering   Clustering is a way to group records in your data set by using an algorithm to detect common characteristics between the records that might be difficult to discover manually. Once the algorithm identifies the clusters, you can analyze each cluster separately. Clustering is also a useful way to evaluate new data. If a record doesn't fit into an existing cluster, you might have an anomaly.

Microsoft Decision Trees   A decision tree is a popular data mining tool because the results are easy to interpret by business people. We like to explain this algorithm as a giant "if-then-else" rule that progressively splits your data set by levels. At each level, the algorithm selects one or more columns to create groupings of your data. A data record can belong to only one group per level. Not only does the Microsoft Decision Trees algorithm support this type of classification, it also can use linear regression to predict continuous values.

Microsoft Linear Regression   Speaking of linear regression, this algorithm was added to Analysis Services specifically to augment the Microsoft Decision Trees algorithm. To use it in the Data Mining Add-in, you must use the Advanced button in the Data Modeling group of the Data Mining tab to create a mining structure, and then add a linear regression model to the structure. When you create a linear regression mining model, you can use only continuous columns, but the Microsoft algorithm discretizes this numeric input.

Microsoft Logistic Regression   The Microsoft Logistic Regression algorithm develops mining models much like classic statistical logistic regression used to predict the probability of an event based on detected patterns in the data set. This particular algorithm is a variant of the Microsoft Neural Network algorithm, but is restricted to a single level of relationships. Many of the tools that you can use in the Data Mining Add-ins rely on the Microsoft Logistic Regression algorithm, which demonstrates the range of utility this particular algorithm provides.

Microsoft Naïve Bayes   Put simply, the Naïve Bayes algorithm counts the correlations between each value in a target column and values in all other columns. It's useful for simple exploration of your data, and has the additional advantage of processing quickly, compared to other algorithms. However, it cannot handle continuous data, so you can either create your own discretization buckets for a continuous data column or allow Analysis Services to determine the number of buckets automatically.

Microsoft Neural Network   Neural networks were originally developed to simulate the way our brains function, with neurons operating in a highly parallel and distributed fashion. The Microsoft Neural Network algorithm is an advanced algorithm that requires more skill to use effectively. In addition, the results of a neural network model can be more difficult to interpret than other algorithms. On the other hand, it has the advantage of potentially finding complex patterns in your data.

Microsoft Sequence Clustering   Sequence clustering is a variation of the clustering algorithm. This algorithm requires you to provide data that links related records together in a sequence. You can use it to predict the next step in a sequence or to uncover deviations in a sequence pattern.

Microsoft Time Series   Analyzing changes in data over periods of time is a common activity in business intelligence solutions, but the type of analysis is historical in nature. You might find it easier to source data for this algorithm from an OLAP cube than from a relational data source because time series queries are simpler to create using MDX.

Chapter 12: Data Mining

Regardless of the method you use to derive your data, the Microsoft Time Series algorithm uses the historical time series patterns in a different way to forecast values for future time periods. For example, if your historical data represents daily sales, then the forecast will project a specified number of days into the future. Similarly, if your historical data is monthly, the forecast time series will also be monthly.

Evaluation

When the modeling process is complete, it's time to evaluate the results. Both the Data Mining Add-ins and Analysis Services project types include tools to help you during this phase. You associate the tool with a data mining model and then identify the variable to predict. In the Data Mining Add-ins, you can access the tools on the Data Mining tab of the ribbon in the Accuracy and Validation group. In Business Intelligence Development Studio (BIDS), you access the tools by using the Mining Accuracy Chart tab of the mining model designer.

Accuracy Chart   You use an accuracy chart, see Figure 12-4, to evaluate a predictive model, as long as the model is not based on a time series or association rules algorithm.

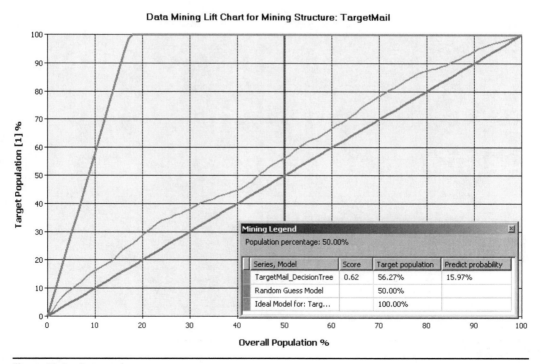

Figure 12-4   *Accuracy chart*

The chart shows the improvement in accuracy of the prediction as the population size increases. It also compares the predictive accuracy of your data mining model to an ideal model and a random guess model. You can see the ideal model as the steepest line in the accuracy chart shown in Figure 12-4, which achieves 100 percent accuracy with approximately 18 percent of the data. The straight line that bisects the chart is the random guess model, which achieves 50 percent accuracy with 50 percent of the data. The data mining model appears slightly better than the random guess model, which typically indicates that the data does not provide enough information to build a suitable model. When you encounter this situation with your own models, you might return to the Data Preparation phase to gather more data.

Profit Chart   The profit chart, shown in Figure 12-5, is a variation of the accuracy chart that you use to estimate profits by the percentage of the population contacted in

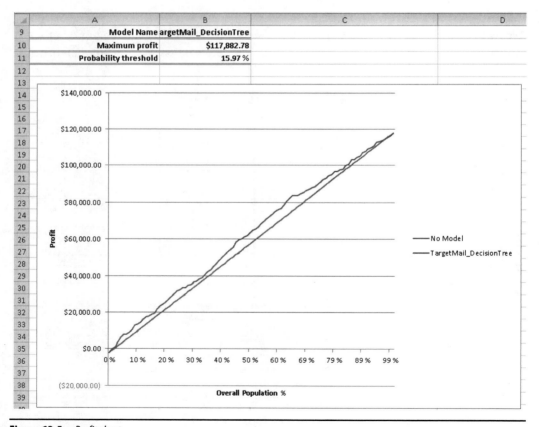

Figure 12-5   *Profit chart*

a marketing campaign. To create the profit chart, you specify the target population, the fixed costs of the campaign, the additional cost per person to contact, and the amount of revenue per person if that person makes a purchase as a result of your campaign. This tool allows you to measure the costs and benefits associated with taking action on your mining model. In this example, you can see that the model is profitable, but it's also not much improved over a random guess.

Classification Matrix   Another way to assess the accuracy of a model is to use a classification matrix. The version in the Data Mining Add-ins, shown in Figure 12-6, provides more information than the corresponding one in an Analysis Services project. Quite simply, it shows the number of correct and incorrect predictions as percentage values and counts. Let's say that you iterate through the Data Preparation and Modeling phases multiple times as you fine-tune the data and the mining model parameters. You can use the classification matrix to determine if the percentage of misclassified records increases or decreases as a result of your changes.

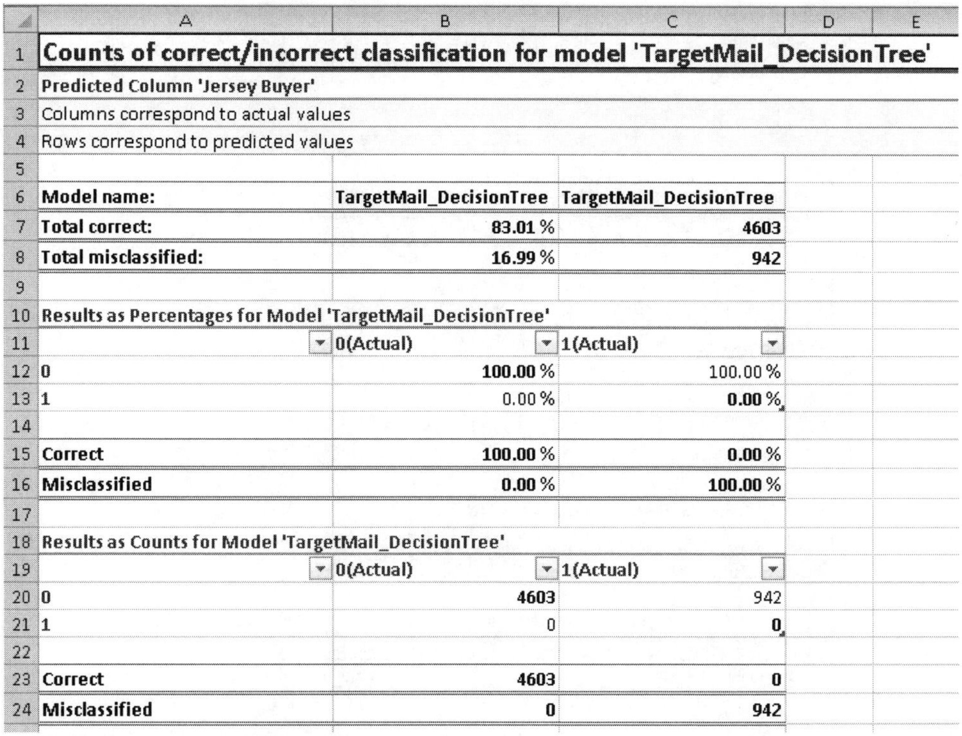

	A	B	C	D	E
1	**Counts of correct/incorrect classification for model 'TargetMail_DecisionTree'**				
2	Predicted Column 'Jersey Buyer'				
3	Columns correspond to actual values				
4	Rows correspond to predicted values				
5					
6	Model name:	TargetMail_DecisionTree	TargetMail_DecisionTree		
7	Total correct:	83.01 %	4603		
8	Total misclassified:	16.99 %	942		
9					
10	Results as Percentages for Model 'TargetMail_DecisionTree'				
11		0(Actual)	1(Actual)		
12	0	100.00 %	100.00 %		
13	1	0.00 %	0.00 %		
14					
15	Correct	100.00 %	0.00 %		
16	Misclassified	0.00 %	100.00 %		
17					
18	Results as Counts for Model 'TargetMail_DecisionTree'				
19		0(Actual)	1(Actual)		
20	0	4603	942		
21	1	0	0		
22					
23	Correct	4603	0		
24	Misclassified	0	942		

Figure 12-6   *Classification matrix*

Cross-Validation   Cross-validation is a more advanced tool for evaluating the accuracy of your mining model. Using parameters you specify, cross-validation automatically creates partitions of the data set of approximately equal size. For each partition, a mining model is created for the entire data set with one of the partitions removed, and then tested for accuracy using the partition that was excluded. If the variations are subtle, then the model generalizes well. If there is too much variation, then the model is not useful. When cross-validation processing is complete, you can view a report of the results, as shown in Figure 12-7. You cannot use cross-validation to test models created with the time series or sequence clustering algorithms.

	A	B	C	D	E
1	**Cross-Validation Report for 'TargetMail'**				
2	**For Target 'Jersey Buyer = 1'**				
3					
4	Models	TargetMail_DecisionTree			
5	Fold Count	10			
6	Maximum Rows	0			
7	Rows Used	12939			
8	Target Attribute	Jersey Buyer			
9	Target State	1			
10					
11	**Cross-Validation Summary for True Positive**				
12	Model Name	Mean	Standard Deviation		
13	TargetMail_Decis	0.0000	0.0000		
14					
15	**Cross-Validation Summary for False Positive**				
16	Model Name	Mean	Standard Deviation		
17	TargetMail_Decis	0.0000	0.0000		
18					
19	**Cross-Validation Summary for True Negative**				
20	Model Name	Mean	Standard Deviation		
21	TargetMail_Decis	1068.9001	0.2999		
22					
23	**Cross-Validation Summary for False Negative**				
24	Model Name	Mean	Standard Deviation		
25	TargetMail_Decis	225.0000	0.0000		
26					
27	**Cross-Validation Summary for Log Score**				
28	Model Name	Mean	Standard Deviation		
29	TargetMail_Decis	-0.4618	0.0007		
30					

Figure 12-7   *Cross-validation report*

Deployment

The requirements of the business problem driving your data mining project dictate the tasks you perform during the Deployment phase. Deployment can be as simple as deploying a report from the Data Mining Add-ins to Excel Services to share the results with SharePoint users. You can also integrate your Analysis Services data mining projects with other Microsoft BI components as part of a more comprehensive solution. Consider some of the following deployment options:

- ▶ Using Integration Services, you can create packages that automate the data preparation process for you using a combination of control flow and data flow transformations or to automate the data mining model training process. Another option is to use the Data Mining Query Task to execute queries against existing mining models. You could use this technique to categorize new customers and thereby associate them with marketing campaigns that focus on specific customer segments.

- ▶ If you built the mining model using the Decision Tree, Clustering, or Association Rules algorithm, you can create an OLAP dimension and add it to a cube to facilitate analysis of the groupings discovered by the model. For example, after developing clusters of customers, you can analyze sales trends by cluster.

- ▶ Reporting Services allows you to write Data Mining Extensions (DMX) statements to query a mining model. (DMX is a both a data definition language and a data manipulation language that you can use to query and manage data mining models.) You can then use standard Reporting Services features such as parameterized queries to display results of data mining. You might use subscriptions to distribute results, such as a list of customer prospects.

- ▶ Whether you use Excel Services or Reporting Services to share reports in SharePoint, remember that you can also incorporate these reports in SharePoint or PerformancePoint dashboards.

- ▶ The Analysis Services data mining engine has a variety of application programming interfaces (APIs) that you can use to develop custom applications.

Data Mining Add-Ins

As we noted previously, the Data Mining Add-ins add desktop data mining capabilities to Excel 2010. The add-ins provide an easy way to start learning about data mining. If you're also developing data mining models using Analysis Services projects, you can use the add-ins as a client viewer for those models.

Architecture

To use the add-ins, you must install the Microsoft SQL Server 2008 Data Mining Add-ins for Office 2007, available as a free download, on the client computer. In turn, the client computer must have access to a server hosting either Analysis Services 2008 or Analysis Services 2008 R2. The add-ins work not only with Office 2007, but also with the 32-bit version of Office 2010. When you install the add-ins, you can choose whether to install the table analysis tools, the data mining tools, or both.

An administrator must also use a configuration utility to enable features on the Analysis Services server supporting the creation of temporary and permanent data mining models and storage of mining structures in an Analysis Services database. The utility also grants administrative access to specified users to a default database dedicated to data mining projects, DMAddinsDB, so they can add and delete objects during the modeling process. If you want users to access models stored in other databases, an administrator must manually grant permissions to those databases. When you create a data mining model using the add-ins, you can create it as a temporary model, which removes the model from the server when you close Excel. Otherwise, your models are permanently available on the server, but you can delete them using the Manage Models command on the Data Mining tab of the ribbon.

Figure 12-8 illustrates the client-server architecture of the add-ins and Analysis Services. On the client, you'll first need to install Excel 2010. If you're using an operating system other than Windows 7, you will also need to install Microsoft .NET Framework 3.5. Then you're ready to install the add-ins. You won't need to establish a connection to Analysis Services until you're ready to use a tool or algorithm that requires the server.

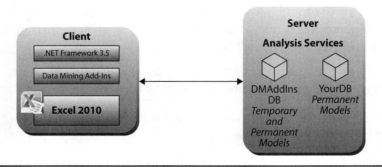

Figure 12-8 *Data Mining Add-ins, client-server architecture*

Data Preparation Tools

After installing the add-ins, you'll notice the Data Mining tab appears on the ribbon when you open Excel. The first group on the Data Mining tab is the Data Preparation group, as shown in Figure 12-9. You can use the commands in this group to perform specific tasks before starting the modeling process. If you anticipate a need to reuse cleansed data in other data mining projects, you should consider performing your cleansing activities in the database, using either SQL scripts or Integration Services. You'll find the data preparation capabilities of Excel are somewhat limited, but remember that the target audience for this tool is the business analyst who needs the ability to manipulate data without creating new dependencies on the IT department. For more permanent cleansing, of course, you can formalize the process and use Integration Services not only to perform the more complex tasks, but also to store the cleansed data in a database table permanently for reuse.

Explore Data

Rather than write queries to explore your data, this tool gives you quick insight into the content of your data by displaying basic statistics in addition to a visualization of the discrete values for a selected column, as shown in Figure 12-10. Your primary goal with this tool is to determine if your data is reasonably balanced and if the data looks reasonably accurate. For example, if you expect to see only two discrete values for marital status but the Explore Data tool reveals five discrete values, you know that you must take steps to clean the data before proceeding with the Modeling phase.

Clean Data

Using the *Outliers* option under Clean Data, you have multiple options for displaying results of an automated data assessment. You can view the distribution of numeric data types, which you'll see in the next exercise, or the discrete values for any data type. This latter capability resembles the Explore Data option, but includes an option to set a minimum threshold of counts to keep the discrete value in the table. The distribution view gives you the option to set both minimum and maximum values to include in the algorithm. You then specify what action to take with rows that will be excluded as a

Explore Data	Classify	Associate	Accuracy Chart	Cross - Validation	Browse	Manage Models		Help
Clean Data	Estimate	Forecast	Classification Matrix		Document Model		Connection	
Sample Data	Cluster	Advanced	Profit Chart		Query			
Data Preparation	Data Modeling		Accuracy and Validation		Model Usage	Management		Help

Figure 12-9 *Data Mining tab of the Excel ribbon*

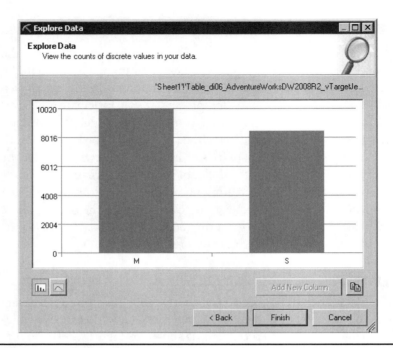

Figure 12-10 *Using the Explore Data option to view counts*

result of the settings. Your options include changing the value to the specified limits, the mean, or null, or eliminating the rows from the table. You can preserve the original data by adding a new column to hold the changed data, copying your data set to a new worksheet and applying those changes, or changing the data in place.

The other Clean Data option is *Re-label,* which lets you change values in a column, as shown in Figure 12-11. Less intrusive options include adding a new column to the data and then copying the entire data set to move it to a separate data set for analysis. You can also use this tool to create smaller groups if the number of groupings that you have in the raw data is too high.

Sample Data

You use this tool to generate a random sample or to add rows to the data set in an effort to enable oversampling. In Excel 2010, a random sample generates two copies of your data. One copy is the data selected as the sample, and the other copy is the remaining data that you can use later for testing purposes. When you choose the option to oversample, you artificially increase the number of underrepresented values by duplicating rows in your data set to produce a more balanced distribution than naturally

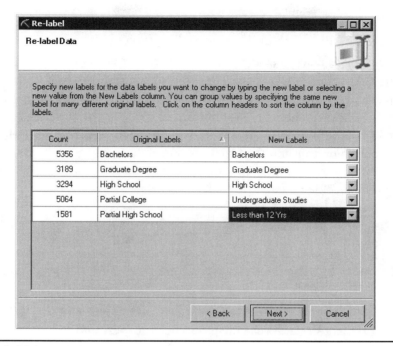

Figure 12-11 *Re-label*

exists in the data. You should run your data mining algorithm against the original sample as well as the oversampled data to determine how the adjustment affects results.

Let's prepare data for our data mining project by importing data from SQL Server into Excel and then use the add-ins tools to convert income to value ranges, establish a threshold for age values, and generate training and test partitions for your data.

Exercise 12-2: Data Cleansing and Partitioning in Excel 2010

1. Open a copy of Excel 2010 that has the Data Mining Add-ins installed.
2. In the Data ribbon, click From Other Sources, and click From SQL Server.
3. In the Data Connection Wizard, in the Server Name box, type the name of your database server, provide a user name and password if applicable, and click the Next button.
4. On the Select Database And Table page of the wizard, in the drop-down list, select AdventureWorksDW2008R2.
5. In the table list, select vTargetJerseyBuyers, click the Next button, and then click the Finish button.

6. In the Import Data dialog box, ensure Table is selected, and click the OK button.

7. On the Data Mining tab of the ribbon, click Explore Data.

8. On the Explore Data welcome page, click the Next button.

9. On the Select Source Data page, click the Next button.

10. On the Select Column page, select YearlyIncome in the Select Column drop-down list, and then click the Next button.

11. On the Explore Data page, change the number of buckets to 5, click the Add New Column button, and then click the Finish button.

12. Notice the new column that appears between YearlyIncome and TotalChildren to contain the income ranges.

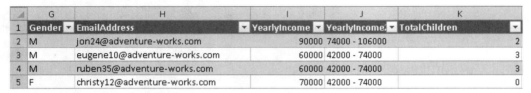

	G	H	I	J	K	
1	Gender	EmailAddress	YearlyIncome	YearlyIncome.	TotalChildren	
2	M	jon24@adventure-works.com	90000	74000 - 106000		2
3	M	eugene10@adventure-works.com	60000	42000 - 74000		3
4	M	ruben35@adventure-works.com	60000	42000 - 74000		3
5	F	christy12@adventure-works.com	70000	42000 - 74000		0

13. On the Data Mining tab of the ribbon, click Clean Data, and click Outliers.

14. On the Outliers Wizard welcome page, click the Next button.

15. On the Select Source Data page, click the Next button.

16. In the Select Column drop-down list, select Age, change Maximum to 80, and click the Next button.

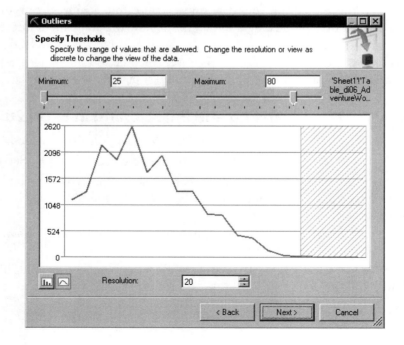

17. On the Outlier Handling page, click the Next button.
18. On the Select Destination page, select Change Data In Place, and click the Finish button.

Table Analysis Tools

The Table Analysis tools are data mining tools with a user-friendly interface. That is not to say they don't provide useful results. Rather, they're easy to use and simple to interpret. The Table Analysis tools can be a great introduction to data mining for business users. You must have a table in the Excel worksheet to view and access the Analyze tab for Table Tools in the ribbon, shown in Figure 12-12. You must also create a connection to Analysis Services before selecting a tool.

When you use the Table Analysis tools in the Data Mining Add-ins, you won't see a reference in the user interface to the specific algorithm at work. Table 12-2 describes the purpose of each tool and identifies the applicable algorithm.

Each tool uses a similar wizard interface, prompting you to select the columns for the algorithm to consider as it builds the model. For example, in the next exercise, we'll be considering which columns contain values that can determine whether someone is likely to buy a jersey or not. You should eliminate columns that are merely used as pass-through information for the end result, such as an e-mail address or unique identifiers. By restricting the algorithm to pertinent columns, you can speed up processing and eliminate noise. Let's look at some of the more commonly used Table Analysis tools.

Analyze Key Influencers

This tool looks for a correlation between the value in the column that you want to analyze and values in all other columns. When the analysis is complete, the tool adds a new sheet to your workbook to display the Key Influencers Report shown in Figure 12-13. In this example, the Pacific region more strongly favors jersey buyers (a value of 1 in the JerseyBuyer column), while the North America region more strongly favors people who don't buy jerseys. If a strong correlation between JerseyBuyer and other columns besides Region were found in the model, you would see those columns listed in this report in descending order of relative impact.

Figure 12-12 *Table Analysis Tools section of ribbon*

This Tool	Does This	Using This Algorithm
Analyze Key Influencers	Shows discrimination between strongest attributes	Microsoft Naïve Bayes
Detect Categories	Shows key characteristics of each category	Microsoft Naïve Bayes
Fill From Example	Predicts a column value based on examples found in existing data	Microsoft Logistic Regression
Forecast	Predicts continuous data over time	Microsoft Time Series
Highlight Exceptions	Shows improbable values	Microsoft Clustering
Scenario Analysis: Goal Seek	Predicts values that must change to support a goal	Microsoft Logistic Regression
Scenario Analysis: What If	Predicts change in predicted value if input value changes	Microsoft Logistic Regression
Prediction Calculator	Predicts whether a column will contain a specific value using a scorecard tool that prompts the user for attribute scores	Microsoft Logistic Regression
Shopping Basket Analysis	Shows groups of items that appear together frequently in transactions	Microsoft Association Rules

Table 12-2   *Description of Table Analysis Tools*

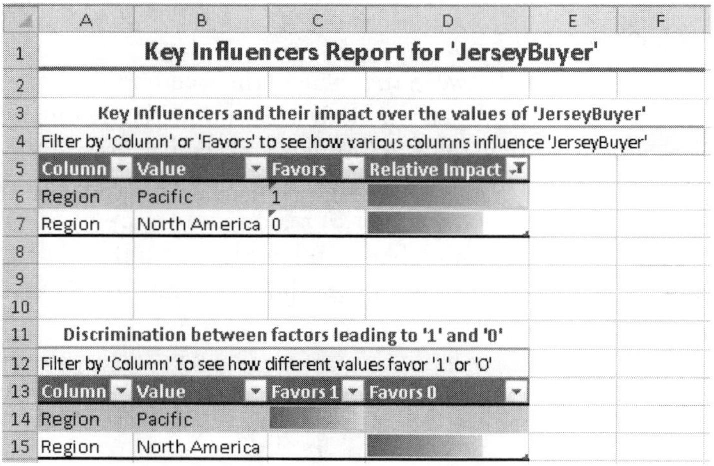

Figure 12-13   *Key Influencers Report*

The discrimination section of the report uses the column values to compare any two discrete values (known as *states*) for JerseyBuyer. In the previous example, there are only two possible states, 1 and 0. If there were other states, you could use the filter list in either of the last two columns to display a different comparison.

Detect Categories

In a sense, category detection tells a story about groups of customers. Each group shares common characteristics. After the tool finishes processing the model that determines the patterns for each category, a set of reports displays. In the first report, shown in Figure 12-14, you can see the distribution of rows by category. You can replace the generic category names with a more meaningful name, as you'll see in the next exercise, which you can then use to filter your source table.

The tool also produces a Category Characteristics report, shown in Figure 12-15. This report helps you see which columns and values in those columns had the greatest impact on the rows included in the selected category. This report is also useful for determining whether you need to perform more data cleansing.

Another report that the tool produces is the category profiles chart, shown in Figure 12-16. Because it's a PivotChart, you can interact with the chart by changing filters. In this report, you can focus on a particular column in the table and then review the distribution of values in that column for the selected category.

Fill From Example

The Fill From Example tool is similar to Excel's AutoFill feature. You start by populating cells in a table with values, as shown in Figure 12-17. The tool then analyzes patterns in the rows for which you have provided values, develops a model to describe those patterns, and then applies the model to the remaining rows in the table.

6 categories were detected

To rename a category, edit the 'Category Name' below.
('Category Name' changes are visible in the 'Category' column of the source Excel table)

Category Name	Row Count
Category 1	4521
Category 2	3709
Category 3	3367
Category 4	2505
Category 5	2198
Category 6	2184

Figure 12-14 *Categories Detected report*

Category Characteristics			
Filter the table by 'Category' to see the characteristics of different categories.			
Category ▼	**Column** ▼	**Value** ▼	**Relative Importance** ▼
Category 1	YearlyIncome	Low:38896 - 70501	
Category 1	YearlyIncome2	42000 - 74000	
Category 1	Age	Low:36 - 44	
Category 1	NumberCarsOwned	0	
Category 1	TotalChildren	1	
Category 1	EnglishOccupation	Skilled Manual	
Category 1	NumberCarsOwned	1	
Category 1	EnglishEducation	Graduate Degree	
Category 1	Region	North America	
Category 1	NumberChildrenAtHome	0	
Category 1	EnglishEducation	Bachelors	
Category 1	CommuteDistance	0-1 Miles	
Category 1	CommuteDistance	2-5 Miles	
Category 1	EnglishOccupation	Professional	
Category 1	NumberChildrenAtHome	2	
Category 1	HouseOwnerFlag	1	
Category 1	TotalChildren	0	

Figure 12-15 *Category Characteristics report*

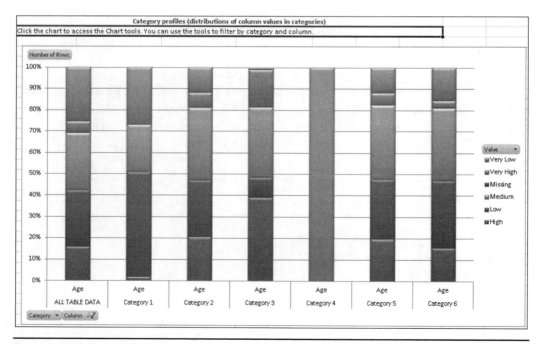

Figure 12-16 *Category Profiles chart*

3	Income	Childre	Education	Occupation	Home Owner	Cars	Commute Distance	Region	Age	High Value Customer
4	40000	1	Bachelors	Skilled Manual	Yes	0	0-1 Miles	Europe	42	Yes
5	30000	3	Partial College	Clerical	Yes	1	0-1 Miles	Europe	43	Yes
6	80000	5	Partial College	Professional	No	2	2-5 Miles	Europe	60	Yes
7	70000	0	Bachelors	Professional	Yes	1	5-10 Miles	Pacific	41	No
8	30000	0	Bachelors	Clerical	No	0	0-1 Miles	Europe	36	Yes
9	10000	2	Partial College	Manual	Yes	0	1-2 Miles	Europe	50	No
10	160000	2	High School	Management	Yes	4	0-1 Miles	Pacific	33	No
11	40000	1	Bachelors	Skilled Manual	Yes	0	0-1 Miles	Europe	43	Yes
12	20000	2	Partial High School	Clerical	Yes	2	5-10 Miles	Pacific	58	No
13	20000	2	Partial College	Manual	Yes	1	0-1 Miles	Europe	48	Yes
14	30000	3	High School	Skilled Manual	No	2	1-2 Miles	Pacific	54	
15	90000	0	Bachelors	Professional	No	4	10+ Miles	Pacific	36	
16	170000	5	Partial College	Professional	Yes	4	0-1 Miles	Europe	55	
17	40000	2	Partial College	Clerical	Yes	1	1-2 Miles	Europe	35	
18	60000	1	Partial College	Skilled Manual	No	1	0-1 Miles	Pacific	45	
19	10000	2	High School	Manual	Yes	1	0-1 Miles	Europe	38	

Figure 12-17 *Preparing data for Fill From Example*

To help you understand how the tool decides how to generate values for the table, it also creates a pattern report for you, as shown in Figure 12-18. Notice the similarity between this report and the Key Influencers Report. For example, the more columns that have values favoring a No value, as shown in this report, the more likely a value of No will be assigned to the High Value Customer column.

Pattern Report for 'High Value Customer'			
Key Influencers and their impact over the values of 'High Value Customer'			
Filter by 'Column' or 'Favors' to see how various columns influence 'High Value Customer'			
Column	Value	Favors	Relative Impact
Region	Pacific	No	
Commute Distance	5-10 Miles	No	
Gender	Female	No	
Education	Partial High School	No	
Education	Bachelors	No	
Commute Distance	1-2 Miles	No	
Occupation	Professional	No	
Commute Distance	2-5 Miles	Yes	
Children	5	Yes	
Region	Europe	Yes	
Home Owner	No	Yes	
Education	Partial College	Yes	
Children	3	Yes	
Cars	2	Yes	

Figure 12-18 *Pattern report generated by Fill From Example*

Forecast

The Forecast tool lets you use historical data to extrapolate data for a fixed number of columns. To use this tool, your table must include a time-based column, such as a date or a month-year combination. You identify the column for which you want to forecast values and specify how far into the future the tool should calculate. When the model completes processing, the tool creates a chart to display the results using dashed lines for the projections, as shown in Figure 12-19, and adds rows to your table with the projected values.

Highlight Exceptions

A good place to start analyzing your data, even during the Data Preparation phase, is with the Highlight Exceptions tool. It uses a clustering algorithm to determine what rows are more similar to one another while at the same time more unlike any other

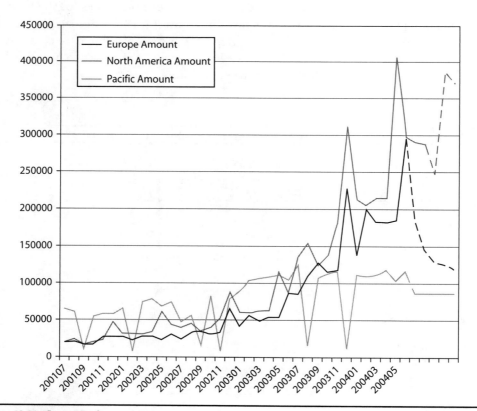

Figure 12-19 *Forecasting future sales*

row in the table. After developing clusters, the tool looks at the values in each column, cluster by cluster, to determine which values appear to be incorrect according to the patterns detected within the same cluster. If the value doesn't match, the tool highlights the row in the cell and uses yellow fill to identify the cell with the outlier value, as shown in Figure 12-20. Either the value is incorrect and you can fix it on the spot, or it really is correct and might be an interesting point for analysis. If you change the data to a value that first the detected pattern, the highlighting is removed from the cell.

In addition to highlighting each row in the table with an exception, the Highlight Exceptions tool produces an exceptions report that lists each column in the table along with the number of exceptions found in the column with a relatively liberal approach to determining whether a value fits the detected patterns. For a more strict approach, change the exception threshold to 0 to increase the number of exceptions detected, as shown in Figure 12-21. That is, the range of values within the valid pattern is smaller when you decrease the exceptions threshold.

In the following exercise, we'll use the Highlight Exceptions tool to find anomalies in the data that might require additional cleansing before we begin the modeling phase, and then we'll use the Analyze Key Influencers and Detect Categories tools to uncover information about AdventureWorks clients that could help the company sell more jerseys.

Exercise 12-3: Using Table Analysis Tools in Excel

1. Click anywhere in the table to activate the Table Tools tab on the ribbon.
2. On the Analyze tab (below the Table Tools tab), click <No Connection>.
3. In the Analysis Services Connections dialog box, click the New button.
4. Type your server name for Analysis Services, select DMAddinsDB in the Catalog Name drop-down list, and click the OK button.
5. In the Analysis Services Connections dialog box, click the Close button.
6. On the Analyze tab, click Highlight Exceptions.
7. Clear the MiddleName check box, and then click the Run button.
8. In the Highlight Exceptions report, note the attributes identified with exceptions.

	EmailAddress	YearlyIncome	YearlyIncome	TotalChildren	NumberChildren	EnglishEducation
88	ryan43@adventure-works.com	70000	42000 - 74000		2	1 Partial College
89	tamara6@adventure-works.com	70000	42000 - 74000		3	2 Partial College
90	hunter64@adventure-works.com	80000	74000 - 106000		2	1 Bachelors
91	abigail25@adventure-works.com	80000	74000 - 106000		2	1 Bachelors
92	trevor18@adventure-works.com	90000	74000 - 106000		2	0 Partial College

Figure 12-20 *Rows identified as exceptions by Highlight Exceptions*

◢	A	B	C	D
1	**Highlight Exceptions Report for Table_AdventureWorksDW2008R2_vTargetJerseyBuyers**			
2	The outlier cells are highlighted in the original table.			
3				
4	Exception threshold (more or fewer exceptions)	0		
5				
6	Column ▼	Outliers ▼		
7	MaritalStatus	597		
8	Gender	25		
9	YearlyIncome	1428		
10	YearlyIncome2	548		
11	TotalChildren	1442		
12	NumberChildrenAtHome	1419		
13	EnglishEducation	1438		
14	EnglishOccupation	803		
15	HouseOwnerFlag	928		
16	NumberCarsOwned	1506		
17	YearsAsCustomer	1708		
18	CommuteDistance	2155		
19	Region	733		
20	Age	1894		
21	JerseyBuyer	1860		
22	Total	18484		

Figure 12-21 *Highlight Exceptions report*

9. Open the Sheet1 tab and note the highlighted rows by scrolling vertically through the table and scrolling horizontally to locate the outlier cells.

10. On the Analyze tab of the ribbon, click Analyze Key Influencers.

11. In the Analyze Key Influencers dialog box, in the Column Selection drop-down list, select JerseyBuyer.

12. Click the Choose Columns To Be Used For Analysis link.

13. Clear the following columns: CustomerKey, CustomerAlternateKey, FirstName, MiddleName, LastName, EmailAddress, YearlyIncome, AddressLine1, AddressLine2, and DateFirstPurchase.

14. Click the OK button, and then click the Run button.

15. When the analysis is complete, click the Add Report button, and then click the Close button.

16. Notice in the Key Influencers Report that the Pacific region is more likely to favor jersey buyers than the North America region.

17. Open the Sheet1 tab, and click anywhere in the table.

18. On the Analyze tab of the ribbon, click Detect Categories.

19. Clear the MiddleName check box, and then click the Run button.

20. Review the Category Characteristics list for Category1 and decide on a name to describe this category, such as "Middle Income."

21. At the top of the Categories Report sheet, in cell A6, replace Category1 with the new category name.

22. Review the other reports created by the tool: Category Characteristics and Category Profile.

23. Change the filter on Category Characteristics to select another category for review.

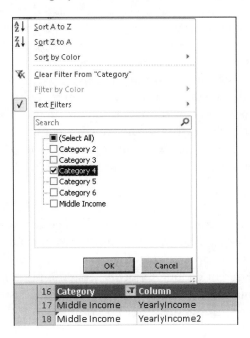

24. Return to Sheet1, and then scroll horizontally to view the contents of the new column appended to the table.

	T	U	V	W	X	Y	Z
1	DateFirstPurchase	YearsAsCustomer	CommuteDis	Regi	Age	JerseyE	Category
2	2005-07-22		5 1-2 Miles	Pacific	40	1	Category 6
3	2005-07-18		5 0-1 Miles	Pacific	41	1	Middle Income
4	2005-07-10		5 2-5 Miles	Pacific	40	0	Middle Income
5	2005-07-01		5 5-10 Miles	Pacific	38	0	Middle Income
6	2005-07-26		5 1-2 Miles	Pacific	37	0	Category 6
7	2005-07-02		5 5-10 Miles	Pacific	40	0	Middle Income

Data Mining Tools

The Data Mining tab of the ribbon includes a variety of tools. For now, we'll focus on the data modeling tools and the model viewers, shown in Figure 12-22. Before working with any of these tools, however, you must create a connection to Analysis Services using the Connection button on the ribbon.

Table 12-3 describes the purpose of each data modeling tool and identifies the applicable algorithm.

The data modeling tools available on the Data Mining tab create models just like the mining models in an Analysis Services project that are based on the same algorithm. With the data modeling tools, you use an Excel table as a data source, whereas your Analysis Services project requires you to create a data source view from a relational source. After you use the wizard to create the model, the Analysis Services data mining engine processes and stores the model on the server.

Unlike the Table Analysis tools that produce reports after processing the model, there is nothing to see in Excel when you use the data modeling tools. Instead, you can use the model viewer tools to examine models, capture details about the models for documentation purposes, and perform ad hoc queries against the models. You can use the model viewer tools with any model on the server, regardless of whether they were created from the add-ins or an Analysis Services project.

Cluster

The Cluster tool produces a model similar to the Detect Categories tool that we discussed earlier, but it uses a different algorithm to group data. The Microsoft Clustering algorithm will identify clusters that contain rows of data that are most like one another, but still different enough to justify separation into a unique cluster. There are four viewers that you can use to view a cluster model—Cluster Diagram, Cluster Profile, Cluster Characteristics, and Cluster Discrimination.

Cluster Diagram   The Cluster Diagram, shown in Figure 12-23, allows you to see at a glance the density difference among the clusters. The darker the color of the cluster, the higher the number of records it represents based on your selection of a shading

Figure 12-22 *Data Mining tab of the ribbon*

This Tool	Does This	Using This Algorithm
Cluster	Shows groups of rows with common characteristics	Clustering
Associate	Shows items found together in multiple transactions	Association Rules
Classify	Predicts tendency towards a particular outcome	Decision Trees
Estimate	Predicts factors affecting continuous values	Decision Trees
Forecast	Predicts continuous data over time	Time Series

Table 12-3 *Description of Data Modeling Tools*

variable and the target state. The links between clusters show you which clusters are more like one another than the other clusters. You can adjust the slider to focus only on the strongest links.

Cluster Profile   Of all the viewers, Cluster Profiling is a really great way just to look at your data and see what information it reveals. It allows you to see, cluster by cluster,

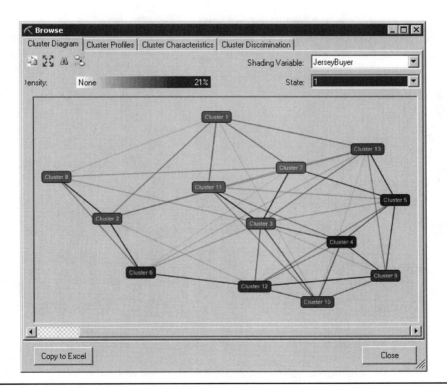

Figure 12-23 *Cluster Diagram*

the range of values associated with each column. For example, in Figure 12-24, you can see what age group is predominant in each cluster as well as the entire population of the source data. If you enabled drill-through when you created the model, you can right-click a cluster to view the individual rows associated with it.

Cluster Characteristics   The Cluster Characteristics viewer is useful for visualizing the values by column that distinguish the selected cluster or the entire population in descending order of probability. In the example shown in Figure 12-25, you can see that the NumberCarsOwned value of 2 has the highest probability, compared to other column values. The next highest probability is Jerseybuyer, with a value of 0, followed by a high probability of NumberChildrenAtHome equal to 0. That is, in this cluster, there is a strong correlation between owning two cars, not buying jerseys, and having no children at home.

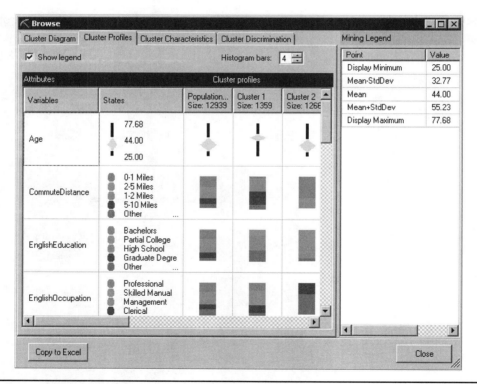

Figure 12-24 *Cluster Profiling*

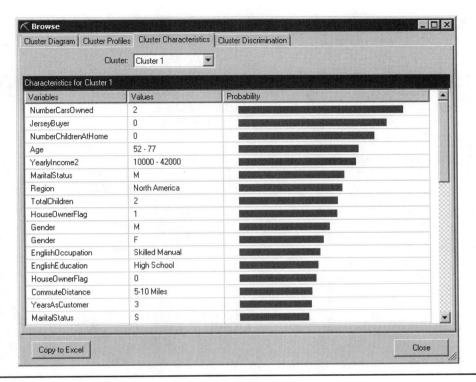

Figure 12-25 *Cluster Characteristics*

Cluster Discrimination   You can determine whether the high-probability column values in the Cluster Characteristics viewer are meaningful by comparing one cluster to all other clusters using the Cluster Discrimination viewer, shown in Figure 12-26. As it turns out, the number of cars owned remains the distinguishing characteristic of this cluster, but then the next most important factor is the total number of children. You can use this viewer to compare one cluster to another.

Associate

The Associate tool is similar to the Shopping Basket Analysis tool, with both using the Microsoft Association Rules algorithm. The rules viewer shows you the probability that an item that displays to the right of the -> symbol will be associated with other items that display to the left of that symbol. In Figure 12-27, the rules illustrate associations of product sales where the sale of a Bottles and Cages item has a 0.788 probability of selling with Hydration Packs and Road Bikes. That rule also has a relatively high importance score, which strengthens its reliability.

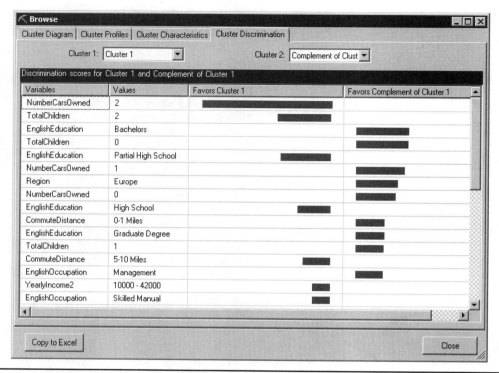

Figure 12-26 *Cluster Discrimination*

Classify

The Classify tool, which uses the Microsoft Decision Trees algorithm, has no counterpart in the Table Analysis tools. You use it to separate records into multiple levels of groups based on the value that you want the model to predict. Each level may or may not contain groups that are based on the same column. For example, notice in Figure 12-28 that two groups in the third level are based on age values while the other two groups are based on whether the number of cars is equal to 0 or not. Like the Cluster Diagram, the Decision Tree viewer uses color to illustrate the density of records within each group. In this case, the largest number of bike buyers is in the group for which the number of cars is 0.

Estimate

The Estimate tool is similar to the Classify tool, except you must specify a continuous column to predict. Like the Classify tool, it also uses the Microsoft Decision Trees algorithm and also has no counterpart in Table Analysis tools. After processing the model, you can use the Decision Tree viewer to see how the values in the target column

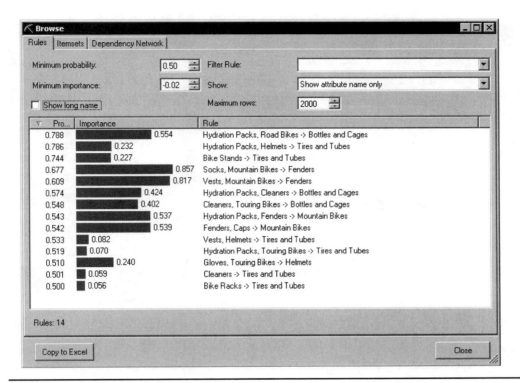

Figure 12-27 *Association rules*

are influenced by other column values in the model. When you click a node, you can see the predicted value for the combination of column values associated with the selected node. In Figure 12-29, the predicted value is Income.

Forecast

The Forecast data modeling tool produces the same result as the Forecast tool in Table Analysis tools. However, the viewer, shown in Figure 12-30, provides more interactivity. You can adjust the number of periods to project by changing a parameter value in the viewer. You can also overlay historic predictions onto the chart. That way, you can compare historic predictions to known values to assess how well the model might predict values for future time periods.

NOTE

To use the viewer, you will need to download and install the Office 2003 Web Components add-in.

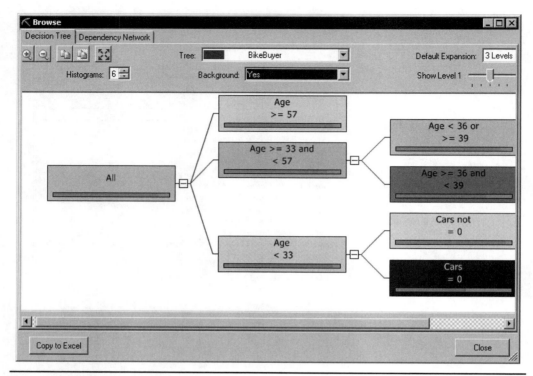

Figure 12-28 *Decision Tree viewer*

In the following exercise, we'll add data from the vTimeSeries view that represents historical sales by product model and region. We'll use that data to create a forecast model using the data modeling tools of the Data Mining Add-ins.

Exercise 12-4: Using Data Mining Tools in Excel

1. Open the Sheet2 tab.
2. In the Data ribbon, click From Other Sources, and click From SQL Server.
3. In the Data Connection Wizard, in the Server Name box, type the name of your database server, provide a user name and password if applicable, and click the Next button.

```
Occupation = 'Manual' and
Education = 'High School'
Existing Cases: 26
Missing Cases: 0
Income = 20,384.615
```

Figure 12-29 *Income estimate*

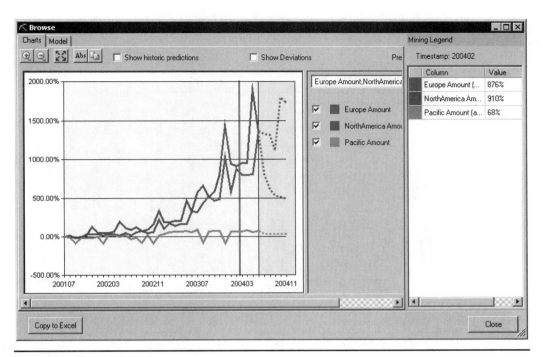

Figure 12-30 *Forecast viewer*

4. On the Select Database And Table page, in the drop-down list, select AdventureWorksDW2008R2.

5. In the table list, select vTimeSeries, click the Next button, and then click the Finish button.

6. In the Import Data dialog box, ensure Table is selected, and click the OK button.

7. Click any cell in the table.

8. On the Data tab of the ribbon, click Sort.

9. In the Sort By drop-down list, select TimeIndex, and click the OK button.

10. On the Data Mining tab of the ribbon, click Forecast.

11. On the welcome page of the wizard, click the Next button.

12. On the Select Source Data page, click the Next button.

13. On the Forecasting page, clear the Month and ReportingDate check boxes.

14. Notice the selection of TimeIndex in the Time Stamp drop-down list.

15. Click the Next button, and then click the Finish button.

16. Widen the viewer window if necessary and adjust the prediction steps to 12, as shown in the following illustration.

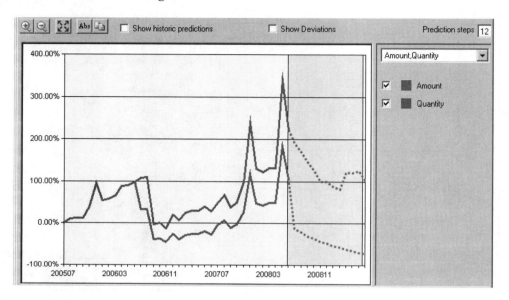

PowerPivot for Excel

As you learned in Chapter 5, PowerPivot for Excel is also an add-in for Excel 2010. Remember that the Data Mining Add-ins require the 32-bit version of Excel, so you'll need to use the 32-bit version of PowerPivot for Excel if you want to have access to both add-ins in the same workbook. Keep in mind also that the memory constraints of the 32-bit version of PowerPivot for Excel limit the size of your PowerPivot data to 400MB or less.

Notwithstanding the restrictions on data, there are some advantages to using PowerPivot for Excel in your Excel-based data mining projects. For example, you can use the Data Mining Add-ins to modify data in a table using the Add Column option in Explore Data or using the Clean Data Wizard, and then use PowerPivot to convert the table into a linked table. Alternatively, you can convert data mining results into a linked table. Either way, you can import the data from a linked table into PowerPivot, where you can create relationships with other data to support powerful analysis.

You can, of course, keep charts and reports generated by the modeling process in a PowerPivot workbook for reference purposes, even if you don't import the data into PowerPivot. In that case, however, the PowerPivot workbook does not maintain a connection to the data mining model. If you publish the workbook to SharePoint, you won't be able to schedule a data refresh for the data mining model. Instead, you must open the workbook and manually rebuild the model to update the reports as needed.

Data Mining in Analysis Services

For enterprise-scale managed data mining, you can create an Analysis Services project in BIDS to use the data mining engine in Analysis Services. You have access to the same algorithms that the Data Mining Add-ins provide, which is no surprise because the add-ins also use the Analysis Services data mining engine to process models. You start an Analysis Services project for data mining much like an OLAP project by creating a data source and a data source view to identify the source location and the table or view for the data that you want to model, but then you use the Mining Model designer to select an algorithm, configure the algorithm's parameters, and access the model viewers to evaluate a completed model.

Architecture

To build data mining models in an Analysis Services project, you must install BIDS on a client computer that can connect to an Analysis Services server, as shown in Figure 12-31. You also need a connection to the relational data source that you want to mine. BIDS requires a connection to the relational source when you create the data source, and a connection to both the relational source and Analysis Services when you process the model. Otherwise, you can work on the model design in disconnected mode.

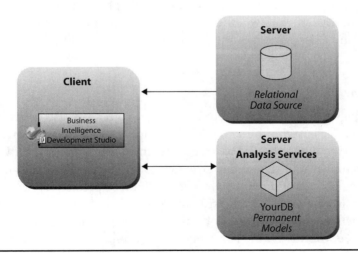

Figure 12-31 *Analysis Services, data mining client-server architecture*

Mining Model Designer

You use the Mining Model designer in an Analysis Services project to build a mining structure and a mining model, which are two database objects that the data mining engine requires to process a model. After the model is processed, you can use the Mining Model designer to access model viewers specific to each mining model's algorithm and to review the evaluation tools, such as the Accuracy Chart and Classification Matrix. The viewers and the evaluation tools are the same as those you can access using the Data Mining Add-ins. The Mining Model designer also includes a prediction query designer with a graphical interface that you can use to create and execute ad hoc queries using the model as a source.

Mining Structure

In Analysis Services, the mining structure is the foundation for the business problem that you want to solve. When you build a mining structure, you generally use only a single table from a data source view. You can use nested tables when data is spread across multiple transaction tables, such as you might find when sales data is stored in both a header and a detail table. In that case, you'll need to identify the header table, which uniquely identifies each transaction by flagging it as a case table, and specify the other table as a nested table. Alternatively, you can use a cube that exists in the same project as the source for your mining structure.

The purpose of the mining structure is to describe the columns that contain data to model. Each column has a collection of properties that store information required by the modeling process, such as whether the data in the column is continuous or discrete, the data type, and a description of the distribution of data within the column, among others.

Mining Model

For each mining structure in the Analysis Services project, you can create one or more mining models. Each mining model either applies a different algorithm or uses the same algorithm with different parameter settings. You can also specify a unique selection of columns from the mining structure for each mining model and define the usage of each column as an input column or a column to predict. By using different mining models for the same mining structure, you can easily compare model results to determine which one best helps you solve the business problem at hand.

Let's continue working on the jersey marketing campaign project by using BIDS to develop a decision tree model.

Exercise 12-4: Developing Mining Models in BIDS

1. Open BIDS.
2. On the File menu, click New, and then click Project.
3. In the New Project dialog box, select Analysis Services Project, name the project, and click the OK button.
4. In Solution Explorer, right-click the Data Sources folder, and click New Data Source.
5. In the Data Source Wizard, click the Next button on the Welcome page (if it displays).
6. On the Select How To Define A Connection page, select the connection for AdventureWorksDW2008R2 if it exists. Otherwise, click the New button and use the Connection Manager dialog box to create a connection to AdventureWorksDW2008R2, and then click the OK button.
7. Click the Next button.
8. On the Impersonation Information page, select Use The Service Account, and click the Next button.

NOTE

Make sure that the account running the Analysis Services service has read permissions on the AdventureWorksDW2008R2 database.

9. Click the Finish button.
10. In Solution Explorer, right-click the Data Source Views folder, and click New Data Source View.
11. Click the Next button on the Welcome page if necessary.
12. On the Select A Data Source page, click the Next button.
13. On the Select Tables And Views page, scroll to locate vTargetJerseyBuyers, double-click it to add it to the Included Objects list, and then click the Next button.
14. Click the Finish button.
15. In Solution Explorer, right-click the Mining Structures folder, and click New Mining Structures.
16. On the Welcome page of the wizard, click the Next button.
17. On the Select The Definition Method page, click the Next button.
18. On the Create The Data Mining Structure page, keep the selection of Microsoft Decision Trees, and click the Next button.
19. On the Select Data Source View page, click the Next button.
20. On the Specify Table Types page, click the Next button.

21. On the Specify The Training Data page, select the following columns as input columns: Age, CommuteDistance, EmailAddress, EnglishEducation, EnglishOccupation, FirstName, Gender, HouseOwnerFlag, JerseyBuyer, LastName, Marital Status, NumberCarsOwned, NumberChildrenAtHome, Region, TotalChildren, YearlyIncome, and YearsAsCustomer.

22. Select the Jersey Buyer column as a predictable column, and then click the Next button.

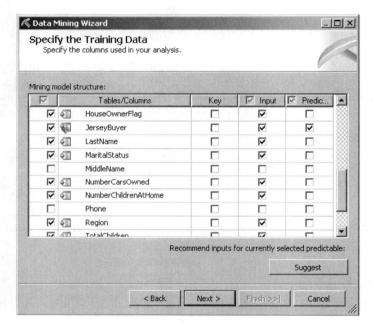

23. On the Specify Columns Content And Data Type page, click the Detect button, and then click the Next button.

24. On the Create Testing Set page, keep 30% as the testing data set percentage, and then click the Next button.

25. On the Completing The Wizard page, type **TargetMail** in the Mining Structure Name box, type **TargetMail_DecisionTree** in the Mining Model Name box, select the Allow Drill Through check box, and then click the Finish button.

26. In the designer, click the Mining Models tab, and then change the column type for each of the following columns to Ignore: EmailAddress, FirstName.

NOTE

By changing the column type to Ignore, you will have access to these columns in the model results to produce a list of customers for the marketing campaign, but the modeling process will ignore data in the columns.

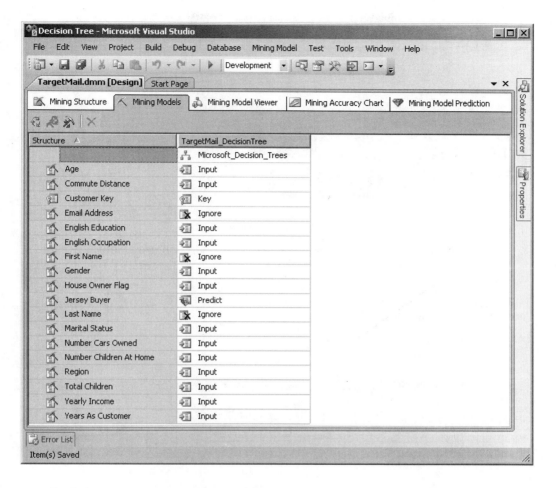

27. In Solution Explorer, right-click TargetMail.dmm, and click Process.
28. In the message box, click the Yes button to build and deploy the project.
29. In the Process Mining Structure dialog box, click the Run button.
30. When processing completes, click the Close button in the Process Progress dialog box, and then click the Close button in the Process Mining Structure dialog box.
31. Click the Mining Model Viewer tab in the designer.

32. In the Background drop-down list, select 1 to focus the decision tree on customers likely to buy jerseys.

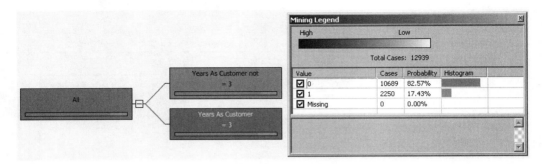

The viewer tells us that few people are likely to be jersey buyers, but more exist in the group of customers that have been buying from AdventureWorks for three years.

33. Right-click the Years As Customers = 3 node, click Drill Through, and then click Model And Structure Columns.

34. Right-click the grid, and then click Copy All. You can paste the results into Excel to build a mailing list.

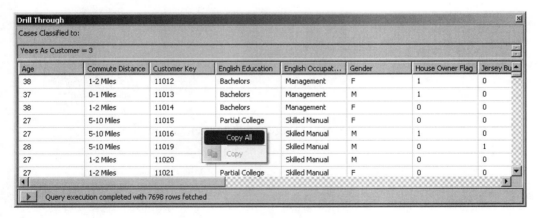

Summary

Data mining is a much more complex topic than we can cover adequately in a single chapter, but we hope that this introduction to data mining inspires you to try it out with your own data. Data mining tools in general have evolved a lot over the last decade, and Microsoft has made incredible strides in making the technology more accessible to business users. Don't let the simplicity of the tools fool you, nor absolve you of the responsibility to make sure you're working with good data and drawing proper conclusions about the results. Our advice is to start small; experiment with a variety of algorithms to learn how they work; and validate, validate, validate before making business decisions based on data mining results. You can find in-depth information about both the Data Mining Add-ins and Analysis Services data mining in *Data Mining with Microsoft SQL Server 2008* by Jamie MacLennan, ZhaoHui Tang, and Bogdan Crivat (Wiley Publishing, 2009).

Chapter 13

Master Data Services

In This Chapter

- ► **Introduction to Master Data Management**
- ► **Master Data Preparation**
- ► **Master Data Stewardship**
- ► **Master Data Administration**
- ► **Summary**

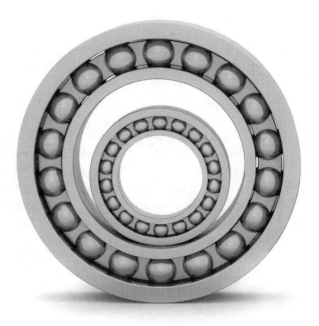

I n the ideal world of business intelligence, the data for your dimension tables comes from a single source system, perhaps an enterprise resource planning (ERP) system. If, on the other hand, your data comes from multiple source systems, your ideal solution conforms the dimensional data nicely using best-practice techniques. However, the real world sometimes doesn't correspond to the ideal scenario. Even if you have a customer's address in an ERP, what do you do if it doesn't match the address stored in the customer relationship management (CRM) system? Furthermore, what happens when the marketing manager wants to view sales by a customer grouping that is stored only in an analyst's spreadsheet?

When your source systems have no mechanisms for reconciling data between systems or for allowing users to set up custom data groupings, you need to develop a process for working through these types of data management problems so that your BI solution can be more effective. One option is to build a custom application, but you need to devote resources to developing and maintaining that application when those resources are already overtaxed with other tasks. Another option to consider is Master Data Services, a new component in the Microsoft BI suite introduced with SQL Server 2008 R2 in the Datacenter, Enterprise, and Developer editions.

Introduction to Master Data Management

Master Data Services (MDS) is a platform for master data management. As a platform, it provides not only an application that you can use out of the box, but also a web service and application programming interfaces (APIs) that you can use to build your own applications or to integrate master data management processes into existing applications. It's based on technology that Microsoft acquired as a result of its purchase of Stratature in 2007.

In more general terms, *master data management* is a set of processes and tools that organizations use to create and maintain nontransactional reference data. That is, master data management focuses on the data related to the people, places, and things that transactions reference. That reference data is exactly the same type of data that we refer to as a dimension in a BI solution. Although master data management is often used to solve problems with conflicting or missing data across multiple business applications, it is also quite useful for managing dimension data, especially dimension data that doesn't have a home in any of those business applications. In this chapter, we'll focus on using MDS for dimension management.

Using MDS, you can create a master data hub to manage your dimensions, as shown in Figure 13-1. The master data hub is a database that you maintain separately from the data warehouse. It contains a superset of all the master data records that exist across multiple systems, and consolidates all information about each *business entity* (person, place, or thing) in a single location.

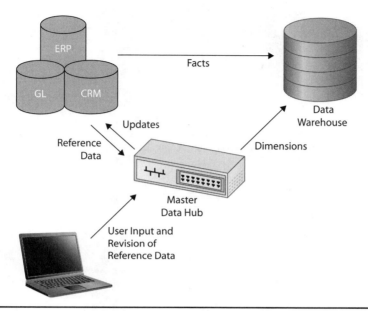

Figure 13-1   *Master data hub for dimensions*

MDS provides the flexibility to manage a master data hub in many different ways, but we'll limit our consideration in this chapter to a simple scenario. In this scenario, you initially populate the master data hub by importing reference data from your source systems. Then you allow business users to review the data in the master data hub, make any necessary changes, and add data that was never available in the source systems. The master data hub returns these revisions and additions to the source systems and updates the dimension tables in the data warehouse. Meanwhile, ETL processes continue to populate the data warehouse with fact data that comes directly from the source systems.

If any conflict arises in the future in the line-of-business applications, you use the data in the master data hub as the *system of record* to resolve the conflict. Eventually, you might require users to add new reference data exclusively in the master data hub, making it the *system of entry*. With MDS, the master data hub isn't limited to one role or the other; it can serve both purposes.

Although you can create your own applications to perform all the functions that we describe in this chapter, a faster way to get started with MDS is to use Master Data Manager. The functional areas that you can access in Master Data Manager depend on the permissions assigned to you. If you are designated as a system administrator for MDS, you have access to all areas, as shown in Figure 13-2. By contrast, users with permissions to view or update a model will see only the Explorer area.

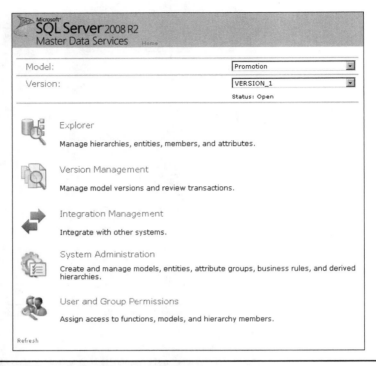

Figure 13-2 *An administrator's view of Master Data Manager*

Master Data Preparation

Although the intent of MDS is to give users the responsibility for managing master data, an administrator must first prepare the environment. Some configuration tasks are necessary, such as creating a database for the master data hub. Then an administrator defines the structure of the master data in preparation to load the data and establishes the criteria for data validation, known as *business rules*. Once the structure is in place, users can begin entering master data, but an administrator can optionally bulk-load master data into the hub.

Configuring Master Data Services

Following the installation of MDS on a server, there are a few additional steps that you must perform before you can allow users to begin managing master data. The first step is to use the MDS Configuration Manager to create the MDS database and configure one or more web applications. The database is the central repository for your master data, or master data hub, as we referred to it earlier. The MDS database also stores the settings for the Master Data Manager application and the MDS web service.

When you create the database, you must be ready to provide two Windows accounts, one to use as a service account and the other to specify a system administrator for the application. The service account must be assigned to the sysadmin role on the SQL Server instance hosting your MDS database. When anyone uses Master Data Manager or the web service, the service account connects to the MDS database to retrieve data or make changes.

The system administrator account has access to all web applications associated with the MDS database. This account can create and update any model, modify model data, and access all areas of Master Data Manager. Although this account has full access, the person assigned as the system administrator more typically prepares a model for business users and configures security, restricting the tasks that business users can perform rather than taking responsibility for managing the individual master data records.

After the database wizard creates the database, you can configure system settings for the MDS web service and Master Data Manager. For example, you can change time-out values for the database or the MDS server, or configure batch and logging settings related to staging data for import into MDS, among others. If you plan to use e-mail notifications with MDS, you must configure a database mail profile, which allows you to specify an e-mail account and the Simple Mail Transport Protocol (SMTP) server to use when sending notifications.

To get started with MDS, we'll need to create a database for a Master Data Services application and create a website for Master Data Manager.

Exercise 13-1: Configuring Master Data Services

1. Open the Master Data Services Configuration Manager in the Master Data Services folder of the Microsoft SQL Server 2008 R2 program group.
2. Click Databases in the left pane, and then click the Create Database button.
3. Type the name of your server in the SQL Server Instance box, change the authentication method if necessary, and click the Next button.
4. Type a database name, like **MDS**, and click the Next button.
5. Type a Windows account for the service account, and click the Next button.
6. Type a Windows account for the administrator account, and click the Next button.
7. On the Summary page, click the Next button.
8. When the database tasks are complete, click the Finish button.
9. Click the Apply button to save the default settings.

10. Click Web Configuration in the left pane, and then click the Create Site button.

11. Type a name for your website, change the port number and provide a host header if necessary, and supply credentials for the application pool identity. (Typically, the application pool identity is the same account that you specify as the service account when creating the database.)

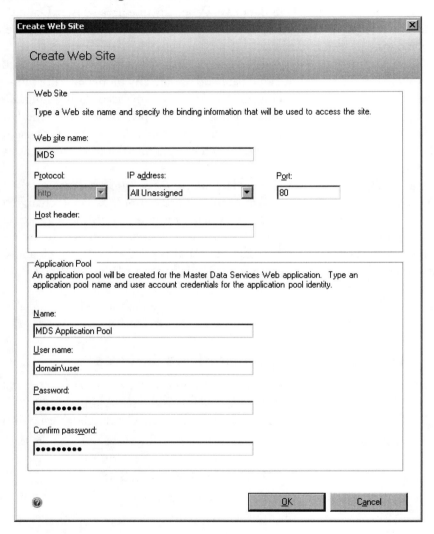

12. Click the OK button to create the website, and then click the OK button to close the message box explaining that you must use the IIS Manager to configure Secure Sockets Layer (SSL).

13. Click the Select button.

14. Click the Connect button in the Connect To Database dialog box.

15. In the Master Data Services Database drop-down list, select the MDS database that you specified in step 4, and click the OK button.

16. Click the Apply button, and then click the OK button in the Configuration Complete message box.

17. Click the Open The Master Data Manager Home Page link, and leave the browser window open for the next exercise. If you plan to perform the exercise at a later time, bookmark the URL address of the home page so that you can access it easily later.

Creating Model Objects

The second step after installing MDS is to use Master Data Manager to create a model to contain the objects that define the structure of the master data as well as the master data itself. A model is typically domain-specific, containing only the data for a single dimension, such as product or customer data. MDS does not provide any predefined templates for common domains, which allows you to set up a domain that matches the way you do business rather than force you to conform to an industry standard.

Entities

After you create a model, you then add one or more entities to the model. Within some domains, you might require several entities to structure the master data properly, while other domains require only a single entity. Don't confuse these entities with the business entities that we described earlier in this chapter. A *model entity* is instead analogous to a table. When you view the master data for an entity, each row represents a *member* and each column represents an *attribute,* as shown in Figure 13-3.

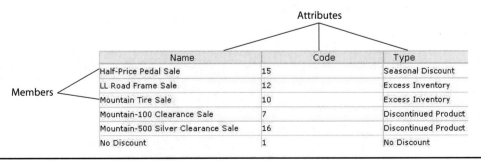

Figure 13-3   *Members and attributes of the Promotion entity*

> **NOTE**
>
> *Throughout the exercises in this chapter, we'll build a model with a single entity to help you get familiar with the application interface and the master data management workflow. The MDS installation also installs sample files, which you can use to study more complex domains. Click the Help icon in the top-right corner of the Master Data Manager, click Getting Started With Master Data Services, click the Model Deployment Wizard link, click Deploy, and browse to the C:\Program Files\Microsoft SQL Server\Master Data Services\Samples\Packages folder to select a package.*

Attributes

When you first create an entity, MDS automatically adds two attributes to the entity's structure—Name and Code. The Name attribute is the label for a member that users typically reference in reports, whereas the Code attribute is a unique identifier for a member, such as a primary key. You can add as many attributes as you need.

The process to add an attribute is similar to adding a column to a table. You define a data type, such as text or number, and length. Some attribute settings depend on the attribute type, as described in the following list:

▶ The free-form attribute type is the one most commonly used and accepts any data type.

▶ A domain-based attribute type requires you to first create a separate entity and load it with members, such as the ProductCategory entity shown in Figure 13-4. The ProductCategory attribute in the ProductSubcategory entity is configured as a domain-based attribute and can contain only the Code attribute from the ProductCategory entity and a valid value from that entity.

▶ A file attribute type stores either a file or an image. This attribute type requires you to specify a file extension that applies to the values that you load into this attribute, such as *.bmp or *.png.

ProductSubcategory Entity

	Name	Code▲	ProductCategory
Mountain Bikes		1	1
Forks		10	2
Headsets		11	2

ProductCategory Entity

	Name	Code▲	ProductGroup
Bikes		1	2
Components		2	1
Clothing		3	2
Accessories		4	2

Figure 13-4   *ProductCategory as a domain-based attribute*

Marketing	Inventory			
X	Name	Code▴	ProductSubCategory	ProductLine
☐ ▾ ✓	Adjustable Race	AR-5381	38	NA
☐ ▾ ✓	Bearing Ball	BA-8327	38	NA
☐ ▾ ✓	LL Bottom Bracket	BB-7421	5	NA

Marketing	Inventory			
X	Name	Code▴	StandardCost	DealerCost
☐ ▾ ✓	Adjustable Race	AR-5381	0	0
☐ ▾ ✓	Bearing Ball	BA-8327	0	0
☐ ▾ ✓	LL Bottom Bracket	BB-7421	23.97	27.57

Figure 13-5   *Using attribute groups to organize attributes of the Promotion entity*

Attribute Groups

Remember that the purpose of setting up a master data hub in MDS is to allow users
to manage master data. If you have users who can make changes to some attributes but
not to others, you can use *attribute groups* to organize attributes into groups for which
you can configure security separately. Or you might use attribute groups as a way to
logically group attributes when you have many attributes, as shown in Figure 13-5.
Each attribute group includes the Name and Code attributes by default. You can
create as many attribute groups as you need, although the use of attribute groups is
completely optional.

Hierarchies

A hierarchy organizes an entity's members either as a flat list of all members or as a
multilevel structure. An *explicit* hierarchy includes members from a single entity, such
as the Promotion entity shown in Figure 13-6. There are two types of members in
an explicit hierarchy: a *leaf member,* such as Half-Price Pedal Sale, and a *consolidated
member,* such as Customer-Seasonal Discount. You use a consolidated member to group
the leaf members or lower-level consolidated members. You can associate a leaf member
with a consolidated member using the graphical interface for the explicit hierarchy or
by coding the data in staging tables when you import data in bulk.

Figure 13-6   *Explicit hierarchy based on a single entity*

Incidentally, there are two types of explicit hierarchies. A *mandatory explicit hierarchy* requires you to include all leaf members in the tree. The parent member can either be the root node or a consolidated member. In a *nonmandatory explicit hierarchy,* a special unused node is the default parent for all leaf members. You can then rearrange members to assign them to a consolidated member as you like.

The structure of a *derived hierarchy* depends on multiple entities. Domain-based attributes define the levels of the hierarchy. In Figure 13-7, you can see a derived hierarchy from the Product model provided as sample data for MDS. The LL Fork and ML Fork members are leaf members that have a domain-based attribute value to relate them to the Forks subcategory. In turn, the Forks member has a domain-based attribute value to relate it to the Components category, which itself has a domain-based attribute value to relate it to the Wholesale product group.

You supply the domain-based attribute values for each member when you add the member manually or when you import the data as part of a staging batch. To create the derived hierarchy, you drag an entity or hierarchy from the list of available items to the Current Levels tree, starting with a leaf-level entity, as shown in Figure 13-8. As you add each level, the list of available items displays only the entities related to the topmost level of the derived hierarchy. If you try to work from the top to the bottom of the hierarchy, you won't have access to the item that you want to add to the next level down.

Collections

A collection is another way to group an entity's members. Whereas a hierarchy includes all members, a collection is a subset of members. A user might create a collection of members for which he or she is responsible to make it easier to work with the members as a group. This collection might contain only leaf members or both consolidated and leaf members. It might even combine nodes from different explicit hierarchies. The only requirement is that all members must belong to the same entity.

Now that we've introduced the various model objects, let's create a model for the Promotion dimension and set up the supporting objects.

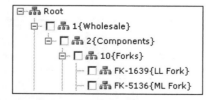

Figure 13-7   *Derived hierarchy based on multiple entities*

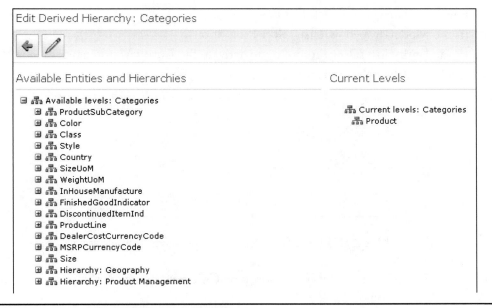

Figure 13-8 *Starting a derived hierarchy with a leaf-level entity*

Exercise 13-2: Creating Model Objects

1. Open the Master Data Manager home page, and click the System Administration link.
2. In the Model Explorer, click the Models node at the top of the tree.
3. Click the Add Item button to add a new model.

4. Type **Promotion** in the Model Name box, and click the Save Model button.

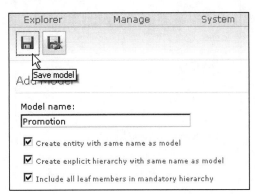

5. Point to Manage, and click Entities.

6. In the Model drop-down list, select Promotion.

7. In the Entity list, select Promotion to activate the Entity Maintenance toolbar.

8. Click the Edit Selected Entity button.

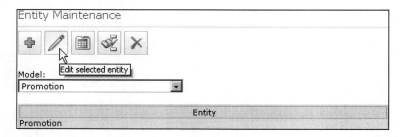

9. Click the Add Explicit Hierarchy button (the plus symbol below Explicit Hierarchies).

10. In the Explicit Hierarchy Name box, type **Category**, and click the Save Hierarchy button.

11. Click the Add Leaf Attribute button.

12. In the Name box, type **Type**, change Display Pixel Width and Length fields to 50, and click the Save Attribute button.

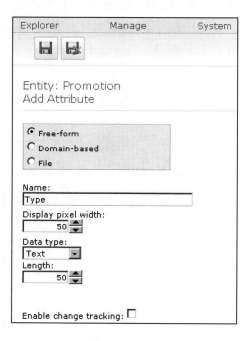

13. Repeat the previous two steps to add the following leaf attributes:

Name	Display Pixel Width	Data Type	Length	Decimals	Input Mask
Category	50	Text	50		
Manager	50	Text	50		
DiscountPct	25	Number		2	-####
MinQty	25	Number		0	-####
MaxQty	25	Number		0	-####

14. Click the Save Entity button.
15. Point to Manage, and click Attribute Groups.
16. Click Leaf Groups.
17. Click the Add Attribute Group button.
18. In the Leaf Group Name box, type **Marketing**, and then click the Save Group button.
19. In the Leaf Groups tree, expand the Marketing folder, select Attributes, and click the Edit Selected Item button.
20. In the Available list, select Type, and then click the Add button (the arrow pointing to the right) to move the attribute to the Assigned list.
21. Move Category, Manager, and DiscountPct to the Assigned list.

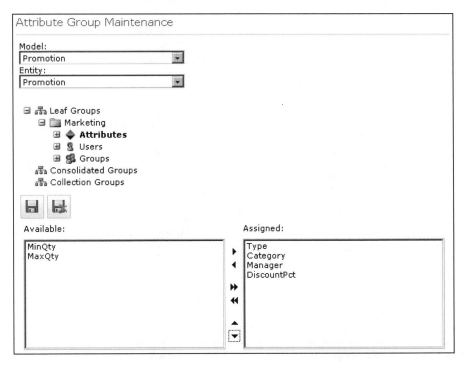

22. Click the Save button.

23. Repeat steps 16 to 22 to create another leaf group named Quantity Levels and assign MinQty and MaxQty to that leaf group.

Assigning Business Rules

MDS is more than a centralized database for master data. It also applies business rules to ensure that data is valid according to the conditions that an administrator specifies. A condition can be as simple as a list of required attributes or a more complex expression that describes invalid data, as shown in Figure 13-9.

The expression is in the form of an IF-THEN statement. The IF clause can include multiple conditions joined by the AND or OR logical operators, but can be empty if the actions in the THEN clause always apply. There are four types of actions that you can specify in the THEN clause:

▶ **Default value** Rather than create a validation issue when a business rule is violated, you can define a default value for an attribute when the user fails to supply a value. A default value can be blank, a specific value that you set, an incremental value generated by MDS, or a value based on a concatenation of specified attribute values.

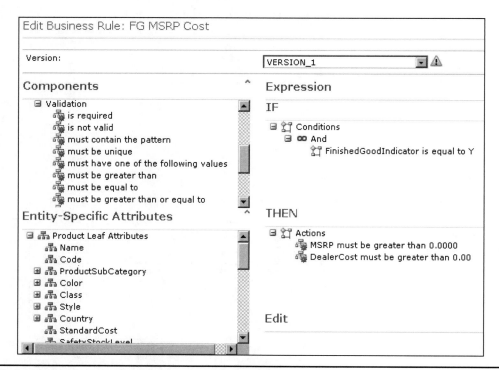

Figure 13-9 *Business rule defining conditions that render an attribute value invalid*

▶ **Change value** This action is similar to the default value. It overrides a value input by the user with either a specific value or a concatenation of specified attribute values.

▶ **Validation** You can use validation to flag required attributes or attributes that meet certain conditions, such as having a specific value, matching a pattern, or having a value shorter or longer than a specified length.

▶ **Start workflow** When MDS invokes this action, it sends data to SharePoint and starts a SharePoint workflow.

When you create a business rule with a validation action, the business rule simply flags the associate attribute as invalid and does not attempt to modify the data. Nor does it prevent a user from saving a member with invalid or missing data. That way, the user can proceed unimpeded with the process of capturing data and can return later to make corrections. Alternatively, you can enable notification for a business rule by double-clicking the notification column in the business rule list, as shown in Figure 13-10, and selecting a group or user to receive notification by e-mail.

In the next exercise, we'll add a business rule to the Promotion entity that specifies the required fields.

Exercise 13-3: Defining a Business Rule

1. In the System Administration area of Master Data Manager, point to Manage, and click Business Rules.
2. Keep the default selections of Promotion model, Promotion entity, Leaf member type, and All attribute; and click the Add Business Rule button.
3. Click the Edit Selected Business Rule button.

Priority	Excluded	Name
10	Edit selected business rule	New rule (1)

4. In the Components section, expand Actions.

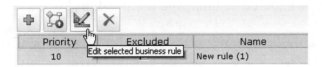

Priority	Excluded	Name	Description	Expression	Status	Notification	Modified Date
10	☐	Required fields	Required fields	🔲	Active		8/10/2010 7:38:52 AM
20	☐	DaysToManufacture	Days to manufacture	🔲	Active	—**None**	
30	☐	Std Cost	Std cost must be &gt	🔲	Active	—Groups	
40	☐	FG MSRP Cost	FG's must have msrp & de	🔲	Active	⊞—Users	

Figure 13-10 *Setting the notification recipient for a business rule*

5. In the Validation group, select Is Required and drag it to the Actions label in the THEN pane on the right side of the browser window. When you release the mouse button, a plus symbol appears.

6. Click Actions to add the rule.

NOTE

You might find the interface to create business rules is very different from other web applications. Although you follow the correct series of steps, the addition of a condition, action, or attribute does not always work as we describe. Just keep trying.

7. In the Entity-Specific Attributes on the left, select Name, drag it to the Select Attribute label in the Edit Action section, release the mouse button, click the Select Attribute label, and then click the Save Item button.

8. Repeat the previous step to make the following attributes required: Code, Type, Category, DiscountPct, and Manager.

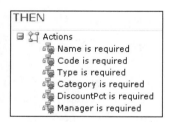

9. Click the Back button to return to the Business Rule list and notice the status of the edited rule is now "Activation pending."

10. Double-click the business rule name, New rule (1), and type a new name: **Required fields**.

11. Click the Publish Business Rules button (the second button on the toolbar), and click the OK button to confirm.

Importing Data

Most likely, you already have data sources for dimensional data. Rather than have someone manually enter this data into MDS using Master Data Manager, you can load data into staging tables in the MDS database and use the MDS import process to transform the staged data into the structures required by MDS. If you have a small number of source tables, you can use the SQL Server Import and Export Wizard in SQL Server Management Studio to copy data into the staging tables. You can save the package created by the wizard to repeat the staging process at a later time if necessary. To stage dimension data from a larger number of tables using more complex transformations, you should use SSIS.

Regardless of which method you use to populate the staging tables, the tables to load and the required values for those tables are the same. For more detailed information, refer to the topic "Importing Data (Master Data Services)" in SQL Server Books Online (http://msdn.microsoft.com/en-us/library/ee633726.aspx). Let's review some of the key points about each table:

- ▶ **tblStgMember**   Use this table to load records as leaf members, consolidated members, or collections. The ModelName, EntityName, MemberType_ID, MemberCode, and Status_ID columns are required. The HierarchyName column is required only for consolidated members. For the MemberType_ID column, use a value of 1 for a leaf member, 2 for a consolidated member, and 3 for a collection. Set the Status_ID column to a value of 0 to indicate the records are ready for staging. Figure 13-11 shows an example of records that are ready to load into tblStgMember.

- ▶ **tblStgMemberAttribute**   Use this table to load the name and value pairs for each attribute of a member. The ModelName, EntityName, MemberType_ID, MemberCode, AttributeName, and Status_ID columns are required. The possible MemberType_ID values are the same as those you can use to stage records for the tblStgMember table. If an attribute is domain-based, the AttributeValue column must contain the MemberCode value of the attribute that it represents. The import process will generate errors if the AttributeValue is blank for attributes with a numeric or date data type or for the Name attribute. You must use Master Data Manager to stage file attributes. You can see an example of records to load into tblStgMemberAttribute in Figure 13-12.

ModelName	EntityName	HierarchyName	MemberType_ID	MemberName	MemberCode	Status_ID
Promotion	Promotion	NULL	1	Touring-1000 Promotion	14	0
Promotion	Promotion	NULL	1	Touring-3000 Promotion	13	0
Promotion	Promotion	NULL	1	Volume Discount 11 to 14	2	0
Promotion	Promotion	NULL	1	Volume Discount 15 to 24	3	0
Promotion	Promotion	NULL	1	Volume Discount 25 to 40	4	0
Promotion	Promotion	NULL	1	Volume Discount 41 to 60	5	0
Promotion	Promotion	NULL	1	Volume Discount over 60	6	0
Promotion	Promotion	Category	2	Customer	Customer	0
Promotion	Promotion	Category	2	Discontinued Product	Reseller-Discontinued Product	0

Figure 13-11 *Records to load into tblStgMember*

ModelName	EntityName	MemberType_ID	MemberCode	AttributeName	AttributeValue	Status_ID
Promotion	Promotion	1	1	Category	No Discount	0
Promotion	Promotion	1	1	DiscountPct	0.00	0
Promotion	Promotion	1	1	MinQty	0	0
Promotion	Promotion	1	1	Type	No Discount	0
Promotion	Promotion	1	10	Category	Customer	0
Promotion	Promotion	1	10	DiscountPct	0.50	0
Promotion	Promotion	1	10	MinQty	0	0
Promotion	Promotion	1	10	Type	Excess Inventory	0

Figure 13-12 *Records to load into tblStgMemberAttribute*

▶ **tblStgRelationship** Use this table to specify the parent-child or sibling relationships between members in a hierarchy or a collection. The following columns are required: ModelName, EntityName, MemberType_ID, MemberCode, TargetCode, TargetType_ID, and Status_ID. HierarchyName is required only when the record describes a relationship in an explicit hierarchy. In this table, you use 4 as the MemberType_ID value for an explicit hierarchy and use 5 for a collection. The TargetCode requires the MemberCode of a sibling member or a parent member, ROOT to add a member to the root of the hierarchy without a parent, or the code of the collection to which you are adding the member. For TargetType_ID, use 1 to specify that the target member is a parent member or a collection, or use 2 to indicate that the target member is a sibling member. Refer to Figure 13-13 for an example of tblStgRelationship records.

After loading records into the respective staging tables, you use the Process Unbatched Data command in the Integration Management area of Master Data Manager. When you execute this command, MDS creates a batch, assigns the batch identifier to each record in the staging tables, and then processes each of the tables sequentially in the order in which the tables are listed above. When the batch completes processing, MDS updates the Status_ID column of each record with 1 to indicate success or 2 to indicate failure. The records remain in the staging tables for review, and are ignored during subsequent

ModelName	EntityName	HierarchyName	MemberType_ID	MemberCode	TargetCode	TargetType_ID	Status_ID
Promotion	Promotion	Category	4	1	No Discount-No Discount	1	0
Promotion	Promotion	Category	4	10	Customer-Excess Inventory	1	0
Promotion	Promotion	Category	4	11	Reseller-Seasonal Discount	1	0
Promotion	Promotion	Category	4	12	Reseller-Excess Inventory	1	0

Figure 13-13 *Records to load into tblStgRelationship*

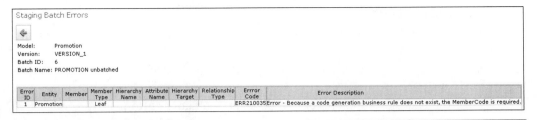

Figure 13-14 *Reviewing staging batch errors*

batch processing as long as you leave the Status_ID as a non-zero value. You can remove them any time, either by performing a manual truncate operation or incorporating a step to truncate the tables in an SSIS package.

The Integration Management area includes a Staging Batches section, which lists the processed batches, the number of records processed, and the number of errors encountered. If a staging batch has errors, you can review the error message by selecting the batch in the list and clicking the View Details For Selected Batch button. In Figure 13-14, you can see an example of an error message that displays when the MemberCode is missing.

Next, we'll import data into the Promotion model using the SQL Server Import and Export Wizard to load data in the staging tables and then process the staging batch.

Exercise 13-4: Importing Model Data

1. Open SQL Server Management Studio in the Microsoft SQL Server 2008 R2 program group and connect to the Database Engine.

2. In Object Explorer, expand the Databases folder, right-click the Master Data Services database that you created in Exercise 1, point to Tasks, and click Import Data.

3. In the wizard, click the Next button on the Welcome page if it displays.

4. On the Choose A Data Source page, select the SQL Server instance hosting the AdventureWorks2008R2 database, set the authentication method, select that database in the Database drop-down list, and click the Next button.

5. On the Choose A Destination page, select the SQL Server instance hosting the MDS database, set authentication, select the MDS database, and click the Next button.

6. On the Specify Table Copy Or Query page, select the Write A Query To Specify The Data To Transfer option, and click the Next button.

7. On the Provide A Source Query page, click the Browse button, navigate to the folder containing the files for this chapter, select the tblStgMember.sql file, and click the Open button.

8. Click the Next button.

9. In the Destination drop-down list, select [mdm].[tblStgMember] and then click the Next button.

10. On the Save And Run Package page, click the Next button, and then click the Finish button.

11. When the package completes execution, click the Close button.

12. Repeat steps 2 through 11 twice more, once using the tblStgMemberAttribute.sql file to load to the [mdm].[tblStgMemberAttribute] table and once using the tblStgRelationship.sql file to load to the [mdm].[tblStgRelationship] table.

13. Open the home page of the Master Data Manager, and click the Integration Management link.

14. In the Unbatched Staging Records section, select Promotion in the Model drop-down list, and select VERSION_1 in the Version drop-down list.

15. Click the Process Unbatched Data button.

16. Refresh the browser page to monitor the batch processing. The Started and Completed columns in the Staging Batches table will display the date and time that MDS completed processing the batch.

Master Data Stewardship

Thus far, we've explored the tasks that an administrator performs to prepare a model for master data management. To restrict the users to specific areas of Master Data Manager, to particular models, and even to subsets of data within a model, you configure user and group permissions, which we'll explain further in the next chapter. After the model is prepared and permissions granted, business users typically take responsibility for proactively managing the master data using Master Data Manager.

Working with Master Data

As a user, once you have the appropriate permissions, you can use Master Data Manager to easily update entities by adding new members. After selecting a model and version on the home page, you can open the Explorer area to access the Model View. From the Model View page, you can see a list of an entity's attributes, hierarchies, or collections in the model.

Members and Attributes

Let's say that you want to add a new member to an entity. First, you select the entity from the Entities menu at the top of the page, click the second button on the toolbar to add a new item, and then select whether you want to add a leaf member or consolidated member. Master Data Manager then displays a page allowing you to enter a code and a name for the new member, as shown in Figure 13-15. You can also click the magnifying glass icon to locate a parent member in a hierarchy to assign to the new member. After you save the member, you can use the Edit button in the Attributes section on the same page to add values for each of the member's attributes.

If, instead of adding a new member, you want to edit an existing member, select the entity from the Entities menu, and then use the Edit Selected Item button. A list of leaf members displays, but you can switch the view to a list of consolidated members if you like. You can then select a specific member in the list to edit. On the member list page, you can also use the toolbar, shown in Figure 13-16, to add a new member, delete a selected member, apply business rules, export members to Excel, or view metadata, respectively.

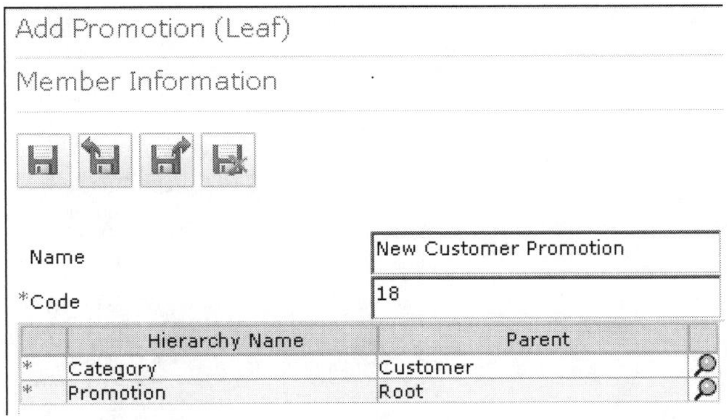

Figure 13-15 *Adding a new member*

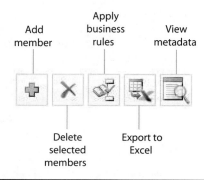

Figure 13-16 *Toolbar for entity members*

Hierarchies

When you want to review the list of members in a hierarchy or reassign a member to a different parent, you can open the hierarchy page from the Model View. The hierarchy page, whether an explicit or derived hierarchy, displays a tree view in the top-left section, as shown in Figure 13-17. After locating a member in the tree view, you can drag it to a different parent to change its position in the hierarchy.

The bottom-right section of the page displays a list of members for the parent member currently selected in the tree view. In the bottom-left section, you can use the clipboard functions to copy nodes of the hierarchy tree and paste the node as a child or a sibling elsewhere in the tree.

In a large hierarchy, you might not know where to find a particular member or group of members. You can use the Filter Criteria section in the top-right section.

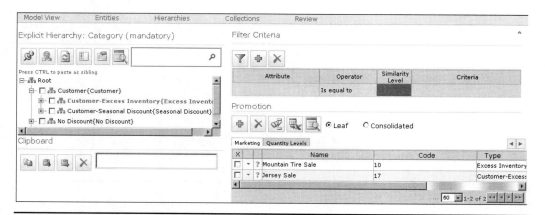

Figure 13-17 *Explicit Hierarchy page*

Just double-click in the Attribute column to select from a list of attributes. Double-click in the Operator section to use a different operator, such as "is not equal to" or "is NULL." When you double-click the Criteria column, you'll see a list of values for the selected attribute. You can add as many rows to the Filter Criteria section as you need. When you're ready, click the Apply Filter button. The members that correspond to your criteria will display in the tree view.

Business Rules

There are several ways that you can respond to issues identified by business rules. If you are a recipient of an e-mail notification, you can use the Review menu in the Explorer Area to access a list of validation issues, as shown in Figure 13-18. After you select a row in the table, you can click a button to go to a page that allows you to view the specific reasons for the failed validation and to resolve the issues by editing the attribute values.

Alternatively, you can take a more proactive approach by accessing a list of members on the Entity or Hierarchy page and using a button to apply the business rules. The user interface then flags each member with a validation icon to indicate success or failure. You can then edit the invalid members to address the identified issues.

Transactions

As users add members to an entity or modify attribute values, MDS captures each change in a transaction log. The transaction log provides an audit trail of activity, including a value of an attribute before and after a change, as well as the name of the user making the change and the date and time of the change. To review all activity in the transaction log for a model, use the Review menu on the Explorer area. If you want to view only transactions related to a specific member, you can use the context menu

Explorer: My Validation Issues

ⓘ Only issues for which you are a notification recipient are shown.

Explicit Hierarchy	Entity Name	Member Code	Member Type	Description	Notification Status
	Promotion	12	Leaf	None	True
	Promotion	10	Leaf	None	True
	Promotion	7	Leaf	None	True

Figure 13-18 *Notifications generated by a business rule*

for a member that you select in a list on the Entity or Hierarchy page. If a change was made erroneously, you have the option to reverse it by using the Reverse Selected Transaction button on the Transactions page.

Annotations

You can use annotations to add a comment to a member or to a transaction as part of an audit trail. Adding an annotation to a member generates a transaction. To view an annotation later, you must open the transaction view and locate transactions with the type of "Member annotated." If you use the Review Transactions option to see all transactions, rather than the View Member Transactions option, you can use a filter to find the "Member annotated" transactions. Unfortunately, an annotation added to a transaction does not generate a transaction. You must select a specific transaction in the log to see whether an annotation exists.

Now let's continue working on the model that we loaded with data in the previous exercise. First, we'll review the master data that we imported in the previous exercise and validate the data using the business rule that we created earlier. Then we'll add a new member and assign it to a specific parent in the Category hierarchy.

Exercise 13-5: Making Changes to Master Data

1. On the Master Data Manager Home page, select the Promotion model in the Model drop-down list, and select VERSION_1 in the Version drop-down list.
2. Click the Explorer link.
3. In the Explicit Hierarchies list, click Promotion.
4. In the member list in the bottom-right corner, click the Apply Business Rules button, and then click the OK button to confirm.

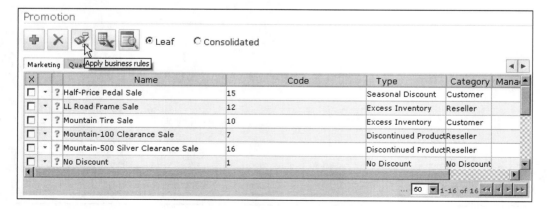

5. Notice the exclamation mark on all rows indicating that validation has failed.

6. In the second column of the first row, click the arrow, and then click Edit Member.

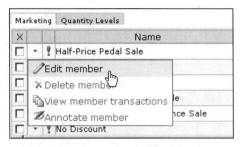

7. Scroll to the bottom of the page to note the validation issues.

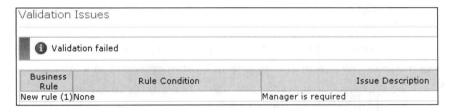

8. Click the Edit button in the Attributes section.

9. In the Manager box, type **Welcker**, and then click the Save button.

10. Click the Back button at the top of the page.

11. Notice the first row now validates properly.

12. In the second column of the first row, click the arrow, and then click View Member Transactions.

13. Notice the transaction for the update to the Manager attribute. Scroll to the right to view all columns in the transaction log, including Prior Value and New Value.

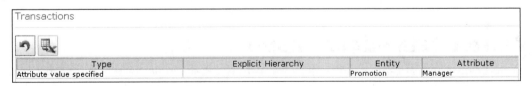

14. Close the Transactions window.

15. Click the Add Member button above the member list.

16. In the Name box, type **Jersey Sale**.

17. In the Code box, type **17**.

18. Click the Save And Edit button.
19. Click the Edit button in the Attributes section.
20. Type values for the attributes as shown in the following table:

Attribute Name	Attribute Value
Type	Customer-Excess Inventory
Category	Customer
DiscountPct	0.2

21. Click the Save button.
22. Click the Quantity Levels tab, and then click the Edit button.
23. In the MinQty box, type **2**, and click the Save button.
24. Click the Back button.
25. Point to Hierarchies, and click Explicit:Category.
26. Expand Customer, and then expand Customer-Excess Inventory.
27. Drag the Jersey Sale item and drop it on Customer-Excess Inventory.
28. When the plus symbol appears, click Customer-Excess Inventory to add Jersey Sale as a child of this promotion type.

Master Data Administration

Periodically, there are some additional administrative tasks to perform. After users have made changes to master data, you must share this data with your data warehouse, and optionally send changes back to the source systems. You can also use versioning to keep historical copies of your master data separate from the current version.

Exporting Master Data

MDS provides a simple, database-driven mechanism to allow other systems to consume data from the master data hub. In the Integration Management area, you can create a subscription view to support this export capability, as shown in Figure 13-19. In the subscription view definition, you specify the filters used to restrict the data that appears in the view. For example, you can select a specific model version or you can use a version flag. Using a version flag is a simpler approach, because it allows you to reference a current version rather than create a new subscription view each time a new version of the model becomes the current version.

The subscription view requires you to select either an entity or a derived hierarchy. You can then specify one of the following formats to construct the subscription view:

- ▶ Leaf attributes, to show only leaf members and all attributes
- ▶ Consolidated attributes, to show only consolidated members and their attributes
- ▶ Collection attributes, to show a list of collections in the model
- ▶ Collections, to show all members added to collections
- ▶ Explicit parent child, to show each parent-child relationship in the hierarchy
- ▶ Explicit levels, to show the names of each level in the hierarchy

The subscription view creates a denormalized view of the master data in the MDS database that you can use in a variety of ways. You can reference the view directly in an Analysis Services data source view or even in a Reporting Services report. More commonly, you'll use the view in an ETL process to update dimension tables in a data warehouse.

Let's complete our work with Master Data Services by creating a subscription view for the members in the Promotion entity.

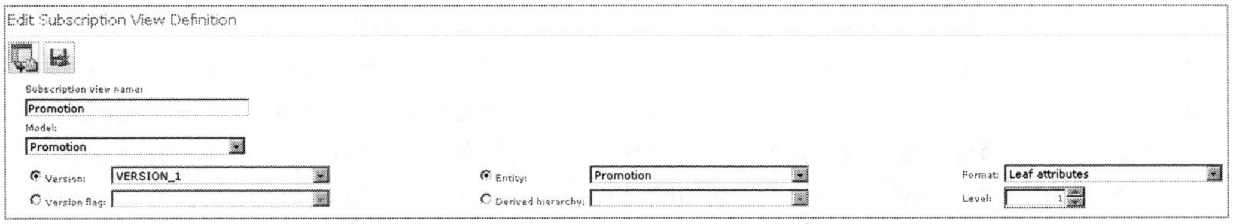

Figure 13-19 *Subscription view definition*

Exercise 13-6: Creating a Subscription View

1. On the Master Data Manager Home page, click the Integration Management link.
2. Click the Export link.
3. Click the Add Subscription View button.
4. In the Subscription View Name box, type **Promotion**.
5. In the Model drop-down list, select Promotion.
6. In the Version drop-down list, select VERSION_1.
7. In the Entity drop-down list, select Promotion.
8. In the Format drop-down list, select Leaf attributes.
9. Click the Save button.
10. Open SQL Server Management Studio, and connect to the database engine.
11. Click the New Query button, and type the following query into the query editor:

```
select * from mdm.Promotion
```

12. In the Available Databases drop-down list, select the Master Data Services database.
13. Press F5 to execute the query.

	Member_ID	VersionName	VersionNumber	VersionFlag	Name	Code	ChangeTrackingMask	Type	Category	Manager	DiscountF
1	1	VERSION_1	1	NULL	Half-Price Pedal Sale	15	0	Seasonal Discount	Customer	Welcker	0.50
2	2	VERSION_1	1	NULL	LL Road Frame Sale	12	0	Excess Inventory	Reseller	NULL	0.35
3	3	VERSION_1	1	NULL	Mountain Tire Sale	10	0	Excess Inventory	Customer	NULL	0.50
4	4	VERSION_1	1	NULL	Mountain-100 Clearance Sale	7	0	Discontinued Product	Reseller	NULL	0.35
5	5	VERSION_1	1	NULL	Mountain-500 Silver Clearance Sale	16	0	Discontinued Product	Reseller	NULL	0.40
6	6	VERSION_1	1	NULL	No Discount	1	0	No Discount	No Discount	NULL	0.00

Managing Versions

The version management feature of MDS allows you to maintain multiple copies of master data if you like. Versioning doesn't save only a copy of the schema, but actually saves the master data itself. That means you can go back to an earlier version to review the data and its hierarchical structure at any point in time. This capability is an important feature for auditing and reporting purposes.

When you first create a model in MDS, the version is a copy of the data that is a work in progress. Perhaps your model is a chart of accounts from a general ledger system and you can allow changes to the structure of the chart of accounts only before the fiscal year begins. After users complete their adjustments to the model, you use the Version Management area of Master Data Manager to work with the version.

Your next step is to lock the version so that users can no longer make changes. Then you can perform a validation of the version to ensure all issues are resolved.

The Version Management area includes an option to apply the business rules and then displays a summary of the results, as shown in Figure 13-20. You can select an item in the Validation Issues list to go directly to the problem member and make corrections. Only model administrators are permitted to make changes to the master data while the version is in a locked state. If necessary, you can unlock the version if you need to allow users to make corrections themselves.

After the model validates successfully, you can commit the version. At that point, the version can no longer be changed by either users or administrators. Furthermore, once the version is committed, the version cannot be unlocked. A committed version is final. However, you can copy a committed version to start a new unlocked version of your model.

As part of the version management process, you can also create as many version flags as you like. Version flags are useful as filter criteria for subscription views. Figure 13-21 shows examples of version flags that you might create. After creating a version flag, you can double-click the Flag column on the Manage Versions page to assign it to a specific version.

Versions: Validate Version

Model:
Promotion

Version:
VERSION_1

Validation Summary
To validate awaiting items, click the Validate Versions button.

Status	Member Count
Awaiting validation	11
Awaiting revalidation	18
Validation succeeded	1
Validation failed	16
Awaiting dependent member revalidation	0

Validation issues

Explicit Hierarchy	Entity Name	Member Code	Member Type	Description	Notification Status
	Promotion	12	Leaf	None	True
	Promotion	10	Leaf	None	True
	Promotion	7	Leaf	None	True
	Promotion	16	Leaf	None	True

Figure 13-20 *Validating a version*

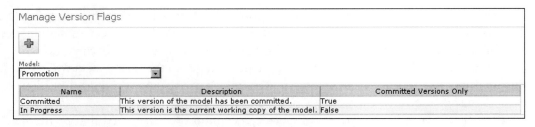

Figure 13-21 *Version flags for the Promotion model*

Summary

As with all the other topics we've covered in this book, there is much more that we could say about MDS, but our purpose in this chapter was to provide you with enough information and hands-on experience to help you start building models for your own master data. Because MDS is so flexible, keep in mind that there is no single way to use it. More important is to establish processes in your organization that rely on a single authoritative source for information related to a business entity, whether that source is the master data hub or elsewhere, and then use MDS to synchronize that data with other systems that rely on the same information in part or as a whole.

Chapter 14

Publishing and Administration

In This Chapter

- ▶ Integration Services
- ▶ Analysis Services
- ▶ Excel Services
- ▶ PowerPivot
- ▶ Reporting Services
- ▶ SharePoint
- ▶ PerformancePoint Services
- ▶ Master Data Services
- ▶ Summary

Throughout this book, we've explored a variety of technologies that you can use to build a business intelligence solution. Your solution might use only some of these technologies, or it might use all of them. Regardless, after building your solution, you'll need to publish the components to production and perform various administrative tasks to keep the solution running effectively. You'll also need to configure security to ensure authorized users have the right access to the solution. In this final chapter, we'll review each of the key technologies that comprise the Microsoft BI stack and explain how you can deploy, maintain, and secure a business intelligence solution.

Integration Services

If you build SQL Server Integration Services (SSIS) packages, as we briefly described in Chapter 3, to populate a data warehouse (or data mart), you will have a collection of DTSX package files stored in a Business Intelligence Development Studio (BIDS) project. To execute these packages in a production environment, you must move the files to a package store. You can move the package files manually or use the SSIS deployment utility to simplify the process. Then you must secure the packages, but the steps you take depend on which package store you use. After storing and securing your files, you can establish a regular schedule for package execution to keep your data warehouse up to date.

Package Store

The package store is essentially a registry for the location of your SSIS packages on a server. The package store supports two types of locations—the file system and the *sysdtspackages* table in the *msdb* database on your SQL Server. There is no requirement to use one or the other exclusively, and it's certainly possible to use both of them. Furthermore, you won't notice any performance difference between the two.

To help you decide which option is better for your environment, let's first consider some advantages of using the file system as your package store. If you frequently make updates to the DTSX files or if you use a source control system, you will likely find using the file system approach fits better with your development processes. You can more easily access the files using BIDS when you need to make changes.

Using *msdb* as a package store also has advantages to consider. Because a standard practice for SQL Server database administrators is to perform a regular backup of the *msdb* database on each SQL Server, any packages that you store in the database are automatically saved in a backup. You can also take advantage of more granular security options for controlling access to packages. In addition, you can encrypt packages that are stored in *msdb* for even higher security.

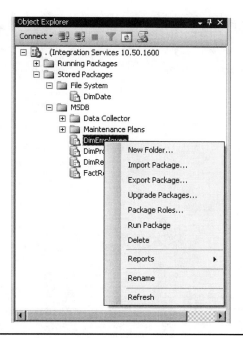

Figure 14-1   *Viewing the SSIS package store in SQL Server Management Studio*

You can use SQL Server Management Studio (SSMS) to manage packages in the SSIS package store. After you connect to Integration Services, you can open the Stored Packages folder to see packages by location, file system, or MSDB, as shown in Figure 14-1.

Incidentally, you do have the option to keep your package files on the file system without using the SSIS package store. If you prefer a file-based storage approach, you still have the same advantages that we provided for the File System package store. However, you cannot use SSMS to view a list of your packages or to run a selected package.

Deploy Packages

To move your files to the package store, you can manually import packages one by one using the Import Package option in SSMS. However, the import process can be rather tedious when you have a lot of packages. A faster method when working with multiple files would be to use the SSIS deployment utility.

First, you must enable the deployment utility by setting the CreateDeploymentUtility property value to True in your project's properties, as shown in Figure 14-2. Then you use the Build menu in BIDS to build the project (or right-click the project in Solution Explorer, and click Build). The build process creates a manifest file with a file extension

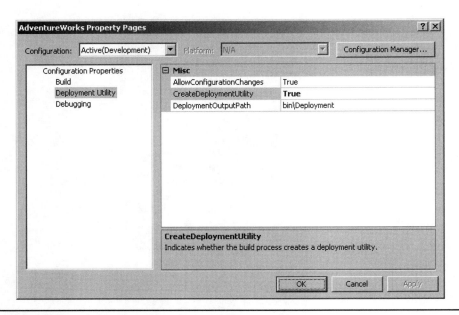

Figure 14-2 *Enabling the SSIS deployment utility*

of SSISDeploymentManifest and copies the project's package files to the path specified in the DeploymentOutputPath property for the project.

Often, package developers are not able to deploy packages directly to a production server, but must hand off script files or installation packages to an administrator who performs the deployment. The SSIS deployment utility was made with that scenario in mind. You simply provide the administrator with the manifest and package files. The administrator can place the files on the host server, or any computer with connectivity to the host server, and then double-click the manifest file to start the Package Installation Wizard. The first page of the wizard (after the Welcome page) prompts for the location to use—file system or SQL Server (see Figure 14-3).

The file system option prompts for a location on the server, which must be the \Program Files\Microsoft SQL Server\100\DTS\Packages folder to load packages into the package store. The SQL Server option prompts for a target server and a folder. The folder must already exist as a path in the MSDB store, which you can add using the Integration Services context menu in SSMS (shown in Figure 14-1).

Secure Packages

If you keep your packages on the file system, regardless of whether you use the package store or not, you should employ two layers of security. First, within the package

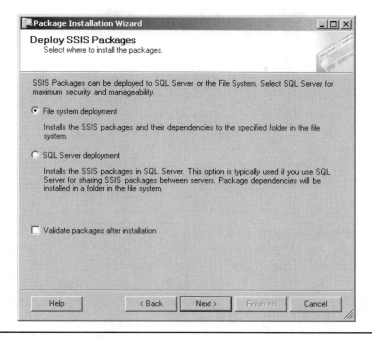

Figure 14-3 *Starting the Package Installation Wizard*

itself, there is a package property called ProtectionLevel. If you set this value to EncryptAllWithPassword, you must provide a password for the package. Then BIDS encrypts the entire package and requires the password when anyone attempts to open it later. Once deployed, no one can execute the package without providing the password. This is the best option when multiple users must have the ability to execute the package. For an additional layer of security, restrict the file system permissions on the folder containing your packages to authorized users.

NOTE

You can learn more about the other ProtectionLevel values by referring to Books Online at http://msdn.microsoft .com/en-us/library/ms141747.aspx.

You set the ProtectionLevel to ServerStorage when you plan to store a package in *msdb* and then assign package roles for the package after you deploy it. In SSMS, open the package store, right-click the package, and click Package Roles. You can then use the drop-down lists, shown in Figure 14-4, for each role to configure security.

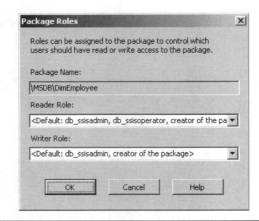

Figure 14-4 *Using package roles to manage package security*

The Reader role can only view the package in the package store list or execute the package, while the Writer role can perform any management function, such as renaming the package or configuring package roles. The package roles depend on SQL Server database roles defined for the *msdb* database. The default database roles for the Reader role are db_ssisadmin, db_ssisoperator, and the package's creator. The package's creator is also assigned to the Writer role, along with the db_ssisadmin role. You can add database roles to *msdb*, and then assign the new roles to the Reader or Writer roles.

Schedule Packages

You can execute a package anytime by using the *dtexec* command-line utility, which means you can use any scheduling tool that can execute batch commands, but you have such a tool already built into SQL Server. Using SSMS, you can connect to the database engine, start SQL Server Agent if necessary, and set up a SQL Server Agent job to run one or more packages on a schedule. A job can have one or more "SQL Server Integration Services Package" steps, as shown in Figure 14-5, with each step executing a different package.

In this example, the package will execute using the SQL Server Agent Service Account, which means that this account must have permissions to access any file share or database for which you configured a connection using Windows Authentication in the package. If you prefer to use a different account, you can add a new credential to SQL Server that has the necessary permissions, and then assign this credential as a new proxy in SQL Server Agent. When you configure the new proxy, you can specify that only jobs that run SSIS packages use this proxy account.

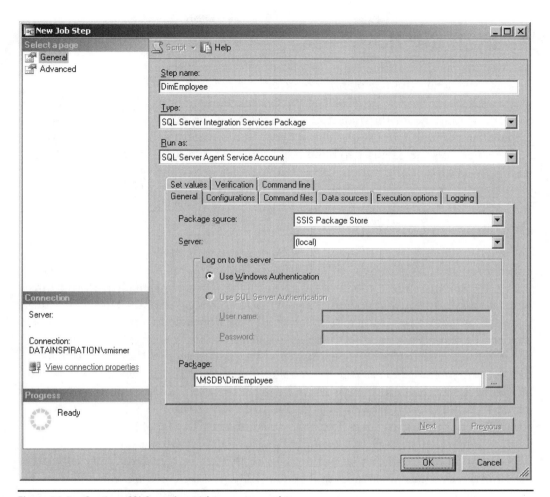

Figure 14-5   *Creating a SQL Server Agent job to execute a package*

After you configure each job step, you can assign a schedule to the job. Typically, SSIS packages for a business intelligence solution run nightly after business hours. To meet this requirement, you can set up a recurring schedule to run daily at midnight or at another time that doesn't interfere with other nightly processes that might be running, such as a backup.

NOTE

For more details, refer to the topic "Scheduling Package Execution in SQL Server Agent" in Books Online at http://msdn.microsoft.com/en-us/library/ms141701.aspx.

Analysis Services

An Analysis Services implementation follows a similar pattern as Integration Services, although the details of implementation are different. You start by moving project files to the server, configure security, and establish a schedule for processing updates. You can use BIDS to deploy the project files directly to the target server, or you can use the Deployment Wizard to move the files for you. Not only must you move files, but you must also process the database to build the database objects and load them with data. As for the security configuration, you can define roles in BIDS or you can wait until you deploy the project and configure roles on the server using SSMS.

Deploy the Database

To use BIDS for deployment, you define the target server and database name in the project properties. When you use the Deploy command on the Build menu (or after you right-click the project in Solution Explorer), the command actually performs three actions—build, deploy, and process. The build action creates four files, but in particular, it creates an asdatabase file that consolidates all the information from the ds, dsv, cube, dim, and other files in the project. The deploy action creates the target folder in the \Program Files\Microsoft SQL Server\MSAS10_50.<instance>\OLAP\Data folder, transfers the single asdatabase file to the target folder, and then extracts all the original files from the single file so that you have a copy of the files from your project on the server. Then the process action reads the files to determine how to build the database objects, queries the data sources, loads the data into the database objects, performs indexing, and calculates aggregations. That's a lot of activity from a single command!

For those situations when you can't deploy directly to the target server, you can perform the same three actions independently. First, in BIDS, you use the Build command on the Build menu or the project's context menu in Solution Explorer to create the asdatabase file and its companion files. You can then give those files to an administrator, who then can place the files on the target server in any location (or on a server with connectivity to the target server) and launch the Deployment Wizard, which is found in the Analysis Services folder of the Microsoft SQL Server 2008 R2 program group.

The wizard prompts for the location of the asdatabase file, which, by default, is in the bin folder of your project, and for the name of the target server and database. Another page of the wizard asks whether to retain or replace partitions and security settings if you are redeploying an existing database. You also have an opportunity to change connection strings or impersonation information for connecting to data sources during processing and to define locations for log files and even the database files, as shown in Figure 14-6. Next, the wizard allows you to decide whether to process the database after deployment.

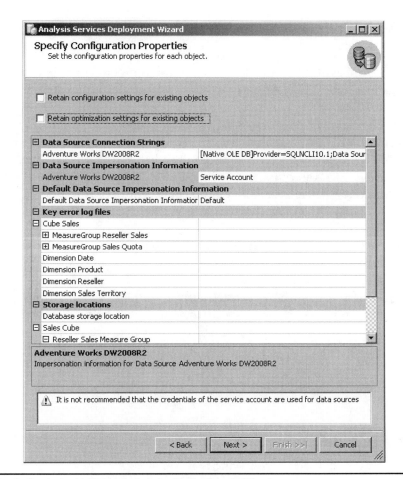

Figure 14-6   *Configuring options in the Analysis Services Deployment Wizard*

At the end of the wizard, you can simply finish the wizard and allow it to complete the deployment and processing (if you selected that option), or you can generate an XMLA script that you can execute at a later time in SSMS or by using the ASCMD command-line utility. If you did not choose the option to process, you can process the database manually in SSMS, create an XMLA script to process, or execute an SSIS package that handles Analysis Services processing. Before users can query the database using any of the front-end tools that we've described throughout this book, you must process the database after deployment to the target server.

Secure the Database

In addition to processing the database, you must configure security for the database before anyone can begin using it, unless you already configured roles in the project. The database is secure by default. Only an Analysis Services administrator can access the database initially.

The creation of a role is identical in BIDS using Solution Explorer and in SSMS using Object Explorer after connecting to the Analysis Services server. In both Explorer windows, you can right-click the Roles folder and click New Role. On the Membership tab of the role designer, you can define Windows user accounts or groups that have permission to access the database. There is no equivalent in Analysis Services to SQL Server database logins. You must use Windows Authentication to grant users access to an Analysis Services database.

Then, on the Cubes tab, shown in Figure 14-7, you typically select Read, unless you intend to support writeback. In that case, you select Read/Write. Notice there is a tab for Mining Structures, which you use when you deploy data mining.

Defining security at the cube level often suffices for many organizations. However, you can get much more restrictive by specifying which dimension members to allow or deny the role to view or even which cells in the cube are accessible to users assigned to the role. This type of security implementation requires planning and a good understanding of MDX to implement correctly. To learn more, see "User Access Security Architecture" in Books Online at http://msdn.microsoft.com/en-us/library/ms174927.aspx.

Schedule Processing

After the processing that occurs following the deployment of the database to the server, you must periodically refresh the data to keep the cube and dimensions up to date. One option is to create an XMLA script in SSMS and then create a batch file that executes the script using the ASCMD utility. That way, you could use a scheduling

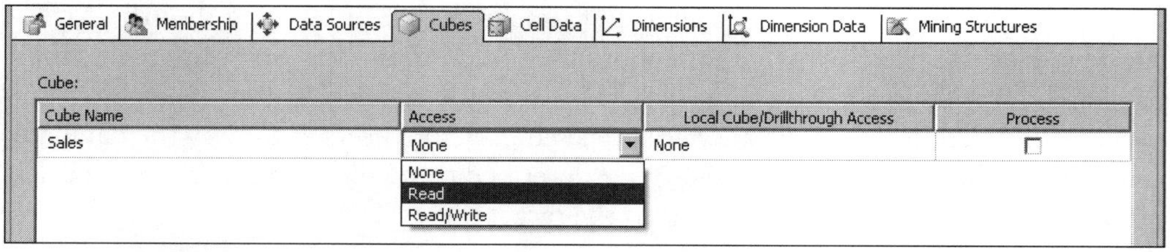

Figure 14-7 *Granting read access to a cube*

tool to execute the batch file—after the SSIS packages finish updating the data warehouse, of course!

To create an XMLA script for processing, as shown in Figure 14-8, you must first connect to the Analysis Services engine in SSMS. Then right-click the object you want to process—the database, the cube, a partition, or a dimension—and click Process. You can use the Change Settings button to specify whether partitions are processed sequentially or in parallel and how to handle dimension errors, among other settings. Then at the top of the dialog box, click the Script button and then save the script to a file.

Another option is to create an SSIS package to process your Analysis Services database. Just add an Analysis Services Processing Task to the control flow. Like the

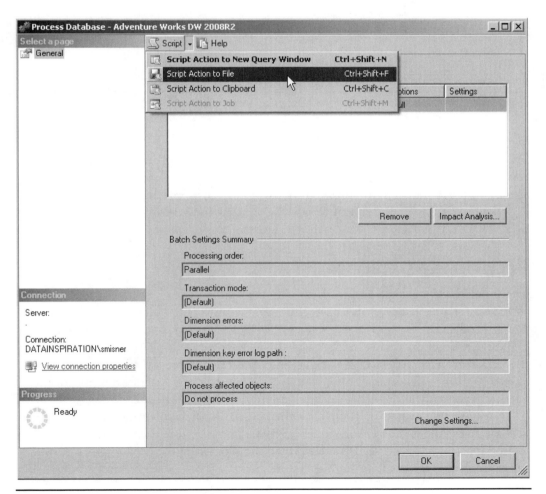

Figure 14-8 *Creating an XMLA script in SSMS*

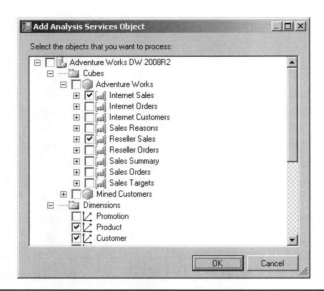

Figure 14-9 *Selecting database objects in the Analysis Services Processing Task*

Process Database dialog in BIDS or SSMS, the Processing Settings page in the task editor includes a section for batch settings. In addition, the task editor allows you to specify whether you want to process the entire database or selected database objects, as shown in Figure 14-9. You can deploy the package and schedule package execution using SQL Server Agent as we described earlier in this chapter.

Back Up the Database

You should have a backup and recovery plan for your Analysis Services database just as you do for a SQL Server database, although the process is a bit different. In SSMS, you right-click the Analysis Services database, and then click Backup. In the Backup Database dialog box, shown in Figure 14-10, you identify the location and name for the backup, which saves to disk as an .abf file. You can compress the backup file, as well as encrypt it for safekeeping of the data. Notice that you can generate a script for the backup process if you prefer to execute it as a script using a scheduling tool.

To restore a database, you right-click the Databases folder, identify the .abf file to use, and name the database. You can choose whether to restore the security information from the backup. Of course, if you encrypted the file during the backup process, you must supply the password during the restore.

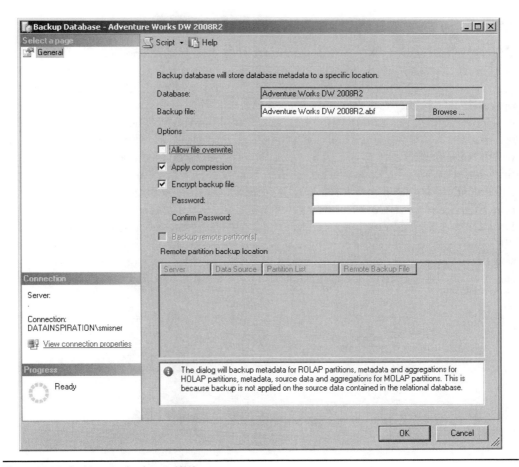

Figure 14-10 *Backing up a database in SSMS*

Excel Services

In Chapter 4, we explained how to publish workbooks to Excel Services. Now it's time to expand on that explanation by providing additional information about Excel Services and security. First, because an external data connection is required when using workbooks as a front-end for Analysis Services, there are some considerations that you should keep in mind as you create workbooks and configure Excel Services to support refreshing external data. Second, you must secure access to workbooks after publishing to ensure that only authorized users can view their contents.

Manage External Data Connections

When you add an Analysis Services connection to a workbook, you decide whether the workbook uses a connection file stored in a Data Connections library in the SharePoint farm or relies on a connection string embedded in the workbook. One of the connection properties is whether to "Always use the connection file," as shown in Figure 14-11, but notice that the connection information is also stored in the workbook. This connection information is ignored when you select the check box. However, if you leave it unchecked, which is the default setting, Excel Services will use the embedded connection information first, and will only use the connection file if that first attempt fails.

You can configure Excel Services to require the workbook to use connection files that are stored in the Data Connections library, which we covered in Chapter 8. The Data Connections library is trusted by default. If you decide to store connections in a different location, you must configure that location as trusted in Excel Services. You can also prevent the workbook from opening if the data refresh fails on opening so that you can prevent the user from viewing cached data in the workbook.

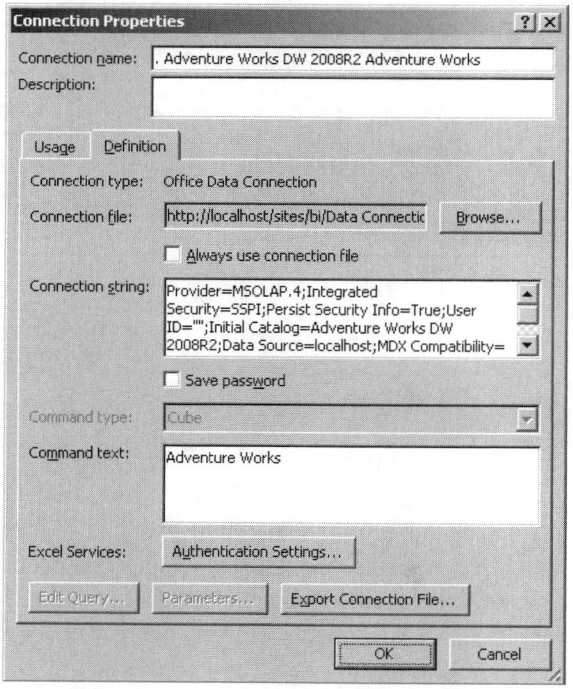

Figure 14-11 *Office Data Connections properties*

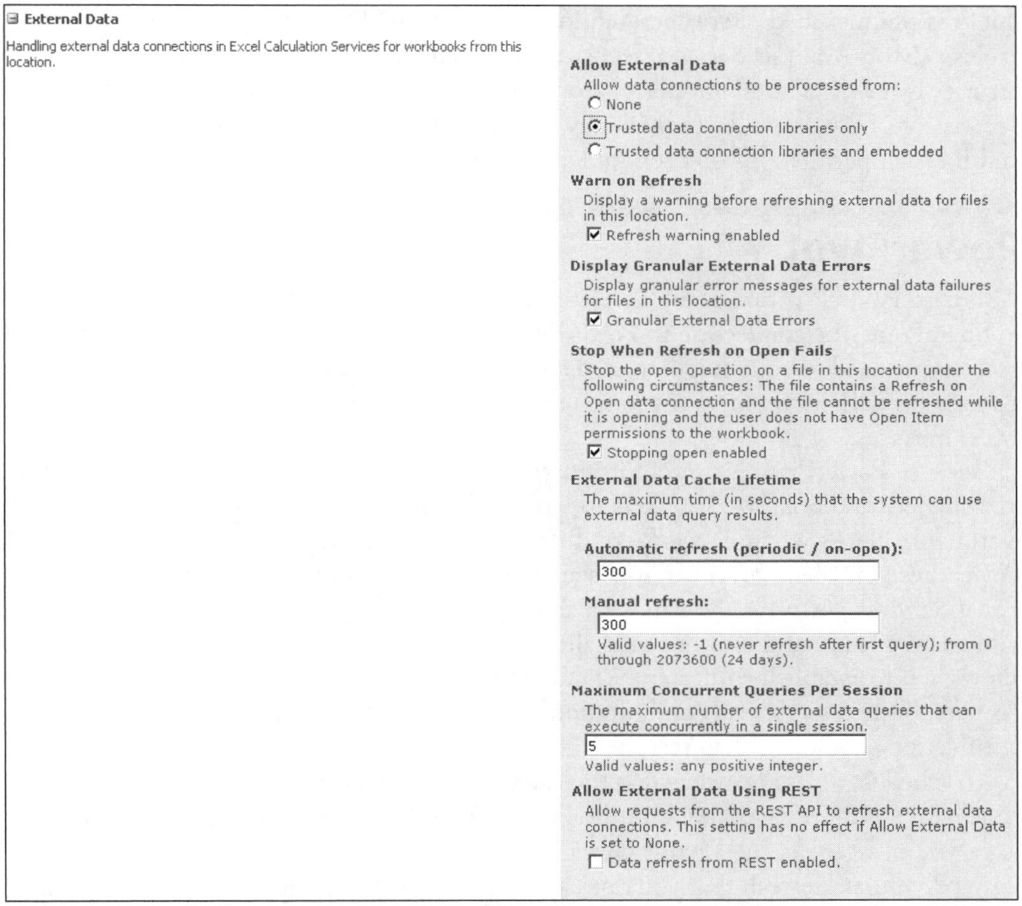

⊟ **External Data**

Handling external data connections in Excel Calculation Services for workbooks from this location.

Allow External Data
Allow data connections to be processed from:
○ None
◉ Trusted data connection libraries only
○ Trusted data connection libraries and embedded

Warn on Refresh
Display a warning before refreshing external data for files in this location.
☑ Refresh warning enabled

Display Granular External Data Errors
Display granular error messages for external data failures for files in this location.
☑ Granular External Data Errors

Stop When Refresh on Open Fails
Stop the open operation on a file in this location under the following circumstances: The file contains a Refresh on Open data connection and the file cannot be refreshed while it is opening and the user does not have Open Item permissions to the workbook.
☑ Stopping open enabled

External Data Cache Lifetime
The maximum time (in seconds) that the system can use external data query results.

Automatic refresh (periodic / on-open):
[300]

Manual refresh:
[300]
Valid values: -1 (never refresh after first query); from 0 through 2073600 (24 days).

Maximum Concurrent Queries Per Session
The maximum number of external data queries that can execute concurrently in a single session.
[5]
Valid values: any positive integer.

Allow External Data Using REST
Allow requests from the REST API to refresh external data connections. This setting has no effect if Allow External Data is set to None.
☐ Data refresh from REST enabled.

Figure 14-12 *External Data settings for an Excel Services trusted location*

You configure both of these settings by opening the Manage Service Applications page in SharePoint's Central Administration, and then opening the page for the Excel Services application. From there, open the Trusted File Locations page, and then open an existing location or add a new one. You can then scroll to the External Data section, shown in Figure 14-12, to configure settings as appropriate for your environment.

Secure Workbooks

Analysis Services role security applies to workbooks, as long as you keep the default Windows Authentication, but does not prevent a user from opening a workbook that might contain cached data generated for a user with higher privileges. Rather than rely exclusively on Analysis Services security, you should consider adding another layer of security by using SharePoint permissions to restrict access to workbooks. You can set permissions on workbooks individually or organize workbooks into groups by folder and then set permissions on each folder.

PowerPivot

Although PowerPivot relies on Excel Services when you publish a PowerPivot workbook to SharePoint, the connection to PowerPivot data is maintained entirely by PowerPivot. You simply need to configure a trusted location as we described in Chapter 5. You should also use SharePoint permissions to secure access to workbooks, just as we described for Excel Services.

Because PowerPivot is useful for integrating many different types of data sources in a single workbook, you are likely to have multiple data connections in the same workbook. Here's where PowerPivot differs from a standard Excel workbook—PowerPivot for SharePoint can manage the data refresh for you. For other workbooks, Excel Services performs the data refresh only when a user tries to open the workbook. PowerPivot for SharePoint not only allows you to schedule the data refresh, but also allows you to establish a different schedule for each data source in the workbook. As part of the data refresh configuration, you can specify recipients of an e-mail notification should the data refresh fail.

To schedule a data refresh, click the calendar icon in the upper-right corner of the panel containing the workbook in the PowerPivot Gallery. To edit the fields on this page, you must select the Enable check box, as shown in Figure 14-13. A feature of the PowerPivot data refresh that you don't typically see in other applications is the ability to schedule a refresh after business hours. You can specify the business hours for your organization in the PowerPivot service application configuration in SharePoint Central Administration.

The service application administrator has a global view of the status of all data refresh attempts in the PowerPivot Management Dashboard. At the bottom of the dashboard are two sections related to data refresh, shown in Figure 14-14—Data Refresh – Recent Activity and Data Refresh – Recent Failures. You should check this dashboard periodically to review the status of the data refresh tasks.

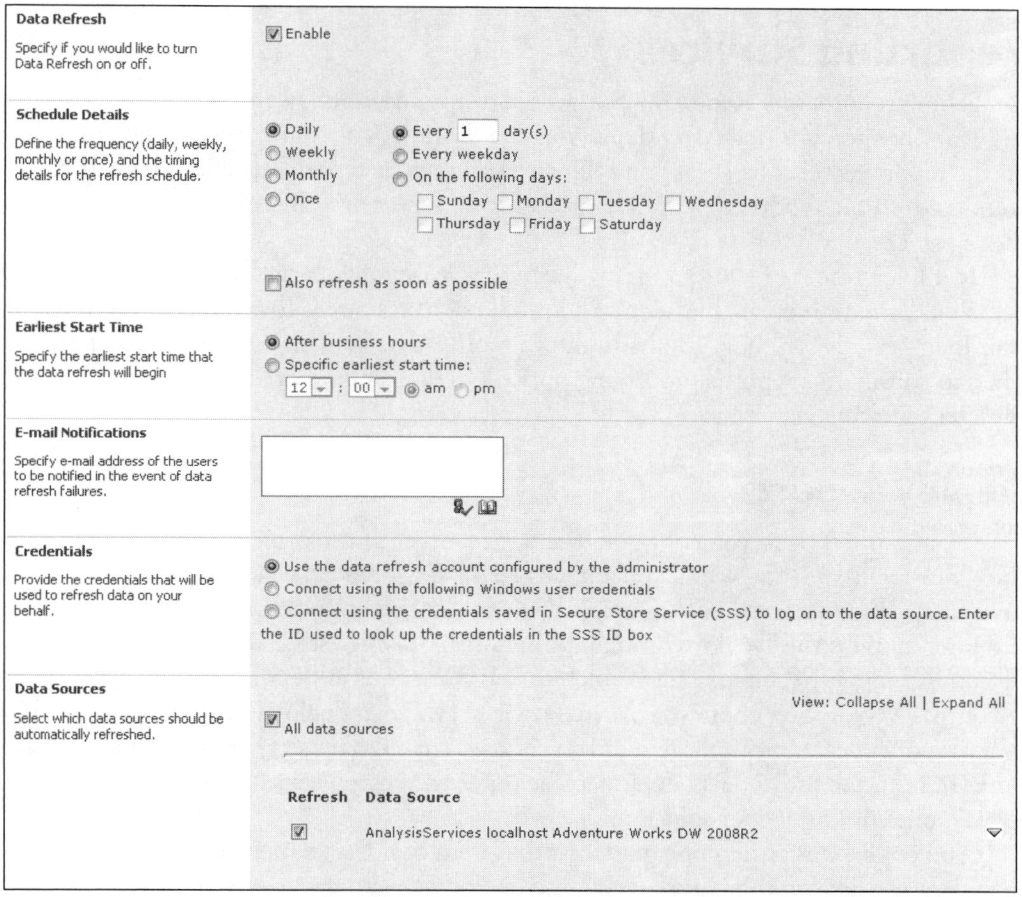

Data Refresh Specify if you would like to turn Data Refresh on or off.	☑ Enable
Schedule Details Define the frequency (daily, weekly, monthly or once) and the timing details for the refresh schedule.	⦿ Daily ⦿ Every ⬚1 day(s) ○ Weekly ○ Every weekday ○ Monthly ○ On the following days: 　　　　　　　☐ Sunday ☐ Monday ☐ Tuesday ☐ Wednesday 　　　　　　　☐ Thursday ☐ Friday ☐ Saturday ☐ Also refresh as soon as possible
Earliest Start Time Specify the earliest start time that the data refresh will begin	⦿ After business hours ○ Specific earliest start time: 　⬚12 ▾ : ⬚00 ▾ ⦿ am ○ pm
E-mail Notifications Specify e-mail address of the users to be notified in the event of data refresh failures.	⬚ 　　　　　　　　　　　　　🔍 📖
Credentials Provide the credentials that will be used to refresh data on your behalf.	⦿ Use the data refresh account configured by the administrator ○ Connect using the following Windows user credentials ○ Connect using the credentials saved in Secure Store Service (SSS) to log on to the data source. Enter the ID used to look up the credentials in the SSS ID box
Data Sources Select which data sources should be automatically refreshed.	View: Collapse All | Expand All ☑ All data sources **Refresh　Data Source** ☑　　　AnalysisServices localhost Adventure Works DW 2008R2　　　▽

Figure 14-13 *Configuring a data refresh schedule for a PowerPivot workbook*

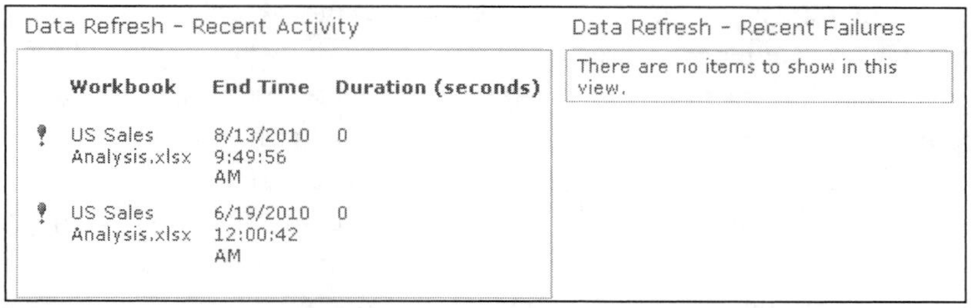

Data Refresh - Recent Activity	Data Refresh - Recent Failures

	Workbook	**End Time**	**Duration (seconds)**
❗	US Sales Analysis.xlsx	8/13/2010 9:49:56 AM	0
❗	US Sales Analysis.xlsx	6/19/2010 12:00:42 AM	0

Data Refresh - Recent Failures: There are no items to show in this view.

Figure 14-14 *Data refresh status in the PowerPivot Management Dashboard*

Reporting Services

Publishing reports to a Reporting Services server is straightforward, but you do have a few options to consider. After deployment, you should, of course, secure the reports on the report server. The steps you follow to secure your reports depend on whether you deployed the reports to a Native mode report server or a SharePoint integrated mode server.

Most likely, most of your reports will run in a reasonable period. However, you might occasionally have reports that require a lot of system resources to render or that must wait long periods for query results to return from a data source. For those situations, you can configure a report's processing options to use caching or snapshots to accelerate the user's viewing experience.

Deploy Reports

Like Analysis Services, you configure the target server in the project properties, as shown in Figure 14-15. When you're ready to deploy a report, you can right-click it in Solution Explorer, and click Deploy. You can also select several reports in Solution Explorer and use the Deploy command to publish only the selected reports. Another option is to deploy the project, in which case BIDS sends all reports to the target server. If your BIDS solution contains multiple projects, you can deploy the solution to publish every report in each project. Shared data sources, shared data sets, report parts, and any other item in the project also deploy to the server when you select them individually or deploy an entire project or solution.

If you deploy a report, report part, or other item besides a data source or data set that already exists on the report server, the deployment process overwrites it on the report server without warning. However, any report parameter settings that you might have changed on the report server are preserved. New report parameters are added to the report on the server, but you must manually adjust parameter properties on the report server to match your report. As an alternative, you can delete the report and then redeploy it to ensure the report server version matches the version in BIDS. On the other hand, if subscriptions or other settings are associated with the report, you will lose that information when you delete the report, so proceed with caution.

The default project properties do not allow you to overwrite data sets and data sources on the report server. Presumably, during your report development process, you used different connection information in data sources than you use for published reports, so these properties protect the connection information that you store on the report server. Likewise, data sets might have dependencies that you want to protect, so you must manually overwrite a data set or change the project properties to proceed with redeployment of a data set.

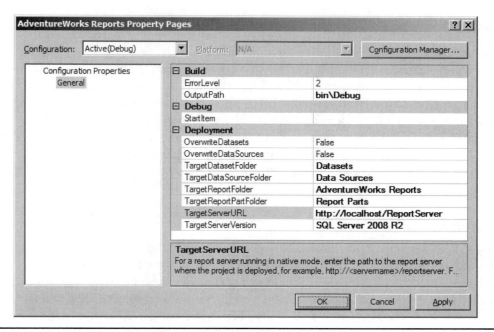

Figure 14-15 *Report server project properties for deployment*

If you don't want to use the built-in Deploy command, you have two other options. You can open either Report Manager or a SharePoint document library if you have a SharePoint integrated mode report server and manually upload a report or other report server item. When you need to deploy multiple report items, you can create a Visual Basic script that calls the Reporting Services web service's Publish method and save the script as an RSS file (not to be confused with an RSS data feed). Then provide the script and the files to deploy to a local administrator who can execute the RS.EXE command-line utility on a report server to complete the deployment. The RS.EXE utility is also useful for scripting other administrative tasks. It's always been available for use with a Native mode report server, but has not been available for a SharePoint integrated mode server until SharePoint 2010.

NOTE

You can download a sample script that shows you how to publish reports from the Codeplex site at http://msftrsprodsamples.codeplex.com/wikipage?title=SS2008!Script Samples (Reporting Services).

Secure Report Server Items

If you're running a SharePoint integrated mode report server, you use SharePoint groups and permissions to control access to report server items: reports, shared data sources, shared data sets, report parts, and report models. A native mode report server uses a role-based authorization system based on Windows accounts. You can organize report server items into folders, and then assign users to different groups or roles for each folder if you need to restrict access to information by subject matter. You can also use roles or groups to secure individual items, but it's much easier to manage security at the folder level. Table 14-1 compares the default native mode roles with SharePoint groups:

Native Mode Security

To assign a user or Windows group to a role on a native mode report server, open Report Manager in your browser. Navigate to the folder for which you want to configure security, and click the Folder Settings button the toolbar. If you're working on the Home folder, click the New Role Assignment button. You can then enter a Windows login or a Windows group and select one or more role assignments, as shown in Figure 14-16.

If you're working on a folder other than the Home folder, there are a few more steps involved. Click the Security tab, click the Edit Item Security button, and click the OK button to confirm that you want to override the security settings inherited from the parent folder. Then you can click the New Role Assignment button and continue with the role assignment settings as described previously.

Allowed Action	Native Mode Role	SharePoint Group
All content management activity (add, change, or delete content) and permissions management	Content Manager	Owner
All content management activity except subscriptions	Publisher	Members
Report access and personal subscription management	Browser	Visitors
Report access, personal subscription management, and Report Builder access	Report Builder	No equivalent (Owners and Members can access Report Builder)
All content management activity within My Reports folder	My Reports	No equivalent

Table 14-1   *Reporting Services Security Model*

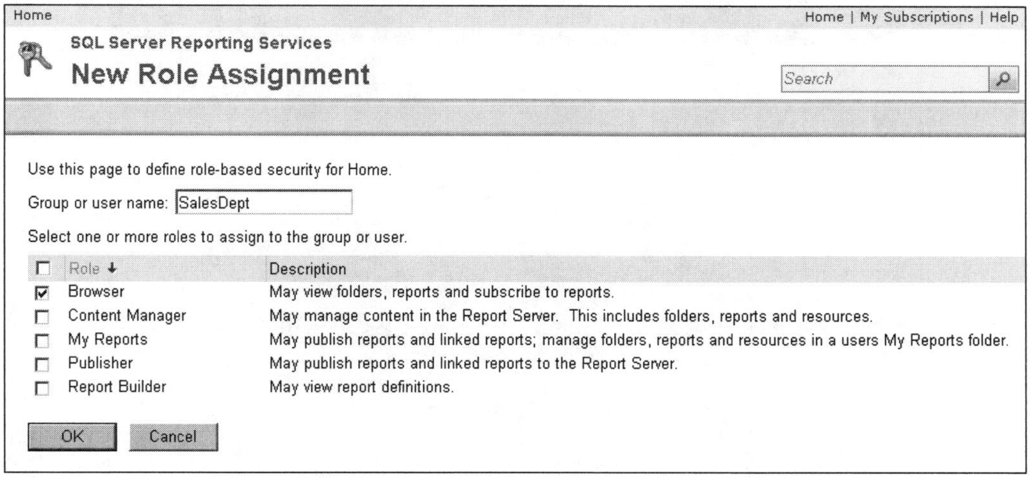

Figure 14-16 *Configuring role security in Reporting Services*

SharePoint Integrated Mode Security

A report server running in SharePoint integrated mode relies on SharePoint's security model, so you may already have groups and permission levels configured for other purposes. Recall from Chapter 8 that you publish reports to document libraries. You can configure report security for the document library, create folders to separate reports into groups, and then manage different security levels by report group, or manage permissions for each report individually.

If you want to use folder-level or report-level security, right-click the folder or report in the document library, and click Manage Permissions. Click the Stop Inheriting Permissions button, and click the OK button to confirm. Then click the Grant Permissions button, type in multiple users or groups, and then assign them to a SharePoint group, as shown in Figure 14-17.

Configure Stored Credentials

To use Reporting Services features that execute reports on behalf of users, you must first configure any shared data source in the report to use stored credentials. These features include subscriptions, cached reports, cache refresh plans, and report snapshots. You can configure stored credentials for a data source only after you deploy it to the report server. Just open the shared data source properties and specify a user name and password for an account with read permissions on the data source. You can use either a database login, as shown in Figure 14-18, or you can use a Windows login if you select

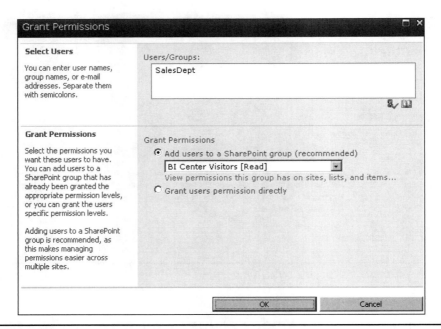

Figure 14-17 *Configuring permissions for a SharePoint integrated mode report server*

the Use As Windows Credentials When Connecting To The Data Source check box. A similar page is available for managing the shared data source properties in SharePoint.

Configure Processing Options

When reports execute quickly on the report server, you can keep the default processing options to run reports on demand and display content that is as current as the information in the source database. On the other hand, if the report execution process is slow, you might consider using cache or snapshot execution instead. In Report Manager, point to a report, open the menu, click Manage, and click Processing Options to open the configuring page shown in Figure 14-19. In SharePoint, you can access a similar page when you point to a report, open the menu, and click Manage Processing Options.

Use the cache option when you want a report to display relatively fresh data. The first person to request a report when no cache version of the report exists must wait for the report to execute, but every subsequent request for the report will render more quickly by accessing the cached copy of the report. You can configure the cache to expire after a fixed period or on a regular schedule. If the report has parameters, Reporting Services creates a different cache copy for each combination of parameter

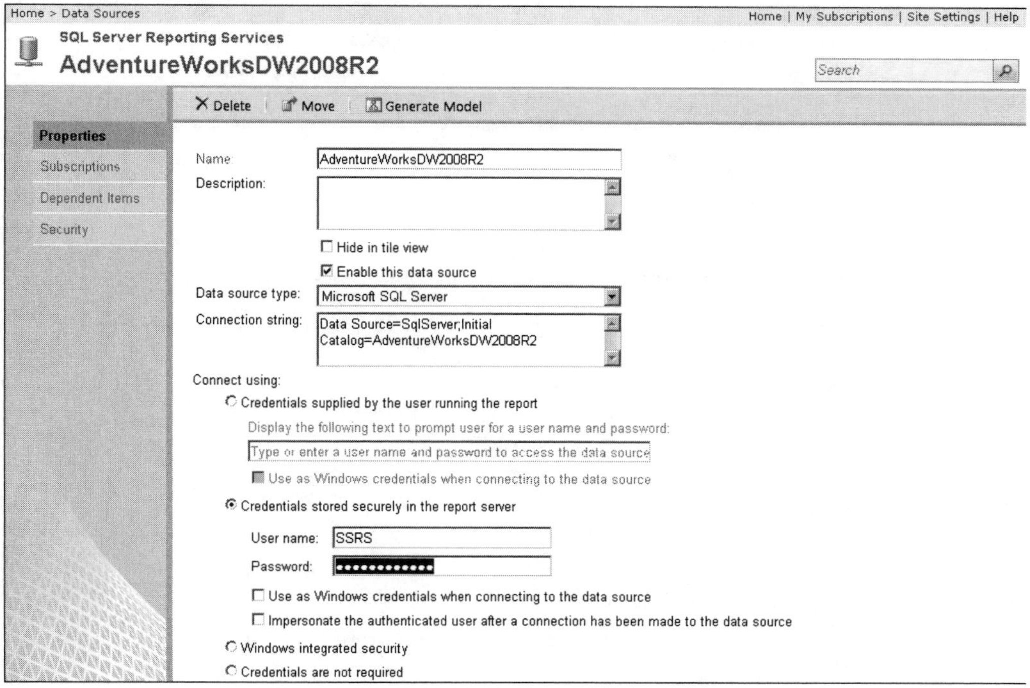

Figure 14-18 *Configuring stored credentials for a shared data source*

values that users request. That means it is possible for a cache version of the report to exist, and yet users must wait for Reporting Services to create another cache version.

You can minimize the impact of the first user's request for a report, or the first request for a particular combination of parameter values, by scheduling a cache refresh, as shown in Figure 14-20. You can create a cache refresh plan by clicking the Cache Refresh Options tab on any report management page on a Native mode report server, or by clicking Manage Cache Refresh Plans from the report's menu on a SharePoint integrated mode server. You can configure a different plan for each combination of parameter values that users are likely to request frequently.

When data changes less frequently, use report snapshots instead. Whereas a cache version of a report is temporary, a report snapshot is a permanent copy of a report. Reporting Services keeps a snapshot available until you change the report's processing options to on demand or caching, or until the report snapshot schedule generates an updated copy. You configure the schedule on the Processing Options page, but specify whether to accumulate the snapshots in report history on the Snapshot Options page, shown in Figure 14-21. The current snapshot is always accessible from the report link

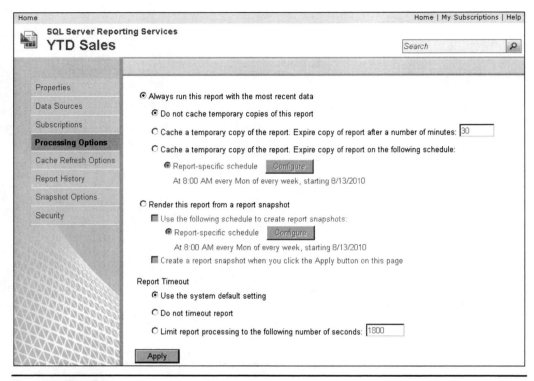

Figure 14-19 *Configuring report processing options*

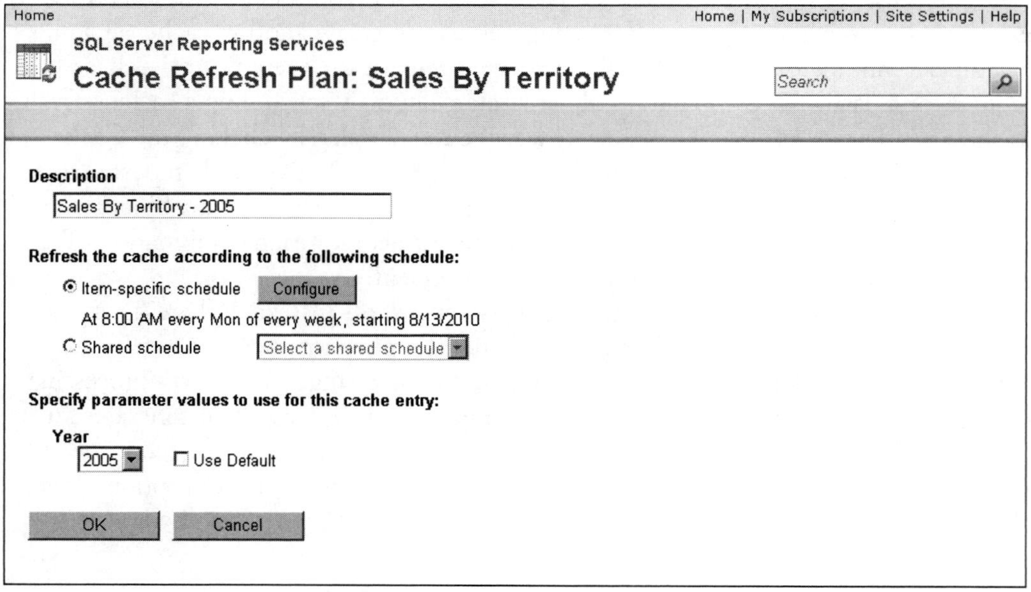

Figure 14-20 *Configuring a cache refresh plan*

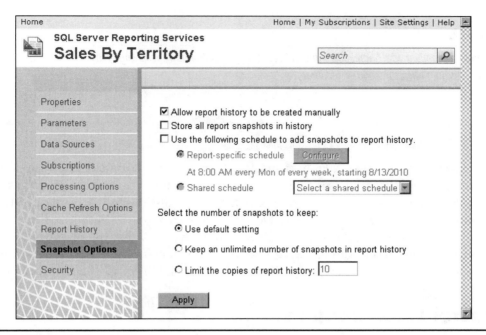

Figure 14-21 *Configuring snapshot options*

in Report Manager or the SharePoint document library, but users must open the Report History page to see earlier copies of the snapshot.

A disadvantage of using report snapshots is the inability to use query parameters in the report. Reporting Services applies the query parameter value only during report execution. You might consider redesigning your report to use a report parameter in combination with a data set filter to achieve the same results. The report query will take longer to execute and the size of the report snapshot will be larger, but users can then dynamically change report parameters to change the content of the report when viewing a snapshot.

SharePoint

In Chapter 8, we explained how to upload Excel workbooks and Reporting Services reports directly to SharePoint, how to create status lists, and how to create dashboard pages to consolidate multiple types of content. After you add these items to SharePoint and assign the appropriate permissions levels to the individual items or to the containing folder, users have immediate access. If you prefer, you can take advantage of SharePoint workflows to require approval from specified users before making a new or edited document available to the user community.

NOTE

If you're unfamiliar with SharePoint workflows, read "Approval Workflow: A Scenario (SharePoint 2010)" at http://technet.microsoft.com/en-us/library/ee704556.aspx.

PerformancePoint Services

As you learned in Chapter 9, PerformancePoint Services stores content in a SharePoint list, so the same approach to securing PerformancePoint items that we described in the previous section applies. You must grant Contribute permissions to users authorized to create PerformancePoint items, and Design permissions to users authorized to deploy a PerformancePoint dashboard. Recall from Chapter 9 that you can save a PerformancePoint dashboard to the PerformancePoint content list, but it's not available to users until you use the Deploy To SharePoint command in the Dashboard Designer.

Master Data Services

Whereas the other technologies we've addressed up to this point in the chapter allow you to create files, database objects, or other types of content that you must then deploy to a server, the focus in Master Data Services (MDS) is on data. Nonetheless, you can build an MDS model on a development server and then deploy the model—data and the object definitions or just the object definitions—to a test or production server. In each of these server environments, you control access to functional areas of Master Data Manager and to master data models using a role-based authorization system.

Deploy a Model

In the System Administration area of Data Manager, you can access the Deployment Wizard from the System menu. The Deployment Wizard allows you to create a package of a specific model and version. You can create a package of the model only, or the model with the data. The wizard prompts you to download the package, which you can hand off to an administrator of the target server. The administrator can then launch the Deployment Wizard on the target server to deploy the package, which unpacks the file and creates the necessary database objects in the MDS database. If the model already exists on the target server, you have the option to update the existing model or create a new model. Of course, if you create a package that contains only the model, you will need to load the model with data on the target server, either manually or using the staging process that we described in Chapter 13.

Secure Master Data Services

MDS uses a role-based authorization system that is similar conceptually to the one used in Reporting Services. Using this system, which you configure in the User And Group Permissions area in Master Data Manager, you can control what users can see and what actions they can perform. The minimum security that you can configure is to grant a user access to one functional area and to one model. For easier security administration, you can create a group in MDS, add users to the group, and then assign permissions by group rather than by individual user.

Functional Area Permissions

After adding a user or a group in Master Data Manager, you use the Functions tab on the Manage Users or Manage Groups page to assign a functional area, as shown in Figure 14-22. When a user opens Master Data Manager, the only areas visible will be the areas assigned.

Model Object Permissions

You use the Models tab on the same page to assign permissions for model objects. Starting at the model level, you can assign read-only, update, or deny permissions. Permissions that you assign at the model level cascade downward to lower levels of the model. However, you can override permissions at any level, as shown in Figure 14-23.

Figure 14-22 *Assigning functional area permissions to a group*

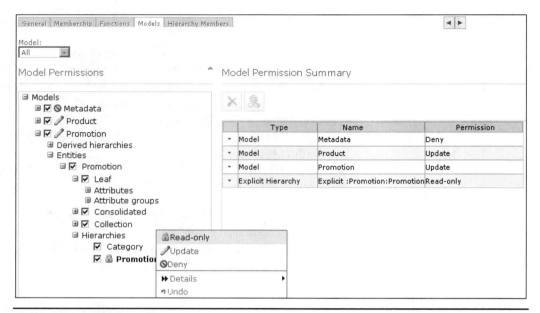

Figure 14-23 *Assigning model permissions*

Summary

With only a few exceptions, the process for putting your business intelligence solution into production is similar for each of the technologies that you include in your solution. You have several options for deploying components to a production server. If you have only a single file, you can opt to manually deploy it, but for larger-scale solutions, you can automate the process with scripts or deployment wizards. Following deployment, you must implement security to give users access to the components of your solution applicable to them, and then schedule any tasks that must recur on a regular basis. That's when your user community can begin experiencing the promise of collaborative business intelligence.

Keep in mind that putting the solution into production is not the end of the process, but merely the end of a cycle. As users become familiar with the capabilities of the solution, they'll clamor for additional reports, scorecards, or dashboards, which will drive the development of new SSIS packages or the addition of new dimensions and measures to the cubes, which, of course, leads to modifications of the master data model. It's a never-ending cycle of development, but easily accomplished by using Microsoft's business intelligence and collaboration tools not only to build flexible and extensible solutions, but solutions that help users make better decisions faster, together.

Appendix

Chart Types

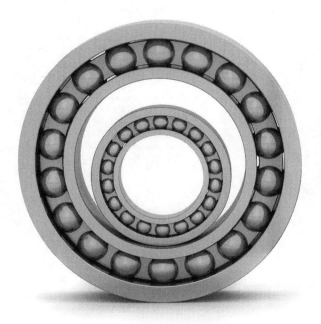

Use the following table to find the product that supports the chart type that you would like to use.

Type	Subtype	Example	Excel	SharePoint Chart Web Part	Reporting Services	Performance Point Services
Column	Clustered Column		●	●	●	●
	Stacked Column		●	●	●	●
	100% Stacked Column		●	●	●	●
	3-D Clustered Column		●	●	●	
	3-D Stacked Column		●	●	●	
	3-D 100% Stacked Column		●	●	●	
	3-D Column		●	●	●	
	Clustered Cylinder		●		●	
	Stacked Cylinder		●		●	
	100% Stacked Cylinder		●		●	

Type	Subtype	Example	Product			
			Excel	SharePoint Chart Web Part	Reporting Services	Performance Point Services
	3-D Cylinder		●	●	●	
	Clustered Cone		●			
	Stacked Cone		●			
	100% Stacked Cone		●			
	3-D Cone		●			
	Clustered Pyramid		●			
	Stacked Pyramid		●			
	100% Stacked Pyramid		●			
	3-D Pyramid		●			
Line	Line		●	●	●	●
	Stacked Line		●			
	100% Stacked Line		●			

Type	Subtype	Example	Excel	SharePoint Chart Web Part	Reporting Services	Performance Point Services
	Line with Markers		●	●	●	●
	Stacked Line with Markers		●			
	100% Stacked Line with Markers		●			
	3-D Line		●	●	●	
	3-D Spline			●	●	
	Stepped Line			●	●	
	3-D Stepped Line			●	●	
Pie	Pie		●	●	●	●
	3-D Pie		●	●	●	
	Pie of Pie		●		●	
	Exploded Pie		●		●	
	3-D Exploded Pie		●		●	
	Bar of Pie		●			

			Product		
Type	**Subtype**	**Example**	**Excel**	**SharePoint Chart Web Part**	**Reporting Services**	**Performance Point Services**
Ratio	Funnel			●	●	
	3-D Funnel			●	●	
	Pyramid			●	●	
	3-D Pyramid				●	●
	Cylinder			●	●	
Bar	Clustered Bar		●	●	●	
	Stacked Bar		●	●	●	
	100% Stacked Bar		●	●	●	
	3-D Clustered Bar		●	●	●	
	3-D Stacked Bar		●	●	●	
	3-D 100% Stacked Bar		●	●	●	
	Clustered Horizontal Cylinder		●		●	
	Stacked Horizontal Cylinder		●		●	

Type	Subtype	Example	Product		
			Excel	SharePoint Chart Web Part	Reporting Services	Performance Point Services
	100% Stacked Horizontal Cylinder		●		●	
	Horizontal Cylinder			●	●	
	Clustered Horizontal Cone		●			
	Stacked Horizontal Cone		●			
	100% Stacked Horizontal Cone		●			
	Clustered Horizontal Pyramid		●			
	Stacked Horizontal Pyramid		●			
	100% Stacked Horizontal Pyramid		●			
Area	Area		●	●	●	
	Smooth Area (Spline Area)			●	●	
	Stacked Area		●	●	●	
	100% Stacked Area		●	●	●	

Type	Subtype	Example	Product		
			Excel	**SharePoint Chart Web Part**	**Reporting Services**	**Performance Point Services**
	3-D Area		●	●	●	
	3-D Smooth Area (Spline Area)			●	●	
	3-D Stacked Area		●	●	●	
	3-D 100% Stacked Area		●	●	●	
X,Y (Scatter)	Scatter with Only Markers		●	●	●	
	3-D Point			●	●	
	Scatter with Smooth Lines and Markers (Spline)		●	●	●	
	Scatter with Smooth Lines (Spline)		●	●	●	
	Scatter with Straight Lines and Markers		●		●	
	Scatter with Straight Lines		●		●	
Stock	High-Low-Close		●	●	●	
	3-D Stock			●	●	
	Open-High-Low-Close (Candlestick)		●	●	●	

Type	Subtype	Example	Excel	Product		
				SharePoint Chart Web Part	**Reporting Services**	**Performance Point Services**
	3-D Candlestick			●	●	
	Volume-High-Low-Close		●		●	
	Volume-Open-High-Low-Close		●		●	
	Stock Triangle Markers			●	●	
	3-D Stock Triangle Markers			●	●	
	Price Volume			●	●	
Range	Range			●	●	
	3-D Range			●	●	
	Smooth Range (Spline Range)			●	●	
	3-D Smooth Range (Spline Range)			●	●	
	Range Column			●	●	
	3-D Range Column			●	●	
	Clustered Range Column			●	●	
	Cylinder Range Column			●	●	

Type	Subtype	Example	Excel	Product		
				SharePoint Chart Web Part	Reporting Services	Performance Point Services
	Range Bar			●	●	
	3-D Gantt			●	●	
	3-D Clustered Gantt			●	●	
	Cylinder Gantt			●	●	
	Error Bar			●	●	
	Boxplot			●	●	
Surface	3-D Surface		●			
	Wireframe 3-D Surface		●			
	Contour		●			
	Wireframe Contour		●			
Doughnut	Doughnut		●	●	●	
	3-D Doughnut			●	●	
	Exploded Doughnut		●		●	

Type	Subtype	Example	Product			
			Excel	SharePoint Chart Web Part	Reporting Services	Performance Point Services
	Thick Doughnut			●	●	
	Ring			●	●	
	3-D Ring			●	●	
Bubble	Bubble		●	●	●	
	3-D Bubble		●	●	●	
Radar	Radar 1 (Polar)		●	●	●	
	Radar 2 (Polar)			●	●	
	Radar with Markers		●	●	●	
	Filled Radar (Radar Area)		●	●	●	
	3-D Radar				●	
Multi axis chart			●		●	●
Decomp tree						●

Index

References to figures are in italics.